Rick Steves'

HIDDEN EUROPE

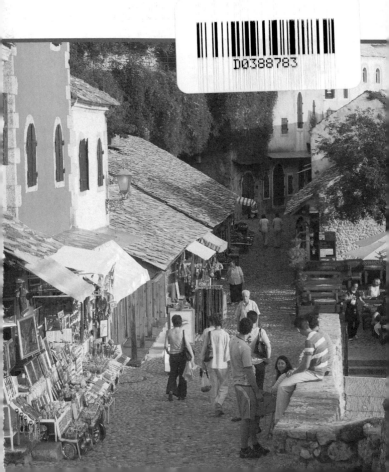

CONTENTS

Hidden Europe

Ærø

Český Krumlov

Hallstatt

Rovinj

Julian Alps

Lucca

Plitvice

San Sebastián

Volterra

Civita

Mostar

Tangier

Hydra

INTRODUCTION

By Rick Steves

I've never published a book like this. Rather than cover a region and lay out all the stops for putting together a smart itinerary, I've assembled chapters on a dozen or so examples of "Hidden Europe." It's a varied, disparate collection of places giving travelers like you the spirit of the culture in each country. Stops range all across Europe, from Scandinavia to Slovenia, and from Spain to Greece.

For the first time in history, more humans live in big cities than in villages, towns, and rural areas. I love cities. But cities have  a commonality that trumps many of the traditions and quirky characteristics of local cultures. People go to cities to leave their traditions; they stay in villages to keep them. And for us, experiencing Europe's genuine, living traditions helps make a better trip.

Understandably, many tourists fall for the mass appeal of Europe's big-name towns and sights. In the same way that everyone will tune into a YouTube video that's gone viral, all the tourists know exactly where the masses are visiting...and that's where they go. The most popular places take on a kind of touristic gravitational pull. And in this age of discount airlines and bullet trains, it's almost too easy for us to lace major cities together and think we are maximizing a far-ranging multicultural experience. The irony is that we're zipping right past some of the best stuff.

I've noticed over the years that when I'm designing a tour itinerary or writing a public television script, I'll do the big cities with all the must-see sights and blockbuster icons—but then I'll retreat

Map Legend

↙	Viewpoint	✈ Airport		Tunnel
↑	Entry Arrow	ⓣ Taxi Stand		Pedestrian Zone
✿	Tourist Info	Ⓣ Tram Stop		Railway
WC	Restroom	Ⓑ Bus Stop		Ferry/Boat Route
♜	Castle	Ⓟ Parking		Tram
⌂	Church	)(Mtn. Pass		Stairs
☪	Mosque	Park		Walk/Tour Route
▪	Statue/Point of Interest	◎ Fountain		Trail
			•—•—•	Mtn. Lift
			o⊢⊢⊢⊢o	Funicular

Use this legend to help you navigate the maps in this book.

an hour or two away to a small town or village scene that's like stepping back in time. This contrast is simply essential for understanding a country or region as a whole.

This book covers some of those lesser-known sights: relatively undiscovered corners of Europe that have, for various reasons, missed the modern parade. With no promotional budgets to attract travelers, they're ignored as they quietly make their traditional way through just another century. Many of these places won't hit you over the head with their cultural razzle-dazzle. Their charms are too subtle to be enjoyed by the tour-bus crowd. But good travelers know that meeting local people kindles all kinds of great travel memories. Without the trample of tourist crowds, you'll find it's easier to make these connections. While these places lack the famous blockbuster sights and museums of the big cities, good travelers know how to make their own fun in these hidden destinations.

That's the joy of this book. The collection of destinations includes places handy to the crowded tourist traps—yet a world away. Rather than linger in Athens, we use that city as a springboard for the two-hour catamaran ride to the time-passed isle of Hydra. While Rome is eternally enchanting, we head two hours north and climb up the donkey path to the hill-capping Italian village of Civita di Bagnoregio. Instead of Copenhagen, with all of its big-city Danish-ness, we go three hours south to the ship-in-a-bottle isle of Ærø and its queen-

Key to This Book

Sights are rated:

▲▲▲	**Don't miss**
▲▲	**Try hard to see**
▲	**Worthwhile if you can make it**
No rating	**Worth knowing about**

Tourist information offices are abbreviated as **TI,** and bathrooms are **WCs.**

Like Europe, this book uses the **24-hour clock.** It's the same through 12:00 noon, then keep going: 13:00 (1:00 p.m.), 14:00 (2:00 p.m.), and so on.

For **opening times,** if a sight is listed as "May-Oct daily 9:00-16:00," it should be open from 9 a.m. until 4 p.m. from the first day of May until the last day of October (but expect exceptions).

For **updates** to this book, visit www.ricksteves.com /update. For a valuable list of reports and experiences—good and bad—from fellow travelers, check www.ricksteves.com /feedback.

of-quaint village capital, Ærøskøbing. Rather than visit Venice, we curl around the corner of the Adriatic to its Croatian little sister, Rovinj. Instead of fighting the cruise-ship crowds for a patch of inundated Dubrovnik, we drive two and a half hours east, into Bosnia-Herzegovina and the town of Mostar—where a new generation is rebuilding after a brutal war. Rather than elbow the mobs

for a piece of sand on Spain's Costa del Turismo (a.k.a. Costa del Sol), we zip across the Strait of Gibraltar to Tangier for a Moroccan welcome as sweet as its mint tea. Instead of waiting in long lines at the great museums of Florence, we settle into nearby Lucca—a town whose wall seems built to corral its charm and its history. While hordes of tourists battle with aggressive cabbies and waiters in Prague, we'll enjoy a mellower small-town Czech charm in Český Krumlov. And while the tour groups take the *Sound of Music* bus tour in Salzburg, we'll sing "Doe, a deer" with real deer—communing with nature two hours east at Hallstatt in the Salzkammergut Lake District.

An often hidden and underappreciated dimension of Europe is its natural wonderlands. While Europeans love nature and are fanatic sun-worshippers, they have an impressive knack for enjoying themselves amid hellish crowds. Some of the destinations in this book offer rare opportunities to enjoy Europe's sun, beaches, mountains, and natural wonders, but without the glitz. After a lifetime of exploring Europe, I'm always impressed with how, when I return from my latest trip, I have a longer list of things I still want

to see than when I departed. And sampling the natural wonders—such as the quirky and breathtaking Julian Alps of Slovenia and the watery wonderland of Plitvice Lakes National Park in Croatia—stokes my appreciation for the importance of getting away from the cities in Europe.

Of course, a good trip is built upon a smart and well-designed itinerary that covers the obvious icons, uses your precious vacation time wisely, gets the most variety and diversity, and maximizes contact with both the people and the authentic cultures. Given its far-ranging nature, this book doesn't give you all the pieces to connect the dots. But it covers with enthusiasm a dozen overlooked places of Europe—many of my favorite discoveries in a continent that has so much to offer. Use it as a starting point for sampling a few flavors that you can later assemble into a well-rounded European feast.

Be warned that some of the places in this book are noncom-

mercial only in a relative sense, and can even suffer from congestion at times. But every year or so, I revisit my poster-child village discoveries (such as Ærø, Civita, Rovinj, and Hydra) and, while more crowded now, they are still great. And, at least from my experience, my Back Door readers are pleasant travelers to share Europe with.

This book was printed as a companion to my public television special, *Hidden Europe*, which aired across the US in 2012. You probably have the book because you contributed during a pledge drive. Thank you for supporting your local public television station. If you missed the program, you can see it any time for free at Hulu.com (search "Rick Steves Hidden Europe") to make the places in this book come vividly to life.

These destinations—unforgettable alternatives to urban Europe—combine to give you a chorus line of travel thrills. And it's my hope that this book will help you splice a slice of Hidden Europe into your next trip. Bon voyage!

AUSTRIA

The following chapter is excerpted from *Rick Steves' Vienna, Salzburg & Tirol.*

HALLSTATT
and the SALZKAMMERGUT

Commune with nature in the Salzkammergut, Austria's Lake District. "The hills are alive," and you're surrounded by the loveliness that has turned on everyone from Emperor Franz Josef to Julie Andrews. This is *Sound of Music* country. Idyllic and majestic but not rugged, it's a gentle land of lakes, forested mountains, and storybook villages, rich in hiking opportunities and inexpensive lodging. Settle down in the postcard-pretty, lake-cuddling town of Hallstatt.

Planning Your Time

While there are plenty of lakes and charming villages in the Salzkammergut, Hallstatt is really the only one that matters. One night and a few hours to browse are all you'll need to fall in love. To relax or take a hike in the surroundings, give it two nights and a day. It's a relaxing break between Vienna and Salzburg.

Orientation to Hallstatt

(area code: 06134)

Lovable Hallstatt (HAHL-shtaht) is a tiny town bullied onto a ledge between a selfish mountain and a swan-ruled lake, with a waterfall ripping furiously through its middle. It can be toured on foot in about 15 minutes. Salt veins in the mountain rock drew people here centuries before Christ. The symbol of Hallstatt, which you'll see all over town, consists of two adjacent spirals—a design based on jewelry found in Bronze Age Celtic graves high in the nearby mountains.

Hallstatt has two parts: the tightly packed medieval town

center (which locals call the Markt) and the newer, more car-friendly Lahn, a few minutes' walk to the south. A lakeside promenade connects the old center to the Lahn. The tiny "main" boat dock (a.k.a. Market Dock), where boats from the train station arrive, is in the old center of town. Another boat dock is in the Lahn, next to Hallstatt's bus stop and grocery store.

The charms of Hallstatt are the village and its lakeside setting. Come here to relax, nibble, wander, and paddle. While tourist crowds can trample much of Hallstatt's charm in August, the place is almost dead in the off-season. The lake is famous for its good fishing and pure water.

Tourist Information

At the helpful TI, Claudia and her staff can explain hikes and excursions, and find you a room (July-Aug Mon-Fri 9:00-17:00, Sat 10:00-14:00, closed Sun; Sept-June Mon-Fri 9:00-12:00 & 14:00-17:00, closed Sat-Sun; one block from Market Square, across from museum at Seestrasse 169, tel. 06134/8208, www.dachstein -salzkammergut.at).

In the summer, the TI offers 1.5-hour **walking tours** of the town in English and German (€4, mid-May-Sept Sat at 10:00). They can arrange private tours for €75.

Arrival in Hallstatt

By Train: If you're coming on the main train line that runs between Salzburg and Vienna, you'll change trains at Attnang-Puchheim to get to Hallstatt (you won't see Hallstatt on the schedules, but any train to Ebensee and Bad Ischl will stop at Hallstatt). Day-trippers can check their bags at the Attnang-Puchheim station (follow signs for *Schliessfächer*, coin-op lockers are at the street, curbside near track 1, €2.50/24 hours, a ticket serves as your key).  Note: Connections can be fast—check the TV monitor.

Hallstatt's train station is a wide spot on the tracks across the lake from town. *Stefanie* (a boat) meets you at the station and glides scenically across the lake to the old town center (€2.20, meets each train until 18:48—don't arrive after that, www.hallstattschifffahrt .at). The last departing boat-train connection leaves Hallstatt at 18:15, and the first boat goes in the morning at 6:50 (8:50 Sat-Sun).

Once in Hallstatt, walk left from the boat dock for the TI; you're steps away from the hotels in the old center, and a 15-minute walk from accommodations in the Lahn.

By Bus: Hallstatt's bus stop is by the boat dock in the Lahn. It takes 15 minutes to walk from the bus stop into the old center along the lakeside path.

By Car: The main road skirts Hallstatt via a long tunnel above the town. Gates close off traffic to the old center, but if you have a hotel reservation, the guard will let you drive into town to drop your bags. Ask your hotel for parking suggestions. There are numbered parking areas outside the center (P1 through P5). Parking there is free with a guest card (available from your hotel), and it's a laid-back system—just show your card later. The problem is that the lots are often full, especially P1 (in the tunnel above town); try P2 or P3, in the Lahn, a lovely 15- to 20-minute lakeside walk from the old center. Without a guest card, per-day parking is still quite reasonable (lot P1: €4.20/day, lot P2: €6/day; less after 14:00). Off-season (Nov-April), parking is free and easy. All of the accommodations I recommend in the Lahn have free parking.

Helpful Hints

Internet Access: Try **Hallstatt Umbrella Bar** (€4/hour, summers only, weather permitting—since it's literally under a big umbrella, halfway between the old center and the Lahn along the lake at Seestrasse 145). For free Wi-Fi, drop by the café at the recommended **Heritage Hotel.**

Laundry: The staff of the **campground** in the Lahn will wash and dry (but not fold) your clothes for €8/load (drop off mid-April–mid-Oct daily 8:00-10:00 & 16:00-18:00, pick up in afternoon or next morning, closed off-season, tel. 06134/83224). In the center, the recommended **Hotel Grüner Baum** does laundry for non-guests (€13/load, on Market Square).

Boat Rental: Two places rent electric boats; both rent from two locations in high season. **Riedler** is next to the main boat dock, and 75 yards past Bräugasthof (€13/hour, tel. 06134/20619). **Hemetsberger** is near Gasthof Simony, and by the Lahn boat dock (€12/hour, tel. 06134/8228). Both are open daily until 19:00 in peak season and in good weather. Boats have two speeds: slow and stop. Spending an extra €3/hour gets you a faster, 500-watt boat. Both places also rent rowboats and paddleboats (slightly cheaper).

Parks and Swimming: Green and peaceful lakeside parks line the south end of Lake Hallstatt. If you walk 15 minutes south of the old center to the Lahn, you'll find a grassy public park, playground, mini-golf, and swimming area *(Badestrand)* with the fun Badeinsel play-island.

Views: For a great view over Hallstatt, hike above the recommended Helga Lenz B&B as far as you like, or climb any path

HALLSTATT

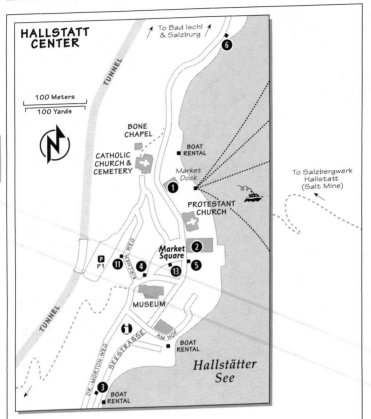

HALLSTATT CENTER

To Bad Ischl & Salzburg

100 Meters
100 Yards

N

TUNNEL

BONE CHAPEL

CATHOLIC CHURCH & CEMETERY

BOAT RENTAL

Market Dock

❶

PROTESTANT CHURCH

To Salzbergwerk Hallstatt (Salt Mine)

❷

Market Square

P P1

❶❶

KIRCHEN WEG

❹

❶❸

❺

MUSEUM

ℹ

AM HOF

BOAT RENTAL

BEESTRASSE

DR. MORTON-WEG

TUNNEL

❸

BOAT RENTAL

Hallstätter See

❶ Heritage Hotel
❷ Hotel/Rest. Grüner Baum
❸ Bräugasthof Hallstatt
❹ Gasthof Zauner
❺ Gasthof Simony
❻ Pension Sarstein
❼ Gasthof Pension Grüner Anger
❽ Helga Lenz Rooms
❾ Haus Trausner
❿ Herta Höll Rooms
⓫ Gasthaus zur Mühle Hostel & Pizza
⓬ Strand Café
⓭ Ruth Zimmerman Pub
⓮ Internet Access
⓯ Campground (Laundry Service)

ECHERNTAL

ECHERNTALWEG

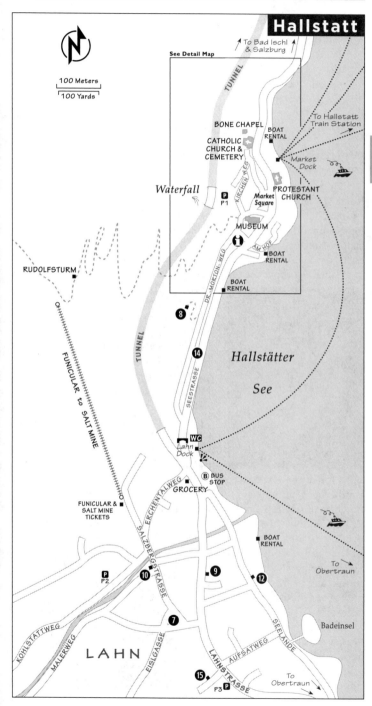

Hallstatt

100 Meters
100 Yards

See Detail Map

To Bad Ischl & Salzburg

TUNNEL

To Hallstatt Train Station

BONE CHAPEL

BOAT RENTAL

CATHOLIC CHURCH & CEMETERY

Market Dock

Waterfall

KIRCHEN-WEG

P P1

Market Square

PROTESTANT CHURCH

MUSEUM

AM HOF

BOAT RENTAL

DR. MORTON-WEG

RUDOLFSTURM

BOAT RENTAL

8

Hallstätter

14

See

FUNICULAR to SALT MINE

TUNNEL

SEESTRASSE

WC

Lahn Dock

12

B BUS STOP

ERCHENTALWEG

GROCERY

FUNICULAR & SALT MINE TICKETS

BOAT RENTAL

SALZBERGSTRASSE

P P2

10

9

12

To Obertraun

KOHLSTATTWEG

7

Badeinsel

MALERWEG

EISLGASSE

LAHN

SEELÄNDE

AUFSATZWEG

15

LAHNSTRASSE

P3 P

To Obertraun

leading up the hill. The 40-minute steep hike down from the salt-mine tour gives the best views (see "Sights in Hallstatt," later). While most visitors stroll the lakeside drag between the old and new parts of town, make a point to do the trip once by taking the more higgledy-piggledy high lane called Dr.-Morton-Weg.

Self-Guided Walk

Welcome to Hallstatt

· *This short walk starts at the dock.*

Boat Landing: There was a Hallstatt before there was a Rome. In fact, because of the importance of salt mining here, an entire epoch—the Hallstatt Era, from 800 to 400 B.C.—is named for this important spot. Through the centuries, salt was traded and people came and went by boat. You'll still see the traditional *Fuhr* boats, designed to carry heavy loads in shallow water.

Towering above the town is the **Catholic church.** Its faded St. Christopher—patron saint of travelers, with his cane and baby Jesus on his shoulder—watched over those sailing in and out. Until 1875, the town was extremely remote...then came a real road and the train. The good ship *Stefanie* shuttles travelers back and forth from here to the Hallstatt train station, immediately across the lake. The *Bootverleih* sign advertises boat rentals. By the way, *Schmuck* is not an insult...it means jewelry.

Notice the one-lane road out of town (below the church). Until 1966, when a bigger tunnel was built above Hallstatt, all the traffic crept single-file right through the town.

Look down the shore at the huge homes. Several families lived in each of these houses, back when Hallstatt's population was about double its present 1,000. Today, the population continues to shrink, and many of these generally underused houses rent rooms to visitors.

Parking is tight here in the tourist season. Locals and hotels have cards getting them into the prime town-center lot. From November through April, the barricade

is lifted and anyone can park here. Hallstatt gets about three months of snow each winter, but the lake hasn't frozen over since 1981.

See any swans? They've patrolled the lake like they own it since the 1860s, when Emperor Franz Josef and Empress Sisi—the Princess Diana of her day—made this region their annual holiday retreat. Sisi loved swans, so locals made sure she'd see them here. During this period, the Romantics discovered Hallstatt, many top painters worked here, and the town got its first hotel (now the Heritage Hotel).

Tiny Hallstatt has two big churches: Protestant (bordering the square on the left, with a grassy lakeside playground) and Catholic (up above, with its fascinating bone chapel).

• *Walk over the town's stream, and pop into the...*

Protestant Church: The Catholic Counter-Reformation was very strong in Austria, but pockets of Protestantism survived, especially in mining towns like Hallstatt. In 1860, Emperor Franz Josef finally allowed non-Catholic Christians to build churches. Before that, they were allowed to worship only in low-key "houses of prayer." In 1863, Hallstatt's miners pooled their humble resources and built this fine church. Step inside (free and often open). It's very plain, emphasizing the pulpit and organ rather than fancy art and saints. Check out the portraits: Martin Luther (left of altar), the town in about 1865 with its new church (left wall), and a century of pastors.

• *Continue past the church to the...*

Market Square (Marktplatz): In 1750, a fire leveled this part of town. The buildings you see now are all late 18th-century structures built of stone rather than flammable wood. The three big buildings on the left are government-subsidized housing (mostly for seniors and people with health problems). Take a close look at the two-dimensional, up-against-the-wall pear tree (it likes the sun-warmed wall). The statue features the Holy Trinity.

• *Continue a block past Gasthof Simony. At the first corner, just before the* Gemeindeamt *(City Hall), jog left across the little square and then right down the tiny lane marked* Am Hof, *which leads through an intimate bit of domestic town architecture, boat houses, lots of firewood, and maybe a couple of swans hanging out. The lane circles back to the main drag and the...*

Museum Square: Because 20th-century Hallstatt was of no industrial importance, it was untouched by World War II. But once upon a time, its salt was worth defending. High above, peeking out of the trees, is Rudolfsturm (Rudolf's Tower). Originally a 13th-century watchtower protecting the salt mines, and later the mansion of a salt-mine boss, it's now a restaurant with a great view. A zigzag trail connects the town with Rudolfsturm and the salt mines just beyond. The big, white houses by the waterfall were water-powered mills that once ground Hallstatt's grain. (If you hike up a few blocks, you'll see the river raging through town.)

Around you are the town's TI, post office, museum, City Hall, and Dachstein Sport Shop (described later). A statue recalls the mine manager who excavated prehistoric graves in about 1850. Much of the *Schmuck* sold locally is inspired by the jewelry found in the area's Bronze Age tombs.

The memorial wooden stairs in front of the museum are a copy of those found in Hallstatt's prehistoric mine—the original stairs are more than 2,500 years old. For thousands of years, people have been leaching salt out of this mountain. A brine spring sprung here, attracting Bronze Age people in about 1600 B.C. Later, they dug tunnels to mine the rock (which was 70 percent salt), dissolved it into a brine, and distilled out the salt—precious for preserving meat. For a look at early salt-mining implements and the town's story, visit the museum (described later).

Across from the TI, Pension Hallberg has a quirky hallway full of Nazi paraphernalia and other stuff found on the lake bed (€1). Only recently did local divers realize that, for centuries, the lake had been Hallstatt's garbage can. If something was *kaputt,* locals would just toss it into the lake. In 1945, Nazi medals decorating German and Austrian war heroes suddenly became dangerous to own. Throughout the former Third Reich, hard-earned medals floated down to lonely lake beds, including Hallstatt's.

Under the TI is the "Post Partner"—a government-funded attempt to turn inefficient post offices into something more viable (selling souvenirs, renting bikes, and employing people with disabilities who otherwise wouldn't work). The *Fischerei* provides the town with its cherished fresh lake fish. The county allows two commercial fishermen on the lake. They spread their nets each morning and sell their catch here to town restaurants, or to any locals cooking up a special dinner (Mon-Fri 9:00-12:00, closed Sat-Sun).

• *Nearby, still on Museum Square, find the...*

Dachstein Sport Shop: During a renovation project, the builders dug down and hit a Celtic and ancient Roman settlement. Peek through the glass pavement on the covered porch to see where the Roman street level was. If the shop is open, pop in and go downstairs (free). You'll walk on Roman flagstones and see the small gutter that channeled water to power an ancient hammer mill (used to pound iron into usable shapes). In prehistoric times, people lived near the mines. Romans were the first Hallstatt lakeside settlers. The store's owners are committed to sharing Hallstatt's fascinating history, and often display old town paintings and folk art.

• *From this square, the first right (after the bank) leads up a few stairs to...*

Dr.-Morton-Weg: House #26A dates from 1597. Follow the lane uphill to the left past more old houses. Until 1890, this was the town's main drag, and the lake lapped at the lower doors of these houses. Therefore, many main entrances were via the attic, from this level. Enjoy this back-street view of town. Just after the arch, near #133, check out the old tools hanging outside the workshop, and the piece of wooden piping. It's a section taken from the 25-mile wooden pipeline that carried salt brine from Hallstatt to Ebensee. This was in place from 1595 until the last generation, when the last stretch of wood was replaced by plastic piping. At the pipe, enjoy the lake view and climb down the stairs. From lake level, look back up at the striking traditional architecture (the fine woodwork on the left was recently rebuilt after a fire; parts of the old house on the right date to medieval times).

• *Your tour is finished. From here, you have boat rentals, the salt-mine tour, the town museum, and the Catholic church (with its bone chapel) all within a few minutes' walk.*

Sights in Hallstatt

▲▲**Catholic Church and Bone Chapel**—Hallstatt's Catholic church overlooks the town from above. From near the main boat dock, hike up the covered wooden stairway and follow the *Kath. Kirche* signs. The lovely church has twin altars. The one on the left was made by town artists in 1897. The one on the right is more historic—dedicated in 1515 to Mary, who's flanked by St. Barbara (on right, patron of miners) and St. Catherine (on left, patron of foresters—a lot of wood was needed to fortify the many miles of tunnels, and to boil the brine to distill the salt).

Behind the church, in the well-tended graveyard, is the 12th-century Chapel of St. Michael (even older than the church). Its bone chapel—or charnel house *(Beinhaus)*—contains more than 600 painted skulls. Each skull has been lovingly named, dated, and decorated (skulls with dark, thick garlands are oldest—18th century; those with flowers are more recent—19th century). Space was so limited in this cemetery that

bones had only 12 peaceful, buried years here before making way for the freshly dead. Many of the dug-up bones and skulls ended up in this chapel. They stopped this practice in the 1960s, about the same time the Catholic Church began permitting cremation. But one woman (who died in 1983) managed to sneak her skull in later (dated 1995, under the cross, with the gold tooth). The skulls on the books are those of priests.

Cost and Hours: €1.50, free English flier, daily May-Sept 10:00-18:00, Oct 10:00-16:00, closed Nov-April, tel. 06134/8279.

▲**Hallstatt Museum**—This pricey but high-quality museum tells the story of Hallstatt. It focuses on the Hallstatt Era (800-400 B.C.), when this village was the salt-mining hub of a culture that spread from France to the Balkans. Back then, Celtic tribes dug for precious salt, and Hallstatt was, as its name means, the "place of salt." While its treasures are the countless artifacts excavated from prehistoric gravesites around the mine, you'll get the whole gamut—with 26 displays on everything from the region's flora and fauna to local artists and the surge in Hallstatt tourism during the Romantic Age. Everything is labeled in English, and the ring binders have translations of the longer texts.

Cost and Hours: €7.50, May-Sept daily 10:00-18:00, shorter hours off-season, closed Mon-Tue Nov-March, adjacent to TI at Seestrasse 56, tel. 06134/828-015, www.museum-hallstatt.at. On Thursdays in summer, when candlelit boats run, the museum stays open until 20:00 (see "Nightlife in Hallstatt," later).

▲**Lake Trip**—For a quick boat trip, you can ride the *Stefanie* across the lake and back for €4.40. It stops at the tiny Hallstatt train station for 30 minutes (note return time in the boat's window), giving you time to walk to a hanging bridge (ask the captain to point you to the *Hängebrücke*—HENG-eh-brick-eh—a 10-minute lakeside stroll to the left). Longer lake tours are also available (€8/50 minutes, €9.50/75 minutes, sporadic schedules—especially off-season—so check chalkboards by boat docks for today's times). Those into relaxation can rent a sleepy electric motorboat to enjoy town views from the water.

▲**Salt-Mine Tour**—If you have yet to tour a salt mine, consider visiting Hallstatt's, which claims to be the oldest in the world. To get to the mine, take the funicular railway, which starts in the Lahn, close to the bus stop and Lahn boat dock.

After riding the funicular above town, you'll hike 10 minutes to the mine (past excavation sites of many prehistoric tombs and a glass case with 2,500-year-old bones—but there's little to actually see). Report back 10 minutes before the tour time on your ticket, check your bag, and put on old miners' clothes. Then hike 200 yards higher in your funny outfit to meet your guide, who escorts your group down a tunnel dug in 1719. Inside the mountain, you'll watch a slide show, follow your guide through several caverns as

you learn about mining techniques over the last 7,000 years, see a silly laser show on a glassy subterranean lake, peek at a few waxy cavemen with pickaxes, and ride the train out. The highlight for most is sliding down two banisters (the second one is longer and ends with a flash for an automatic souvenir photo that clocks your speed—see how you did compared to the rest of your group after the tour).

The presentation is very low-tech, as the mining company owns all three mine tours in the area and sees little reason to invest in the experience when they can simply mine the tourists. While the tour is mostly in German, the guide is required to speak English if you ask...so ask. Be sure to dress for the constant 47-degree temperature.

Cost and Hours: €24 combo-ticket includes mine and funicular round-trip, €16 for mine tour only, buy all tickets at funicular station—note the time and tour number on your ticket, daily May-mid-Sept 9:00-16:00, mid-Sept-Oct 9:00-14:30, later funicular departures miss the last tour of the day, closed Nov-April, no children under age 4, arrive early or late to avoid summer crowds, tel. 06132/200-2400, www.salzwelten.at.

Funicular: You can also just take the funicular without going on the mine tour (€7 one-way, €12 round-trip, 4/hour, daily May-mid-Sept 9:00-18:00, mid-Sept-Oct 9:00-16:30, closed Nov-April).

Returning to Hallstatt: If you skip the funicular down, the scenic 40-minute hike back into town is (with strong knees) a joy. At the base of the funicular, notice the train tracks leading to the Erbstollen tunnel entrance. This lowest of the salt tunnels goes many miles into the mountain, where a shaft connects it to the

Salzkammergut

Map showing the Salzkammergut region with labeled locations:

Mondsee · Mondsee

Fuschlsee

GERMANY

A-1 · 158

Freilassing ·

TRAIN STATION

A-8

To Munich

Salzburg

Schafberg

St. Gilgen · **St. Wolfgang**

Wolfgangsee

Untersberg ∧

Hallein ∎

AUSTRIA

305

· Berchtesgaden

∎ ▲ Kehlstein

HITLER'S EAGLE'S NEST

Königsee ·

A-10

162

Königsee

166

Bischofshofen ·

To Innsbruck ← 311   To Italy →

tunnels you just explored. Today, the salty brine from these tunnels flows 25 miles through the world's oldest pipeline—made of wood until quite recently—to the huge modern salt works (next to the highway) at Ebensee.

▲**Local Hikes**—Mountain-lovers, hikers, and spelunkers who use Hallstatt as their home base keep busy for days (ask the TI for ideas). A good, short, and easy walk is the two-hour round-

trip up the Echern Valley to the Waldbachstrub waterfall and back: From the parking lot, follow signs to the salt mines, then follow the little wooden signs marked *Echerntalweg*. With a car, consider hiking around nearby Altaussee (flat, 3-hour hike) or along Grundlsee to Toplitzsee. Regular buses connect Hallstatt with Gosausee for a pleasant hour-long walk around that lake. Or consider walking nine miles halfway around Lake Hallstatt via the town of Steeg (boat to train station, walk left along lake and past idyllic farmsteads, returning to Hallstatt along the old salt trail, *Soleleitungsweg*); for a shorter hike, walk to Steeg along either side of the lake, and catch the train from Steeg back to Hallstatt's station. The TI can also recommend a great two-day hike with an overnight in a nearby mountain hut.

Biking—The best two bike rides take nearly the same routes as the hikes listed previously: up the Echern Valley, and around the lake (bikers do better going via Obertraun along the new lakeside bike path—start with a ride on the *Stefanie*). There's no public bike rental in Hallstatt, but some hotels have loaner bikes for guests.

Near Hallstatt

▲▲Dachstein Mountain Cable Car and Caves

From Obertraun, three miles beyond Hallstatt on the main road (or directly across the lake as the crow flies), a cable car glides up to the Dachstein Plateau. Along the way, you

can hop off to tour two different caves: the refreshingly chilly Giant Ice Caves and the less-impressive Mammoth Caves.

Getting to Obertraun: The cable car to Dachstein leaves from the outskirts of Obertraun. To reach the cable car from Hallstatt, the handiest and cheapest option is the bus (€1.70, 5-6/day, leaves from Lahn boat dock, drops you directly at cable-car station). Romantics can take the boat from Hallstatt's main boat dock to Obertraun (€5, 5/day July-Aug, 3/day in June and Sept, 30 minutes, www.hallstattschifffahrt.at)—but it's a 40-minute hike from there to the lift station. The impatient can consider hitching a ride—virtually all cars leaving Hallstatt to the south will pass through Obertraun in a few minutes.

Returning to Hallstatt: Plan to leave by midafternoon. The last bus from the cable-car station back to Hallstatt (at 17:05 in summer) inconveniently leaves before the last cable car down—if you miss the bus, try getting a ride from a fellow cable-car passenger. Otherwise, you can either call a taxi (€13, ask cable-car staff for help), or simply walk back along the lakefront (about one hour).

Dachstein Cable Car—From Obertraun, this mighty gondola goes in three stages high up the Dachstein Plateau—crowned by Dachstein, the highest mountain in the Salzkammergut (9,800 ft). The first segment stops at **Schönbergalm** (4,500 ft, runs May-late Oct), which has a mountain restaurant and two huge caves (described next). The second segment goes to the summit of **Krippenstein** (6,600 ft, runs mid-May-late Oct). The third segment descends to **Gjaidalm** (5,800 ft, runs mid-June-late Oct), where several hikes begin. For a quick high-country experience, Krippenstein is better than Gjaidalm.

From **Krippenstein,** you'll survey a scrubby, limestone, karstic landscape (which absorbs, through its many cracks, the rainfall that ultimately carves all those caves), with 360-degree views of the surrounding mountains.

Cost and Hours: Round-trip cable-car ride to Schönbergalm and the caves-€15, to Krippenstein-€23, to Gjaidalm-€25; cheaper family rates available, last cable car back down usually at about 17:00, tel. 06131/51310, www.dachsteinwelterbe.at.

Combo-Ticket Tips: The several combo-tickets available for the cable car and caves generally won't save you any money over buying individual tickets. But if you're gung-ho enough to want to visit one or both caves, and plan to ride the cable car farther up the mountain, the €33 same-day combo-ticket makes sense (covers the cable car all the way to Gjaidalm and back, as well as entry to both caves; it's slightly cheaper to buy separate tickets if you're riding only to Krippenstein and skipping one of the caves).

Giant Ice Caves (Riesen-Eishöhle)—Located near the Schönbergalm cable-car stop (4,500 ft), these caves were discovered in 1910. Today, guides lead tours in German and English on an hour-long, half-mile hike through an eerie, icy, subterranean world, passing limestone canyons the size of subway stations.

At the Schönbergalm lift station, report to the ticket window to get your cave appointment. Drop by the little free museum near the lift station—in a local-style wood cabin designed to support 200 tons of snow—to see the cave-system model, exhibits about its exploration, and info about life in the caves. Then hike 10 minutes from the station up to the cave entry. The temperature is just above freezing, and although the 700 steps help keep you warm, you'll want to bring a sweater. The limestone caverns, carved by rushing water, are named for scenes from Wagner's operas—the favorite of the mountaineers who first came here. If you're nervous, note that the iron oxide covering the ceiling takes 5,000 years to form. Things are very stable. Allow 1.5 hours total from the station.

Cost and Hours: €10, €15 combo-ticket with Mammoth Caves, €33 combo-ticket covers the cable car up to Gjaidalm and entry to both caves, open May-late Oct, hour-long tours start at 9:20, last tour at 15:30, stay in front and assert yourself to get English information, tel. 06131/51310.

Mammoth Caves (Mammuthöhle)—While huge and well-promoted, these are much less interesting than the ice caves and—

for most—not worth the time. Of the 30-mile limestone labyrinth excavated so far, you'll walk a half-mile with a German-speaking guide.

Cost and Hours: €10, €15 combo-ticket with ice caves, €33 combo-ticket covers the cable car up to Gjaidalm and entry to both caves, open May-late Oct, hour-long tours in English and German 10:15-14:30, entrance a 10-minute hike from lift station.

Luge Rides (Sommerrodelbahnen) on the Hallstatt-Salzburg Road

If you're driving between Salzburg and Hallstatt, you'll pass two luge rides operated by the same company (www.rodelbahnen.at).

Each is a ski lift that drags you backward up the hill as you sit on your go-cart. At the top, you ride the cart down the winding metal course. It's easy: Push to go, pull to stop, take your hands off your stick and you get hurt.

Each course is just off the road with easy parking. The ride up and down takes about 15 minutes. The one in **Fuschl am See** (closest to Salzburg, look for *Sommer-rodelbahn* sign) is half as long and cheaper (€4.30/ride, 1,970 ft, tel. 06226/8452). The one in **Strobl** near Wolfgangsee (look for *Riesenschutzbahn* sign) is a double course, more scenic with grand lake views (€6.40/ride, €43/10 rides, 4,265 ft, each track is the same speed, tel. 06137/7085). Courses are open May through October from 10:00 to 18:00—but generally close in bad weather. These are fun, but the concrete courses near Reutte are better.

Nightlife in Hallstatt

Locals would laugh at the thought. But if you want some action after dinner, you do have a few options: **Gasthaus zur Mühle** is a youth hostel with a rustic sports-bar ambience in its restaurant when drinks replace the food (open late, closed Tue Sept-mid-May, run by Ferdinand). Or, for your late-night drink, savor the Market Square from the trendy little pub called **Ruth Zimmermann,** where locals congregate with soft music, a good selection of drinks, two small rooms, and tables on the square (daily May-Sept 10:00-2:00 in the morning, Oct-April 11:00-2:00, mobile 0664/501-5631). From late July to late August, **candlelit boat rides** leave at 20:30 on Thursday evenings (€13.50, €16 combo-ticket with Hallstatt Museum).

Sleeping in Hallstatt

Hallstatt's TI can almost always find you a room (either in town or at B&Bs and small hotels outside of town—which are more likely to have rooms available and come with easy parking). Drivers, remember to ask if your hotel has in-town parking when you book your room.

Mid-July and August can be tight. Early August is worst. Hallstatt is not the place to splurge—some of the best rooms are *Zimmer*, just as nice and modern as rooms in bigger hotels, at half the cost. In summer, a double bed in a private home costs about €50 with breakfast. It's hard to get a one-night advance reservation (try calling the TI for help). But if you drop in and they have a spot, one-nighters are welcome. Prices include breakfast, lots of stairs, and a silent night. *"Zimmer mit Aussicht?"* (TSIM-mer mit OWS-zeekt) means "Room with view?"—worth asking for. Unlike many businesses in town, the cheaper places don't take credit cards.

As most rooms here are in old buildings with well-cared-for wooden interiors, dripping laundry is a no-no at Hallstatt pensions. Be especially considerate when hanging laundry over anything but tile—if you must wash larger clothing items here, ask your host about using their clothesline.

$$$ Heritage Hotel, next to the main boat dock, is the town's fanciest place to stay. It has 34 rooms with modern furnishings in a lakeside main building with an elevator; uphill are another 20 rooms in two separate buildings for those willing to

---

Sleep Code

(€1 = about $1.40, country code: 43, area code: 06134)
S = Single, **D** = Double/Twin, **T** = Triple, **Q** = Quad, **b** = bathroom, **s** = shower only. Unless otherwise noted, credit cards are accepted, English is spoken, and breakfast is included.

To help you sort easily through these listings, I've divided the rooms into three categories, based on the price for a double room with bath in high season:

$$$ **Higher Priced**—Most rooms €90 or more.
$$ **Moderately Priced**—Most rooms between €60-90.
$ **Lower Priced**—Most rooms €60 or less.

Prices can change without notice; verify the hotel's current rates online or by email. For other updates, see www .ricksteves.com/update.

climb stairs for better views (Sb-€90, Db-€150, these special prices for Rick Steves readers, free sauna, free cable Internet in rooms and Wi-Fi in lobby, laundry service-€13, parking-€10/day, Landungsplatz 120, tel. 06134/20036, fax 06134/20042, www .heritagehotel.at, info@heritagehotel.at).

$$$ Hotel Grüner Baum, on the other side of the church from the main boat dock, has a great location, fronting Market Square and overlooking the lake in back. The owner, Monika, moved here from Vienna and renovated this stately—but still a bit creaky—old hotel with urban taste. Its 22 rooms are huge, each with a separate living area and ancient hardwood floors, but you may not need so much space and the high price that comes with it (suite-like Db-€140-210, price

depends on view, 8 percent discount with this book, family rooms, Internet access in restaurant, laundry service-€13, closed in Nov, 20 yards from boat dock, tel. 06134/82630, fax 06134/826-344, www.gruenerbaum.cc, contact@gruenerbaum.cc).

$$$ Bräugasthof Hallstatt is like a museum filled with antique furniture and ancient family portraits. This former brewery, now a good restaurant, rents eight clean, cozy upstairs rooms. It's run by Virena and her daughter, Virena. Six of the rooms have gorgeous little lakeview balconies (Sb-€55, Db-€98, Tb-€140, free parking, just past TI along lake at Seestrasse 120, tel. 06134/8221, fax 06134/82214, www.brauhaus-lobisser.com, info@brauhaus -lobisser.com, Lobisser family).

$$$ Gasthof Zauner is run by a friendly mountaineer, Herr Zauner, whose family has owned it since 1893. The 13 pricey, pine-flavored rooms near the inland end of Market Square are decorated with sturdy alpine-inspired furniture (sealed not with lacquer but with beeswax, to let the wood breathe out its calming scent). Lederhosen-clad Herr Zauner recounts tales of local mountaineering lore, including his own impressive ascents (Sb-€60, Db-€107, lakeview Db-€112, cheaper mid-Oct-April, Internet access in office, closed Nov-early Dec, Marktplatz 51, tel. 06134/8246, fax 06134/82468, www.zauner.hallstatt.net, zauner@hallstatt.at).

$$$ Gasthof Simony is a well-worn, grandmotherly, 12-room place on the square, with a lake view, balconies, ancient beds, creaky wood floors, slippery rag rugs, antique furniture, and a lakefront garden for swimming. Reserve in advance, and call if arriving late (S-€35, D-€55, Ds-€65, Db-€95, third person-€30-35 extra, cash only, kayaks for guests, Marktplatz 105, tel. & fax 06134/8231, www.gasthof-simony.at, info@gasthof-simony.at,

Susanna Scheutz and family).

$$ Pension Sarstein is a big, flower-bedecked house right on the water on the edge of the old center. Its seven renovated rooms are bright, and all have lakeview balconies. You can swim from its plush and inviting lakeside garden (D-€50, Db-€65, Tb-€85; apartments with kitchen: Db-€65, Tb-€75, Qb-€85, apartment prices don't include breakfast; €3 extra per person for 1-night stay, cash only, pay Internet access, 200 yards to the right of the main boat dock at Gosaumühlstrasse 83, tel. 06134/8217, www.pension -sarstein.at.tf, pension.sarstein@aon.at, helpful Isabelle and Klaus Fischer).

$$ Gasthof Pension Grüner Anger, in the Lahn near the bus station and base of the funicular, is practical and modern. It's big

 and quiet, with 11 rooms and no creaks or squeaks. There are mountain views, but none of the lake (Sb-€43-48, Db-€76-86, third person-€15, price depends on season, non-smoking, free Internet access and Wi-Fi, free loaner bikes, free parking, Lahn 10, tel. 06134/8397, fax 06134/83974, www.anger.hall statt.net, anger@aon.at, Sulzbacher family). If arriving by train, have the boat captain call Herr Sulzbacher, who will pick you up at the dock. They run a good-value restaurant, too, with discounts for guests.

$ Helga Lenz rents two fine *Zimmer* a steep five-minute climb above Dr.-Morton-Weg (look for the green *Zimmer* sign). This large, sprawling, woodsy house has a nifty garden perch, wins the "Best View" award, and is ideal for those who sleep well in tree houses and don't mind the steps up from town (Db-€50, Tb-€75, €2 more per person for one-night stay, cash only, family room, closed Nov-March, Hallberg 17, tel. 06134/8508, www.hallstatt .net/lenz, haus-lenz@aon.at).

$ Two *Zimmer* are a few minutes' stroll south of the center, just past the bus stop/parking lot and over the bridge. **Haus Trausner** has three clean, bright, new-feeling rooms adjacent to the Trausner family home (Ds/Db-€50, 2-night minimum for reservations, cash only, breakfast comes to your room, free parking, Lahnstrasse 27, tel. 06134/8710, trausner1@aon.at, charming Maria Trausner makes you want to settle right in). **Herta Höll** rents out three spacious, modern rooms on the ground floor of her riverside house crawling with kids (Db-€50, apartment for up to five-€60-90, €2 more per person for one-night stay, cash only, free parking, free cable Internet, Salzbergstrasse 45, tel. 06134/8531, fax 06134/825-533, frank.hoell@aon.at).

$ *Hostel:* **Gasthaus zur Mühle Jugendherberge,** below the waterfall and along the gushing town stream, has 46 of the cheapest good beds in town (bed in 3- to 8-bed coed dorms-€14, twin D-€28, family quads, sheets-€4 extra, breakfast-€5, big lockers with a €15 deposit, closed Nov, reception closed Tue Sept-mid-May—so arrange in advance if arriving on Tue, below P1 tunnel parking lot, Kirchenweg 36, tel. & fax 06134/8318, toeroe-f @hallstatturlaub.at, Ferdinand Törö). It's also popular for its great, inexpensive pizza (described below).

Eating in Hallstatt

In this town, when someone is happy to see you, they'll often say, "Can I cook you a fish?" While everyone cooks the typical Austrian fare, fish is your best bet here. *Reinanke* (whitefish) is caught wild out of Lake Hallstatt and served the same day. *Saibling* (lake trout) is also tasty and costs less. You can enjoy good food inexpensively, with delightful lakeside settings. Restaurants in Hallstatt tend to have unreliable hours and close early on slow nights, so don't wait too long to get dinner. Most of the eateries listed here are run by recommended hotels.

Restaurant Bräugasthof, on the edge of the old center, is a good value. The indoor dining room is cozy in cool weather. On a balmy evening, its great lakeside tables offer the best ambience in town—you can feed the swans while your trout is being cooked (€10-14 three-course daily specials, daily May-Oct 11:30-late, closed Nov-April, Seestrasse 120, tel. 06134/8221).

Hotel Grüner Baum is a more upscale option, with elegant service at tables overlooking the lake inside and out (€15-21 main dishes, daily Dec-Oct 8:00-22:00, closed Nov, at bottom of Market Square, tel. 06134/8263).

Gasthof Simony's Restaurant am See serves Austrian cuisine on yet another gorgeous lakeside terrace, as well as indoors (€12-16 main courses, Thu-Tue 11:30-20:00, until 21:00 June-Sept and on winter weekends, closed Wed, tel. 06134/20646).

Gasthaus zur Mühle serves the best pizza in town. Chow down cheap and hearty here with fun-loving locals and the youth-hostel crowd (€7 pizza, lots of Italian, some Austrian, Wed-Mon in summer 16:00-21:00, closed Tue, Kirchenweg 36, tel. 06134/8318, Ferdinand).

Strand Café, a local favorite, is in the Lahn, near Badeinsel, the town beach (€8-15 main courses, plenty of alcohol, Tue-Sun April-mid-Sept 10:00-21:00, mid-Sept-Oct 11:30-20:00, closed Mon and Nov-March, great garden setting on the lake, Seelände 102, tel. 06134/8234).

Picnics and Cheap Eats: The **Zauner** bakery/butcher/grocer, great for picnickers, makes fresh sandwiches to go (Tue-Fri 7:00-12:00 & 15:00-18:00, Sat and Mon 7:00-12:00, closed Sun, uphill to the left from Market Square). The only **supermarket** is Konsum, in the Lahn at the bus stop (Mon-Fri 7:30-12:00 & 15:00-18:00, Sat 7:30-12:00, closed Sun, July-Aug no midday break and until 17:00 on Sat, Sept-April closed Wed). **Snack stands** near the main boat dock and the Lahn boat dock sell *Döner Kebab* and so on for €3 (tables and fine lakeside picnic options nearby).

Hallstatt Connections

By Public Transportation

From Hallstatt by Train: Most travelers leaving Hallstatt are going to Salzburg or Vienna. In either case, you need to catch the

shuttle boat (€2.20, departs 15 minutes before every train) to the little Hallstatt train station across the lake, and then ride 1.5 hours to **Attnang-Puchheim** (hourly from about 7:00 to 18:00). Trains are synchronized, so after a short wait in Attnang-Puchheim, you'll catch your onward connection to **Salzburg** (50 minutes) or **Vienna** (2.5 hours). The Hallstatt station has no staff or ticket machines, but you can buy tickets from the conductor without a penalty. In town, your hotel or the TI can help you find schedule information, or check www.oebb.at. Train info: tel. 051-717 (to get an operator, dial 2, then 2).

By Bus: The bus ride from Hallstatt to **Salzburg** is cheaper and more scenic than the train, and only slightly slower. You can still start off from Hallstatt by rail, taking the boat across the lake to the station and then the train toward Attnang-Puchheim—but get off after about 20 minutes in **Bad Ischl,** where you catch bus #150 to Salzburg (€8.80, Mon-Fri almost hourly, less Sat-Sun).

Alternatively, you can reach Bad Ischl by bus from the Hallstatt bus stop (€4.20, change in Gosaumühle), and then catch bus #150 to Salzburg. The Hallstatt TI has a schedule. In Salzburg, bus #150 stops at Hofwirt and Mirabellplatz (convenient to Linzergasse hotels) before ending at the Salzburg train station.

Route Tips for Drivers

Hallstatt to Vienna, via Mauthausen, Melk, and Wachau Valley (210 miles): Leave Hallstatt early. Follow the scenic Route 145 through Gmunden to the autobahn and head east. After Linz, take exit #155 at Enns, and follow the signs for *Mauthausen* (five miles from the freeway). Go through Mauthausen town and follow the *Ehemaliges KZ-Gedenkstätte Lager* signs. When leaving Mauthausen for Melk, enjoy the riverside drive along scenic Route 3 (or take the autobahn if you're in a hurry or prone to carsickness). At Melk, signs to *Stift Melk* lead to the abbey. Other *Melk* signs lead into the town.

From Melk (get a Vienna map at the TI), cross the river again (signs to *Donaubrücke*) and stay on Route 3. After Krems, the riverside route (now the S-5) hits the autobahn (A-22), and you'll barrel right into Vienna's traffic.

BOSNIA-HERZEGOVINA

The following chapter is excerpted from *Rick Steves' Croatia & Slovenia.*

MOSTAR

Mostar (MOH-star) represents the best and the worst of Yugoslavia. During the Tito years, it was an idyllic mingling of cultures—Catholic Croats, Orthodox Serbs, and Muslim Bosniaks living together in harmony, their differences spanned by an Old Bridge that epitomized an optimistic vision of a Yugoslavia where ethnicity didn't matter. And yet, as the country unraveled in the early 1990s, Mostar was gripped by a gory three-way war among those same peoples...and that famous bridge crumbled into the Neretva River.

Mostar rearranges your mental furniture. Most startling are the vivid and thought-provoking signs of the war. A few years ago, much of the city was destroyed; today, while still easy to find, the ruins aren't quite as in-your-face as before. Still, especially outside of the tourist zone, burned-out husks of buildings, unmistakable starburst patterns in the pavement, and bullet holes in walls are a constant reminder that the city is still recovering—physically and psychologically. In an age when we watch TV news cover-

age of conflicts abroad with the same detachment we give Hollywood blockbusters, Mostar provides an unpleasant but essential reminder of how real and how destructive war truly is.

Western visitors may also be struck by the immediacy of the Muslim culture that permeates Mostar. Here

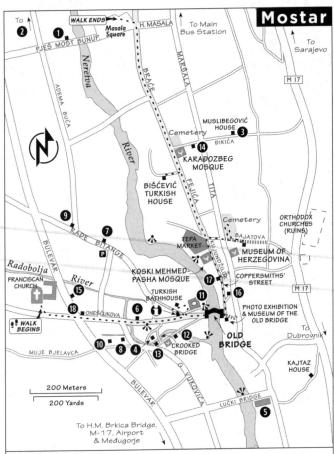

Mostar

MOSTAR

1. Hotel Bristol
2. To Hotel Ero
3. Muslibegović House
4. Motel Kriva Ćuprija
5. Hotel Kriva Ćuprija II
6. Motel Emen
7. Villa Fortuna B&B
8. Pansion Botticelli
9. Pansion Most
10. Dika Kasumačić Rooms
11. Bridge View Eateries
12. Restoran Hindin Han
13. Konoba Dvije Pećine
14. Saray Restaurant
15. Bistro Verona
16. Ali Baba Nightclub
17. Fortuna Tours
18. Future Synagogue Site

at a crossroads of civilizations, minarets share the skyline with church steeples. During the Ottomans' 400-year control of this region, many Slavic subjects converted to Islam. And, although they retreated in the late 19th century, the Ottomans left behind a rich architectural, cultural, and religious legacy that has forever shaped Mostar. Five times each day, loudspeakers on minarets crackle to life, the call to prayer warbles through the streets, and Mostar's Muslim residents flock into the mosques. In many parts of the city, you'd swear you were in Turkey.

If these factors intrigue you, read on—Mostar has so much more to offer. Despite the scars of war, its setting is stunning: straddling the banks of the gorgeous Neretva River, with tributaries and waterfalls carving their way through the rocky landscape. The sightseeing—mosques, old Turkish-style houses, and that spine-tingling Old Bridge—is more engaging than much of what you'll find in Croatia or Slovenia. And it's cheap—hotels, food, and museums are less than half the prices you'll pay in Croatia.

While a visit to Mostar just a few years ago was depressing, these days, more and more, it's uplifting. The city is rebuilding at an impressive pace, and local entrepreneurs are working hard to make Mostar tourist-friendly. Before long, Mostar will reclaim its status as one of the premier destinations in the former Yugoslavia. Visit now, while it still has its rough-around-the-edges charm—and you'll have seen it before it really took off.

Planning Your Time

Because of its cultural hairiness, a detour into Bosnia-Herzegovina feels like a real departure from a Dalmatian vacation. But actually, Mostar is easier to reach from Dubrovnik or Split than many popular Dalmatian islands (it's within a three-hour drive or bus ride from either city).

The vast majority of tourists in Mostar are day-trippers from the coast, which means the Old Town is packed midday, but empty in the morning and evening. You can get a good feel for Mostar in just a few hours, but a full day gives you time to linger and ponder.

You have three basic options: take a package tour from Dalmatia; rent a car for a one-day side-trip into Mostar; or (my favorite) spend the night here en route between Croatian destinations. To work a Mostar overnight into your itinerary, consider a round-trip plan that takes you south along the coast, then back north via Bosnia-Herzegovina (for example, Split-Hvar-Korčula-Dubrovnik-Mostar-back to Split).

Orientation to Mostar

(country code: 387; area code: 036)

Mostar—a mid-sized city with just over 100,000 people—is situated in a basin surrounded by mountains and split down the middle by the emerald-green Neretva River. Bosniaks live mostly on the east side of the river and Croats on the west (though increasingly the populations are mixing again). Visitors move freely throughout the city, and most don't even notice the division. The cobbled, Turkish-feeling Old Town (called the "Stari Grad" or—borrowing a Turkish term—the "Stara Čaršija") surrounds the town's centerpiece, the Old Bridge. Timid tourists feel most comfortable in the Old Town sector, and that's where I've focused my sightseeing, hotel, and restaurant recommendations.

The skyline is pierced by the minarets of various mosques, but none is as big as the two major Catholic (Croat) symbols in town, both erected since the recent war: the giant white cross on the hilltop (placed where Croat forces shelled the Bosniak side of the river, including the Old Bridge); and the enormous (almost 100-foot-tall) bell tower of the Franciscan Church of Sts. Peter and Paul. A monumental Orthodox cathedral once stood on the hillside across the river, but it was destroyed in the war when the Serbs were forced out. Funds are now being collected to rebuild it.

A note about safety: Mostar is as safe as any city its size, but it doesn't always *feel* safe. You'll see bombed-out buildings everywhere, even in the core of the city. Some are marked with *Warning! Dangerous Ruin* signs, but for safety's sake, never wander into any building that appears damaged or deserted.

Tourist Information

The virtually worthless TI shares a building with a tour office, but it does give out a free town map and a few other brochures on Mostar and Herzegovina (sporadic hours, generally open June-Oct daily 9:00-17:00, maybe later in busy times, likely closed Nov-May, just a block from the Old Bridge on Rade Bitange street, tel. 036/580-275, www.bhtourism.ba).

Arrival in Mostar

By Bus or Train: As with many things in Mostar, bus service is divided; most Bosniak (Muslim) buses, and some Croat ones, use the main bus station on the east side of town, while other Croat buses use a different stop, on the west side of town. (For details on this confusing system, see "Mostar Connections," at the end of this chapter.)

The main bus station, which is combined with the train station, is north of the Old Town on the east side of the river (about a 10-KM taxi trip). At the station, you'll find ticket windows in the lobby facing the bus stalls. But you're better off visiting the English-speaking and generally helpful Autoprevoz "tourist agency" (to the left as you face the station, tel. 036/551-900, www.autoprevoz-bus.ba; note that they have good information for Bosniak bus companies, but not necessarily for Croat ones). To find your way to town center, walk through the bus stalls and parking lot and turn left at the big road, which leads you to the Old Town area in about 15 minutes.

By Car: For tips on driving to Mostar from the Dalmatian Coast, see the end of this chapter.

Helpful Hints

Local Cash: Need Convertible Marks (KM)? The most convenient ATM in town is to the left of Fortuna Tours' door, right at the top of Coppersmiths' Street (Croatian kunas and euros are also accepted here). I have given hotel prices in euros; my recommended Mostar hotels will take either Convertible Marks or euros in payment.

Travel Agency: The handy **Fortuna Tours** travel agency, right in the heart of the Old Town (at the top of Coppersmiths' Street), sells all the tourist stuff, can book you a local guide, and answers basic questions (open long hours daily, Kujundžiluk 2, tel. 036/551-887, main office tel. 036/552-197, fax 036/551-888, www.fortuna.ba, fortuna_mostar1@bih.net.ba).

Local Guides: Hiring a guide is an excellent investment to help you understand Mostar. I've enjoyed working with **Alma Elezović,** a warm-hearted Bosniak who loves sharing her city with visitors (€20 per person up to €70 per group for 2-3-hour tour, includes entries into a Turkish house and a mosque, tel. 036/550-514, mobile 061-467-699, aelezovic@gmail.com). If Alma is busy, various companies around town can arrange for a local guide at extremely reasonable prices (€40/2-hour tour); try **Fortuna Tours,** listed above.

If someone approaches you offering to be your guide, ask the price in advance (they often charge ridiculously high rates). If they seem cagey or overpriced, decline politely. The official guides are better anyway.

Local Driver: Ermin Elezović, the husband of local guide Alma Elezović, is a friendly, English-speaking driver who enjoys taking visitors on day trips from Mostar. You can also hire him for a transfer between Mostar and destinations anywhere in Croatia (small car for up to 3 people: €100 for transfer to Split, Dubrovnik, or Sarajevo, or €150 for an all-day excursion; bigger van for up to 8 people: €150 for transfer to Split, Dubrovnik, or Sarajevo, or €200 for all day; tel. 036/550-514, mobile 061-908-597, elezovicermin@gmail.com).

Sights in Mostar

Mostar's major sights line up along a handy L-shaped axis. I've laced them together as an enjoyable orientation walk: From the Franciscan Church, you'll walk straight until you cross the Old Bridge. Then you'll turn left and walk basically straight (with a couple of detours) to the big square at the far end of town.

• *Begin at the...*

▲Franciscan Church of Sts. Peter and Paul

In a town of competing religious architectural exclamation points, this spire is the tallest. The church, which adjoins a working Franciscan monastery, was built after the fighting subsided in 1997 (the same year as the big cross on the hill). The tower, which looks at first glance like a minaret on steroids, is actually modeled after the typical Croatian/Venetian campanile bell towers. Step inside to see how the vast and coarse concrete shell awaits completion. In the meantime, the cavernous interior is already hosting services. (Sunday Mass here is an inspiration.)

• *The church fronts the busy boulevard called...*

▲Bulevar

This "Boulevard" was once the modern main drag of Mostar. In the early 1990s, this city of Bosniaks, Croats, and Serbs began to fracture under the pressure of politicians' propaganda. In October of 1991, Bosnia-Herzegovina—following Croatia's and Slovenia's example, but without the blessing of its large Serb minority—declared independence from Yugoslavia. Soon after, the Serb-dominated Yugoslav National Army invaded. Mostar's Bosniaks

and Croats joined forces to battle the Serbs and succeeded in claiming the city as their own and forcing out the Serb residents.

But even as they defended their city from the final, distant bombardments of Serb forces, the Bosniaks and Croats began to squabble. Neighbors, friends, and even relatives took up arms against each other. As fighting raged between the Croat and Bosniak forces, this street became the front line—and virtually all of its buildings were destroyed. Then as now, the area to the east of here (toward the river) was held by Bosniaks, while the western part of town was Croat territory.

While many of the buildings along here have been rebuilt, some damage is still evident. Stroll a bit, imagining the hell of a split community at war. Mortar craters in the asphalt leave poignant scars. (In Sarajevo, these have been filled with red resin to create monuments called "Sarajevo roses.") During those dark war years, the Croats on this side of the city laid siege to the Bosniaks (Muslims) on the other side, cutting off electricity, blocking roads, and blaring Croatian rabble-rousing pop music and Tokyo Rose-type propaganda speeches from loudspeakers. Through '93 and '94, when the Bosniaks dared to go out, they sprinted past exposed places, for fear of being picked off by a sniper. Local Bosniaks explain, "Night was time to live" (in black clothes). When people were killed along this street, their corpses were sometimes left here for months (because it wasn't safe to retrieve the bodies). Tens of thousands fled (Scandinavian countries were the first to open their doors, but many Bosnians ended up elsewhere in Europe, the US, and Canada).

The stories are shocking, and it's difficult to remain impartial. But looking back on this complicated war, I try not to broadly cast one side as the "aggressors" and another as the "victims." The Bosniaks were victimized in Mostar, just as the Croats were victimized during the siege of Dubrovnik. And, as the remains of a destroyed Orthodox cathedral on the hillside above Mostar (not quite visible from here) attest, the Serbs also took their turn as victims. Every conflict has many sides, and tragically it's the civilians who often pay the highest toll—no matter their affiliation.

Cross the boulevard and head down Onešćukova street. A few steps down on the left, the vacant lot with the menorah-ornamented metal fence will someday be the Mostar Synagogue. While the town's Jewish population has dwindled to a handful of families since World War II, many Jews courageously served as aid workers and intermediaries when Croats and Bosniaks were killing each other. In recognition of their loving help, the community of Mostar gave them this land for a new synagogue.

• *Continue past the synagogue site, entering the Old Town and following the canyon with the small river...*

Radobolja River Valley

The creek called Radobolja winds over waterfalls and several mills on its way to join the Neretva. As you step upon cobbles, you suddenly become immersed in the Turkish heritage of Mostar. From the arrival of the Ottomans all the way through the end of World War II, Mostar had fewer than 15,000 residents. This

compact central zone was pretty much all there was to the city until it became industrialized and grew like crazy during the Tito years. The historic core is cobbled with smooth, ankle-twisting river stones. Until 2004, the stones were simply embedded in loose sand, but now they're held together with concrete. As you explore, survey the atmospheric eateries clinging to the walls of this canyon—and choose one for a meal or drink later in the day (I've noted a couple under "Eating in Mostar," later).

Walk straight ahead until you reach a square viewpoint platform on your right. It's across from a charming little mosque and above a stream. The mosque is one of 10 in town. Before the recent war, there were 36. Many mosques were actually damaged or destroyed in World War II, but were never repaired or replaced (since Tito's communist Yugoslavia discouraged religion). But the recent war inspired Muslims to finally rebuild. Each of the town's newly reconstructed mosques has been financed by a Muslim nation or organization (this one was a gift from an international association for the protection of Islamic heritage). Around you are several fine examples of Mostar's traditional heavy limestone-shingled roofs.

• *Spanning the river below the mosque is the...*

▲Crooked Bridge (Kriva Ćuprija)

This miniature Old Bridge was built nearly a decade before its more famous sibling, supposedly to practice for the real deal. Damaged—but not destroyed—during the war, the bridge was swept away several years later by floods. The bridge you see today is a recent reconstruction.

• *Continue deeper on the same street into the city center. After a few steps, a street to the left (worth a short detour) leads to the* **TI**, *then a copper-domed* hammam, *or Turkish bathhouse, which was destroyed in World War II and only recently rebuilt. A happening nightlife and restaurant scene tumbles downhill toward the river from here, offering spectacular views of the Old Bridge.*

Back on the main drag, continue along the main shopping zone, past several market stalls, to the focal point of town, the...

▲▲▲Old Bridge (Stari Most)

One of the most evocative sights in the former Yugoslavia, this iconic bridge confidently spanned the Neretva River for more than

four centuries. Mostarians of all faiths love the bridge and speak of "him" as an old friend. Traditionally considered the point where East meets West, the Old Bridge is as symbolic as it is beautiful. Dramatically arched and flanked by two boxy towers, the bridge is striking—even if you don't know its history.

Before the Old Bridge, the Neretva was spanned only by a rickety suspension bridge, guarded by *mostari* ("watchers of the bridge"), who gave the city its name. Commissioned in 1557 by the Ottoman Sultan Süleyman the Magnificent, and completed just nine years later, the Old Bridge was a technological marvel for its time..."the longest single-span stone arch on the planet." (In other words, it's the granddaddy of the Rialto Bridge in Venice.) Because of its graceful keystone design—and the fact that there are empty spaces inside the structure—it's much lighter than it seems. And yet, nearly 400 years after it was built, the bridge was still sturdy enough to support the weight of Nazi tanks that rolled in to occupy Mostar. Over the centuries, it became the symbol for the town and region—a metaphor in stone for the way the diverse faiths and cultures here were able to bridge the gaps that divided them.

All of that drastically changed in the early 1990s. When the city became engulfed in war, the Old Bridge frequently got caught in the crossfire. Old tires were slung over its sides to absorb some of the impact from nearby artillery or shrapnel. In November 1993, Croats began shelling the bridge from the top of the mountain (where the cross is now—you can just see its tip peeking over the hill from the top of the bridge). Several direct hits caused the venerable Old Bridge to lurch, then tumble in pieces into the river. The mortar inside, which contained pink bauxite, turned the water red as it fell in. Locals said that their old friend was bleeding.

The decision to destroy the bridge was partly strategic—to cut off a Bosniak-controlled strip on the west bank from Bosniak forces on the east. (News footage from the time shows Bosniak soldiers scurrying back and forth over the bridge.) But there can be no doubt that, like the siege of Dubrovnik, the attack was also partly symbolic: the destruction of a bridge representing the city's Muslim legacy.

After the war, city leaders decided to rebuild the Old Bridge. Chunks of the original bridge were dredged up from the river. But the stone had been compromised by soaking in the water for so long, so it couldn't be used (you can still see these pieces of the old Old

MOSTAR

Bridge on the riverbank below). Staying true to their pledge to do it authentically, restorers quarried new stone (a limestone called *tenelija*) from the original quarry, and each stone was hand-carved. Then they assembled the stones with the same technology used by the Ottomans 450 years ago: Workers erected wooden scaffold-ing and fastened the stones together with iron hooks cast in lead. The project cost over $13 million, funded largely by international donors and overseen by UNESCO.

MOSTAR

It took longer to rebuild the bridge in the 21st century than it did to build it in the 16th century. But on July 23, 2004, the new Old Bridge was inaugurated with much fanfare and was immediately embraced by both the city and the world as a sign of reconciliation. Feel the shivers run down your spine as you walk over the Old Bridge today, and ponder its troubled yet inspirational past.

On a lighter note: One of Mostar's favorite traditions is for young men to jump from the bridge 75 feet down into the Neretva (which remains icy cold even in summer). Done both for the sake of tradition and to impress girls, this custom was carried on even during the time when the destroyed bridge was temporarily replaced by a wooden one. Now the tower on the west side of the bridge houses the office of the local "Divers Club," a loosely run organization that carries on this long-standing ritual. On hot summer days, you'll see divers making a ruckus and collecting donations at the top of the bridge. They tease and tease, standing up on the railing and pretending they're about to jump...then getting down and asking for more money. (If he's wearing trunks rather than Speedos, he's not a diver—just a teaser.) Once they collect about €30, one of them will take the plunge.

Before moving on, see how many of the town's 10 mosques you can spot from the top of the bridge (I counted eight minarets).

• *If you'd like to see one of the best **views** in town—looking up at the Old Bridge from the riverbank below—backtrack the way you came into the shopping zone, take your first left (at Šadran restaurant—a good place to try the powerful "Bosnian coffee"), then find the steps down to the river on the left.*

When you're ready to continue, hike back up to the Old Bridge and cross to the other side. After the bridge on the right are two different exhibits that are worth a quick visit. First is a good, free photo exhibition of powerful images of war-torn Mostar, displayed inside a former mosque for soldiers who guarded the bridge. Just beyond that, tucked into the corner on the right, look for the stairs leading up to the...

Museum of the Old Bridge (Muzej Stari Most)

Located within one of the Old Bridge's towers, this museum features a film and photos about the reconstruction of the bridge, archaeological findings, and a few other paltry exhibits about the history of the town and bridge, all in English. First you'll climb up the stairs just after the bridge and buy your ticket, before hiking the rest of the way up to the top of the tower, where you'll enjoy fine views through grubby windows. Then you'll go around below to the archaeological exhibit. The museum offers more detail than most casual visitors need; consider just dropping into the smaller, free photo exhibition described earlier, then moving along.

Cost and Hours: 5 KM, Tue-Sun 10:00-18:00, closed Mon, lots of stairs, Bajatova 4, tel. 036/551-602.

• *After the Old Bridge, the street swings left and leads you along...*

▲▲Coppersmiths' Street (Kujundžiluk)

This lively strip, with the flavor of a Turkish bazaar, offers some of the most colorful shopping this side of Istanbul. You'll see Mostar's

characteristic bridge depicted in every possible way, along with blue-and-white "evil eyes" (believed in the Turkish culture to keep bad spirits at bay), old Yugoslav army kitsch, and hammered-copper decorations (continuing the long tradition that gave the street its name). Partway up, the homes with the colorfully painted facades double as galleries for local artists. The artists live and work upstairs, then sell their work right on this street. Pop into the *atelier d'art* ("Đul Emina") on the right to meet Sead Vladović and enjoy his impressive iconographic work (daily 9:00-20:00). This is the most touristy street in all of Bosnia-Herzegovina, so don't expect any bargains. Still, it's fun. As you stroll, check out the fine views of the Old Bridge.

• *Continue uphill. About halfway along this street, on the left-hand side, look for the entrance to the...*

▲Koski Mehmed-Pasha Mosque (Koski Mehmed-Paša Džamija)

Mostar's Bosniak community includes many practicing Muslims. Step into this courtyard for a look at one of Mostar's many mosques. This mosque, dating from the early 17th century, is notable for its cliff-hanging riverside location, and because it's particularly accessible for tourists. The following information generally applies to the other mosques in Mostar, as well.

The Muslims of Mostar

While recent Muslim immigrants are becoming a fixture in most European cities, Bosnia-Herzegovina is one place where Muslims have continuously been an integral part of the cultural tapestry for centuries.

During the more than 400 years that Mostar was part of the Ottoman Empire, the Muslim Turks (unlike some Catholic despots at the time) did not forcibly convert their subjects. However, it was advantageous for non-Turks to adopt Islam (for lower taxes and better business opportunities), so many Slavs living here became Muslims. In fact, within 150 years of the start of Ottoman rule, half of the population of Bosnia-Herzegovina was Muslim.

The Ottomans became increasingly intolerant of other faiths as time went on, and uprisings by Catholics and Orthodox Christians eventually led to the end of Ottoman domination in the late 19th century. But even after the Ottomans left, many people in this region continued practicing Islam, as their families had been doing for centuries. These people constitute an ethnic group called "Bosniaks," and many of them are still practicing Muslims today (following the Sunni branch of the Muslim faith). Keep in mind that most Bosniaks are Slavs—of the same ethnic stock as Croats and Serbs—and look pretty much the same as their neighbors, although some Bosniaks have ancestors who married into Turkish families, and they may have some Turkish features.

Due to the recent actions of a small but attention-grabbing faction of Muslim extremists, Islam is burdened with a bad reputation in the Western world. But judging Islam based on Osama bin Laden and al-Qaeda is like judging Christianity based on Timothy McVeigh and the Ku Klux Klan. Visiting Mostar is a unique opportunity to get a taste of a fully Muslim society, made a bit less intimidating because it wears a more-familiar European face.

Here's an admittedly basic and simplistic outline (written

Cost and Hours: 4 KM to enter mosque, 4 KM more to climb minaret, daily April-Oct 9:00-18:00, until 19:00 at busy times, Nov-March 9:00-15:00.

Touring the Mosque: The fountain (*šadrvan*) in the courtyard allows worshippers to wash before entering the mosque, as directed by Islamic law. This practice, called ablution, is both a literal and a spiritual cleansing in preparation for being in the presence of Allah. It's also refreshing in this hot climate, and the sound of running water helps worshippers concentrate.

The minaret—the slender needle jutting up next to the dome—is the Islamic equivalent of the Christian bell tower, used to call people to prayer. In the old days, the *muezzin* (prayer leader) would climb the tower five times a day and chant, "There is only

by a non-Muslim) designed to help travelers from the Christian West understand a very rich but often misunderstood culture worthy of respect:

Muslims, like Christians and Jews, are monotheistic. They call God "Allah." The most important person in the Islamic faith is Muhammad, Allah's most important prophet, who lived in the sixth and seventh centuries A.D.

The "five pillars" of Islam are the same among Muslims in Bosnia-Herzegovina, Turkey, Iraq, Indonesia, the US, and everywhere else. Followers of Islam should:

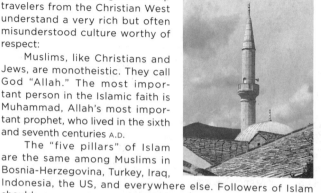

1. Say and believe, "There is only one God, and Muhammad is his prophet."

2. Pray five times a day, facing Mecca. Modern Muslims explain that it's important for this ritual to include several elements: washing, exercising, stretching, and thinking of God.

3. Give to the poor (one-fortieth of your wealth, if you are not in debt).

4. Fast during daylight hours through the month of Ramadan. Fasting is a great social equalizer and helps everyone to feel the hunger of the poor.

5. Visit Mecca. This is interpreted by some Muslims as a command to travel. Muhammad said, "Don't tell me how educated you are, tell me how much you've traveled."

Good advice for anyone, no matter what—or if—you call a higher power.

one God, and Muhammad is his prophet." In modern times, loudspeakers are used instead. Climbing the minaret's claustrophobic staircase is a memorable experience, rewarding you with a grand view at the top (entrance to the right of mosque entry).

Because this mosque is accustomed to tourists, you don't need to take off your shoes to enter (there's a special covering on the floor), women don't need to wear scarves, and it's fine to take photos inside. Near the front of the mosque, you may see some of the small, overlapping rugs that are below this covering (reserved for shoes-off worshippers).

Once inside, notice the traditional elements of the mosque. The niche *(mihrab)* across from the entry is oriented toward Mecca (the holy city in today's Saudi Arabia)—the direction all Muslims

MOSTAR

face to pray. The small stairway *(mimber)* that seems to go nowhere is symbolic of the growth of Islam—Muhammad had to stand higher and higher to talk to his growing following. This serves as a kind of pulpit, where the cleric gives a speech, similar to a sermon or homily in Christian church services. No priest ever stands on the top stair, which is symbolically reserved for Muhammad.

The balcony just inside the door is traditionally where women worship. For the same reason I find it hard to concentrate on God at aerobics classes, Muslim men decided prayer would go better without the enjoyable but problematic distraction of bent-over women between them and Mecca. These days, women can also pray on the main floor with the men, but they still must avoid physical contact.

Muslims believe that capturing a living creature in a painting or a sculpture is inappropriate. (In fact, depictions of Allah and the prophet Muhammad are strictly forbidden.) Instead, mosques are filled with ornate patterns and calligraphy (of the name "Muhammad" and important prayers and sayings from the Quran). Some of the calligraphy is in Arabic, and some is in Bosnian. You'll also see some floral and plant designs, which you'd never see in a more conservative, Middle Eastern mosque.

Before leaving, ponder how progressive the majority of Mostar's Muslims are. Most of them drink alcohol, wear modern European clothing (you'll see virtually no women wearing head scarves or men with beards), and almost never visit a mosque to pray. In so many ways, these people don't fit our preconceived notions of Islam...and yet, they consider themselves Muslims all the same.

The mosque's courtyard is shared by several merchants. When you're done haggling, head to the terrace behind the mosque for the best view in town of the Old Bridge.

• *Just beyond this mosque, the traffic-free cobbles of the Old Town end. Take a right and leave the cutesy tourists' world. Walk up one block to the big...*

▲▲New Muslim Cemetery

In this cemetery, which was a park before the war, every tomb is dated 1993, 1994, or 1995. As the war raged, more exposed cemeteries were unusable. But this tree-covered piece of land was relatively safe from Croat snipers. As the casualties mounted, locals buried their loved ones here under cover of darkness. Many of these people

were soldiers, but some were civilians. Strict Muslim graves don't display images of people, but here you'll see photos of war dead who were young, less-traditional members of the Muslim community. The fleur-de-lis shape of many of the tombstones is a patriotic symbol for the nation of Bosnia. The Arabic squiggles are the equivalent of an American having Latin on his or her tombstone—old-fashioned and formal.

• *Go up the wide stairs to the right of the cemetery (near the mosque). At #4 on the right, just before and across from the bombed-out tower, you'll find the...*

Museum of Herzegovina (Muzej Hercegovine)

This humble but worthwhile little museum holds fragments of this region's rich history, including historic photos and several items from its Ottoman period. There are sparse English descriptions, but without a tour guide the exhibits are a bit difficult to appreciate. Topics include the Turkish period, Herzegovina under the Austro-Hungarian Empire, village life, and local archaeology. One small room commemorates the house's former owner, Dzemal Bijedić, who was Tito's second-in-command during the Yugoslav period until he was killed in a mysterious plane crash in 1977. (If Bijedić had lived, many wonder whether he might have succeeded Tito...and succeeded in keeping Yugoslavia together.)

But the museum is made worthwhile by a deeply moving **film,** rated ▲▲, that traces the history of the town through its Old Bridge: fun circa-1957 footage of the diving contests; harrowing scenes of the bridge being pummeled, and finally toppled, by artillery; and a stirring sequence showing the bridge's reconstruction and grand reopening on that day in 2004—with high-fives, Beethoven's *Ode to Joy*, fireworks, and more divers.

Cost and Hours: 5-KM museum entry includes 12-minute film, no narration—works in any language, ask about "film?" as you enter, Mon-Fri 9:00-14:00, Sat 10:00-12:00, closed Sun, Bajatova 4—walking up these stairs, it's the second door that's marked for the museum, under the overhanging balcony, www.muzejhercegovine.com.

• *Backtrack to where you left the Old Town. Notice the* **Tepa Market,** *with locals buying produce, in the area just beyond the pedestrian zone. Now walk (with the produce market on your left) along the lively street called* **Braće Fejića.** *(There's no sign, but the street is level and busy with cafés.) You're in the "new town," where locals sit out in front of boisterous cafés sipping coffee while listening to the thumping beat of*

MOSTAR

distinctly Eastern-sounding music.

Stroll down this street for a few blocks. At the palm trees (about 50 yards before the minaret), you can side-trip a block to the left to reach...

▲Bišćević Turkish House (Bišćevića Kuća)

Mostar has three traditional Turkish-style homes that are open for tourists to visit. The Bišćević House is the first and most con-

venient for a quick visit, but two others are described at the end of this listing. Dating from 1635, the Bišćević House is typical of old houses in Mostar, which mix Oriental style with Mediterranean features.

Cost and Hours: 4 KM, daily March-Oct 8:00-20:00, Nov-Feb 9:00-15:00, Bišćevića 13.

Touring the House: Notice that the house is surrounded by a high wall—protection from the sun's rays, from thieves... and from prying eyes. First you'll step through the outer (or animals') garden,

then into the inner (or family's) garden. Notice how the smooth river stones are set in geometrical forms in the floor (for example, the five-sided star), and keep an eye out for the house's pet turtles. It's no coincidence that the traditional fountain *(šadrvan)* resembles those at the entrance to a mosque—a reminder of the importance of running water in Muslim culture. The little white building is a kitchen—cleverly located apart from the house so that the heat and smells of cooking didn't permeate the upstairs living area.

Buy your ticket and take off your shoes before you climb up the wooden staircase. Imagine how a stairway like this one could be pulled up for extra protection in case of danger. The cool, shady, and airy living room is open to the east—from where the wind rarely blows. The overhanging roof also prevented the hot sun from reaching this area. The loom in the corner was the women's workplace—the carpets you're standing on would have been woven there. The big chests against the wall were used to bring the dowry when the homeowner took a new wife. Study the fine wood carving and the heavy stonework of the roof.

Continue back into the main gathering room *(divanhan)*. This space—whose name comes from the word "talk"—is designed in a circle so people could face each other, cross-legged, for a good conversation while they enjoyed a dramatic view overlooking the Neretva. The room comes with a box of traditional costumes—great for photo fun. Put on a pair of baggy pants and a fez and really lounge.

Other Turkish Houses: If you're intrigued by this, consider dropping by Mostar's two other Turkish houses. The **Muslibegović House** (Muslibegovića Kuća) feels newer because it dates from 1871, just a few years before the Ottomans left town. This homey house—which also rents out rooms to visitors (see "Sleeping in Mostar," later)—has many of the same features as the Bišćević House. If she's not too busy, Sanela can give you an English tour (4 KM, mid-April-mid-Oct daily 10:00-18:00, closed to visitors off-season, just two blocks uphill from the Karadozbeg Mosque at Osman Dikica 41, tel. 036/551-379, www.muslibegovichouse .com). To find it, go up the street between the Karadozbeg Mosque and the cemetery, cross the busy street, and continue a long block uphill on the alley. The wall with the slate roof on the left marks the house.

The **Kajtaz House** (Kajtazova Kuća), hiding up a very residential-feeling alley a few blocks from the Old Bridge, feels lived-in because it still is (in the opposite direction from most of the other sights, at Gaše Ilića 21).

• *Go back to the main café street and continue to the...*

▲Karadozbeg Mosque (Karadozbegova Džamija)

The city's main mosque was completed in 1557, the same year work began on the Old Bridge. This mosque, which welcomes visitors,

feels less touristy than the one back in the Old Town. Before entering the gate into the complex, look for the picture showing the recent war damage sustained by this mosque (which has since been repaired). You'll see that this mosque has most of the same elements as the Koski Mehmed-Pasha Mosque (described earlier). But here, some of the decorations are original.

Cost and Hours: 4 KM to enter mosque, 4 KM more to climb minaret, daily May-Sept 9:00-19:30, Oct-April 10:00-15:00.

Nearby: Across the street is another cemetery with tombstones from that terrible year, 1993.

• *Now continue into modern, urban Mostar along the street in front of the Karadozbeg Mosque. This grimy, mostly traffic-free street is called...*

▲Braće Fejića

Walking along the modern town's main café strip, enjoy the opportunity to observe this workaday Bosniak town. You'll see the humble offices of the ragtag B&H Airlines; a state-run gambling office taxing its less-educated people with a state lottery; and lots of cafés that serve drinks but no food. People generally eat at home before going out to nurse an affordable drink. (Café ABC has good cakes and ice cream; the upstairs is a popular pizza hangout for students and families.)

Obituary announcements are tacked to trees by the mosque, listing the bios and funeral times for locals who have recently died. A fig tree grows out of the minaret in the small mosque—just an accident of nature illustrating how that plant can thrive with almost no soil.

Walking farther, you see a few ruins—still ugly nearly two decades after the war. There's a messy confusion about who owns what. Surviving companies have no money. Yugo Bank, which held the mortgages, is defunct. No one will invest until clear ownership is established. Until then, the people of Mostar sip their coffee and rip up their dance clubs in the shadow of these jagged reminders of the warfare that wracked this town not so long ago.

Near the end of the pedestrian zone, through the parking lot on the right, look for the building with communist-era reliefs of Bogomil tomb decor from the 12th century—remembering the indigenous culture before the arrival of the Ottomans.

When you finally hit the big street (with car traffic), head left one block to the big **Masala Square** (literally, "Place for Prayer"). Historically this was where pilgrims gathered before setting off for Mecca on their hajj. This is a great scene on balmy evenings, when it's a rendezvous point for the community.

• *For a finale, you can continue one block more out onto the bridge to survey the town you just explored. From here, you can backtrack to linger in the places you found most inviting.*

Nightlife in Mostar

Be sure to enjoy the local scene after dark in Mostar. Though the town is touristy, it's also a real urban center with a young popula-

tion riding a wave of raging hormones. The meat market in the courtyard next to the old Turkish bathhouse near the TI is fun to observe. The Old Bridge is a popular meeting place for locals as well as tourists (and pickpockets). A stroll from the Old Bridge down the Braće Fejića café-lined boulevard, to the modern Masala Square at the far end of town (described earlier), gives a great peek at Mostarians socializing.

Ali Baba is an actual cave featuring a fun, atmospheric, and youthful party scene. Order a cocktail or try a Turkish-style hubbly-bubbly (*šiša*, SHEE-shah). Ask to have one of these big water pipes fired up for you and choose your flavored tobacco: apple, cappuccino, banana, or lemon (20 KM per pipe per group, 8-KM cocktails, open late daily; look for low-profile,

cave-like entrance along Coppersmiths' Street, just down from the Old Bridge—watch for "Open Sesame" sign tucked down a rocky alley).

Sleeping in Mostar

My first two listings are big, full-service hotels, but a bit farther from the charming Old Town. The rest are small, friendly, accessible, affordable guest houses in or very near the Old Town. Mostar's Old Town can be very noisy on weekends, with nightclubs and outdoor restaurants rollicking into the wee hours. If you're a light sleeper, consider Villa Fortuna and the Muslibegović House, which are quieter than the norm.

$$$ Hotel Bristol is the only business-class place near central Mostar, overlooking the river a 10-minute walk from the heart of the Old Town. While it's on a busy street, the windows in its 47 rooms are good (Sb-€60, Db-€100, apartment-€115, extra bed-€16, air-con, elevator, pay Internet access, Mostarskog Bataljona, tel. 036/500-100, fax 036/500-502, www.bristol.ba, info @bristol.ba).

Sleep Code

(€1 = about $1.40, country code: 387, area code: 036)
S = Single, **D** = Double/Twin, **T** = Triple, **Q** = Quad, **b** = bathroom. Unless otherwise noted, prices include breakfast. To help you sort easily through these listings, I've divided the accommodations into three categories based on the price for a double room with bath in high season:

  $$$ Higher Priced—Most rooms €80 or more.
    $$ Moderately Priced—Most rooms between €40-80.
      $ Lower Priced—Most rooms €40 or less.

    Prices can change without notice; verify the hotel's current rates online or by email. For other updates, see www.ricksteves.com/update.

$$$ Hotel Ero, a 20-minute walk north of the Old Town, is a good big-hotel option, with 140 fine rooms and a professional staff. This was one of the only big buildings in the center not damaged during the war, since it hosted journalists and members of the international community and was therefore off-limits (Sb-€50, Db-€85, suite-€110, air-con, elevator, some traffic noise, ulica Dr. Ante Starčevića, tel. 036/386-777, fax 036/386-700, www.ero.ba, hotel.ero@tel.net.ba).

$$ The Muslibegović House, a Bosnian national monument that also invites tourists in to visit during the day, is in an actual

MOSTAR

Turkish home dating from 1871. The complex houses nine homey rooms and two suites, all of which combine classic Turkish style (elegant old beds, old floors, carpets, sofas; guest remove shoes at the outer door) with modern comforts (air-con, free Wi-Fi). Situated on a quiet residential lane just above the bustle of Mostar's main pedestrian drag and Old Town zone, this is the most enticing deal in town and a memorable experience (Sb-€50, Db-€70, "pasha suite"-€95, all prices €15 more in July-Aug, price includes tour of house, 2 blocks uphill from the Karađozbeg Mosque at Osman Dikica 41, tel. 036/551-379, www.muslibegovic house.com).

$$ Motel Kriva Ćuprija ("Crooked Bridge"), by the bridge of the same name, is tucked between waterfalls in a picturesque valley a few steps from the Old Bridge. It's an appealing oasis with seven rooms, three apartments, and a restaurant with atmospheric outdoor seating (Sb-€39, Db-€65, apartment-€70, extra bed-€20, 10 percent discount with this book, can be noisy, air-con, free Wi-Fi, Kriva Ćuprija 2, tel. 036/550-953, mobile 061-135-286, www.motel-mostar.ba, info@motel-mostar.ba, Sami). Their second location—called **Hotel Kriva Ćuprija II**—offers 10 rooms in a Habsburg-style building overlooking the river in a modern neighborhood about 200 yards to the south (same prices, discount, amenities, and contact information as main hotel; Maršala Tita 186, next to the Lučki Bridge).

$$ Motel Emen has six modern, sleek rooms overlooking a busy café street a few cobbled blocks from the Old Bridge (Sb-€40, Db-€60, bigger Db with balcony-€70, air-con, free Internet access and Wi-Fi, Onešćukova 32, tel. 036/581-120, www.motel-emen .com, info@motel-emen.com).

$ Villa Fortuna B&B, in a nondescript urban neighborhood a few minutes' walk farther away from the Old Bridge, has nine tasteful, modern, air-conditioned rooms. The rooms are just above the main office of Fortuna Tours, and you'll reserve through them. There's free, secure parking on the courtyard in front, and a pleasant garden in back (Sb-€30, Db-€40, breakfast-€5, tel. 036/552-197, mobile 063-315-017, fax 036/551-888, fortuna_headoffice@bih .net.ba). Fortuna Tours can also put you in touch with locals renting rooms and apartments.

$ Pansion Botticelli, overlooking a charming waterfall garden just up the valley from the Crooked Bridge, has five colorful rooms (Sb-€30, Db-€40, Tb-€60, breakfast-€3, air-con, Muje Bjelavca 6, enter around back along the alley, mobile 063-319-057, botticelli@bih.net.ba, Snježana and Zoran).

$ Pansion Most rents eight small, older-feeling rooms a few minutes' walk farther from the Old Bridge, above a sportsbook and a travel agency. I'd consider this a last resort for budget travelers (Sb-€25, Db-€38, air-con, Adema Buća 100, tel. 036/552-528, www.pansionmost.dzaba.com, pansion_most@yahoo.com).

$ Dika Kasumačić has five basic, inexpensive rooms on a quiet lane just above the Crooked Bridge action (S-€15, D-€30, cash only, air-con, follow green *pansion* signs from near Pansion Botticelli to Kapetanovina 16, mobile 061-506-443, sanjink@hot mail.com).

Eating in Mostar

Most of Mostar's tourist-friendly restaurants are conveniently concentrated in the Old Town. If you walk anywhere that's cobbled, you'll stumble onto dozens of tempting restaurants charging about the same reasonable prices and serving rustic, traditional Bosnian food. In my experience, the menu at most places is about the same—though quality and ambience can vary greatly. Grilled meats are especially popular. Another specialty here is *dolma*—a pepper stuffed with minced meat, vegetables, and rice. Sarajevsko Pivo beer is on tap.

On the Embankment, with Old Bridge Views

For the best atmosphere, find your way into the several levels of restaurants that clamber up the riverbank with perfect views of the Old Bridge. To reach these, go over the Old Bridge to the west side of the river, and bear right on the cobbles until you get to

MOSTAR

the old Turkish bathhouse, or *hammam* (with the copper domes on the roof). To the right of the bathhouse is the entrance to a lively courtyard surrounded with cafés and restaurants. Continuing toward the river from the courtyard, stairs lead down to several riverfront terraces. While you'll have menus pushed in your face as you walk, don't hesitate—poke around to find your favorite bridge view before settling in for a drink or a meal. If you want a good perch, it's fun and smart to drop by earlier in the day and personally reserve the table of your choice. In terms of the setting and views, this is the most memorable place to dine in Mostar—but be warned that the quality of the food along here is uniformly low.

Away from the Old Bridge

While they lack the Old Bridge views, these places serve food that's generally a step up. The first two places are in the atmospheric Old Town, while the last two are in the modern part of town.

Restoran Hindin Han is pleasantly situated on a woody terrace over a rushing stream. It's respected locally for its good cooking and fair prices (big 10-15-KM salads, 6-12-KM grilled dishes, 10-20-KM fish and other main dishes, Sarajevsko beer on tap, daily 11:00-24:00, Jusovina 10, tel. 036/581-054). To find it, walk west from the Old Bridge, bear left at the Šadrvan restaurant, cross the bridge, and you'll see it on the left.

Konoba Dvije Pećine ("The Two Caves") is a mom-and-pop place woven into a tangle of terraces over a rushing little stream facing the Crooked Bridge. It's known for its home-cooking (*domaća*—"homemade"—is the key word), and the food does taste a cut above the norm (6-18-KM plates, splittable mixed grill for 16 KM, daily 11:00-24:00, on Jusovina street at the end of the Crooked Bridge, mobile 061-558-228, Nuna and Jusa Dizdarević and Cako the charming head waiter).

Saray is a nondescript little eatery just uphill from the Karađozbeg Mosque in the modern part of town. They have a basic menu of very tasty grilled meats—specializing in the classic *ćevapčići* (little sausage-shaped meat patties)—and outdoor seating overlooking a playground that offers good people- and kid-watching while you eat (5-8-KM grilled meat dishes, big 6-7-KM salads, daily 9:00-17:00, mobile 061-529-320).

Bistro Verona sits along the bombed-out but increasingly revitalized Bulevar, in the shadow of the towering Franciscan Church. While as charming as a strip-mall diner, it's a great chance to eat—indoors or out—surrounded by a humble, friendly, and perfectly local scene without a hint of tourism (6-10-KM grilled meat dishes and pastas, Husnije Rebca 3, mobile 062-432-260).

Mostar Connections

By Bus

Not surprisingly for a divided city, Mostar has two different bus terminals, each served by different companies. On the east (Bosniak/Muslim) side of the river, you'll find the main bus station (called "Autobusna Stanica"; about a 15-minute walk north of the Old Town—for details, see "Arrival in Mostar," earlier). On the west (Croat/Catholic) side, the situation is less predictable: Some buses leave from a bus stop near the Franciscan Church, while others use a bus station (called "Kolodvor") on Vukovarska street.

Most Bosniak buses are operated by Autoprevoz (tel. 036/551-900, www.autoprevoz-bus.ba). Many Croat buses are run by Globtour (www.globtour.com). And local or regional buses are operated by Mostar Bus, whose buses depart from across the street from the main bus station (www.mostarbus.ba).

Tracking down reliable **schedule** information in Mostar is next to impossible. There's still tension between the Bosniak and Croat companies, which means there's often a lack of communication and therefore no single, reliable place where you can go to be sure you know all of your options. Start by checking the websites above, but realize that schedules can change unexpectedly. The Autoprevoz "tourist agency" at the main bus station (described earlier, under "Arrival in Mostar") is English-speaking and generally helpful, but they don't have dependable information about Croat-run buses. It's not unheard-of for someone to ride a bus here in the morning from Dubrovnik, expecting to take a late-afternoon bus back the same day—only to find that the day's last departure leaves just a few minutes after they arrive. While this sounds intimidating, it's workable. Just do your best to double-check schedules at both ends to be sure your connection lines up—especially if you'll be cutting it close. Note that buses to seasonal destinations (such as along the Dalmatian Coast) run more frequently in peak season, roughly June through mid-September.

From Mostar by Bus to: Međugorje (7/day Mon-Fri, 3/day Sat, none Sun, 50 minutes, mostly from the west side, 3 KM), **Sarajevo** (about hourly, 2.5 hours, from main bus station, 15 KM), **Zagreb** (daily at about 9:00, 8 hours, plus 1 night bus/day, 9.5 hours, 70 KM), **Split** (4-7/day depending on season, 4-4.5 hours, can be from either side—ask locally about your specific bus, 20-30 KM), **Dubrovnik** (2-5/day depending on season, 4-5 hours, from main bus station, 20-30 KM—but note that except for some weekends, most Dubrovnik buses leave early in the day, making an afternoon return from Mostar to Dubrovnik impossible). Service to **Korčula** is sporadic—sometimes once per week, sometimes none at all.

Enter the Dragon

Reconciliation works in strange and unexpected ways. In the early 2000s, idealistic young Mostarians formed the Urban Movement of Mostar, which searched for a way to connect the still-feuding Catholic and Muslim communities. As a symbol of their goals, they chose Bruce Lee, the deceased kung-fu movie star, who is beloved by both Croats and Bosniaks for his characters' honorable struggle against injustice. A life-size bronze statue of Lee was unveiled with fanfare in November 2005 in Veliki Park. Unfortunately, soon after, the statue was damaged. Whether or not the vandalism was ethnically motivated is unclear, but many locals hope the ideals embodied in the statue will continue to bring the city together.

By Train

Mostar is on the train line that runs from Ploče (on the Croatian coast between Split and Dubrovnik) to Zagreb, via Mostar and Sarajevo. This train—which leaves from next to the main bus station—generally runs once daily, leaving **Ploče** soon after 6:00 in the morning, with stops at **Mostar** (1.5 hours), **Sarajevo** (4.25 hours), and **Zagreb** (13.5 hours; bus is faster). Going the opposite direction, the train leaves Zagreb at about 9:00 in the morning.

Route Tips for Drivers

You have two ways to drive between Mostar and Dubrovnik: easy and straightforward, or adventurous and off the beaten path.

Between Mostar and the Main Coastal Road

The most convenient entry point into Bosnia-Herzegovina from the Dalmatian Coast is the town of **Metković,** about halfway between Dubrovnik and Split. (If you're driving there from Dubrovnik or Korčula, you'll actually cross into Bosnia-Herzegovina twice—including the short stretch of coastline that Bosnia-Herzegovina still controls, with the town of **Neum.**)

Near Metković, the main coastal road jogs away from the coast and around the striking **Neretva River Delta**—the extremely fertile "garden patch of Croatia," which produces a significant portion of Croatia's fruits and vegetables. The Neretva is the same river that flows under Mostar's Old Bridge upstream—but in Metković, it spreads out into 12 branches as it enters the Adriatic, flooding a vast plain and creating a bursting cornucopia in the middle of an otherwise rocky and arid region. Enjoying some of the most plentiful sunshine on the Croatian coast, as well as a steady supply of water for irrigation, the Neretva Delta is as productive as it is beautiful.

After passing through Metković, you'll cross the border into **Bosnia-Herzegovina,** then continue straight on the main road (M-17) directly into Mostar. As you drive, you'll see destroyed buildings and occasional roadside memorials bearing the likenesses of fresh-faced soldiers who died in the recent war.

Along the way are a few interesting detours: In Čapljina, you can turn off toward **Međugorje,** an unassuming little village and important Christian pilgrimage site. Since the first Virgin Mary sighting here in 1981, more than 30 million pilgrims have visited Međugorje. On the hills behind the main St. James Church (Crkva Sv. Jakova), trails lead to Apparition Hill (at Podbrdo), where the sightings occurred (a 1-mile hike, topped by a statue of Mary), and Great Hill (Križevac, or "Cross Mountain"), where a giant hilltop cross has become a secondary site of pilgrimage (1.5-mile hike).

Soon after, a mountaintop castle tower on the right side of the road marks the medieval town of **Počitelj**—an artists' colony with a compelling mix of Christian and Muslim architecture, including a big mosque and a multi-domed bathhouse. It's well worth pulling over and strolling around this steep village (pictured here).

With extra time, just before Mostar (in Buna), you can detour a few miles along the Buna River into **Blagaj**—the historical capital of the region until the arrival of the Ottomans. This is the site of a mountain called Hum, which is topped by the ruins of a hilltop castle that once belonged to Herzog ("Duke") Stjepan, who gave Herzegovina its name. Deep in Blagaj is an impressive cliff face with a scenic house marking the source of the Buna River. The building, called the Tekija, is actually a former monastery for Turkish dervishes (an order that emphasizes poverty and humility, and is famous for the way they whirl when in a worshipful trance); inside is a modest museum with the graves of two important dervishes. Today the area is surrounded by gift shops and a big restaurant with fine views over the river and cliff.

Approaching **Mostar** on M-17, you'll pass the airport, then turn left at your first opportunity to cross the river. After crossing the bridge, bear right onto Bulevar street, and continue on that main artery for several blocks (passing several destroyed buildings). At the street called Rade Bitange (just after the giant church bell tower), turn right to find the public parking lot—less than a 10-minute walk from the Old Bridge. Be warned that signage is poor; if you get lost, try asking for directions to "Stari Most" (STAH-ree most)—the Old Bridge.

Rugged-but-Scenic Backcountry Route Through Serbian Herzegovina

If you're visiting Mostar round-trip from Dubrovnik, consider coming back a different route, mostly through Herzegovina. This feels much more remote and takes an hour or two longer, but the roads are good and the occasional gas station and restaurant break up the journey. Since this route takes you through the Republika Srpska part of Herzegovina, most road signs are exclusively in the Cyrillic alphabet—though, interestingly, much of the advertising you'll see uses the more familiar Roman alphabet. (Because this road goes through the Serbian part of Herzegovina, it's not popular among Bosniaks or Croats—in fact, locals might tell you this road "does not exist." It does.)

This route is narrated from Dubrovnik to Mostar, but you can do it in reverse—just hold the book upside-down. If you want a little taste of Republika Srpska, consider just day-tripping into Trebinje—especially on Saturday, when the produce market is at its liveliest.

From Dubrovnik, head south toward Cavtat, the airport, and Montenegro. Shortly after leaving Dubrovnik, watch for signs on the left directing you to *Gornji Brgat*. Follow this road to the border of Bosnia-Herzegovina, cross the border, and carry on about 20 minutes into **Trebinje** (Требиње). Consider stopping for a break in Trebinje, a pleasant and relatively affluent town with a leafy main square that hosts a fine Saturday market. Overlooking the town from its hilltop perch is the striking Orthodox Church of Nova Gračanica, built to resemble the historically important  Gračanica Monastery in Kosovo. If you have time, drive up to the church's viewpoint terrace for great views over Trebinje and the valley.

From Trebinje, you have two options. One is to drive along the very pretty valley via **Ljubinje** (Љубиње) and **Stolac** (Столац), on the Serb-Muslim boundary, then to **Počitelj** (described earlier) and on to Mostar.

Or, for a longer, more remote, middle-of-nowhere adventure, consider this alternate route: From Trebinje, drive north toward **Bilećko Lake**—a vast, aquamarine lake you'll see on your right (the Vikiovac Restaurant offers a great viewpoint). Then you'll go through the town of **Bileća** (Билећа), turning west at the gloomy industrial town of **Gacko** (Гацко, with a giant coal mine), and onward to the humble but proud little town of **Nevesinje** (Невесиње). From Nevesinje, it's a quick drive up over the mountains, then down into Mostar—passing more familiar Roman-alphabet road signs, then spectacular views of Herzog Stjepan's imposing castle over the town of Buna. Follow signs on into Mostar.

CROATIA

The following two chapters are excerpted from *Rick Steves' Croatia & Slovenia.*

PLITVICE LAKES NATIONAL PARK

Nacionalni Park Plitvička Jezera

Plitvice (PLEET-veet-seh) is one of Europe's most spectacular natural wonders. Imagine Niagara Falls diced and sprinkled over a heavily forested Grand Canyon. There's nothing like this lush valley of 16 terraced lakes, laced together by waterfalls and miles of pleasant plank walks. Countless cascades and water that's both strangely clear and full of vibrant colors make this park a misty natural wonderland. Years ago, after eight or nine visits, I thought I really knew Europe. Then I discovered Plitvice and realized you can never exhaust Europe's surprises.

Planning Your Time

Plitvice deserves at least a good few hours. Since it takes some time to get here (two hours by car or bus from Zagreb), the most sensible plan is to spend the night in one of the park's hotels (no character, but comfortable and convenient) or a nearby private

home (cheaper, but practical only if you're driving). If you're coming from the north (e.g., Ljubljana), you can take the train to Zagreb in the morning, spend a few hours seeing the Croatian capital, then take the bus (generally no buses after about 16:00) or drive to Plitvice in the late afternoon to spend the night at the park. Get up early and hit the trails (ideally by 8:30); by early afternoon, you'll be ready to move on (by bus to the coast, or back to Zagreb). The most interesting and accessible part of the park can be seen very efficiently, in

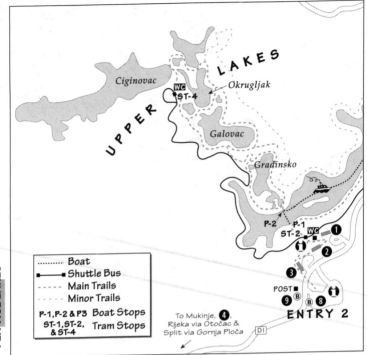

a three- to four-hour hike; while there are other hiking opportunities, they pale in comparison to this "greatest hits" section. Therefore, two nights and a full day at Plitvice is probably overkill for all but the most avid hikers.

Crowd-Beating Tips: Plitvice is swamped with international tour groups, many of whom aren't shy about elbowing into position for the best photos. The park's trails are most crowded between 10:00 and 15:00. It's essential to get an early start to get in front of the hordes. I try to hit the trails by 8:30; that way, the crowds are moving in just as I'm finishing up.

Getting to Plitvice

Plitvice Lakes National Park, a few miles from the Bosnian border, is two hours by car south of Zagreb on the old highway #1 (a.k.a. D-1).

By **car** from Zagreb, you'll take the A-1 expressway south for about an hour, exiting at Karlovac (marked for *1* and *Plitvice*). From here, D-1 takes you directly south about another hour to the park. If you're staying at the park hotels, you can park for free at the hotel lot; to park at the lots at Entrance 1 or Entrance 2, you'll have to pay (7 kn/hour). For information about driving onward from

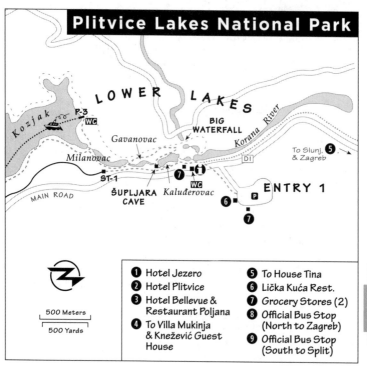

Plitvice Lakes National Park

LOWER LAKES

Kozjak

P-3

WC

Gavanovac

BIG WATERFALL

Korana River

To Slunj ⑤ & Zagreb

Milanovac

D1

ST-1

①

ENTRY 1

WC

P

⑥

MAIN ROAD

ŠUPLJARA CAVE Kaluđerovac

⑦

500 Meters

500 Yards

① Hotel Jezero
② Hotel Plitvice
③ Hotel Bellevue & Restaurant Poljana
④ To Villa Mukinja & Knežević Guest House

⑤ To House Tina
⑥ Lička Kuća Rest.
⑦ Grocery Stores (2)
⑧ Official Bus Stop (North to Zagreb)
⑨ Official Bus Stop (South to Split)

PLITVICE LAKES

Plitvice, see "Route Tips for Drivers" at the end of this chapter.

Buses leave from Zagreb's main bus station in the direction of Plitvice. Various bus companies handle the route; just go to the ticket window and ask for the next departure (about 75–95 kn depending on company, trip takes 2–2.5 hours). Buses run from Zagreb about hourly until about 16:00; while sporadic buses run late at night, they'll get you to the park extremely late and should be avoided. Confirm that your bus will actually stop at Plitvice. (The official Plitvice bus stop is along the main road, about a 5- to 10-minute walk beyond the hotels.) Confirm the schedule online (www.akz.hr) or at the Plitvice office in Zagreb (Mon–Fri 8:00–16:00, closed Sat–Sun, Trg Kralja Tomislava 19, tel. 01/461-3586).

By car or bus, you'll see some thought-provoking terrain between Zagreb and Plitvice. As you leave Karlovac, you'll pass through the village of **Turanj,** part of the war zone from almost two decades ago. The destroyed, derelict houses belonged to Serbs who have not come back to reclaim and repair them. Farther along, about 25 miles before Plitvice, you'll pass through the striking village of **Slunj,** picturesquely perched on travertine formations (like Plitvice's) and surrounded by sparkling streams and waterfalls. If you're in a car, this is worth a photo stop. This town, too, looks very different than it did before the war—when it was 30 percent Serb. As in countless other villages in the Croatian interior, the Orthodox church has been destroyed...and locals still seethe when they describe how occupying Serbs "defiled" the town's delicate beauty.

Orientation to Plitvice

(area code: 053)
Plitvice's 16 lakes are divided into the Upper Lakes (Gornja Jezera) and the Lower Lakes (Donja Jezera). The park officially has two entrances *(ulaz)*, each with ticket windows and snack and gift shops. Entrance 1 is at the bottom of the Lower Lakes, across the busy D-1 road from the park's best restaurant, Lička Kuća (described later, under "Eating in Plitvice"). Entrance 2 is about 1.5 miles south, below the cluster of Plitvice's three hotels (Jezero, Plitvice, and Bellevue; see "Sleeping in Plitvice," later). There is no town at Plitvice. The nearest village, Mukinje, is a residential community mostly for park workers (boring for tourists, but has some good private room options).

Cost: The price to enter the park during peak season (April–Oct) is 110 kn (80 kn Nov–March; covers park entry, boat, and shuttle bus). Park hotel guests pay the entry fee only once for their entire stay; if you're staying off-site and want to visit the park on several days, you'll have to buy separate tickets each day.

Hours: The park is open every day, but the hours vary by season. In summer, it's generally open 7:00–20:00 (last ticket sold at 16:00); in spring and fall, 8:00–18:00 (last ticket sold at 14:00); and in winter, 8:00–16:00 (last ticket sold at 12:00). Night owls should note that the park never really "closes"; these hours are for the ticket booths and the boat and shuttle bus system. You can just stroll right into the park at any time, provided that you aren't using the boat or bus. Again, for fewer tour-group crowds, visit early or late in the day.

Tourist Information
A handy map of the trails is on the back of your ticket, and big maps are posted all over the park. The big map is a good investment; the various English-language guidebooks are generally poorly translated and not very helpful (both sold at entrances, hotels, and shops throughout the park). The park has a good website: www.np-plitvicka-jezera.hr.

Getting Around Plitvice
Of course, Plitvice is designed for hikers. But the park has a few ways (included in entry cost) to help you connect the best parts.

By Shuttle Bus: Buses connect the hotels at Entrance 2 (stop ST2, below Hotel Jezero) with the top of the Upper Lakes (stop ST4) and roughly the bottom of the Lower Lakes (stop ST1, a 10-minute walk from Entrance 1). Buses start running early and continue until late afternoon (frequency depends on demand—generally 3–4/hour; buses run from March until the first snow—often Dec). Note that the park refers to its buses as "trains," which confuses some visitors. Also note that no local buses take you along the major road (D-1) that connects the entrances. The only way to get between them without a car is by shuttle bus (inside the park) or by foot (about a 40-minute walk).

By Boat: Low-impact electric boats ply the waters of the biggest lake, Kozjak, with three stops: below Hotel Jezero (stop P1), at the bottom of the Upper Lakes (P2), and at the far end of Kozjak, at the top of the Lower Lakes (P3). From Hotel Jezero to the Upper Lakes, it's a quick five-minute ride; the boat goes back and forth continuously. The trip from the Upper Lakes to the Lower Lakes takes closer to 20 minutes, and the boat goes  about twice per hour—often at the top and bottom of every hour. (With up to 10,000 people a day visiting the park, you might have to wait for a seat on this boat.) Unless the lake freezes (about every five years), the boat also runs in the off-season—though frequency drops to hourly, and it stops running earlier.

Sights in Plitvice

Plitvice is a refreshing playground of 16 terraced lakes, separated by natural travertine dams and connected by countless waterfalls.

Over time, the water has simultaneously carved out, and, with the help of mineral deposits, built up this fluid landscape.

Plitvice became Croatia's first national park in 1949, and was a popular destination during the Yugoslav period. On Easter Sunday in 1991, the first shots of Croatia's war with Yugoslavia were fired right here—in fact, the war's first casualty was a park policeman, Josip Jović. The Serbs occupied Plitvice until 1995, and most of the Croatians you'll meet here were evacuated and lived near

PLITVICE LAKES

The Science of Plitvice

Virtually every visitor to Plitvice eventually asks the same question: How did it happen? A geologist once explained to me that Plitvice is a "perfect storm" of unique geological, climatic, and biological features you'll rarely find elsewhere on earth.

Plitvice's magic ingredient is calcium carbonate ($CaCO_3$), a mineral deposit from the limestone. Calcium is the same thing that makes "hard water" hard. If you have hard water, you may get calcium deposits on your cold-water faucet. But these deposits build up only at the faucet, not inside the pipes. That's because when hard water is motionless (as it usually is in the pipes), it holds on to the calcium. But at the point where the water is subjected to pressure and movement—as it pours out of the faucet—it releases the calcium.

Plitvice works the same way. As water flows over the park's limestone formations, it dissolves the rock, and the water becomes supersaturated with calcium carbonate. When the water is still, it holds on to the mineral—which helps create the beautiful deep-blue color of the pools. But when the water speeds up and spills over the edge of the lakes, it releases carbon dioxide gas. Without the support of the carbon dioxide, the water can't hold on to the calcium carbonate, so it gets deposited on the lake bed and at the edges of the lakes. Eventually, these deposits build up to form a rock called travertine (the same composition as the original limestone, but formed in a different way). The travertine coating becomes thicker, and barriers—and eventually dams and new waterfalls—are formed. The moss and

the coastline as refugees. During those five years, the park saw virtually no tourists, and was allowed to grow wild—allowing the ecosystem to recover from the impact of so many visitors. Today, the war is a fading memory, and the park is again a popular tourist destination, with nearly a million visitors each year (though relatively few are from the US).

▲▲▲Hiking the Lakes

Plitvice's system of trails and boardwalks makes it possible for visitors to get immersed in the park's beauty. (In some places, the path leads literally right up the middle of a waterfall.) The official park map and signage recommend a variety of hikes, but there's no need to adhere strictly to these suggestions; invest in the big map and create your own route.

Most visitors stick to the main paths and choose between two basic plans: uphill or

grass serve as a natural foundation for the calcification. In other words, the stone hangs down like the foliage because the foliage guides the growth of the stone. Because of this ongoing process, Plitvice's landscape is always changing.

And why is the water so clear? For one thing, it comes directly from high-mountain runoff, giving it little opportunity to become polluted or muddy. And because the water calcifies everything it touches, it prevents the creation of mud—so the bottoms of the lakes are entirely stone. Also, a different mineral in the water, magnesium carbonate, both gives the water its special color (which, park rangers brag, changes based on the direction of the sunshine) and makes it highly basic, preventing the growth of plant life (such as certain algae) that could cloud the water.

The park contains nearly 1,300 different species of plants. Wildlife found in the park include deer, wolves, wildcats, lynx, wild boar, voles, otters, 350 species of butterflies, 42 types of dragonflies, 21 species of bats, and more than 160 species of birds (including eagles, herons, owls, grouse, and storks). The lakes (and local menus) are full of trout, and you'll also see smaller, red-finned fish called *klen* ("chub" in English). Perhaps most importantly, Plitvice is home to about 40 or 50 brown bears—a species now extremely endangered in Europe. You'll see bears, the park's mascot, plastered all over the tourist literature (and in the form of a scary representative in the lobby of Hotel Jezero).

PLITVICE LAKES

downhill. Each one has pros and cons. Park officials generally recommend hiking uphill, from the Lower Lakes to the Upper Lakes, which offers slightly better head-on views of the best scenery (this is the route described below). It also saves the most scenic stretch of lakes and falls—the Upper Lakes—for last. Hiking downhill, from Upper to Lower, is easier (though you'll have to hike steeply up out of the canyon at the end), and since most groups go the opposite way, you'll be passing—but not stuck behind—the crowds. Either way you go, walking briskly and with a few photo stops, figure on an hour for the Lower Lakes, an hour for the Upper Lakes, and a half-hour to connect them by boat.

Lower Lakes (Donja Jezera)—The lower half of Plitvice's lakes are accessible from Entrance 1. If you start here, the route marked *G2* (intended for groups, but doable for anyone) leads you along the boardwalks to Kozjak, the big lake that connects the Lower and the Upper Lakes (described later).

From the entrance, you'll descend a steep path with lots of **switchbacks,** as well as thrilling views over the canyon of the

Lower Lakes. As you reach the lakes and begin to follow the boardwalks, you'll have great up-close views of the travertine formations that make up Plitvice's many waterfalls. Count the trout. If you're tempted to throw in a line, don't. Fishing is strictly forbidden. (Besides, they're happy.)

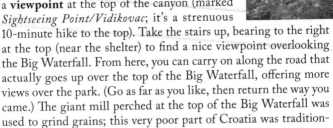

After you cross the path over the first lake, an optional 10-minute detour (to the right) takes you down to the **Big Waterfall** (Veliki Slap). It's the biggest of Plitvice's waterfalls, where the Plitvica River plunges 250 feet over a cliff into the valley below. Depending on recent rainfall, the force of the Big Waterfall varies from a light mist to a thundering deluge.

If you're a hardy hiker, consider climbing the steep steps from the Big Waterfall up to a **viewpoint** at the top of the canyon (marked *Sightseeing Point/Vidikovac*; it's a strenuous 10-minute hike to the top). Take the stairs up, bearing to the right at the top (near the shelter) to find a nice viewpoint overlooking the Big Waterfall. From here, you can carry on along the road that actually goes up over the top of the Big Waterfall, offering more views over the park. (Go as far as you like, then return the way you came.) The giant mill perched at the top of the Big Waterfall was used to grind grains; this very poor part of Croatia was traditionally inhabited by farmers.

After seeing the Big Waterfall, backtrack up to the main trail and continue on the boardwalks. After you pass another bank of waterfalls, a smaller trail branches off (on the left) toward **Šupljara Cave.** You can actually climb through this slippery cave all the way up to the trail overlooking the Lower Lakes (though it's not recommended). This unassuming cavern is a surprisingly big draw. In the 1960s, several German and Italian "Spaghetti Westerns" were filmed at Plitvice and in other parts of Croatia (which, to European eyes, has terrain similar to the American West). The most famous, *Der Schatz im Silbersee (The Treasure in Silver Lake)*, was filmed here at Plitvice, and the treasure was hidden in this cave. The movie—complete with *Deutsch*-speaking "Native Americans"—is still a favorite in Germany, and popular theme tours bring German tourists to movie locations here in Croatia. (If you drive the roads near Plitvice, keep an eye out for strange, Native American–sounding names such as Winnetou—fictional characters from these beloved stories of the Old West, by the German writer Karl May.)

After Šupljara Cave, you'll stick to the east side of the lakes, then cross over one more time to the west, where you'll cut through a comparatively dull forest. You'll emerge at a pit-stop-perfect clearing with WCs, picnic tables, a souvenir shop, and a self-service restaurant. Here you can catch the shuttle boat across Lake Kozjak to the bottom of the Upper Lakes (usually every 30 min).

Lake Kozjak (Jezero Kozjak)—The park's biggest lake, Kozjak, connects the Lower and Upper Lakes. The 20-minute boat ride between Plitvice's two halves offers a great chance for a breather. You can hike between the lakes along the west side of Kozjak, but the scenery's not nearly as good as in the rest of the park.

Upper Lakes (Gornja Jezera)—Focus on the lower half of the Upper Lakes, where nearly all the exotic beauty is. From the boat dock, signs for *B* direct you up to Gradinsko Lake through the most striking scenery in the whole park. Enjoy the stroll, taking your time...and lots of photos.

After Gradinsko Lake, you'll have two options:

1. Make your hike a loop by continuing around the far side of Gradinsko Lake and back to the P2 boat dock, where you can take the boat back over to the hotels (P1 stop).

2. Continue hiking up to the top of the Upper Lakes (following the icon for the shuttle bus); you'll get away from the crowds and feel like you've covered the park thoroughly. From here on up, the scenery is less stunning, and the waterfalls are fewer and farther between. At the top, you'll finish at shuttle bus stop ST4 (with food stalls and a WC), where the bus zips you back to the entrances and hotels.

Nice work!

Sleeping in Plitvice

At the Park

The most convenient way to sleep at Plitvice is to stay at the park's lodges, which are run by the same office (reservation tel. 053/751-015, fax 053/751-013, www.np-plitvicka-jezera.hr, info @np-plitvicka-jezera.hr; reception numbers for each hotel listed below). Warning: Because of high volume in peak season, the booking office often doesn't respond to emails. Instead, to make a reservation, use the park's website to book your room (look for the "Online booking" box). In a pinch, try calling the booking office or the hotel directly (they speak English), or emailing the park information office in Zagreb (np.zg.info@np-plitvicka-jezera.hr), which is more likely to respond in the busy summer months.

$$$ Hotel Jezero is big and modern, with all the comfort—and charm—of a Holiday Inn. It's well-located right at the park entrance and offers 200 rooms that feel newish, but generally have at least one thing that's broken. Rooms facing the park have big

PLITVICE LAKES

Sleep Code

(€1 = about $1.40, country code: 385, area code: 053)
English is spoken, credit cards are accepted, and breakfast is included at each place. The tourist tax (€1 per person, per day) is not included in these prices.

To help you sort easily through these listings, I've divided the accommodations into three categories based on the price for a double room with bath in high season:

$$$ **Higher Priced**—Most rooms €100 or more.
$$ **Moderately Priced**—Most rooms between €50-100.
$ **Lower Priced**—Most rooms €50 or less.

---

glass doors and balconies (July–Aug: Sb-€83, Db-€118; May–June and Sept–Oct: Sb-€76, Db-€108; Nov–April: Sb-€61, Db-€86; elevator, reception tel. 053/751-400).

$$ Hotel Plitvice, a better value than Jezero, offers 50 rooms and mod, wide-open public spaces on two floors with no elevators. For rooms, choose from economy (fine, older-feeling; July–Aug: Sb-€72, Db-€96; May–June and Sept–Oct: Sb-€65, Db-€82; Nov–April: Sb-€50, Db-€70), standard (just a teeny bit bigger; July–Aug: Sb-€77, Db-€106; May–June and Sept–Oct: Sb-€70, Db-€96; Nov–April: Sb-€55, Db-€74), or superior (bigger still, with a sitting area; July–Aug: Sb-€82, Db-€116; May–June and Sept–Oct: Sb-€75, Db-€106; Nov–April: Sb-€60, Db-€84, reception tel. 053/751-100).

$$ Hotel Bellevue is simple and bare-bones (no TVs or elevator). It has an older feel to it, but the price is right and the 80 rooms are perfectly acceptable (July–Aug: Sb-€55, Db-€74; May–June and Sept–Oct: Sb-€50, Db-€68; Nov–April: Sb-€40, Db-€54, reception tel. 053/751-700).

Sobe near the Park

While the park's lodges are the easiest choice for non-drivers, those with a car should consider sleeping at a **$–$$** *sobe* (room in a private home). You'll see *sobe* signs for miles on either side of the park. A few that have good reputations include **Villa Mukinja** (in the village of Mukinje just south of the park, tel. 01/652-1857, www.plitvice-lakes.com, info@plitvice-lakes.com), **House Tina** (just north of the park in the village of Grabovac, tel. 04/778-4197), and **Kneževic Guest House** (also in the village of Mukinje, tel. 053/774-081, mobile 098-168-7576, www.knezevic.hr, guest_house@vodatel.net, daughter Kristina speaks English).

Eating in Plitvice

The park runs all of the restaurants at Plitvice. These places are handy, and the food is affordable and decent. If you're staying at the hotels, you have the option of paying for half-board with your room (lunch or dinner, €12 each). This option is designed for the restaurants inside hotels Jezero and Plitvice, but you can also use the voucher at other park eateries (you'll pay the difference if the bill is more). The half-board option is worth doing if you're here for dinner, but don't lock yourself in for lunch—you'll want more flexibility as you explore Plitvice (excellent picnic spots and decent food stands abound inside the park).

Hotel Jezero and **Hotel Plitvice** both have big restaurants with adequate food and friendly, professional service (half-board for dinner, described above, is a good deal; or order à la carte; both open daily until 23:00).

Lička Kuća, across the pedestrian overpass from Entrance 1, has a wonderfully dark and smoky atmosphere around a huge open-air wood-fired grill (pricey, daily 11:00–24:00, tel. 053/751-024).

Restaurant Poljana, behind Hotel Bellevue, has the same boring, park-lodge atmosphere in both of its sections: cheap, self-service cafeteria and sit-down restaurant with open wood-fired grill (same choices and prices as the better-atmosphere Lička Kuća, above; both parts open daily but closed in winter, tel. 053/751-092).

For **picnic** fixings, there's a small grocery store at Entrance 1 and another one with a larger selection across road D-1 (use the pedestrian overpass). At the P3 boat dock, you can buy grilled meat and drinks. Friendly old ladies sell homemade goodies (such as strudel or hunks of cheese) throughout the park, including at Entrance 1.

Plitvice Connections

To reach the park, see "Getting to Plitvice," earlier in this chapter. Moving on from Plitvice is trickier. **Buses** pass by the park in each direction—northbound (to **Zagreb,** 2–2.5 hours) and southbound (to coastal destinations such as **Split,** 4–6 hours).

There is no bus station—just a low-profile *Plitvice Centar* bus stop shelter. To reach it from the park, go out to the main road from either Hotel Jezero or Hotel Plitvice, then turn right; the bus stops are just after the pedestrian overpass. The one on the hotel side of the road is for buses headed for the coast (southbound); the stop on the opposite side is for Zagreb (northbound). Try to carefully confirm the bus schedule with the park or hotel staff, then head out to the bus stop and wave down the bus. (It's easy to confuse public buses with private tour buses, so don't panic if a bus doesn't stop for you—look for a bus with your final destination marked in the windshield.)

But here's the catch: If the bus is full, they won't stop to pick you up at Plitvice. This is most common on days when the buses are jammed with people headed to or from the coast. For example, on Fridays—when everyone is going from Zagreb to Split—you'll have no luck catching a southbound bus at Plitvice after about 12:00, as they are likely to be full. Similarly, on Sunday afternoons, northbound buses are often full.

While this sounds risky, and there is a chance that you'll miss a bus and have to wait for the next one, in practice it usually works...if you're patient.

Route Tips for Drivers

Plitvice's biggest disadvantage is that it's an hour away from the handy A-1 expressway that connects northern Croatia to the Dalmatian Coast. You have three ways to access this expressway from Plitvice, depending on which direction you're heading.

Going North: If you're heading north (to Zagreb or Slovenia), you'll get on the expressway at **Karlovac.** From Plitvice, drive about one hour north on D-1 to the town of Karlovac, where you can access A-1 northbound. Alternatively, you can take A-1 southbound to A-6, which leads west to Rijeka, Opatija, and Istria (though this route is more boring and only slightly faster than the route via Otočac, next).

Going to Central Croatia: If you're going to central destinations, such as Istria, Rijeka, Opatija, or Rab, get on the expressway at **Otočac.** From Plitvice, go south on D-1, then go west on road #52 to the town of Otočac (about an hour through the mountains from Plitvice to Otočac). After Otočac, you can get on A-1 (north to Zagreb, south to the Dalmatian Coast); or continue west and twist down the mountain road to the seaside town of Senj, on the main coastal road of the Kvarner Gulf. From Senj, it's about an hour north along the coast to Rijeka, then on to Opatija or Istria; or an hour south to Jablanac, where you can catch the ferry to Rab Island.

During the recent war, the front line between the Croats and Serbs ran just east of **Otočac** (OH-toh-chawts), and bullet holes still mar the town's facades. (Watch for minefield warning signs just east of Otočac, but don't be too nervous—it's safe to drive here, but not safe to get out of your car and wander through the fields.) Today Otočac is putting itself back together, and it's a fine place to drop into a café for a coffee, or pick up some produce at the outdoor market. The Catholic church in the center of town, destroyed in the war but now rebuilt, has a memorial out back with its damaged church bells. Notice that the crucifix nearby is made of old artillery shells. Just up the main street, beyond

the big, grassy park, is the Orthodox church. Otočac used to be about one-third Serbian, but the Serbs were forced out during the war, and this church fell into disrepair. But, as Otočac and Croatia show signs of healing, about two dozen Serbs have returned to town and reopened their church.

Going South: If you're heading south (to Split and the rest of Dalmatia) from Plitvice, catch the expressway at **Gornja Ploča.** Drive south from Plitvice on D-1, through Korenica, Pećane, and Udbina, then follow signs for the A-1 expressway (and *Lovinac*) via Kurjak to the Gornja Ploča on-ramp. Once on A-1, you'll twist south through the giant Sveti Rok tunnel to Dalmatia.

PLITVICE LAKES

ROVINJ

Rising dramatically from the Adriatic as though being pulled up to heaven by its grand bell tower, Rovinj (roh-VEEN, Rovigno/roh-VEEN-yoh in Italian) is a welcoming Old World oasis in a sea of tourist kitsch. Among the villages of Croatia's coast, there's something particularly romantic about Rovinj—the most Italian town in Croatia's most Italian region. Rovinj's streets are delightfully twisty, its ancient houses are characteristically crumbling, and its harbor—lively with real-life fishermen—is as salty as they come. Like a little Venice on a hill, Rovinj is the stage set for your Croatian seaside dreams.

Rovinj was prosperous and well-fortified in the Middle Ages. It boomed in the 16th and 17th centuries, when it was flooded with refugees fleeing both the Ottoman invasions and the plague. Because the town was part of the Republic of Venice for five centuries (13th to 18th centuries), its architecture, culture, and even language are strongly Venetian. The local folk groups sing in a dialect actually considered more Venetian than what the Venetians themselves speak these days. (You can even see Venice from Rovinj's church bell tower on a very clear day.)

After Napoleon seized the region, then was defeated, Rovinj became part of Austria. The Venetians had neglected Istria, but the Austrians invested in it, bringing the railroad, gas lights, and a huge Ronhill tobacco factory. (This factory—recently replaced by an enormous, state-of-the-art facility you'll pass on the highway farther inland—is one of the town's most elegant structures, and is slated for extensive renovation in the coming years.) The Austrians chose Pula and Trieste to be the empire's major ports—cursing those cities with pollution and sprawl, while allowing Rovinj to linger in its trapped-in-the-past quaintness.

Before long, Austrians discovered Istria as a handy escape for a beach holiday. Tourism came to Rovinj in the late 1890s, when a powerful Austrian baron bought one of the remote, barren islands offshore and brought it back to life with gardens and a grand villa. Before long, another baron bought another island...and a tourist boom was underway. In more recent times, Rovinj has become a top destination for nudists. The resort of Valalta, just to the north, is a popular spot for those seeking "southern exposure"... as a very revealing brochure at the TI illustrates (www.valalta.hr). Whether you want to find PNBs (pudgy nude bodies), or avoid them, remember that the German phrase *FKK* (*Freikörper Kultur*,

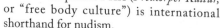

or "free body culture") is international shorthand for nudism.

Rovinj is the most atmospheric of all of Croatia's small coastal towns. Maybe that's because it's always been a real town, where poor people lived. You'll find no fancy old palaces here—just narrow streets lined with skinny houses that have given shelter to humble families for generations. While it's becoming known on the tourist circuit, Rovinj retains the soul of a fishermen's village; notice that the harbor is still filled not with glitzy yachts, but with a busy fishing fleet.

Planning Your Time

Rovinj is hardly packed with diversions. You can get the gist of the town in a one-hour wander. The rest of your time is for enjoying the ambience or pedaling a rental bike to a nearby beach. When you're ready to overcome your inertia, there's no shortage of day trips (the best are outlined in this chapter). Be aware that much of Rovinj closes down from November through Easter.

Orientation to Rovinj

(area code: 052)

Rovinj, once an island, is now a peninsula. The Old Town is divided in two parts: a particularly charismatic chunk on the oval-shaped peninsula, and the rest on the mainland (with similarly time-worn buildings, but without the commercial cuteness that comes with lots of tourist money). Where the mainland meets the peninsula is a broad, bustling public space called Tito Square (Trg Maršala Tita). The Old Town peninsula—traffic-free except for the occasional moped—is topped by the massive bell tower of the Church of St. Euphemia. At the very tip of the peninsula is a small park.

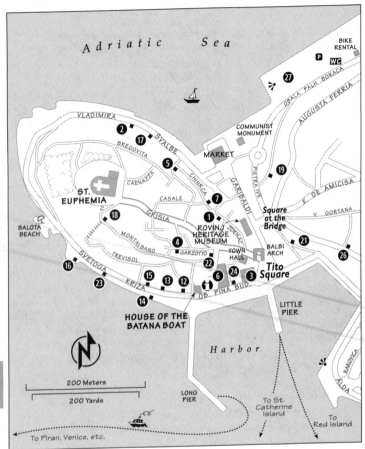

Tourist Information

Rovinj's helpful TI, facing the harbor, has several handy, free materials, including a town map and an info booklet (June-Sept daily 8:00-22:00; Oct-May Mon-Fri 8:00-15:00, Sat 8:00-13:00, closed Sun; along the embankment at Obala Pina Budičina 12, tel. 052/811-566, www.tzgrovinj.hr).

Arrival in Rovinj

By Car: To make a beeline to the Old Town, follow *Centar* signs through the little roundabout to the big parking lot on the water-front (5 kn/hour, or 4 kn/hour from 1:00-6:00 in the morning; as cars are not allowed into the Old Town itself, this is as close as you'll get). While this lot is the most convenient—and comes with the classic Rovinj view—the cost adds up fast if you're parking overnight. If it's full, you'll be pushed to another pay lot farther

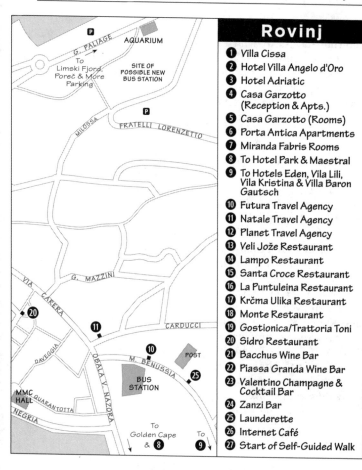

Rovinj

1. Villa Cissa
2. Hotel Villa Angelo d'Oro
3. Hotel Adriatic
4. Casa Garzotto (Reception & Apts.)
5. Casa Garzotto (Rooms)
6. Porta Antica Apartments
7. Miranda Fabris Rooms
8. To Hotel Park & Maestral
9. To Hotels Eden, Vila Lili, Vila Kristina & Villa Baron Gautsch
10. Futura Travel Agency
11. Natale Travel Agency
12. Planet Travel Agency
13. Veli Jože Restaurant
14. Lampo Restaurant
15. Santa Croce Restaurant
16. La Puntuleina Restaurant
17. Krčma Ulika Restaurant
18. Monte Restaurant
19. Gostionica/Trattoria Toni
20. Sidro Restaurant
21. Bacchus Wine Bar
22. Piassa Granda Wine Bar
23. Valentino Champagne & Cocktail Bar
24. Zanzi Bar
25. Launderette
26. Internet Café
27. Start of Self-Guided Walk

ROVINJ

out, along the bay northwest of the Old Town (a scenic 15-minute walk from town; 5 kn/hour in summer, 2 kn/hour off-season). If you're sleeping at a hotel away from the Old Town, carefully track individual blue hotel signs as you approach town.

By Bus: The bus station is on the south side of the Old Town, close to the harbor. Leave the station to the left, then walk on busy Carera street directly into the center of town. Note that there are plans to move the bus station to the other side of the Old Town, just above the long waterfront parking lots. If your bus stops here instead, simply head down to the main road and walk along the parking lots into town.

By Boat: The few boats connecting Rovinj to Venice, Piran, and other Istrian towns dock at the long pier protruding from the Old Town peninsula. Just walk up the pier, and you're in the heart of town.

Helpful Hints

Internet Access: A-Mar Internet Club has several terminals and long hours (40 kn/hour, Mon-Fri 8:00-22:00, Sat-Sun 9:00-23:00, on the main drag in the mainland part of the Old Town, Carera 26, tel. 052/841-211).

Laundry: The full-service **Galax** launderette hides up the street beyond the bus station. You can usually pick up your laundry after 24 hours, though same-day service might be possible if you drop it off early enough in the morning (70 kn/load wash and dry, daily 6:00-20:00, even longer hours in summer, closed Sun Oct-Easter, up Benussia street past the bus station, on the left after the post office, tel. 052/816-130).

Local Guides: Vukica Palčić is a very capable guide who knows her town intimately and loves to share it with visitors (€50 for a 2-hour tour, mobile 098-794-003, vukica.palcic@pu.t-com .hr). **Renato Orbanić** is a laid-back musician (sax) who also enjoys wandering through town with visitors. While light on heavy-hitting facts, his casual tour somehow suits this easy-going little town (€60 for a 2-hour tour, mobile 091-521-6206, rorbanic@inet.hr).

Best Views: The town is full of breathtaking views. Photography buffs will be busy in the "magic hours" of early morning and evening, and even by moonlight. The postcard view of Rovinj is from the parking lot embankment at the north end of the Old Town (at the start of the "Self-Guided Walk," next). For a different perspective on the Old Town, head for the far side of the harbor on the opposite (south) end of town. The church bell tower provides a virtual aerial view of the town and a grand vista of the outlying islands.

Self-Guided Walk

▲▲▲Rovinj Ramble

This orientation walk introduces you to Rovinj in about an hour. Begin at the parking lot just north of the Old Town.

Old Town View

Many places offer fine views of Rovinj's Old Town, but this is the most striking. Boats bob in the harbor, and behind them Venetian-looking homes seem to rise from the deep. (For an aerial perspective, notice the big billboard overhead and to the left.)

The Old Town is topped by

the church, whose bell tower is capped by a weathervane in the shape of Rovinj's patron saint, Euphemia. Local fishermen look to this saintly weathervane for direction: When Euphemia is looking out to sea, it means the stiff, fresh Bora wind is blowing, bringing dry air from the interior...a sailor's delight. But if she's facing the land, the humid Jugo wind will soon bring bad weather from the sea. After a day or so, even a tourist learns to look to St. Euphemia for the weather report.

As you soak in this scene, ponder how the town's history created its current shape. In the Middle Ages, Rovinj was an island, rather than a peninsula, and it was surrounded by a double wall—a protective inner wall and an outer seawall. Because it was so well-defended against pirates and other marauders (and carefully quarantined from the plague), it was extremely desirable real estate. And yet, it was easy to reach from the mainland, allowing it to thrive as a trading town. With more than 10,000 residents at its peak, Rovinj became immensely crowded, explaining today's pleasantly claustrophobic Old Town.

Over the centuries—as demand for living space trumped security concerns—the town walls were converted into houses, with windows grafted on to their imposing frame. Gaps in the wall, with steps that seem to end at the water, are where fishermen would pull in to unload their catch directly into the warehouses on the bottom level of the houses. (Later you can explore some of these lanes from inside the town.) Today, if you live in one of these houses, the Adriatic is your backyard.

• *Now head into town. In the little park near the sea, just beyond the end of the parking lot, look for the big, blocky...*

Communist-Era Monument

Dating from the time of Tito, this celebrates the Partisan Army's victory over the Nazis in World War II and commemorates the

victims of fascism. The minimalist reliefs on the ceremonial tomb show a slow prisoners' parade of victims prodded by a gun in the back from a figure with a Nazi-style helmet. Notice that one side of the monument is in Croatian, and the other is in Italian. With typical Yugoslav grace and subtlety, this jarring block shatters the otherwise harmonious time-warp vibe of Rovinj. Fortunately, it's the only modern structure anywhere near the Old Town.

• *Now walk a few more steps toward town, stopping to explore the covered...*

Market

The front part of the market, near the water, is for souvenirs. But natives delve deeper in, to the local produce stands. Separating the gifty stuff from the nitty-gritty produce is a line of merchants aggressively pushing free samples. Everything is local and mostly homemade. Consider this snack-time tactic: Loiter around, joking with the farmers while sampling their various tasty walnuts, figs, cherries, grapes, olive oils, honey, *rakija* (the powerful schnapps popular throughout the Balkans), and more. If the sample is good, buy some more for a picnic. In the center of the market, a delightful and practical fountain from 1908 reminds locals of the infrastructure brought in by their Habsburg rulers a century ago. The hall labeled *Ribarnica/Pescheria* at the back of the market is where you'll find fresh, practically wriggling fish. This is where locals gather ingredients for their favorite dish, *brodet*—a stew of various kinds of seafood mixed with olive oil and wine...all of Istria's best bits rolled into one dish. It's slowly simmered and generally served with polenta (unfortunately, it's rare in restaurants).

• *Continue up the broad street, named for* **Giuseppe Garibaldi**—*one of the major players in late-19th-century Italian unification. Imagine: Even though you're in Croatia, Italian patriots are celebrated in this very Italian-feeling town (see the "Italo-Croatia" sidebar). After one long block, you'll come to the wide cross-street called...*

Square at the Bridge (Trg na Mostu)

This marks the site of the medieval bridge that once connected the fortified island of Rovinj to the mainland (as illustrated in the small painting above the door of the Kavana al Ponto—"Bridge Café"). Back then, the island was populated mostly by Italians, while the mainland was the territory of Slavic farmers. But as Rovinj's strategic importance waned, and its trading status rose, the need for easy access became more important than the canal's protective purpose—so in 1763, it was filled in. The two populations integrated, creating the bicultural mix that survives today.

Notice the breeze? Via Garibaldi is nicknamed Val de Bora ("Valley of the Bora Wind") for the constant cooling wind that blows here. On the island side of Trg na Mostu is the Rovinj Heritage Museum (described later, under "Sights in Rovinj"). Next door, the town's cultural center posts lovingly hand-lettered signs in Croatian and Italian announcing upcoming musical events (generally free, designed for locals, and worth noting and enjoying).

Nearby (just past Kavana al Ponto, on the left), the Viecia Batana Café—named for Rovinj's unique, flat-bottomed little fishing boats—has a retro interior with a circa-1960 fishermen mural that evokes an earlier age. The café is popular for its chocolate cake and "Batana" ice cream.

ROVINJ

Italo-Croatia

Apart from its tangible attractions, one of Istria's hallmarks is its biculturalism: It's an engaging hybrid of Croatia and Italy. Like most of the Croatian Coast, Istria has variously been controlled by Illyrians, Romans, Byzantines, Slavs, Venetians, and Austrians. After the Habsburgs lost World War I, most of today's Croatia joined Yugoslavia—but Istria became part of Italy. During this time, the Croatian vernacular was suppressed, while the Italian language and culture flourished. This extra chapter of Italian rule left Istrians with an identity crisis. After World War II, Istria joined Yugoslavia, and Croatian culture and language returned. But many people here found it difficult to abandon their ties to Italy.

Today, depending on who you ask, Istria is the most Italian part of Croatia...or the most Croatian part of Italy. Istria pops up on Italian weather reports. A few years ago, Italy's then-Prime Minister Silvio Berlusconi declared that he still considered Istria part of Italy—and he wanted it back. When I wrote an article about Istria for a newspaper recently, some Italian readers complained that I made it sound "too Croatian," while some Croatians claimed my depiction was "too Italian."

People who actually live here typically don't worry about the distinction. Locals insist that they're not Croatians and not Italians—they're Istrians. They don't mind straddling two cultures. Both languages are official (and often taught side-by-side in schools), street signs are bilingual, and most Istrians dabble in each tongue—often seeming to foreign ears as though they're mixing the two at once.

As a result of their tangled history, Istrians have learned how to be mellow and take things as they come. They're gregarious, open-minded, and sometimes seem to thrive on chaos. A twentysomething local told me, "My ancestors lived in Venice. My great-grandfather lived in Austria. My grandfather lived in Italy. My father lived in Yugoslavia. I live in Croatia. My son will live in the European Union. And we've all lived in the same town."

ROVINJ

• *Now proceed to the little fountain in the middle of the square (near Hotel Adriatic).*

Tito Square (Trg Maršala Tita)

This wide-open square at the entrance to the Old Town is the crossroads of Rovinj. The **fountain,** with a little boy holding a water-spouting fish, celebrates the government-funded water system that finally brought running water to the Old Town in 1959. Walk around the fountain, with your eyes on the relief, to see a successful socialist society at the inauguration of this new water system. Despite the happy occasion, the figures are pretty stiff—

conformity trumped most other virtues in Tito's world.

Now walk out to the end of the concrete pier, called the **Mali Molo ("Little Pier")**. From here, you're surrounded by Rovinj's crowded harbor, with fishing vessels and excursion boats that shuttle tourists out to the offshore islands. If the weather's good, a **boat trip** can be a memorable way to get out on the water for a different angle on Rovinj. In Rovinj's own little archipelago, the two most popular islands to visit are St. Catherine (Sv. Katarina—the lush, green island just across the harbor, about a 5-minute trip, boats run about hourly in summer, 20 kn) and Red Island (Crveni Otok—farther out, about a 15-minute trip, boats run hourly in summer, 30 kn). Each island has a hotel and its own share of beaches. If you're more interested in the boat trip than the destination, it's also fun to simply go for a cruise to the various coves and islands around Rovinj. Your two basic options are a straightforward 1.5-hour loop trip around the offshore islands for around 100 kn; or a four-hour, 150-kn sail north along the coast and into the disappointing "Limski Canal" (a.k.a. "Limski Fjord"), where you'll have two hours of free time. To sort through your options, chat with the captains nearby hawking excursions.

Scan the **harbor**. On the left is the MMC, the local meeting and concert hall (described later, under "Nightlife in Rovinj"). Above and behind the MMC, the highest bell tower inland marks the Franciscan monastery, which was the only building on the mainland before the island town was connected to shore. Along the waterfront to the right of the MMC is Hotel Park, a typical monstrosity from the communist era, now tastefully renovated on the inside. A recommended bike path starts just past this hotel, leading into a nature preserve and the best nearby beaches (which you can see in the distance; for more on bike rental, see "Activities in Rovinj," later).

Now head back to the base of the pier. If you were to walk down the **embankment** between the harbor and the Old Town (past Hotel Adriatic), you'd find the TI and a delightful "restaurant row" with several tempting places for a drink or a meal. Many fishermen pull their boats into this harbor, then simply carry their catch across the street to a waiting restaurateur. (This self-guided walk finishes with a stroll down this lane.)

Backtrack 10 paces past the fountain and face the Old Town entrance gate, called the **Balbi Arch**. The winged lion on top is a reminder that this was Venetian territory for centuries.

• *Head through the gate into the Old Town. Inside and on the left is the red...*

Town Hall

On the old Town Hall, notice another Venetian lion, as well as other historic crests embedded in the wall. The Town Hall actually sports an Italian flag (along with ones for Croatia and Rovinj) and faces a square named for Giacomo Matteotti, a much-revered Italian patriot.

Continue a few more steps into town. Gostionica/Trattoria Cisterna faces another little square, which once functioned as a cistern (collecting rainwater, which was pulled from a subterranean reservoir through the well you see today). On your left, the building with a *batana* boat out front is the Italian Union—yet another reminder of how Istria has an important bond with Italy.
• *Now begin walking up the street to the left of Gostionica/Trattoria Cisterna.*

Grisia Street

The main "street" (actually a tight lane) leading through the middle of the island is choked with tourists during the midday rush and

lined with art galleries. This inspiring town has attracted many artists, some of whom display their works along this colorful stretch. Notice the rusty little nails speckling the walls—each year in August, an art festival invites locals to hang their best art on this street. With paintings lining the lane, the entire community comes out to enjoy each other's creations.

As you walk, keep your camera cocked and ready, as you can find delightful scenes down every side lane. Remember that, as crowded as it is today, little Rovinj was even more packed in the Middle Ages. Keep an eye out for arches that span narrow lanes (such as on the right, at Arsenale street)—the only way a walled city could grow was up. Many of these additions created hidden little courtyards, nooks, and crannies that make it easy to get away from the crowds and claim a corner of the town for yourself. Another sign of Rovinj's overcrowding are the distinctive chimneys poking up above the rooftops. These chimneys, added long after the buildings were first constructed, made it possible to heat previously underutilized rooms...and squeeze in even more people.
• *Continue up to the top of Grisia. Capping the town is the can't-miss-it...*

▲Church of St. Euphemia (Sv. Eufemija)

Rovinj's landmark Baroque church dates from 1754. It's watched over by an enormous 190-foot-tall campanile, a replica of the famous bell tower on St. Mark's Square in Venice. The tower is topped by a copper weathervane with the weather-predicting St. Euphemia, the church's name-sake.

Cost and Hours: Free, generally open May-Sept daily 10:00-18:00, Easter-April and Oct-Nov open only for Mass and with demand, generally closed Dec-Easter.

Touring the Church: Go inside. The vast, somewhat gloomy interior boasts some fine altars of Carrara marble (a favorite medium of Michelangelo's). Services here are celebrated using a combination of Croatian and Italian, suiting the town's mixed population.

To the right of the main altar is the church's highlight: the chapel containing the relics of St. Euphemia. Before stepping into the chapel, notice the altar featuring Euphemia—depicted, as she usually is, with her wheel (a reminder of her torture) and a palm frond (symbolic of her martyrdom), and holding the fortified town of Rovinj, of which she is the protector.

St. Euphemia was the virtuous daughter of a prosperous early fourth-century family in Chalcedon (near today's Istanbul). Euphemia used her family's considerable wealth to help the poor. Unfortunately, her pious philanthropy happened to coincide with anti-Christian purges by the Roman Emperor Diocletian. When she was 15 years old, Euphemia was arrested for refusing to worship the local pagan idol. She was brutally tortured, her bones broken on a wheel. Finally she was thrown to the lions as a public spectacle. But, the story goes, the lions miraculously refused to attack her—only nipping her gently on one arm. The Romans murdered Euphemia anyway, and her remains were later rescued by Christians. In the year 800, a gigantic marble sarcophagus containing St. Euphemia's relics somehow found its way into the Adriatic and floated all the way up to Istria, where Rovinj fishermen discovered it bobbing in the sea. They towed it back to town, where a crowd gathered. The townspeople realized what it was and wanted to take it up to the hilltop church (an earlier version of the one we're in now). But nobody could move it...until a young boy with two young calves showed up. He said he'd had a dream of St. Euphemia—and, sure enough, he succeeded in dragging her relics to where they still lie.

The small chapel behind the altar is dominated by Euphemia's famous sarcophagus. The front panel (with the painting of Euphemia) is opened with much fanfare every September 16, St. Euphemia's feast day, to display the small, withered, waxen face of Rovinj's favorite saint. The sarcophagus is flanked by frescoes depicting her most memorable moment (protected by angels, as a bored-looking lion tenderly nibbles at her right bicep) and her arrival here in Rovinj (with burly fishermen looking astonished as the young boy succeeds in moving the giant sarcophagus). Note the depiction of Rovinj fortified by a double crenellated wall—looking more like a castle than like the creaky fishing village of today. At the top of the hill is an earlier version of today's church.

• *If you have time and energy, consider climbing the...*

Bell Tower

Scaling the church bell tower's creaky wooden stairway requires an enduring faith in the reliability of wood. It rewards those who

brave the climb with a commanding view of the town and surrounding islands (10 kn, same hours as church, enter from inside church—to the left of the main altar). The climb doubles your altitude, and from this perch you can also look down—taking advantage of the quirky little round hole in the floor to photograph the memorable staircase you just climbed.

• *Leave the church through the main door. A peaceful café on a park terrace (once a cemetery) is a bit to your right. Farther to the right, a winding lane leads down toward the water, then forks. A left turn zigzags you past a WWII pillbox and leads along the "restaurant row," where you can survey your options for a drink or a meal (see "Eating in Rovinj," later). A right turn curls you down along the quieter northern side of the Old Town peninsula. Either way, Rovinj is yours to enjoy.*

Sights in Rovinj

▲**House of the Batana Boat (Kuća o Batani)**—Rovinj has a long, noble shipbuilding tradition, and this tiny but interesting museum gives you the story of the town's distinctive *batana* boats. Locals say this museum puts you in touch with the soul of this town.

Cost and Hours: 5 kn; June-Sept daily 9:00-13:00 & 19:00-22:00; Oct-Dec and March-May Tue-Sun 10:00-13:00 & generally also 15:00-17:00, closed Mon; closed Jan-Feb; Obala Pina Budicina

2, tel. 052/812-593, www.batana.org.

Touring the Museum: The flat-bottomed vessels are favored by local fishermen for their ability to reach rocky areas close to shore that are rich with certain shellfish. The museum explains how the boats are built, with the help of an entertaining elapsed-time video showing a boat built from scratch in five minutes. You'll also meet some of the salty old sailors who use these vessels (find the placemat with wine stains, and put the glass in different red circles to hear various seamen talk in the Rovinj dialect). Another movie shows the boats at work. Upstairs is a wall of photos of *batana* boats still in active use, a tiny library (peruse photos of the town from a century ago), and a video screen displaying *bitinada* music—local music with harmonizing voices that imitate instruments. Sit down and listen to several (there's a button for skipping ahead). The museum has no posted English information, so pick up the comprehensive English flyer as you enter.

Activities: The museum, which serves as a sort of cultural heritage center for the town, also presents a variety of engaging *batana*-related activities. On some summer evenings, you can take a **boat trip** on a *batana* from the pier near the museum. The trip, which is accompanied by traditional music, circles around the end of the Old Town peninsula and docks on the far side, where a traditional wine cellar has a fresh fish dinner ready,

with local wine and more live music (June–mid-Sept, generally 2 days per week—likely Tue and Thu at 20:30, boat trip-50 kn, dinner-120 kn extra, visit or call the museum the day before to reserve). Also on some summer evenings, you can enjoy an outdoor **food market** with traditional Rovinj foods and live *bitinada* music. The centerpiece is a *batana* boat being refurbished before your eyes (in front of museum, 20–30-kn light food, mid-June–early Sept generally Tue and Sat 20:00–23:00—but confirm details at museum). Even if you're here off-season, ask at the museum if anything special is planned.

Rovinj Heritage Museum (Zavičajni Muzej Grada Rovinja)—

This ho-hum museum combines art old (obscure classic painters) and new (obscure contemporary painters from Rovinj) in an old mansion. Rounding out the collection are some model ships and a small archaeological exhibit.

Cost and Hours: 15 kn; summer Tue-Fri 9:00-15:00 & 19:00-22:00, Sat-Sun 9:00-14:00 & 19:00-22:00, closed Mon; winter Tue-Sat 9:00-15:00, closed Sun-Mon; Trg Maršala Tita 11, tel.

052/816-720, www.muzej-rovinj.com.

Aquarium (Akvarij)—This century-old collection of local sea life is one of Europe's oldest aquariums. Unfortunately, it's also tiny (with three sparse rooms holding a few tanks of what you'd see if you snorkeled here), disappointing, and overpriced.

Cost and Hours: 20 kn, daily June–Aug 9:00-21:00, Sept 9:00-20:00, Oct–May 10:00-16:00 or longer depending on demand, across the street from the end of the waterfront parking lot at Obala G. Paliage 5, tel. 052/804-712.

Activities in Rovinj

▲**Swimming and Sunbathing**—The most central spot to swim or sunbathe is at **Balota Beach,** on the rocks along the embank-

ment on the south side of the Old Town peninsula (no showers, but scenic and central). For bigger beaches, go to the wooded **Golden Cape** (Zlatni Rt) south of the harbor (past the big, waterfront Hotel Park). This cape is lined with walking paths and beaches, and shaded by a wide variety of trees and plants. For a scenic and

memorable sunbathing spot, choose a perch facing Rovinj on the north side of the Golden Cape. Another beach, called **Kuvi,** is beyond the Golden Cape. To get away from it all, take a boat to an island on Rovinj's little archipelago (described earlier, on my self-guided walk).

▲**Bike Ride**—The TI's free, handy biking map suggests a variety of short and long bike rides. The easiest and most scenic is a quick loop around the Golden Cape (Zlatni Rt, described above). You can do this circuit and return to the Old Town in about an hour (without stops). Start by bik-

ing south around the harbor and past the waterfront Hotel Park, where you leave the cars and enter the wooded Golden Cape. Peaceful miniature beaches abound. The lane climbs to a quarry (much of Venice was paved with Istrian stone), where you're likely to see beginning rock climbers inching their way up and down. Cycling downhill from the quarry and circling the peninsula, you hit the Lovor Grill (open daily

ROVINJ

in summer 10:00-16:00 for drinks and light meals)—a cute little restaurant housed in the former stables of the Austrian countess who planted what today is called "Wood Park." From there, you can continue farther along the coast or return to town (backtrack two minutes and take the right fork through the woods back to the waterfront path).

Bike Rental: Bikes are rented at subsidized prices from the city parking lot kiosk (5 kn/hour, open 24 hours daily except no rentals in winter, fast and easy process; choose a bike with enough air in its tires or have them pumped up, as the path is rocky and gravelly). Various travel agencies around town rent bikes for quadruple the price (20 kn/hour); look for signs or ask around.

Nightlife in Rovinj

Rovinj After Dark

Rovinj is a delight after dark. Views that are great by day become magical in the moonlight and floodlight. The streets of the Old Town are particularly inviting when empty and under stars.

Concerts—Lots of low-key, small-time music events take place right in town (ask at the TI, check the events calendar at www.tzgrovinj.hr, and look for handwritten signs on Garibaldi street near the Square at the Bridge). Groups perform at various venues around town: right along the harborfront (you'll see the bandstand set up); in the town's churches (especially St. Euphemia and the Franciscan church); in the old cinema/theater by the market; at the House of the Batana Boat (described earlier, under "Sights in Rovinj"); and at the Multi-Media Center (a.k.a. the "MMC," which locals call "Cinema Belgrade"—its former name), in a cute little hall above a bank across the harbor from the Old Town.

Wine Bars—Rovinj has two good places to sample Istrian and Croatian wines, along with light, basic food—such as prosciutto-like *pršut*, truffles, and olive oil. Remember, two popular local wines worth trying are *malvazija* (a light white) and *teran* (a heavy red). At **Bacchus Wine Bar,** owner Paolo is happy to explain how the local wine has improved since communist times, when wine production stagnated (15-40 kn per deciliter, most cost around 20-30 kn, 70-250-kn bottles, daily 7:00-23:00, Carera 5, tel. 052/812-154). **Piassa Granda,** on a charming little square right in the heart of the Old Town, has a classy, cozy interior and 140 types of wine (18-25-kn glasses, 30-70-kn Istrian small plates, more food than Bacchus, daily 10:00-24:00, Veli trg 1, mobile 098-824-322, Helena).

Lounging—**Valentino Champagne and Cocktail Bar** is a memorable, romantic, justifiably pretentious place for a late-

night waterfront drink with jazz. Fish, attracted by its underwater lights, swim by from all over the bay...to the enjoyment of those nursing a cocktail on the rocks (literally—you'll be given a small seat cushion and welcomed to find your own seaside niche). Or you can choose to sit on one of the terraces. Classy candelabras twinkle in the twilight, as couples cozy up to each other and the view. Patricia opens her bar nightly from 19:00 until as late as there's any action. While the drinks are extremely pricey, this place is unforgettably cool (50-65-kn cocktails, 50-kn non-alcoholic drinks, Via Santa Croce 28, tel. 052/830-683). **La Puntuleina**—next door and listed later, under "Eating in Rovinj"—has a similarly rocky ambience, with lower prices (30-40-kn drinks) but a bit less panache than Valentino. **Zanzi Bar,** while named for an African archipelago, has a Havana ambience. Stepping over its threshold, you enter a colonial Caribbean world, with seating indoors or out on the tropical veranda (80 different cocktails for 45-60 kn each, nightly until 1:00 in the morning, near the TI on Obala Pina Budicina).

Batana Boat Activities—In summer, the House of the Batana Boat often hosts special events such as a boat trip and traditional dinner, and an outdoor food court. For details, see the listing earlier, under "Sights in Rovinj."

ROVINJ

Sleeping in Rovinj

Most Rovinj accommodations (both hotels and *sobe*) prefer longer stays of at least four or five nights, so in peak season (mid-July-mid-Sept), you'll likely run into strict minimum-stay requirements or high surcharges for shorter stays. Unfortunately, you'll probably have to simply eat this extra cost for a short stay. Hoteliers and *sobe* hosts are somewhat more flexible in the shoulder season. Don't just show up here without a room in August—popular Rovinj is packed during that peak month.

In the Old Town

All of these accommodations are on the Old Town peninsula, rather than the mainland section of the Old Town. Rovinj has no real hostel, but *sobe* are a good budget option.

Sleep Code

(5 kn = about $1, country code: 385, area code: 052)
S = Single, **D** = Double/Twin, **T** = Triple, **Q** = Quad, **b** = bathroom.

The modest tourist tax (7 kn per person, per night, lower off-season) is not included in these rates. Hotels accept credit cards and include breakfast in their rates, while most *sobe* accept only cash and don't offer breakfast. Everyone listed here speaks at least enough English to make a reservation (or knows someone nearby who can translate).

To help you sort easily through these listings, I've divided the accommodations into three categories based on the price for a double room with bath in high season:

$$$ Higher Priced—Most rooms 800 kn or more.
$$ Moderately Priced—Most rooms between 500-800 kn.
$ Lower Priced—Most rooms 500 kn or less.

Prices can change without notice; verify the hotel's current rates online or by email. For other updates, see www.ricksteves.com/update.

ROVINJ

$$$ Hotel Villa Angelo d'Oro is your Old Town splurge. The location—on a peaceful street just a few steps off the water—is ideal, and the public spaces (including a serene garden bar and sauna/whirlpool area) are rich and inviting. The 23 rooms don't quite live up to the fuss, but if you want your money to talk your way into the Old Town, this is the place (mid-July-Aug: Sb-950 kn, Db-1,600 kn; June-mid-July and Sept: Sb-860 kn, Db-1,450 kn; cheaper Oct-Dec and March-May, closed Jan-Feb, pricier suites also available, no extra charge for 1-night stays, no elevator, air-con, free Wi-Fi in lobby, bike rental for guests, Vladimira Švalbe 38-42, tel. 052/840-502, fax 052/840-111, www.angelodoro.hr, hotelangelo@vip.hr).

$$$ Porta Antica rents 15 comfortable, nicely decorated apartments in five different buildings around the Old Town (two houses—Porta Antica and Marco Polo—are on the peninsula, while the others are on the mainland). Review your options on their website and be specific in your request—though in busy times (July-Aug), they might not be able to guarantee a particular apartment. The underwhelming sea views aren't worth the extra expense. You'll pay less per night the longer you stay; I've listed rates per night for two-night stays, but you can check specific rates on their website (most of Aug: Db-1,000 kn; July: Db-920 kn; late May-June and late Aug-late Sept: Db-675 kn; rest of year: Db-570 kn; sea views-70-140 kn extra, extra person-180 kn, no breakfast, air-con, tries to be non-smoking, open year-round, reception and main building next door to TI on Obala Pina Budičina, tel. 052/812-548, mobile 099-680-1101, www.portaantica.com, porta antica@yahoo.it).

$$$ Hotel Adriatic, a lightly renovated holdover from the communist days, features 27 rooms overlooking the main square, where the Old Town peninsula meets the mainland. The quality of the drab, worn rooms doesn't justify the outrageously high prices...but the location might. Of the big chain of Maistra hotels, this is the only one in the Old Town (rates flex with demand, in top season figure Sb-1,125 kn, Db-1,700 kn; these prices are per night for 1- or 2-night stays—cheaper for 3 nights or more, all Sb are non-view, most Db are twins and have views—otherwise 150 kn less, closed mid-Oct-March, no elevator, air-con, pay Wi-Fi, some nighttime noise—especially on weekends, Trg Maršala Tita, tel. 052/803-520, fax 052/813-573, www.maistra.hr, adriatic @maistra.hr).

$$ Villa Cissa, run by Zagreb transplant Veljko Despot, has three apartments with tastefully modern, artistic decor above an art gallery in the Old Town. Kind, welcoming Veljko—who looks a bit like Robin Williams—is a fascinating guy who had an illustrious career as a rock-and-roll journalist (he was the only Eastern Bloc reporter to interview the Beatles) and record-company executive. Now his sophisticated, artistic style is reflected in these comfortable apartments. Because the place is designed for longer stays, you'll pay a premium for a short visit (50 percent extra for 2-night stays, prices double for 1-night stays), and it comes with some one-time fees, such as for cleaning. Veljko lives off-site, so be sure to clearly communicate your arrival time (July-early Sept: Db-700 kn; most of Sept: Db-625 kn; May-June and late Sept-Oct: Db-550 kn; April: Db-480 kn; rest of the year: Db-410 kn; about 650-700 kn more for bigger apartment; cash only, air-con, free Wi-Fi, some night noise from café across the street, Zdenac 14, tel. 052/813-080, www.villacissa.com, info@villacissa.com).

$$ Casa Garzotto is an appealing mid-range option, with four apartments, four rooms, and one large family apartment in three different Old Town buildings. These classy and classic lodgings have modern facilities but old-fashioned charm, with antique furniture and historic family portraits on the walls. Thoughtfully run by a friendly staff, it's a winner (rooms—mid-June-late Sept: Sb-370 kn, Db-520 kn; rest of year: Sb-300 kn, Db-450 kn; apartments—mid-July-Aug: 1,030 kn, mid-June-mid-July and Sept: 920 kn, mid-May-mid-June and early Oct: 780 kn, less off-season; 2-bedroom family apartment—mid-June-Sept: Db-890-1,030 kn, Tb-1,110 kn, Qb-1,470 kn; mid-May-mid-June and early Oct: Db-780 kn, Tb-960 kn, Qb-1,180; includes breakfast,

ROVINJ

off-site parking, loaner bikes, and other thoughtful extras; no extra charge for 1-night stays, air-con, lots of stairs, free Wi-Fi in main building, reception and most apartments are at Garzotto 8, others are a short walk away, tel. 052/811-884, mobile 098-616-168, www .casa-garzotto.com, casagarzotto@gmail.com).

$ Miranda Fabris is an outgoing local teacher who rents four cheap, basic, tight apartments with kitchenettes. While rough around the edges, the rooms are affordable and pleasantly located in the thick of the Old Town (July-Aug: Db-370 kn; Sept-June: Db-300 kn; no extra charge for 1- or 2-night stays, cash only, no breakfast, lots of steep stairs, across from Villa Val de Bora at Chiurca 5, mobile 091-881-8881, miranda_fabris@yahoo.com).

$ Other *Sobe:* Try looking for your own room online (www .inforovinj.com is helpful). Several agencies rent private rooms in the Old Town for good prices (figure Db-150-300 kn, depending on season, location, and size). But remember that in peak season, you'll pay about 70 percent extra for a one-night stay, and 30 percent extra for a two- or three-night stay. Just about everyone in town has a line on rooms. These two agencies are English-friendly and handy to the bus station (open sporadic hours, based on demand): **Futura Travel** (across from bus station at Benussi 2, tel. 052/817-281, fax 052/817-282, www.futura-travel.hr) and **Natale** (Carducci 4, tel. & fax 052/813-365, www.rovinj.com). In the Old Town, try **Planet,** near the TI (Sv. Križa 1, tel. 052/840-494, www .planetrovinj.com).

On the Mainland

To escape the high prices of Rovinj's Old Town, consider the resort neighborhood just south of the harbor. While the big hotels themselves are an option, I prefer cheaper alternatives in the same area. The big hotels are signposted as you approach town (follow signs for *hoteli,* then your specific hotel). Once you're on the road to Hotels Eden and Park, the smaller ones are easy to reach: Villa Baron Gautsch is actually on the road to Hotel Park (on the right, brown *pansion* sign just before Hotel Park itself); Hotel Vila Lili and Vila Kristina are a little farther on the main road toward Eden (to the left just after turnoff for Hotel Park, look for signs). All of these options are about a 15-minute uphill walk from the Old Town.

$$$ Maistra Hotels: The local hotel conglomerate, Maistra, has several hotels in the lush parklands just south of the Old Town. Most of my readers—looking for proximity to the Old Town rather than predictable rooms, a big lounge, and hotel-based activities—will prefer to save money and stay at one of my other listings. These hotels have extremely slippery pricing, based on the hotel, the type of room, the season, and how far ahead you book (for starters, in July-Aug figure non-view Sb-925 kn, non-view Db-1,240 kn, view

Db-1,450 kn, more for 1- or 2-night stays, cheaper off-season), but you'll have to call or check the website for specifics (www.maistra .hr). **Hotel Park** has 202 thoroughly renovated but dull rooms in a colorized communist-era hull, and a seaside swimming pool with sweeping views to the Old Town. From here, you can walk in about 15 minutes along the scenic harborfront promenade into town (tel. 052/811-077, fax 052/816-977, park@maistra.hr). **Hotel Eden** offers 325 upscale, imaginatively updated rooms with oodles of contemporary style behind a brooding communist facade. This flagship hotel is the fanciest one in the Maistra chain, but it's a bit farther from the Old Town—frustrating without a car (10 percent extra for fancier rooms, tel. 052/800-400, fax 052/811-349, eden@maistra.hr). Both hotels have air-conditioning, elevators, free parking, and pay Internet access. The Maistra chain also has several other properties (including the Old Town's Hotel Adriatic, described earlier, and other more distant, cheaper options). Only one branch of the Maistra chain remains open through the winter.

$$$ **Hotel Vila Lili,** a lesser value, is a family-run hotel with 20 overpriced rooms above a restaurant on a quiet, leafy lane (April-Oct: Sb-450 kn, Db-800 kn; shoulder season: Sb-370 kn, Db-550 kn; cheaper off-season, pricier suites also available, 10 percent discount with this book except in July-Aug, no extra charge for 1-night stays, elevator, air-con, parking-30 kn/day, Mohorovičića 16, tel. 052/840-940, fax 052/840-944, www.hotel -vilalili.hr, info@hotel-vilalili.hr, Petričević family).

$$ **Vila Kristina,** run by friendly Kristina Kiš and her family, has 10 rooms and five apartments along a busy road (July-Aug: Db-590 kn, extra bed-295 kn; Sept-June: Db-520 kn, extra bed-260 kn; includes breakfast, air-con, no elevator, free Wi-Fi, Luje Adamovića 16, tel. 052/815-537, www.kis-rovinj.com, kristinakis @mail.inet.hr).

$$ **Villa Baron Gautsch,** named for a shipwreck, is a German-owned pension with 17 comfortable rooms and an inviting, shared terrace with a view (late July-early Sept: Db-570 kn; late June-late July and early Sept-early Oct: Db-500 kn; off-season: Db-400-440 kn; they also have two Sb for half the Db price, 20 percent more for 1- or 2-night stays, 35 kn less without balcony, non-balcony rooms have air-con, closed Nov-Easter, cash only, no elevator, free Wi-Fi, Ronjgova 7, tel. 052/840-538, fax 052/840-537, www.baron-gautsch.com, baron.gautsch@gmx.net).

Eating in Rovinj

It's expensive to dine in Rovinj—don't expect great value for your money. Interchangeable restaurants cluster where Rovinj's Old Town peninsula meets the mainland, and all around the harbor.

ROVINJ

Be warned that most eateries—like much of Rovinj—close for the winter (roughly November to Easter).

Along Rovinj's "Restaurant Row"

The easiest dining option is to stroll the Old Town embankment overlooking the harbor (Obala Pina Budičina), which changes its name to Svetoga Križa and cuts behind the buildings after a few blocks. Window-shop the pricey but scenic eateries along here, each of which has its own personality (all open long hours daily). I've listed these in the order you'll reach them. You'll pay top dollar, but the ambience is memorable.

Veli Jože, with a few outdoor tables and a rollicking, folksy interior decorated to the hilt, is in all the guidebooks but still delivers on its traditional, if overpriced, Istrian cuisine (35-80-kn pastas, 60-120-kn main courses, Sv. Križa 1, tel. 052/816-337).

Lampo is simpler, with scenic seating right on the water—fine for a big salad, pizza, or pasta at a reasonable price (30-45-kn pastas, 60-100-kn main courses, Sv. Križa 22).

Santa Croce, with tables scenically scattered along a terraced incline that looks like a stage set, is well-respected for its pricey seafood and pastas (50-70-kn pastas, 70-160-kn main courses, daily 18:00-24:00, Sv. Križa 11, tel. 052/842-240).

La Puntuleina, at the end of the row, is the most scenic option. This upscale restaurant/cocktail bar/wine bar features pricey Italo-Mediterranean cuisine served in the contemporary dining room, or outside—either on one of the many terraces, or at tables literally scattered along the rocks overlooking a swimming hole. The menu is short, and the selection each day is even less, since Miriam and Giovanni insist on serving only what's fresh in the market. I wouldn't pay these prices unless I got a nice table out on a terrace. Reservations are recommended (80-100-kn pastas, 100-160-kn main courses, Thu-Tue 12:00-15:00 & 18:00-22:00, closed Wed except in peak season, closed Nov-Easter, on the Old Town embankment past the harbor at Sv. Križa 38, tel. 052/813-186). You can also order just a drink to sip while sitting down on the rocks.

Just before La Puntuleina, don't miss the inviting **Valentino Champagne and Cocktail Bar**—with no food but similar "drinks on the rocks" ambience (described earlier, under "Nightlife in Rovinj"). If you're on a tight budget, dine cheaply elsewhere, then come here for an after-dinner finale.

ROVINJ

International Fare in the Old Town Peninsula

Offering upscale, international (rather than strictly Croatian) food and presentation, these options are expensive but memorable.

Krčma Ulika, a classy hole-in-the-wall run by Inja Tucman, has a mellow, cozy, art-strewn interior. Inja enjoys surprising diners with unexpected flavor combinations. While the lack of a real kitchen in the back makes this less than a gourmet experience, the food preparation area in a corner of the tight, six-table dining room adds to the ambience. The food is a bit overpriced and can be hit-or-miss, but the experience feels like an innovative break from traditional Croatian fare. Explore your options with Inja's help before ordering (12-kn cover, 100-130-kn main courses, daily 19:00-1:00 in the morning, Sun-Thu also 13:00-15:00, until 23:00 in shoulder season, closed Nov-Easter, cash only, Vladimira Švalbe 34, tel. 052/818-089, mobile 098-929-7541).

Monte Restaurant is your upscale, white-tablecloth splurge—made to order for a memorable dinner out. With tables strewn around a covered terrace just under the town bell tower, this atmospheric place features inventive cuisine that melds Istrian products with international techniques. Come here only if you value a fine dining experience, polished service, and the chance to learn about local food and wines more than you value the price tag (plan to spend 300-500 kn per person for dinner, daily 12:00-14:30 & 18:30-23:00, reserve ahead in peak season, Montalbano 75, tel. 052/830-203, Đekić family).

Affordable Alternatives on the Mainland

These options are a bit less expensive than those described above. I've listed them in the order you'll reach them as you walk around Rovinj's harbor.

Gostionica/Trattoria Toni is a hole-in-the-wall serving up small portions of good Istrian and Venetian fare. Choose between the cozy interior (tucked down a tight lane), or their terrace on a bustling, mostly pedestrian street (40-60-kn pastas, 50-120-kn main courses, Thu-Tue 12:00-15:00 & 18:00-22:30, closed Wed, just up ulica/via Driovier on the right, tel. 052/815-303).

Sidro offers a break from pasta, pizza, and fish; it's well-respected for its Balkan meat dishes such as *ćevapčići* (minced meat formed into a sausage-like shape, then grilled) and a spicy pork-and-onion stew called *mućkalica*. With unusually polite service and a long tradition (run by three generations of the Paoletti family since 1966), it's a popular local hangout (45-70-kn pastas, 55-90-kn grilled meat dishes, 75-140-kn steaks and fish, daily 11:00-23:00, closed Nov-Feb, harborfront at Rismondo 14, tel. 052/813-471).

Maestral combines affordable, straightforward pizzas and seafood with Rovinj's best view. If you want an outdoor table

ROVINJ

overlooking bobbing boats and the Old Town's skyline—without breaking the bank—this is the place. It fills a big building surrounded by workaday shipyards about a 10-minute walk from the Old Town, around the harbor toward Hotel Park (30-kn sandwiches, 45-60-kn pizzas and pastas, 45-100-kn fish and meat dishes, May-Sept open long hours daily, Oct-April drinks only and open until 20:00, obala N. Nazora b.b., look for *Bavaria* beer sign).

Breakfast

Most rental apartments come with a kitchenette handy for breakfasts (stock up at a neighborhood grocery shop). Cafés and bars along the waterfront serve little more than an expensive croissant with coffee. The best budget breakfast (and a fun experience) is a picnic. Within a block of the market, you have all the necessary stops: the Brionka bakery (fresh-baked cheese or apple strudel); mini-grocery stores (juice, milk, drinkable yogurt, and so on); market stalls (cherries, strawberries, walnuts, and more, as well as an elegant fountain for washing); an Albanian-run bread kiosk/café between the market and the water...plus benches with birds chirping, children playing, and fine Old Town views along the water. For a no-fuss alternative, you can shell out 60 kn for the buffet breakfast at Hotel Adriatic (daily 7:00-10:00, until 11:00 July-Aug; described earlier, under "Sleeping in Rovinj").

Rovinj Connections

From Rovinj by Bus to: Pula (about hourly, 45 minutes), **Poreč** (6-9/day, 1 hour), **Umag** (5/day, 1.5 hours), **Rijeka** (4-7/day, 3 hours), **Zagreb** (6-9/day, 5-8 hours), **Venice** (1/day Mon-Sat departing very early in the morning, none Sun, 5 hours). In the summer, you can reach Slovenia—including **Piran** (2.5 hours) and **Ljubljana** (5.5 hours)—by hopping on the 8:00 bus from Rovinj (June-late Sept only, no buses off-season). You can also reach Piran (and other Slovenian destinations) with a transfer in Umag and Portorož. A bus departs Rovinj every evening at 19:00 for the Dalmatian Coast, arriving in **Split** at 6:00 and **Dubrovnik** at 11:00. (If this direct bus isn't running, you might have to take an earlier bus to Pula, from where this night bus leaves at 20:00; also note that Pula has two daytime connections to Split.) As always, confirm these times before planning your trip. Bus information: tel. 052/811-453.

Route Tips for Drivers

Just north of Rovinj, on the coastal road to Poreč, you'll drive briefly along a seven-mile-long inlet dubbed the **Limski "Fjord"** (Limski Zaljev). Supposedly the famed pirate Captain Morgan was so enchanted by this canal that he retired here, founding the nearby namesake town of Mrgani. Local tour companies sell boat excursions into the fjord, which is used to raise much of the shellfish that's slurped down at local restaurants. Calling this little canal a "fjord" outrages Norwegians—it's not worth going out of your way to see. Along the road above the canal, you'll pass kiosks selling grappa (firewater, a.k.a. *rakija*), honey, and other home-made concoctions.

CZECH REPUBLIC

The following chapter
is excerpted from
*Rick Steves' Prague &
the Czech Republic.*

ČESKÝ KRUMLOV

Lassoed by its river and dominated by its castle, this enchanting town feels lost in a time warp. While Český Krumlov is the Czech Republic's answer to Germany's Rothenburg, it has yet to be turned into a medieval theme park. When you see its awe-inspiring castle, delightful Old Town of shops and cobbled lanes, characteristic little restaurants, and easy canoeing options, you'll understand why having fun is a slam-dunk here.

Český Krumlov (CHESS-key KROOM-loff) means, roughly, "Czech Bend in the River." Calling it "Český" for short sounds silly to Czech-speakers (since dozens of Czech town names begin with "Český"). However, "Krumlov" for short is OK.

The sharp bend in the Vltava provides a natural moat, so it's no wonder Český Krumlov has been a choice spot for eons. Celtic tribes first settled here a century before Christ. Then came German tribes. The Slavic tribes arrived in the ninth century. The Rožmberks—Bohemia's top noble family—ran the city from 1302 to 1602. You'll see their rose symbol all over town.

In many ways, the 16th century was the town's Golden Age, when Český Krumlov hosted artists, scientists, and alchemists from all over Europe. In 1588, the town became home to an important Jesuit college. The Habsburgs bought the region in 1602, ushering in a more Germanic period. After that, as many as 75 percent of the town's people were German—until 1945, when most Germans were expelled.

Český Krumlov's rich mix of Gothic, Renaissance, and Baroque buildings is easy to miss. As you wander, look up...notice the surviving details in the stonework. Step into shops. Snoop into back lanes and tiny squares. Gothic buildings curve with the winding streets. Many precious Gothic and Renaissance frescoes were whitewashed in Baroque times (when the colorful trimmings of earlier periods were way out of style). Today, these frescoes are being rediscovered and restored.

With the town's rich German heritage, it was easy for Hitler to claim that this region—the Sudetenland—was rightfully part of Germany, and in 1938, the infamous Munich Agreement made it his. Americans liberated the town in 1945. Due to Potsdam Treaty-approved ethnic cleansing, three million Germans in Czech lands were sent west to Germany. Emptied of its German citizenry, Český Krumlov turned into a ghost town, partially inhabited by Roma (Gypsies—see the "Roma in Eastern Europe" sidebar, later).

In the post-WWII world drawn up by Stalin, Churchill, and FDR at Yalta, the border of the Soviet and American spheres of influence fell about here. While the communist government established order, the period from 1945 to 1989 was a smelly interlude, as the town was infamously polluted. Its now-pristine river was foamy with effluent from the paper mill just upstream, while the hills around town were marred with prefab-concrete apartment blocks. The people who moved in never fully identified with the town—in Europe, a place without ancestors is a place without life. But the bleak years of communism paradoxically provided a cocoon to preserve the town. There was no money, so little changed, apart from a build-up of grime.

In the early 1990s, tourists discovered Český Krumlov, and the influx of money saved the buildings from ruin. Color returned to the facades, waiters again dressed in coarse linen shirts, and the main drag was flooded with souvenir shops.

With its new prosperity, the center of today's Český Krumlov looks like a fairy-tale town. In fact, movie producers consider it ideal for films. *The Adventures of Pinocchio* was filmed here in 1995, as was the opening sequence for the 2006 film *The Illusionist*.

After Prague, Český Krumlov is the Czech Republic's second-biggest tourist magnet (1.5 million visits annually), with enough tourism to make things colorful and easy—but not so much that it tramples the place's charm. This town of 15,000 attracts a young, bohemian crowd, drawn here for its simple beauty, cheap living, and fanciful bars.

Planning Your Time

Because you can visit the castle and theater only with a guide (and English-language tours are offered just a few times a day), serious sightseers should reserve both tours first thing in the morning in person at the castle and theater (or call the castle), and then build your day around your tour times. Those who hate planning ahead on vacation can join a Czech tour anytime

ČESKÝ KRUMLOV

(English information sheets provided).

A paddle down the river to Zlatá Koruna Abbey is a highlight (three hours), and a 20-minute walk up to the Křížový Vrch (Hill of the Cross) rewards you with a fine view of the town and its unforgettable riverside setting. Other sights are quick visits and worthwhile only if you have a particular interest (Viennese artist Egon Schiele, puppets, torture, and so on).

The town itself is the major attraction. Evenings are for atmospheric dining and drinking. Sights are generally open 10:00-17:00 and closed on Monday.

Orientation to Český Krumlov

Český Krumlov is extremely easy to navigate. The twisty Vltava River, which makes a perfect S through the town, ropes the Old Town into a tight peninsula. Above the Old Town is the Castle Town. Český Krumlov's one main street starts at the isthmus and heads through the peninsula. It winds through town and continues across a bridge before snaking through the Castle Town, the castle complex (a long series of courtyards), and the castle gardens high above. The main square, Náměstí Svornosti—with the TI, ATMs, and taxis—dominates the Old Town and marks the center of the peninsula. All recommended restaurants and hotels are within a few minutes' walk of this square. No sight in town is more than a five-minute stroll away.

Tourist Information

The helpful TI is on the **main square** (daily 9:00-19:00, July-Aug until 20:00, shorter hours in winter, tel. 380-704-622, www .ckrumlov.info). Pick up the free city map. The 129-Kč *City Guide* book explains everything in Český Krumlov and includes a fine town and castle map in the back. The TI has a baggage-storage desk and can check train, bus, and flight schedules. Ask about concerts, city walking tours in English, and canoe trips on the river. A second, less-crowded TI—actually a private business—is just below the **castle** (daily 9:00-19:00, tel. 380-725-110).

Arrival in Český Krumlov

By Train: The train station is a 20-minute walk from town (turn right out of the station, then walk downhill onto a steep cobbled path leading to an overpass into the town center). Taxis are standing by to zip you to your hotel (about 100 Kč), or call 602-113-113 to summon one.

By Bus: The bus station is just three blocks away from the Old Town. To walk from the bus-station lot to the town center, drop down to the main road and turn left, then turn right at the grocery

Parting of the Roses

A five-petal rose is not just the distinctive mark of Český Krumlov and the Rožmberk rulers (literally, "Lords from the Rose Mountain"). You'll find it, in five-color combinations, all over South Bohemia.

A medieval legend, depicted inside Český Krumlov's castle, explains the division of the roses in the following way: A respected nobleman named Vítek split the property he had accumulated during his lifetime among five sons. Each son was also assigned his own coat of arms, all of which shared the motif of a five-petal rose. The oldest son, Jindřich, received a golden rose in a blue field, along with the lands of Hradec and Telč. Vilém received a silver rose in a red field, with the lands of Landštejn and Třeboň. Smil was given a blue rose in a golden field and the lands of Stráž and Bystřice. Vok kept his father's coat of arms, a red rose in a white field, and became the lord in Rožmberk and Český Krumlov. Finally, the out-of-wedlock Sezima had to make do with a black rose and the tiny land of Ústí.

Over generations, the legend—which is corroborated by historical sources—served as a constant warning to the ambitious Rožmberks not to further split up their land. The Lords from the Rose Mountain were the rare Czech noble family that, for 300 years, strictly adhered to the principle of primogeniture (the oldest son gets all, and younger sons are subservient to him). Unlike Vítek, the patriarch, each successive ruler of the Rožmberk estates made sure to consolidate his possessions, handing more to his eldest son than he had received. As a result, the enterprising Rožmberks grew into the most powerful family in Bohemia. In 1501, their position as "first in the country after the king" became law.

store *(potraviny)*. Figure on 60 Kč for a taxi from the station to your hotel.

Helpful Hints

Festivals: Locals drink oceans of beer and celebrate their medieval roots at big events such as the Celebration of the Rose (Slavnosti Růže), where blacksmiths mint ancient coins, jugglers swallow fire, mead flows generously, and pigs are roasted on open fires (June 22-24 in 2012). The summer also brings a top-notch international jazz and alternative music festival to town, performed in pubs, cafés, and the castle gardens (Aug 20-25 in 2012, www.festivalkrumlov.cz). During the St. Wenceslas celebrations, the square becomes a medieval market and the streets come alive with theater and music (Sept 28-30 in 2012). Reserve a hotel well in advance if you'll be in town for these events.

Internet Access: Fine Internet cafés are all over town, and many of my recommended accommodations offer Wi-Fi or Internet access. The TI on the main square has several fast, cheap, stand-up stations. Perhaps the best cybercafé is behind the TI by the castle (tel. 380-725-117).

Bookstore: Shakespeare and Sons is a good little English-language bookstore (daily 11:00-19:00, a block below the main square at Soukenická 44, tel. 380-711-203, www.shakes.cz).

Laundry: Pension Lobo runs a self-service launderette near the castle. Since there are only a few machines, you may have to wait (200 Kč to wash and dry, includes soap, daily 9:00-20:00, Latrán 73).

Bike Rental: You can rent bikes at the **train station** (150 Kč/day with train ticket, prices slightly higher otherwise, tel. 380-715-000), **Vltava Sport Service** (see listing under "Canoeing and Rafting the Vltava" on page 118), and the recommended **Hostel 99.**

Tours in Český Krumlov

Walking Tours—Since the town itself, rather than its sights, is what it's all about here, taking a guided walk is the key to a meaningful visit. The TI sells tickets for two different guided walks. They are affordable, in English, and well worth your time. Both meet in front of the TI on the main square. No reservations are necessary—just drop in and pay the guide. The **Old Town Tour** offers the best general town introduction and is most likely to run (250 Kč, daily May-Oct at 10:30 and 15:00, Nov-April at 11:00, weekends only in Feb, 1.5 hours). The **Brewing History Tour,** which is the most intimate of the many brewery tours in this land that so loves its beer, takes you through the Eggenberg Brewery (200 Kč, daily May-Oct at 12:30, Nov-April at 13:00, weekends only in Feb, 1 hour). For a self-guided town walk, consider renting an **audioguide** from the TI (100 Kč/one hour).

Local Guides—**Oldřiška Baloušková** is a hardworking young guide who offers a wonderful tour around her hometown (400 Kč/hour, mobile 737-920-901, oldriskab@gmail.com). **Jiří (George) Václavíček,** a gentle and caring man who perfectly fits mellow Český Krumlov, is a joy to share this town with (450 Kč/hour, mobile 603-927-995, www.krumlovguide.cz, jiri.vaclavicek @gmail.com). **Karolína Kortušová** is an enthusiastic woman with great organizational skills. Her company, Krumlov Tours, can set you up with a good local tour guide, palace and theater admissions, river trips, and more (guides-400 Kč/hour, mobile 723-069-561, www.krumlovtours.com, info@krumlovtours.com).

Self-Guided Walk

▲▲▲Welcome to Český Krumlov

The town's best sight is its cobbled cityscape, surrounded by a babbling river and capped by a dramatic castle. All of Český Krumlov's

modest sights are laced together in this charming walk from the top of the Old Town, down its spine, across the river, and up to the castle.

• *Start at the bridge over the isthmus, which was once the fortified grand entry gate to the town.*

Horní Bridge: From this "Upper Bridge," note the natural fortification provided by the tight bend in the river. The last building in town (just over the river) is the Eggenberg Brewery (with daily tours—see "Tours in Český Krumlov," earlier). Behind that, on the horizon, is a pile of white apartment high-rises—built in the last decade of the communist era and considered the worst places in town to call home. Left of the brewery stands a huge monastery (not generally open to the public). Behind that, on Kleť Mountain, the highest hilltop, stands a TV tower that locals say was built to jam Voice of America broadcasts. Facing the town, on your left, rafters take you to the river for the sloppy half-hour float around town to the takeout spot just on your right.

• *A block downhill on Horní (Upper) street is the...*

Museum of Regional History: This small museum gives you a quick look at regional costumes, tools, and traditions. When you pay, pick up the English translation of the displays (it also includes a lengthy history of Krumlov). Start on the top floor, where you'll see a Bronze Age exhibit, old paintings, a glimpse of noble life, and a look at how the locals rafted lumber from Krumlov all the way to Vienna (partly by canal). Don't miss the fun-to-study ceramic model of Český Krumlov in 1800 (note the extravagant gardens high above the town). The lower floor comes with fine folk costumes and domestic art (50 Kč, daily 10:00-17:00, July-Aug until 18:00, Horní 152, tel. 380-711-674).

• *Below the museum, a little garden overlook affords a fine castle view. Immediately across the street, notice the Renaissance facade of...*

Hotel Růže: This former Jesuit college hides a beautiful courtyard. Pop inside to see a couple of bronze busts that stand like a shrine to the founders of Czechoslovakia. The one on the right, dedicated by the Czech freedom fighters, commemorates the first Czechoslovak president, Tomáš Garrigue Masaryk (in office 1918-1934). The bust on the left recalls Masaryk's successor,

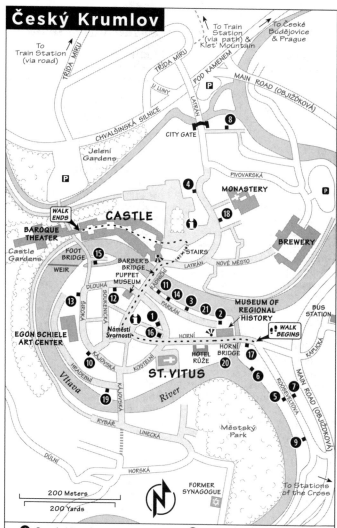

Český Krumlov

ČESKÝ KRUMLOV

1. Castle View Apartments
2. Hotel Mlýn
3. Pension Olšakovský
4. Pension Danny & Launderette
5. Pension Teddy
6. Pension Myší Díra & Maleček Boat Rental
7. Pension Anna
8. Hostel 99 & Hospoda 99 Rest.
9. Krumlov House Hostel
10. Na Louži Restaurant
11. Krčma u Dwau Maryí
12. Cikánská Jizba
13. Restaurace u Dobráka
14. Laibon Restaurant
15. Rybářská Restaurace
16. Krčma v Šatlavské
17. Restaurace Barbakán
18. Dobrá Čajovna Teahouse
19. Vltava Sport Service
20. Start Quickie River Float
21. End Quickie River Float & Start Zlatá Koruna Float

Edvard Beneš and the German Question

Czechoslovakia was created in 1918, when the vast, multi-ethnic Habsburg Empire broke into smaller nations after losing World War I. The principle that gave countries such as Poland, Czechoslovakia, and Romania independence was called "self-determination": Each nation had the right to its own state within the area in which its people formed the majority. But the peoples of Eastern Europe had mixed over the centuries, making it impossible to create functioning states based purely on ethnicity. In the case of Czechoslovakia, the borders were drawn along historical rather than ethnic boundaries. While the country was predominantly Slavic, there were also areas with overwhelmingly German and Hungarian majorities. One of these areas—a fringe around the western part of the country, mostly populated by Germans—was known as the Sudetenland.

At first, the coexistence of Slavs and Germans in the new republic worked fine. German parties were important power brokers and participated in almost every coalition government. Hitler's rise to power, however, led to the growth of German nationalism, even outside Germany. Soon 70 percent of Germans in Czechoslovakia voted for the Nazis. In September 1938, the Munich Agreement ceded the Sudetenland to Germany, and the Czech minority had to leave.

Edvard Beneš was the first Czechoslovak secretary of state (1918-1934) and later became the country's second president (1934-1948), leading the Czechoslovak exile government in London during World War II. Like most Czechs and Slovaks, Beneš believed that after the hard feelings produced by the Munich Agreement, peaceful coexistence of Slavs and Germans in a single state was impossible. His postwar solution: move the Sudeten Germans to Germany, much as the Czechs had been forced out of the Sudetenland before. Through skillful diplomacy,

Edvard Beneš (in office 1934-1948; see sidebar, above).

• *Walk another block down the main drag, until you reach steps on the left leading to the...*

Church of St. Vitus: Český Krumlov's main church was built as a bastion of Catholicism in the 15th century, when the Roman Catholic Church was fighting the Hussites. The 17th-century Baroque high altar shows a totem of religious figures: the Virgin Mary (crowned in heaven); St. Vitus (above Mary); and, way up on top, St. Wenceslas, the patron saint of the Czech people—long considered their ambassador in heaven. The canopy in the back, though empty today, once supported a grand statue of a Rožmberk atop a horse. The statue originally stood at the high altar. (Too egotistical for Jesuits, it was later moved to the rear of the nave, and then lost for good.) As you listen to the river, notice the empty

Beneš got the Allies to sign on to this idea.

Shortly after the end of World War II, three million people of German ancestry were forced to leave their homes in Czechoslovakia. Millions of Germanic people in Poland, Romania, Ukraine, and elsewhere met with a similar fate. Many of these families had been living in these areas for centuries. The methods employed to expel them included murder, rape, and plunder. (Today, we'd call it "ethnic cleansing.")

In 1945, Český Krumlov lost 75 percent of its population, and Czechs moved into the vacated German homes. Having easily acquired the property, the new residents didn't take care of the houses. Within a few years, the once-prosperous Sudetenland was reduced to shabby towns and uncultivated fields—a decaying, godforsaken region. After 1989, displaced Sudeten Germans—the majority of whom now live in Bavaria—demanded that the Czechoslovak government apologize for the violent way in which the expulsion was carried out. Some challenged the legality of the decrees, and for a time the issue threatened otherwise good Czech-German relations.

Although no longer such a hot-button diplomatic issue, the so-called Beneš Decrees remain divisive in Czech politics. While liberals consider the laws unjust, many others—especially the older generations—see them as fair revenge for the behavior of the Sudeten Germans prior to and during the war. In the former Sudetenland, where Czech landowners worry that the Germans will try to reclaim their property, Beneš is a hugely popular figure. His bust in Český Krumlov's Hotel Růže is one of the first memorials to him in the country. The bridge behind the Old Town has been named for Beneš since the 1990s. The main square—the center of a thriving German community 70 years ago—is now, ironically, called "Square of Concord."

organ case. While the main organ is out for restoration, the cute little circa-1716 Baroque beauty is getting plenty of use (see photos of the restoration work on the far wall, church open daily 10:00-19:00, Sunday Mass at 9:30, tel. 380-711-336).

• *Continuing on Horní street, you'll come to the...*

Main Square (Náměstí Svornosti): Lined with a mix of Renaissance and Baroque homes of burghers (all built on 12th-century Gothic foundations), the main square has a grand charm. There's continuity here. Lékárna, with the fine red Baroque facade on the lower corner of the square, is still a pharmacy, as it has been since 1620. McDonald's tried three times to get a spot here but was turned away each time. The Town Hall flies both the Czech flag and the town flag, which shows the rose symbol of the Rožmberk family, who ruled the town for 300 years.

Imagine the history that this square has seen: In the 1620s, the rising tide of Lutheran Protestantism threatened Catholic Europe. Krumlov was a seat of Jesuit power and learning, and the intellectuals of the Roman church allegedly burned books on this square. Later, when there was a bad harvest, locals blamed witches—and burned them, too. Every so often, terrible plagues rolled through the countryside. In a nearby village, all but two residents were killed by a plague.

But the plague stopped before devastating the people of Český Krumlov, and in 1715—as thanks to God—they built the plague

monument that stands on the square today. Much later, in 1938, Hitler stood right here before a backdrop of long Nazi banners to celebrate the annexation of the Sudetenland. And in 1968, Russian tanks spun their angry treads on these same cobblestones to intimidate locals who were demanding freedom. Today, thankfully, this square is part of an unprecedented time of peace and prosperity for the Czech people.

• *The following three museums are grouped around the main square.*

Puppet Museum: In three small rooms, you'll see fascinating displays of more than 200 movable creations (overwhelmingly of Czech origin, but also some from Burma and Rajasthan). At the model stage, children of any age can try their hand at pulling the strings on their favorite fairy tale (80 Kč, daily 10:00-18:00, longer hours in July-Aug, Dlouhá 29, tel. 380-713-422, www.krumlov skainspirace.cz).

Torture Museum: This is just a lame haunted house: dark, with sound effects, cheap modern models, and prints showing off the cruel and unusual punishments of medieval times (100 Kč, daily 9:00-20:00, shorter hours off-season, English descriptions, Náměstí Svornosti 1, tel. 380-766-343).

Egon Schiele Art Center: This classy contemporary art gallery has temporary exhibits, generally featuring 20th-century Czech artists. The top-floor permanent collection celebrates the Viennese artist Egon Schiele (pronounced "Sheila"), who once spent a few weeks here during a secret love affair. A friend of Gustav Klimt and an important figure in the Secession movement in Vienna, Schiele lived a short life, from 1890 to 1918. His cutting-edge lifestyle and harsh art of graphic nudes didn't always fit the conservative, small-town style of Český Krumlov, but townsfolk are happy today to charge you to see this relatively paltry collection of his work (120 Kč, daily 10:00-18:00 except closed Mon in Jan, café, Široká 71, tel. 380-704-011, www.schieleartcentrum.cz).

• *From the main square, walk up Radniční street and cross the...*

Barber's Bridge (Lazebnicky Most): This wooden bridge, decorated with two 19th-century statues, connects the Old Town and the Castle Town. In the center stands a statue of St. John of Nepomuk, who's also depicted by a prominent statue on Prague's Charles Bridge. Among other responsibilities, he's the protector against floods. In the great floods of August 2002, the angry river submerged the bridge (but removable banisters minimized the damage). Stains just above the windows of the adjacent building show you how high the water rose.

• *After crossing the bridge, hike up the hill. Your next stop is Krumlov Castle.*

Sights in Český Krumlov

▲▲Krumlov Castle (Krumlovský Zámek)

No Czech town is complete without a castle—and now that the nobles are gone, their mansions are open to us common folk. The Krumlov Castle complex includes bear pits, a rare Baroque theater, groomed gardens—and the castle itself (www.castle.ckrumlov.cz).

Round Tower (Zâmecká Věž)— The strikingly colorful round tower marks the location of the first castle, built here to guard the medieval river crossing. With its 16th-century Renaissance paint job colorfully restored, it looks exotic, featuring fancy astrological decor, terra-cotta symbols of the zodiac, and a fine arcade. Climb its 162 steps for a great view.

Cost and Hours: 50 Kč, daily 9:00-18:00, last entry at 17:30.

Bear Pits (Medvědí Příkop)—At the site of the castle draw-bridge, the bear pits hold a family of European brown bears, as they have since the Rožmberks added bears to their coat of arms in the 16th century to demonstrate their (fake) blood relation to the distinguished Italian family of Orsini (the name means "bear-like"). Featured on countless coats of arms, bears have long been totemic animals for Europeans. Pronouncing the animal's real name was taboo in many cultures, and Czechs still refer to bears only indirectly. For example, in most Germanic languages the word "bear" is derived from "brown," while the Slavic medvěd literally means "honey-eater."

Roma in Eastern Europe

Numbering 12 million, the Roma people constitute a bigger European nation than the Czechs, Hungarians, or the Dutch. The term "Gypsies," which used to be the common name for this group, is now considered both derogatory and inaccurate. It was derived from "Egypt"—the place that medieval Roma were mistakenly thought to have originated. In the absence of written records, the solution to the puzzle of Roma ancestry had to wait for 19th-century advances in the science of linguistics.

The Roma are now thought to be descended from several low north-Indian castes (one of which may have given the Roma their name). A thousand years ago, the Roma began to migrate through Persia and Armenia into the Ottoman Empire, which later stretched across much of southeastern Europe. Known for their itinerant lifestyle, expertise in horse trading, skilled artisanship, and flexibility regarding private property, the Roma were both sought out and suspected in medieval Europe. In a similar way, *gadjos* (non-Roma) and their customs came to be distrusted by the Roma.

The Industrial Revolution removed the Roma's few traditional means of earning a livelihood, making their wandering lifestyle difficult to sustain. In the 1940s, Hitler sent hundreds of thousands of Roma to the gas chambers. After the war, communist governments in Eastern Europe implemented a policy of forced assimilation: Roma were required to speak the country's major language, settle in *gadjo* towns, and work in new industrial jobs. Today, few Roma can speak their own language well. Rather than producing well-adjusted citizens, the policy eroded time-honored Roma values and shattered the cohesiveness of their

Castle (Zámek)—The immense castle is a series of courtyards with shops, contemporary art galleries, and tourist services. The interior is accessible only by tour, which gives you a glimpse of the places where the Rožmberks, Eggenbergs, and Schwarzenbergs dined, studied, worked, prayed, entertained, and slept. (By European standards, the castle's not much, and the tours move slowly.) Imagine being an aristocratic

guest here, riding the dukes' assembly line of fine living: You'd promenade through a long series of elegant spaces and dine in the sumptuous dining hall before enjoying a concert in the Hall of Mirrors, which leads directly to the Baroque Theater (described next). After the play, you'd go out into the château garden for a fireworks finale.

traditional communities. It left the new Roma generation prone to sexual, alcohol, and drug abuse, and filled state-run orphanages with deprived Roma toddlers. When the obligation and right to work disappeared with the communist regimes in 1989, rampant unemployment and dependence on welfare joined the list of Roma afflictions.

As people all over Eastern Europe found it difficult to adjust to the new economic realities, they again turned on the Roma as scapegoats, fueling the latent racism that is so characteristic of European history. Many Roma now live in segregated ghettos, where even the most talented of their children are forced to attend schools for the mentally disabled. Those who make it against the odds and succeed in mainstream society typically do so by turning their backs on their Roma heritage.

In this context, the Roma in Český Krumlov are a surprising success story. The well-integrated, proud Roma community here (numbering 1,000 strong, or 5 percent of the town's population) is considered a curious anomaly even by experts. Their success could be due to a number of factors: It could be the legacy of the multicultural Rožmberks, or the fact that almost everyone in Český Krumlov is a relative newcomer. Or maybe it's that local youngsters, regardless of skin color, tend to resolve their differences over a beer in the local "Gypsy Pub" (Cikánská Jizba), with a trendy Roma band setting the tune.

While provincial politicians throughout the rest of Eastern Europe become national leaders by moving Roma into ghettos, Český Krumlov is living proof that Roma and *gadjos* can coexist happily.

Cost and Hours: To see the interior, you must take a one-hour escorted tour: Tour I (Gothic and Renaissance rooms, of the most general interest) or Tour II (19th-century castle life). Tours run June-Aug Tue-Sun 9:00-12:00 & 13:00-18:00, spring and fall until 17:00, closed Mon and Nov-March. Tours in Czech cost 150 Kč plus a 10-Kč reservation fee, leave regularly, and include an adequate flier in English that contains about half the information imparted by the guide (generally a student who's simply memorized the basic script). English tours are preferable, but cost more (200 Kč plus a 10-Kč reservation fee), run less frequently, and are often booked solid. Make your reservation when you arrive in town—just walk up to the castle office—or you can call 380-704-721, though the number is often busy. You'll be issued a ticket with your tour time printed on it. Be in the correct courtyard at that time, or you'll be locked out.

▲▲**Baroque Theater (Zámecké Divadlo)**—Europe once had several hundred Baroque theaters. Using candles for light and fireworks for special effects, most burned down. Today, only two survive in good shape and open to tourists: one at Stockholm's Drottningholm Palace; and one here, at Krumlov Castle. During the 40-minute tour, you'll sit on benches in the theater and then go under the stage to see the wood-and-rope contraptions that enabled scenes to be scooted in and out within seconds (while fireworks and smoke blinded the audience). Due to the theater's fragility, the number of visitors is strictly regulated. There are only five English tours a day, limited to 20 people per group, and generally sold out in advance. While it's a lovely little theater with an impressive 3-D effect that makes the stage look deeper than it really is, I wouldn't bother with the tour unless you can snare a spot on an English one. The theater is used only once a year for an actual performance, with attendance limited to Baroque theater enthusiasts. You can call 380-704-721 to get English-language tour times and reserve a space; but as with the castle tour, you will likely do best visiting the ticket office in person.

Cost and Hours: 300 Kč plus a 10-Kč reservation fee for English tour, 250 Kč plus a 10-Kč reservation fee for Czech tour, tours Tue-Sun May-Oct, no tours Mon and Nov-April; English departures at 10:00, 11:00, 13:00, 14:00, and 15:00; buy theater tour tickets at castle ticket office.

Castle Museum (Hradní Muzeum)—A newly opened exhibit assembled from the castle's archives focuses on key moments in the lives of the town's various ruling families. While generally skippable, on summer Mondays it provides the only chance to peek inside the castle.

Cost and Hours: 100 Kč, April-Aug daily 9:00-17:00, Sept-March Tue-Sun 9:30-16:00, closed Mon.

Castle Gardens (Zámecká Zahrada)—This 2,300-foot-long garden crowns the castle complex. It was laid out in the 17th century, when the noble family would have it lit with 22,000 oil lamps, torches, and candles for special occasions. The lower part is geometrical and symmetrical—French garden-style. The upper is rougher—English garden-style.

Cost and Hours: Free, May-Sept Tue-Sun 8:00-19:00, April and Oct Tue-Sun 8:00-17:00, closed Mon and Nov-March.

Near Český Krumlov

Zlatá Koruna Abbey (Klášter Zlatá Koruna)—Directly above the river at the end of a three-hour float by raft or canoe (see "Activities in Český Krumlov," later), this abbey was founded in the 13th century by the king to counter the growing influence of the Vítek family, the ancestors of the mighty Rožmberks. As you enter the grounds, notice the central linden tree, with its strange, cape-like leaves; it's said to have been used by the anti-Catholic

Hussites when they hanged the monks. The short guided abbey tour takes you through the rare two-storied Gothic Chapel of the Guardian Angel, the main church, and the cloister. After the order was dissolved in 1785, the abbey functioned shortly as a village school, before being turned into a factory during the Industrial Revolution. Damage from this period is visible on the cloister's crumbling arches. The abbey was restored in the 1990s and opened to the public only a few years ago.

Cost and Hours: 95 Kč for a tour in Czech—generally runs hourly, 180 Kč for an English tour, Tue-Sun 9:00-15:30, until 16:30 June-Aug, closed Mon and Oct-March, call 380-743-126 to pre-arrange an English tour, access via river float, www.klaster-zlata koruna.eu.

Šumava Mountains—The well-rounded Šumava Mountains (SHOO-mah-vah) are, geologically, one of Europe's oldest ranges. Separating Bohemia from Bavaria, this long ridge, known in German on the Bohemian side as the Böhmerwald ("Bohemian Forest") and on the Bavarian side as the Bayerischer Wald ("Bavarian Forest"), also separates rivers that flow to the North Sea from those that empty into the Black Sea. This range was the physical embodiment of the Iron Curtain for 40 years: The first 10 miles or so within the Czech border were a forbidden no-man's-land, where hundreds of Czechs were shot as they tried to run across to Germany. In 1989, the barbed wire was taken down, and the entire area—more than 60 miles long—was declared the Šumava-Bayerischer Wald National Park. No development is permitted within the park, and visitors can't camp outside of designated areas. Since there's little industry nearby, these mountains preserve some of the most pristine woods, creeks, and meadows in Eastern Europe.

The gateway most easily accessible from Český Krumlov is the trailhead village of **Nová Pec,** a scenic 1.5-hour train ride away (5 direct trains/day). Nová Pec is located just beneath the slopes of the tallest mountain on the Czech side of the border, Plechý, a popular destination for hiking, biking, and cross-country skiing. Nová Pec's TI, which is 100 yards to the right of the train station, sells hiking and biking maps. You can rent bikes at the Pec train station (150 Kč/day with train ticket, slightly more without one, reserve a few days ahead by calling 972-543-891 or emailing zstvlrdop@mail.cd.cz) or three miles away toward Plechý next to the Plešný parking lot (mobile 723-380-138). Since bikes can be in high demand in Nová Pec, it may be a better bet to rent a bicycle at the Český Krumlov train station and bring it—for a 30 Kč surcharge—along with you on the train. You can then return the bike at the station in Nová Pec. Helmets are not included.

Sleeping near Nová Pec: Both of these recommended B&Bs

are about a mile outside of Nová Pec. Like almost everywhere else in this border region, German and Czech are the only ways to communicate.

$$ Pension Za Pecí has five new, tastefully decorated rooms (Sb-450 Kč, Db-900 Kč, optional dinner-100 Kč, tel. 388-336-103, mobile 775-977-469, www.zapeci.com, mifudy@seznam.cz).

$$ Pension Hubertus sits on a sloping meadow and operates its three rooms on solar power. Owner Eva will pick you up from the train station if you ask (Sb-450 Kč, Db-900 Kč, mobile 602-253-572, www.ubytovani.net/hubertus).

Activities in Český Krumlov

Český Krumlov lies in the middle of a valley popular for canoe-ing, rafting, hiking, and horseback riding. Boat-rental places are convenient to the Old Town, and several hiking paths start right in town.

▲▲▲Canoeing and Rafting the Vltava

Splash a little river fun into your visit by renting a rubber raft or fiberglass canoe for a quick 30-minute spin around Český Krumlov.

Or go for a three-hour float and paddle through the Bohemian forests and villages of the nearby countryside. You'll end up at Zlatá Koruna Abbey (described earlier), where the rafting com-pany will shuttle you back to town—or provide you with a bicycle to pedal back on your own along a bike path. This is a great hot-weather activity. Though the river is far from treacherous, be prepared to get wet.

You'll encounter plenty of inviting pubs and cafés for breaks along the way. There's a little whitewater, but the river is so shal-low that if you tip, you can simply stand up and climb back in. (When that happens, pull the canoe up onto the bank to empty it, since you'll never manage to pour the water out while still in the river.)

Choose from a kayak, a canoe (faster, less work, more likely to tip), or an inflatable raft (harder rowing, slower, but very stable). Prices are per boat (2-6 people) and include a map, a waterproof container, and transportation to or from the start and end points. Here are your options:

Quickie Circle-the-Town Float: The easiest half-hour experience is to float around the city's peninsula, starting and ending at opposite sides of the tiny isthmus. Heck, you can do it twice (400 Kč for 1-2 people in a canoe or raft).

Three-Hour Float to Zlatá Koruna Abbey: This is your best basic trip, with pastoral scenery, a riverside pub about two hours down on the left, and a beautiful abbey as your destination (about 9 miles, 700 Kč for 1-2 people). From there you can bike back or catch a shuttle bus home—simply arrange a return plan with the rental company.

Longer and Faster Trips: If you start upriver from Krumlov (direction: Rožmberk), you'll go faster with more whitewater, but the river parallels a road, so it's a little less idyllic. Longer trips in either direction involve lots of paddling, even though you're going downstream. Rafting companies can review the many day-trip options with you.

Rental Companies: Several companies offer this lively activity. Perhaps the handiest are **Půjčovna Lodí Maleček Boat Rental** (open long hours daily April-Oct, closed Nov-March, at recommended Pension Myší Díra, Rooseveltova 28, tel. 380-712-508, www.malecek.cz, lode@malecek.cz) and **Vltava Sport Service** (April-Oct daily 9:00-18:00, closed Nov-March, Hradební 60, tel. 380-711-988, www.ckvltava.cz). Vltava also rents mountain bikes (320 Kč/day) and can bring a bike to the abbey for you to ride back.

Hiking

For an **easy 20-minute hike** to the Křížový Vrch (Hill of the Cross), walk to the end of Rooseveltova street, cross at the traffic light, then head straight for the first (empty) chapel-like Station of the Cross. Turning right, it's easy to navigate along successive Stations of the Cross until you reach the white church on the hill (closed), set in the middle of wild meadows. Looking down into the valley at the medieval city nestled within the S-shaped river, framed by the rising hills, it's hard to imagine any town with a more powerful *genius loci* (spirit of the place). The view is best at sunset.

For **longer hikes,** start at the trailhead by the bear pits below the castle. Red-and-white trail markers guide you on an easy six-mile hike around the neighboring slopes and villages. The green-and-yellow stripes mark a five-mile hiking trail up Kleť Mountain—with an altitude gain of 1,800 feet. At the top, you'll find the Kleť Observatory, the oldest observatory in the country (now a leading center for discovering new planets). On clear days, you can see the Alps (observatory tours-30 Kč, hourly July-Aug Tue-Sun 10:30-15:30, closed Mon, www.hvezdarna.klet.cz).

ČESKÝ KRUMLOV

Horseback Riding

Head about a mile and a half out of town, beyond the Křížový Vrch (Hill of the Cross), for horseback rides and lessons at Slupenec Horseback Riding Club.

Cost and Hours: One hour outdoors or in the ring-300 Kč, all-day ride-2,200 Kč, helmets provided, Tue-Sun 10:00-18:00, closed Mon, Slupenec 1, worth a taxi trip, tel. 380-711-052, www .jk-slupenec.cz, René Srncová.

Sleeping in Český Krumlov

Krumlov is filled with small, good, family-run pensions offering doubles with baths from 1,000 to 1,500 Kč and hostel beds for 300 Kč. Summer weekends and festivals (see "Helpful Hints," earlier) are busiest and most expensive; reserve ahead when possible. Hotels (not a Krumlov forte) have staff that speak some English and accept credit cards; pensions rarely have or do either. While you can find a room upon arrival here, it's better to book at least a few days ahead if you want to stay in the heart of town. Cars are not very safe overnight—locals advise paying for a garage.

In the Old Town

$$$ Castle View Apartments, run by local guide Jiří Václavíček, rents seven apartments. These are the plushest and best-equipped rooms I found in town—the bathroom floors are heated, all come with kitchenettes, and everything's done just right. Their website describes each stylish apartment (1,800-4,500 Kč depending on size, view, and season; the big 4,500-Kč apartment sleeps up

---

Sleep Code

(18 Kč = about $1, country code: 420)
S = Single, **D** = Double/Twin, **T** = Triple, **Q** = Quad, **b** = bathroom, **s** = shower only. Unless otherwise noted, prices include breakfast.

To help you sort easily through these listings, I've divided the accommodations into three categories based on the price for a double room with bath in high season:

$$$ Higher Priced—Most rooms 1,500 Kč or more.
$$ Moderately Priced—Most rooms between 1,000-1,500 Kč.
$ Lower Priced—Most rooms 1,000 Kč or less.

Prices can change without notice; verify the hotel's current rates online or by email. For other updates, see www .ricksteves.com/update.

---

to six, complex pricing scheme, reserve direct with this book for 10 percent off online prices, non-smoking, breakfast in a nearby hotel, Šatlavská 140, tel. 380-727-015, mobile 731-108-677, www .castleview.cz, info@castleview.cz).

On Parkán Street, Below the Square

Secluded Parkán street, which runs along the river below the square, has a row of pensions with three to five rooms each. These places have a family feel and views of the looming castle above.

$$$ Hotel Mlýn, at the end of Parkán, is a newly opened and tastefully furnished hotel with more than 30 rooms and all the amenities (Sb-2,400 Kč, Db-3,000 Kč, elevator, free Wi-Fi, pay parking, Parkán 120, tel. 380-731-133, fax 380-747-054, www .hotelmlyn.eu, info@hotelmlyn.eu).

$$ Pension Olšakovský, which has a delightful breakfast area on a terrace next to the river, treats visitors as family guests (Db-1,000-1,250 Kč, includes parking, Parkán 114, tel. & fax 380-714-333, mobile 604-430-181, www.olsakovsky.cz, J.Olsakovsky@post.cz).

On Latrán Street, at the Base of the Castle

A quiet, cobbled pedestrian street (Latrán) runs below the castle just over the bridge from the Old Town. It's a 10-minute walk downhill from the train station. Lined with cute shops, the street has a couple of fine little family-run, eight-room pensions.

$$ Pension Danny is a little funky place, with homey rooms and a tangled floor plan above a restaurant (Db-1,050 Kč, apartment Db-1,250 Kč, breakfast in room, Latrán 72, tel. 380-712-710, www.pensiondanny.cz, recepce@pensiondanny.cz).

On Rooseveltova Street, Between the Bus Station and the Old Town

Rooseveltova street, midway between the bus station and the Old Town (a four-minute walk from either), is lined with several fine little places, each with easy free parking. The key here is tranquility—the noisy bars of the town center are out of earshot.

$$ Little **Pension Teddy** offers three deluxe rooms that share a balcony overlooking the river and have original 18th-century furniture. Or stay in one of four modern-style rooms, some of which also face the river (Db-1,250 Kč, deluxe Db-1,400 Kč, cash only, staff may be unhelpful, free Wi-Fi and Internet access, parking-200 Kč, Rooseveltova 38, tel. 380-711-595, mobile 724-003-981, www.pensionteddy.cz, info@pensionteddy.cz).

$$ Pension Myší Díra ("Mouse Hole") hides eight sleek, spacious, bright, and woody Bohemian contemporary rooms overlooking the Vltava River just outside the Old Town (Db-900-1,400 Kč, bigger deluxe riverview Db-1,900 Kč, prices include transfer

ČESKÝ KRUMLOV

to/from bus or train station, Internet access, Rooseveltova 28, tel. 380-712-853, fax 380-711-900, www.malecek.cz). The no-nonsense reception, which closes at 20:00, runs the recommended boat rental company (Půjčovna Lodí Maleček, at the same address), along with three similar pensions with comparable prices: **Pension Wok** down by the river, **Pension Margarita** farther along Rooseveltova, and **Pension u Hada.**

$$ Pension Anna is well-run, with two doubles, five apartments, and a restful little garden. Its apartments are spacious suites, with a living room and stairs leading to the double-bedded loft. The upstairs rooms can get stuffy during the summer (Db-1,250 Kč, Db apartment-1,550 Kč, extra bed-350 Kč, Rooseveltova 41, tel. & fax 380-711-692, www.pensionanna-ck.cz, pension.anna@quick .cz). If you book a standard Db and they bump you up to an apartment, don't pay more than the Db rate.

Hostels

There are several hostels in town. Hostel 99 (closest to the train station) is clearly the high-energy, youthful party hostel. Krumlov House (closer to the bus station) is more mellow. Both are well-managed, and each is a five-minute walk from the main square.

$ Hostel 99's picnic-table terrace looks out on the Old Town. While the gentle sound of the river gurgles outside your window late at night, you're more likely to hear a youthful international crowd having a great time. The hostel caters to its fun-loving young guests, offering a day-long river rafting and pub crawl, with rental bikes and a free keg of beer each Wednesday (65 beds in 4- to 10-bed coed rooms-300 Kč, D-700 Kč, T-990 Kč, Internet access-1 Kč/minute, laundry-200 Kč/load, use the lockers, no curfew or lockout, recommended Hospoda 99 restaurant, 10-minute downhill walk from train station or two bus stops to Spicak, Vezni 99, tel. & fax 380-712-812, www.hostel99.cz, hostel99@hotmail.com).

$ Krumlov House Hostel is take-your-shoes-off-at-the-door, shiny, hardwood-with-throw-rugs mellow. Efficiently run by a Canadian, it has a hip and trusting vibe and feels welcoming to travelers of any age (24 beds, 6 beds in two dorms-300 Kč per bed, Db-800 Kč, 2-person apartment-900 Kč, family room, no breakfast but there is a guests' kitchen, DVD library, Wi-Fi, laundry facilities, Rooseveltova 68, tel. 380-711-935, www.krumlovhostel .com, info@krumlovhostel.com).

Eating in Český Krumlov

Krumlov, with a huge variety of creative little restaurants, is a fun place to eat. In peak times, the good places fill fast, so make reservations or eat early.

Na Louži seems to be everyone's favorite little Czech bistro, with 40 seats in one 1930s-style room decorated with funky old advertisements. They serve inexpensive, tasty local cuisine and hometown Eggenberg beer on tap. If you've always wanted to play the piano for an appreciative Czech crowd in a colorful little tavern...do it here (daily 10:00-23:00, Kájovská 66, tel. 380-711-280).

Krčma u Dwau Maryí ("Tavern of the Two Marys") is a characteristic old place with idyllic riverside picnic tables, serving ye olde Czech cuisine and drinks. The fascinating menu explains the history of the house and makes a good case that the food of the poor medieval Bohemians was tasty and varied. Buck up for buckwheat, millet, greasy meat, or the poor-man's porridge (daily 11:00-23:00, Parkán 104, tel. 380-717-228).

Cikánská Jizba ("Gypsy Pub") is a Roma tavern filling one den-like, barrel-vaulted room. The Roma staff serves Slovak-style food (Slovakia is where most of the Czech Republic's Roma population came from). Krumlov has a long Roma history, and even today 1,000 Roma people live in the town. While this rustic little restaurant—which packs its 10 tables under a mystic-feeling Gothic vault—won't win any cuisine awards, you never know what festive and musical activities will erupt, particularly on Friday nights, when the owner's son's band, Cindži Renta (Wet Rag), performs here (Mon-Sat 15:00-24:00, closed Sun, 2 blocks toward castle from main square at Dlouhá 31, tel. 380-717-585).

Restaurace u Dobráka ("Good Man") is like eating in a medieval garage, with a giant poster of Karl Marx overseeing the action. Lojza, who's been tossing steaks on his open fire for years, makes sure you'll eat well. Locals know it as the best place for grilled steak and fish—expect to pay 350 Kč for a full meal. He charges too much for his beer in order to keep the noisy beer-drinkers away (open daily 17:30-24:00 from Easter until Lojza "has a shoebox full of money," Široká 74, tel. 380-717-776).

Laibon is the modern vegetarian answer to the carnivorous Middle Ages. Settle down inside or head out onto the idyllic river terrace, and lighten up your pork-loaded diet with soy goulash or Mútábúr soup (daily 11:00-23:00, Parkán 105).

Rybářská Restaurace ("Fisherman's Restaurant") doesn't look particularly inviting from the outside, but don't get discouraged. This is *the* place in town to taste freshwater fish you've never heard of (and never will again). Try eel, perch, shad, carp, trout, and more. Choose between indoor tables under fishnets or riverside picnic benches outside (daily 11:00-22:00, on the island by the millwheel, mobile 723-829-089).

Krčma v Šatlavské is an old prison gone cozy, with an open fire, big wooden tables under a rustic old medieval vault, and tables outdoors on the pedestrian lane. It's great for a late drink or roasted game (cooked on an open spit). *Medovina* is the hot honey wine (daily 12:00–24:00, on Šatlavská, follow lane leading to the side from TI on main square, mobile 608-973-797).

Restaurace Barbakán is built into the town fortifications, with a terrace hanging high over the river. It's a good spot for old-fashioned Czech cooking and beer, at the top of town and near the recommended Rooseveltova street accommodations (open long hours daily, reasonable prices, Horní 26, tel. 380-712-679).

Hospoda 99 Restaurace serves good, cheap soups, salads, and meals. It's the choice of hostelers and locals alike for its hamburgers, vegetarian food, Czech dishes, and cheap booze (meals served 10:00–22:00, bar open until 24:00, at Hostel 99, Vezni 99, tel. 380-712-812). This place is booming until late, when everything else is hibernating.

Dobrá Čajovna is a typical example of the quiet, exotic-feeling teahouses that flooded Czech towns in the 1990s as alternatives to smoky, raucous pubs. Though directly across from the castle entrance, it's a world away from the touristic hubbub. As is so often the case, if you want to surround yourself with locals, don't go to a traditional place...go ethnic. With its meditative karma inside and a peaceful terrace facing the monastery out back, it provides a relaxing break (daily 13:00–22:00, Latrán 54, mobile 777-654-744).

Český Krumlov Connections

Almost all trains to and from Český Krumlov require a transfer in the city of České Budějovice, a transit hub just to the north. České Budějovice's bus and train stations are next to each other. All bus and train timetables are online at www.idos.cz.

From Český Krumlov by Train to: České Budějovice (6/day, 1 hour), **Prague** (8/day, 1/day direct, 4 hours; bus is faster, cheaper, and easier—see below), **Brno** (10/day, 1.25 hours), **Vienna** (6/day with at least one change, 5–6 hours), **Budapest** (6/day with at least one change, 10–15 hours).

From Český Krumlov by Bus to: Prague (7/day, 3.5 hours, 180 Kč; 2 of the daily departures—12:00 and 16:45—can be reserved and paid for at TI, tickets can be bought from driver if seats are available), **České Budějovice** (transit hub for other destinations; about 2/hour, 30–50 minutes, 30 Kč). The Český Krumlov bus station, a five-minute walk out of town, is just a big parking lot with

numbered stalls for various buses (bus info tel. 380-711-190). A good place to buy bus tickets online is www.studentagency.cz.

From České Budějovice to Třeboň, Telč, and Třebíč: An express bus goes from České Budějovice to the Moravian city of **Brno** (5/day Mon-Fri, 2/day Sat-Sun, 4.5 hours). Along the way, it stops at **Třeboň** (30 minutes from České Budějovice), **Telč** (2 hours from České Budějovice), and **Třebíč** (3.25 hours from České Budějovice).

By Shuttle Bus or Private Car to Linz and Beyond: If you can get to Linz, Austria, you'll have your choice of the fast trains running hourly from Linz to Munich, Salzburg, and Vienna.

Two companies with similar pricing run shuttle buses to and from Český Krumlov and **Linz** (3/day, 1.25 hours, 400 Kč), **Vienna** (1/day, 3 hours, 1,090 Kč), and **Salzburg** (1/day, 3 hours, 1,090 Kč). Be sure to book in advance, whether you're going with reliable Sebastian Tours (mobile 607-100-234 or 608-357-581, www.sebastianck-tours.com, sebastiantours@hotmail.com) or Pension Lobo (tel. 380-713-153 or 777-637-374, www.shuttlelobo.cz, lobo@ckrumlov.cz; or reserve in person at Pension Lobo at Latrán 73 or at the main square shuttle office; may cancel with short notice—reconfirm the day before).

ČESKÝ KRUMLOV

DENMARK

The following chapter is excerpted from *Rick Steves' Scandinavia.*

ÆRØ

This small (22 by 6 miles) island on the south edge of Denmark is as salty and sleepy as can be. Its tombstones are carved with such sentiments as: "Here lies Christian Hansen at anchor with his wife. He'll not weigh until he stands before God." It's a peaceful and homey island, where baskets of strawberries sit in front of houses—for sale on the honor system.

Ærø statistics: 7,000 residents, 500,000 visitors and 80,000 boaters annually, 350 deer, seven priests, no crosswalks, and three police officers. The three big industries are farming (wheat and dairy), shipping, and tourism—in that order. Twenty percent of the Danish fleet still resides on Ærø, in the town of Marstal. But jobs are scarce, the population is slowly dropping, and family farms are consolidating into larger units.

Ærø, home to several windmills and one of the world's largest solar power plants, is going "green." They hope to become completely wind- and solar-powered. Currently, nearly half the island's heat and electricity is provided by renewable sources, and most of its produce is organically grown. New technology is expected to bring Ærø closer to its goal within the next few years.

Getting Around Ærø

On a short visit, you won't need to leave Ærøskøbing, except for a countryside bike ride—everything is within walking or pedaling distance. But if you have more time or want to explore the rest of the island, you can take advantage of Ærø's **bus** network. Buses leave from a stop just above the ferry dock (leaving the ferry, walk up about a block and look right). Ærø recently made its main bus line, #790, free for visitors (Mon-Fri hourly until about 19:00;

Sat only June-Aug 4/day; Sun 3-4/day). There are two different branches—one going to Marstal at the east end of the island, and the other to Søby in the west (look for the town name under the bus number). The main reason to take the bus is to go to Marstal on a rainy day to visit its maritime museum (see page 143).

You can also take a subsidized **taxi** ride to points around the island—but it requires some planning ahead. To use this "Telebus" system, you have to make the trip between 5:00 and 22:00 (from 7:00 on Sat-Sun). At least two hours in advance, call FynBus at 63 11 22 55 to reserve; a ride to anywhere on Ærø costs just 40 kr per person.

Ærøskøbing

Ærøskøbing is Ærø's village in a bottle. It's small enough to be cute, but just big enough to feel real. The government, recognizing the value of this amazingly preserved little town, prohibits modern building anywhere in the center. It's the only town in Denmark protected in this way. Drop into the 1680s, when Ærøskøbing was the wealthy home port of a hundred windjammers. The many Danes and Germans who come here for the tranquility—washing up the cobbled main drag in waves with the landing of each boat—call it the fairy-tale town. The Danish word for "cozy," *hyggelig*, describes Ærøskøbing perfectly.

Ærøskøbing is simply a pleasant place to wander. Stubby little porthole-type houses, with their birth dates displayed in proud decorative rebar, lean on each other like drunk, sleeping sailors. Wander under flickering old-time lamps. Snoop around town. It's OK. Peek into living rooms (if people want privacy, they shut their drapes). Notice the many "snooping mirrors" on the houses—antique locals are fol-lowing your every move. The har-

bor now caters to holiday yachts, and on midnight low tides you can almost hear the crabs playing cards.

The town economy, once rich with the windjammer trade, hit the rocks in modern times. Kids 15 to 18 years old go to a boarding school in Svendborg; many don't return. It's an interesting discus-sion: Should the island folk pickle their culture in tourism, or for-get about the cuteness and get modern?

Planning Your Time

You'll regret not setting aside a minimum of two nights for your Ærøskøbing visit. In a busy day you can "do" everything you like—except relax. If ever a place was right for recreating, this is it. I'd arrive in time for an evening stroll, dinner, and the Night Watchman's tour (21:00 nightly in summer). The next morning, do the island bike tour, returning by mid-afternoon. You can see the town's three museums in less than two hours (but take note of their closing times—16:00 in summer, even earlier off-season), then browse the rest of your daylight away. Your second evening is filled with options: Stroll out to the summer huts for sunset, watch the classic sailing ships come in to moor for the evening (mostly Dutch and German boats crewed by vacationers), watch a movie in the pint-sized town cinema, go bowling with local teens, or check out live music in the pub.

Note that during the off-season (basically Sept-May), the town is quite dead and may not be worth a visit. Several shops and restaurants are closed, the Night Watchman's tour stops running, and bad weather can make a bike ride unpleasant.

Orientation to Ærøskøbing

Ærøskøbing is tiny. Everything's just a few cobbles from the ferry landing.

Tourist Information

The TI, which faces the ferry landing, is a clearinghouse for brochures promoting sights and activities on the island, has info on other Danish destinations, can help book rooms, rents small electric cars (300 kr/half-day, 500 kr/day, reserve a day or two in advance, available June-Aug only), and offers Internet access and Wi-Fi (late-June-mid-Aug Mon-Fri 9:00-18:00, Sat-Sun 10:00-18:00; off-season Mon-Fri 10:00-16:00, closed Sat-Sun; tel. 62 52 13 00, www.aeroe.dk or www.aeroeisland.com).

Helpful Hints

Money: The town's only cash machine is on Torvet Square.

Internet Access: Try the TI (steady hours) or the library on Torvet Square (sketchy hours).

Laundry: Ærøskøbing's self-service launderette (on Gyden) is looking for a new owner; in the meantime, most of its machines are out of order. You might be able to do laundry, but don't count on it.

Ferries: See "Ærøskøbing Connections," at the end of this chapter.

Bike Rental: Pilebækkens Cykler rents bikes year-round at the gas station at the top of the town. Manager Janne loans read-

ers of this book the 25-kr island *cykel* map so they won't get lost (three-speed bikes-55 kr/24 hours, seven-speed bikes-75 kr/24 hours; Mon-Fri 9:00-16:30, Sat 9:00-12:00, closed Sun except in July—when it's open 10:00-13:00; from Torvet Square,

go through green door at Søndergade end of square, past gar-den to next road, in the gas station at Pilebækken 7; tel. 62 52 11 10). **Hotel Ærøhus** rents seven-speed bikes (75 kr/24 hours, 200-kr deposit, open very long hours). The campground and hostel also rent bikes (see "Sleeping in Ærøskøbing," later). Most people on Ærø don't bother locking up their bikes—if your rental doesn't have a lock, don't fret.

Shopping: The town is speckled with cute little shops, including a funky flea market shop next to the bakery. Each July, local artisans show their creations in a warehouse facing the ferry landing.

Self-Guided Walk

▲▲▲Welcome to Ærøskøbing

Ideally, take this stroll with the sun low, the shadows long, and the colors rich. Start at the harbor.

Harbor: Loiter around the harbor a bit first. German and Dutch vacationers on grand old sailboats come into port each evening. Because Ærø is only nine miles across the water from Germany, the island is popular with Germans who regularly return to this peaceful retreat.

• *From the harbor and TI, walk up the main street a block and go left on...*

Smedegade: This is the poorest street in town, with the most

architectural and higgledy-piggledy charm. Have a close look at the "street spies" on the houses—clever mirrors letting old women inside keep an eye on what's going on out-side. The ship-in-a-bottle Bottle Peter Museum is on the right (described later,

ÆRØ

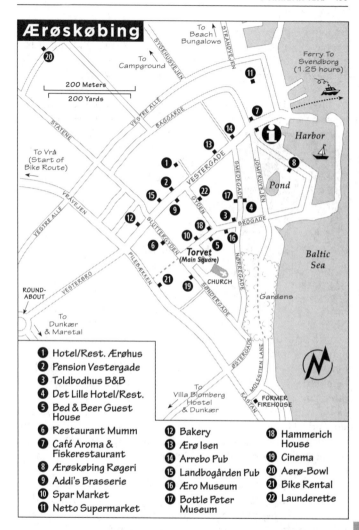

Ærøskøbing

200 Meters
200 Yards

To Beach Bungalows
To Campground
Ferry To Svendborg (1.25 hours)
To Vrå (Start of Bike Route)
Harbor
Pond
Baltic Sea
Torvet (Main Square)
CHURCH
Gardens
ROUND-ABOUT
To Dunkær & Marstal
To Villa Blomberg Hostel & Dunkær
FORMER FIREHOUSE

1 Hotel/Rest. Ærøhus
2 Pension Vestergade
3 Toldbodhus B&B
4 Det Lille Hotel/Rest.
5 Bed & Beer Guest House
6 Restaurant Mumm
7 Café Aroma & Fiskerestaurant
8 Ærøskøbing Røgeri
9 Addi's Brasserie
10 Spar Market
11 Netto Supermarket
12 Bakery
13 Ærø Isen
14 Arrebo Pub
15 Landbogården Pub
16 Ærø Museum
17 Bottle Peter Museum
18 Hammerich House
19 Cinema
20 Aerø-Bowl
21 Bike Rental
22 Launderette

under "Sights in Ærøskøbing"). Notice the gutters—some protect only the doorway. Locals find the rounded modern drainpipes less charming than the old-school ones with hard angles. Appreciate the finely carved old doors. Each is proudly unique—try to find two the same. Number 37 (on the left, after Det Lille Hotel), from the 18th century, is Ærøskøbing's cutest house. Its tiny dormer is from some old ship's poop deck. The plants above the door have a traditional purpose—to keep this part of the house damp and slow to burn in case of fire.

Smedegade ends at the Folkehøjskole (folks' high school). Inspired by the Danish philosopher Nikolaj Gruntvig—who wanted people to be able to say "I am good at being me"—it offers people of any age the benefit of government-subsidized cultural education (music, art, theater, and so on).

• *Jog left, then turn right after the school, and stroll along the peaceful, harborside...*

Molestien Lane: This gravel path is lined with gardens, a quiet beach, and a row of small-is-beautiful houses—beginning

with humble and progressing to captain's class. These fine buildings are a reminder that through the centuries, Ærøskøbing has been the last town in Germany, independent, the first town in Denmark...and always into trade—legal and illegal. (The smuggling spirit survives in residents' blood even today. When someone returns from a trip, friends eagerly ask, "And what did you bring back?") Each garden is cleverly and lovingly designed. The harborfront path, nicknamed "Virgin's Lane," was where teens could court within view of their parents.

The dreamy-looking island immediately across the way is a nature preserve and a resting spot for birds making their long journey from the north to the Mediterranean. There's one lucky bull here (farmers raft over their heifers, who return as cows). Rainbows often end on this island—where plague victims were once buried. In the winter, when the water freezes (about once a decade), locals slip and slide over for a visit. The white building you can see at the end of the town's pier was the cooking house, where visiting sailors (who tried to avoid working with open flame on flammable ships) could do their baking.

At the end of the lane stands the former firehouse (with the tall brick tower, now a place for the high school garage band to practice). Twenty yards before the firehouse, a trail cuts left about 100 yards along the shore to a place the town provides for fishermen to launch and store their boats and tidy up their nets. A bench is strategically placed to enjoy the view.

• *Follow the rutted lane inland, back past the firehouse. Turn right and walk a block toward town. At the first intersection, take a right onto...*

Østergade: This was Ærøskøbing's east gate. In the days of German control, all island trade was legal only within the town. All who passed this point would pay various duties and taxes at a tollbooth that once stood here.

As you walk past the traditional houses, peer into living rooms. Catch snatches of Danish life. (After the bend, you can see right through the windows to the sea.) Ponder the beauty of a society with such a keen sense of civic responsibility that fishing permits commit you "to catch only what you need." You're welcome to pick berries where you like...but "no more than what would fit in your hat."

The wood on these old houses prefers organic coverings to modern paint. Tar painted on beams as a preservative blisters in the sun. An old-fashioned paint of chalk, lime, and clay lets old houses breathe and feel more alive. (It gets darker with the rain and leaves a little color on your fingers.) Modern chemical paint has much less personality.

The first square (actually a triangle, at #55) was the old goose market. Ærøskøbing—born in the 13th century, burned in the 17th, and rebuilt in the 18th—claims (believably) to be the best-preserved town from that era in Denmark. The original plan, with 12 streets laid out by its founder, survives.

• *Leaving the square, stay left on...*

Søndergade: Look for wrought-iron girders on the walls, added to hold together bulging houses. (On the first corner, at

#55, notice the nuts that could be tightened like a corset to keep the house from sagging.) Ærøskøbing's oldest houses (check out the dates)—the only ones that survived a fire during a war with Sweden—are #36 and #32. At #32, the hatch upstairs was where masts and sails were stored for the winter. These houses also have some of the finest doors in town (and in Ærøskøbing, that's really saying something). The red on #32's door is the original paint job—ox blood, which, when combined with the tannin in the wood, really lasts. The courtyard behind #18 was a parking lot in pre-car days. Farmers, in town for their shopping chores, would leave their horses here. Even today, the wide-open fields are just beyond.

• *Wander down to Torvet, Ærøskøbing's main square.*

Torvet (Main Square): Notice the two pumps. Until 1951, townspeople came here for their water. The linden tree is the town symbol. The rocks around it celebrate the reunion of a big chunk of southern Denmark (including this island), which was ruled by Germany from 1864 to 1920. See the town seal featuring a linden tree, over the door of the old

City Hall (now the library, with Internet stations in former prison cells). Read the Danish on the wall: "With law shall man a country build."

• *Our walk is over. Continue straight (popping into recommended Restaurant Mumm, the best place in town, to make a reservation for dinner). You'll return to the main street (Vestergade) and—just when you need it—the town bakery. If you're ready to launch right into a bike ride, go through the green door right of the City Hall to reach the town's bike-rental place (listed earlier, under "Helpful Hints").*

Sights in Ærøskøbing

Museums

Ærøskøbing's three tiny museums cluster within a few doors of each other just off the main square (if visiting all three, buy the 85-kr combo-ticket; tel. 62 52 29 50, www.arremus.dk). In July, they organize daily chatty tours. While quirky and fun (and with sketchy English handouts), these museums would be much more interesting and worthwhile if they translated their Danish descriptions for the rare person on this planet who doesn't speak *Dansk*. (Your gentle encouragement might help get results.)

Ærø Museum—This museum fills two floors of an old house with the island's local history, from seafaring to farming. On the ground

floor, you'll see household objects (such as pottery, kitchenware, and tools), paintings, a loom from 1683, and a fun diorama showing an aerial view of Ærøskøbing in 1862—notice the big gardens behind nearly every house. (This museum carries on the tradition with its own garden out back—be sure to go out and explore it before you leave.) Upstairs are 19th-century outfits, lots more paintings, an 18th-century peasant's living room with colorful furniture, and the gear from a 100-year-old pharmacy.

Cost and Hours: 30 kr; late June-Aug daily 11:00-16:00; mid-April-late June and Sept-late Oct daily 11:00-15:00; late Oct-mid-April Mon-Fri 10:00-13:00, closed Sat-Sun; Brogade 3-5.

▲**Bottle Peter Museum (Flaske-Peters Samling)**—This fascinating house has 750 different bottled ships. Old Peter Jacobsen, who made his first bottle at 16 and his last at 85, created some 1,700 total ships-in-bottles in his lifetime. He bragged that he drank the contents of each bottle...except those containing milk. This museum opened in 1943, when the mayor of Ærøskøbing offered Peter and his wife a humble home in exchange for the right to

display his works. Bottle Peter died in 1960 (and is most likely buried in a glass bottle), leaving a lifetime of tedious little creations for visitors to squint and marvel at.

In two buildings facing each other across a cobbled courtyard, you'll see rack after rack of painstaking models in bottles and cigar boxes. Some are "right-handed" and some are "left-handed" (referring to the direction the bottle faced, and therefore which hand the model-maker relied on to execute the fine details)—Bottle Peter could do it all. In the entrance building, you'll see Peter's "American collection," which he sold to a Danish-American collector so he could have funds to retire. One of Peter's favorites was the "diver-bottle"—an extra-wide bottle with two separate ship models inside: One shipwreck on the "ocean floor" at the bottom of the bottle, and, above that, a second one floating on the "surface." A video shows the artist at work, and nearby you can see some of his tools. In the second building, you can read some English panels about Peter's life (including his mischievous wit, which caused his friends great anxiety when he had an audience with the king) and see the headstone he designed for his own grave: A cross embedded with seven ships-in-bottles, representing the seven seas he explored in his youth as a seaman.

Cost and Hours: 40 kr; mid-April-late Oct daily 10:00-16:00, in summer until 17:00; late Oct-Dec Mon-Fri 10:00-13:00, closed Sat-Sun; Jan-mid-April Tue-Fri 13:00-15:00, Sat 10:00-12:00, closed Sun-Mon; Smedegade 22.

Hammerich House—These 12 funky rooms in three houses are filled with 200- to 300-year-old junk.

Cost and Hours: 30 kr, late May-late Aug daily 12:00-16:00, closed off-season, Gyden 22.

Ærø Island Bike Ride (or Car Tour)

This 15-mile trip shows you the best of this windmill-covered island's charms. The highest point on the island is only 180 feet above sea level, but the wind can be strong and the hills seem long and surprisingly steep. If you'd rather drive the route, you can rent an electric car at the TI (summer only, see page 131).

As a bike ride, it's good exercise, though it may be more exhausting than fun if you've done only light, recreational cycling at home. You'll pay more for seven gears instead of five, but it's worth it.

Rent your bike in town (see "Helpful Hints," earlier). While my map and instructions work, a local cycle map is helpful (free

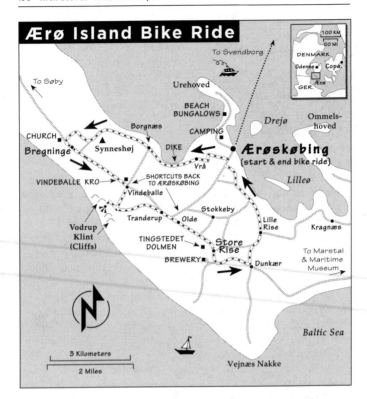

Ærø Island Bike Ride

loaner maps if you rent from Pilebækkens Cykler, or buy one at the TI). Bring along plenty of water, as there are few opportunities to fill up (your first good chance is at the WC at the Bregninge church; there are no real shops until downtown Bregninge).

• *Leave Ærøskøbing to the west on the road to Vrå (Vråvejen, signed Bike Route #90). From downtown, pedal up the main street (Vestergade) and turn right on Vråvejen; from the bike-rental place on Pilebækken, just turn right and pedal straight ahead—it turns into Vråvejen.*

Leaving Ærøskøbing: You'll see the first of many U-shaped farms, typical of Denmark. The three sides block the wind and store cows, hay, and people. *Gård* (farm) shows up in many local surnames.

At Øsemarksvej, bike along the coast in the protection of the dike built in 1856 to make the once-salty swampland to your left farmable. While the weak soil is good for hay and little else, they get the most out of it. Each winter, certain grazing areas flood with seawater. (Some locals claim this makes their cows produce fatter milk and meat.) As you roll along the dike, the land on your left is about eight feet below sea level. The little white pump house—alone in the field—is busy each spring and summer.

• *At the T-junction, go right (over the dike) toward Borgnæs.*

Borgnæs: The traditional old "straw house" (50 yards down, on left) is a café and shop selling fresh farm products. Just past that, a few roadside tables sell farm goodies on the honor system. Borgnæs is a cluster of modern summer houses. In spite of huge demand, a weak economy, and an aging population, development like this is no longer allowed.

• *Keep to the right (passing lots of wheat fields); at the next T-junction, turn right, following signs for Ø.* Bregningemark (*don't turn off for* Vindeballe). *After a secluded beach, head inland (direction: Ø. Bregninge). Pass the island's only water mill, and climb uphill over the island's 2,700-inch-high summit toward Bregninge. The tallest point on Ærø is called Synneshøj ("Seems High"—it sure does, and if you're even a bit out of shape, you'll feel every one of those inches).*

Gammelgård: Take a right turn marked only by a *Bike Route #90* sign. The road deteriorates (turns to gravel—and can be slushy if there's been heavy rain, so be careful). You'll wind scenically and sometimes steeply through "Ærø's Alps," past classic thatched-roofed "old farms" (hence the name of the lane—Gammelgård).

• *At the modern road, turn left (leaving Bike Route #90) and bike to the big village church. Before turning left to roll through Bregninge, visit the church.*

Bregninge Church: The interior of the 12th-century Bregninge church is still painted as a Gothic church would have been.

Find the painter's self-portrait (behind the pulpit, right of front pew). Tradition says that if the painter wasn't happy with his pay, he'd paint a fool's head in the church (above third pew on left). Note how the fool's mouth—the hole for a rope tied to the bell—has been worn wider and wider by centuries of ringing. (During services, the ringing bell would call those who were ill and too contagious to be allowed into the church to come for communion—distributed through the square hatches flanking the altar.)

The altarpiece—gold leaf on carved oak—is from 1528, six years before the Reformation came to Denmark. The cranium carved into the bottom indicates it's a genuine masterpiece by Claus Berg (from Lübeck, Germany). This Crucifixion scene is

such a commotion, it seems to cause Christ's robe to billow up. The soldiers who traditionally gambled for Christ's robe have traded their dice for knives. Even the three wise men (lower right; each perhaps a Danish king) made it to this Crucifixion. Notice the escaping souls of the two thieves—the one who converted on the cross being carried happily to heaven, and the other, with its grim-winged escort, heading straight to hell. The scene at lower left—a bare-breasted, dark-skinned woman with a disciple feeding her child—symbolizes the Great Commission: "Go ye to all the world." Since this is a Catholic altarpiece, a roll call of saints lines the wings. During the restoration, the identity of the two women on the lower right was unknown, so the lettering—even in Latin—is clearly gibberish. Take a moment to study the 16th-century art on the ceiling (for example, the crucified feet ascending, leaving only footprints on earth). In the narthex, a list of pastors goes back to 1505. The current pastor (Agnes) is the first woman on the list.

• *Now's the time for a bathroom break (public WC in the churchyard). Then roll downhill through...*

Bregninge: As you bike through what is supposedly Denmark's "second-longest village," you'll pass many more U-shaped *gårds*. Notice how the town is in a gully. Imagine pirates trolling along the coast, looking for church spires marking unfortified villages. Ærø's 16 villages are all invisible from the sea—their church spires carefully designed not to be viewable from sea level.

• *About a mile down the main road is Vindeballe. Just before the main part of the village (soon after you pass the official* Vindeballe *sign and the* din fart *sign—which tells you "your speed"), take the* Vodrup Klint *turnoff to the right.*

Vodrup Klint: A road leads downhill (with a well-signed jog to the right) to dead-end at a rugged bluff called Vodrup Klint (WC, picnic benches). If I were a pagan, I'd worship here—the sea, the wind, and the chilling view. Notice how the land steps in sloppy slabs down to the sea. When saturated with water, the slabs of clay that make up the land here get slick, and entire chunks can slide.

Hike down to the foamy beach (where you can pick up some flint, chalk, and wild thyme). While the wind at the top could drag a kite-flier, the beach below can be ideal for sunbathing. Because Ærø is warmer and drier than the rest of Denmark, this island is home to plants and animals found nowhere else in the country. This southern exposure is the warmest area. Germany is dead ahead.

• *Backtrack 200 yards and follow the signs to* Tranderup. *On the way, you'll pass a lovely pond famous for its bell frogs and happy little duck houses.*

Popping out in Tranderup, you can backtrack (left) about 300 yards to get to the traditional **Vindeballe Kro**—*a handy inn for a stop if you're hungry or thirsty (30-45-kr lunches served daily July–mid-Aug 12:00-14:00, 150-200-kr dinners served daily year-round 18:00-21:00).*

If you're tired or if the weather is turning bad, you can shortcut from here back to Ærøskøbing: Go down the lane across the street from the Vindeballe Kro, and you'll zip quickly downhill across the island to the dike just east of Borgnæs; turn right and retrace your steps back into town.

But there's much more to see. To continue our pedal, head on into...

Tranderup: Still following signs for *Tranderup*, stay on Tranderupgade parallel to the big road through town. You'll pass a lovely farm and a potato stand. At the main road, turn right. At the Ærøskøbing turnoff (another chance to bail out and head home), side-trip 100 yards left to the big stone (commemorating the return of the island to Denmark from Germany in 1750) and a grand island panorama. Seattleites might find Claus Clausen's rock interesting (in the picnic area, next to WC). It's a memorial to an extremely obscure pioneer from the state of Washington.

• *Return to the big road (continuing in direction: Marstal), pass through Olde, pedal past FAF (the local wheat farmers' co-op facility), and head toward Store Rise (STOH-reh REE-zuh), the next church spire in the distance. Think of medieval travelers using spires as navigational aids.*

Store Rise Prehistoric Tomb, Church, and Brewery: Thirty yards after the Stokkeby turnoff, follow the rough, tree-lined path

on the right to the Langdysse (Long Dolmen) Tingstedet, just behind the church spire. This is a 6,000-year-old **dolmen,** an early Neolithic burial place. Though Ærø once had more than 200 of these prehistoric tombs, only 13 survive. The site is a raised mound the shape and length (about 100 feet) of a Viking ship, and archeologists have found evidence that indicates a Viking ship may indeed have been burned and buried here.

Ting means assembly spot. Imagine a thousand years ago: Viking chiefs representing the island's various communities gathering here around their ancestors' tombs. For 6,000 years, this has been a holy spot. The stones were considered fertility stones. For centuries, locals in need of virility chipped off bits and took them home (the nicks in the rock nearest the information post are mine).

Tuck away your chip and carry on down the lane to the Store Rise **church.** Inside you'll find little ships hanging in the nave, a fine 12th-century altarpiece, a stick with offering bag and a ting-a-ling bell to wake those nodding off (right of altar), double seats (so worshippers can flip to face the pulpit during sermons), and Martin Luther in the stern keeping his Protestant hand on the rudder. The list in the church allows today's pastors to trace their pastoral lineage back to Doctor Luther himself. (The current pastor, Janet, is the first woman on the list.) The churchyard is circular—a reminder of how churchyards provided a last refuge for humble communities under attack. Can you find anyone buried in the graveyard whose name doesn't end in "-sen"?

The buzz lately in Ærø is its **brewery,** located in a historic brewery 400 yards beyond the Store Rise church. Follow the smell of the hops (or the *Rise Bryggeri* signs). It welcomes visitors with free samples of its various beers. The Ærø traditional brews are available in pilsner (including the popular walnut pilsner), light ale, dark ale, and a typical dark Irish-like stout. The *Rise* organic brews come in light ale, dark ale, and walnut (mid-June-mid-Sept daily 10:00-14:00; mid-Sept-mid-June open Wed-Fri only 10:00-14:00, closed Sat-Tue; tel. 62 52 11 32, www.risebryggeri.dk).

• *From here, climb back to the main road and continue (direction: Marstal) on your way back home to Ærøskøbing. The three 330-foot-high modern windmills on your right are communally owned and, as they are a nonpolluting source of energy, state-subsidized. At Dunkær (3 miles from Ærøskøbing), take the small road, signed* Lille Rise, *past the topless windmill. Except for the Lille Rise, it's all downhill from here, as you coast past great sea views back home to Ærøskøbing.*

Huts at the Sunset Beach: Still rolling? Bike past the campground along the Urehoved beach (*strand* in Danish) for a look at the coziest little beach houses you'll never see back in the "big is beautiful" US. This is Europe, where small is beautiful, and the concept of sustainability is neither new nor subversive. (For more details, see "Beach Bungalow Sunset Stroll," later.)

Rainy-Day Options

Ærø is disappointing but not unworkable in bad weather. In addition to the museums listed earlier, you could rent a car (such as the TI's electric cars) to cruise the island. Also, many of the evening options under "Nightlife in Ærøskøbing" (next) are good in bad weather.

If you want to find out more about the island's seafaring history, hop on the free bus #790 to the dreary town of **Marstal** to visit its fine Marstal Maritime Museum (Marstal Søfartsmuseum). Ride the bus all the way to the harbor (about a 20-minute trip), where you'll find the museum. You'll see plenty of model ships, nautical paintings (including several scenes by acclaimed painter Carl Rasmussen), an original ship's galley, a re-created wheel-house (with steering and navigation equipment), a collection of exotic goods brought back from faraway lands, and a children's area with a climbable mast. Designed by, for, and about sailors, the museum presents a warts-and-all view of the hardships of the seafaring life, rather than romanticizing it (50 kr; July-Aug daily 9:00-18:00; June daily 9:00-17:00; May and Sept-Oct daily 10:00-16:00; Nov-April Mon-Fri 10:00-16:00, Sat 11:00-15:00, closed Sun; Prinsensgade 1, tel. 62 53 23 31, www.marmus.dk).

Nightlife in Ærøskøbing

These activities are best done in the evening, after a day of biking around the island.

▲**Town Walk with Night Watchman**—Each evening in summer, Mr. Jan Pedersen becomes the old night watchman and leads visitors through town. The hour-long walk is likely in Danish and English—and often in German, too—so you'll hang around a lot. But it's a fine time to be out, meet other travelers, and be charmed by gentle Jan (25 kr, daily late June-late

Aug, no tours off-season, meet on Torvet near the church at 21:00, Jan also available as private guide, mobile 40 40 60 13, www.aeroe -turguide.dk, jan.leby@mail.dk).

▲▲**Beach Bungalow Sunset Stroll**—At sunset, stroll to Ærøskøbing's sand beach. Facing the ferry dock, go left, following the harbor. Upon leaving the town, you'll pass the Netto

supermarket (convenient for picking up snacks, beer, or wine), a mini-golf course, and a children's playground. In the rosy distance, past a wavy wheat field, is Vestre Strandvejen—a row of tiny, Monopoly-like huts facing the sunset. These tiny beach escapes are privately owned on land rented from the town (no overnight use,

WCs at each end). Each is different, but all are stained with merry memories of locals enjoying themselves Danish-style. Bring a beverage or picnic. It's perfectly acceptable—and very Danish—to borrow a porch for your sunset sit. From here, it's a fine walk out to the end of Urehoved (as this spit of land is called).

Cinema—The cute little 30-seat Andelen Theater (a former grain warehouse near Torvet Square) plays movies in their original language (Danish subtitles, closed Mon and in July—when it hosts a jazz festival, new titles begin every Tue). It's run in a charming community-service kind of way. The management has installed heat, so tickets no longer come with a blanket.

Bowling—Ærø-Bowl is a six-lane alley in a modern athletic club at the edge of town. In this old-fashioned town, where no modern construction is allowed in the higgledy-piggledy center, this hip facility is a magnet for young people. One local told me, "I've never seen anyone come out of there without a smile" (hot dogs, junk food, arcade games, kids on dates; Tue-Thu 16:00-22:00, later on Fri-Sat, closed Sun-Mon, Søndergade 28, tel. 62 52 23 06, www.arrebowl.dk).

Pubs—Ærøskøbing's two bars are at the top and bottom of Vestergade. **Arrebo Pub,** near the ferry landing, attracts a young crowd and is *the* place for live music (but no food). The low-key **Landbogården** was recently taken over by a Sri Lankan family who have made it non-smoking and have started serving food— both Indian and Danish dishes (daily for 45-75-kr lunches and 100-160-kr dinners, near the top of Vestergade).

Sleeping in Ærøskøbing

The accommodations scene here is boom or bust. Summer weekends and all of July are packed (book long in advance). It's absolutely dead in the winter. These places come with family-run personality, and each is an easy stroll from the ferry landing.

In Ærøskøbing

$$$ Hotel Ærøhus is big and sprawling, with 33 rooms. Although it is less personal and cozy than some of the other listings here, it's the closest thing to a grand hotel in this capital of quaint (S-600 kr, Sb-990 kr, D-800 kr, Db-1,250 kr, free Internet access and Wi-Fi, bike rentals-75 kr/day, possible noise from large dinner parties—ask for a quiet room, tel. 62 52 10 03, fax 62 52 21 23, www.aeroehus-hotel.dk, mail@aeroehus.dk, Ole Jensen and family). Their modern holiday apartments nearby are used as overflow accommodations and can be a fine value for groups and families (details on their website).

Sleep Code

(5 kr = about $1, country code: 45)

S = Single, **D** = Double/Twin, **T** = Triple, **Q** = Quad, **b** = bathroom, **s** = shower. Credit cards are accepted (with a 4 percent surcharge), staff speak English, and breakfast is included unless otherwise noted.

To help you sort easily through these listings, I've divided the accommodations into three categories, based on the price for a double room with bath during high season:

$$$ Higher Priced—Most rooms 1,000 kr or more.
$$ Moderately Priced—Most rooms between 450-1,000 kr.
$ Lower Priced—Most rooms 450 kr or less.

Prices can change without notice; verify the hotel's current rates online or by email. For other updates, see www.ricksteves.com/update.

$$ Pension Vestergade is your best home away from home in Ærøskøbing. It's lovingly run by Susanna Greve and her daughters, Henrietta and Celia. Susanna, who's fun to talk with and is always ready with a cup of tea, has a wealth of knowledge about the town's history and takes good care of her guests. Built in 1784 for a sea captain's daughter, this creaky, sagging, and venerable eight-room place—with each room named for its particular color scheme—is on the main street in the town center. Picnic in the back garden and get to know Hector, the live-in hound. Reserve well in advance (S-600 kr year-round but doubles fluctuate, July: D-990 kr; spring and fall: D-890 kr; winter: D-790 kr; cash only, cuddly hot-water bottles, shared bathrooms, free Internet access and Wi-Fi, Vestergade 44, tel. 62 52 22 98, www.vestergade44.com, pensionvestergade44@post.tele.dk).

$$ Toldbodhus B&B, a tollhouse from 1770 to 1906, now rents four delightful rooms. Three rooms share two bathrooms in the main house, and a small garden house has a double room with a detached bathroom. Karin and John Steenberg—who, as avid travelers, understand your needs—named and decorated each room after cities they've lived in: Amsterdam, København, London, and Hong Kong (April-Sept: S-750 kr, Db-890 kr; Oct-March: S-650 kr, Db-790 kr; cash only, near harbor on corner of Smedegade at Brogade 8, tel. 62 52 18 11, www.toldbodhus.com, toldbodhus @mail.dk).

$$ Det Lille Hotel is a former 19th-century captain's home with six tidy but well-worn rooms (June-Sept: S/D-950 kr; Oct-May: S/D-850 kr; extra bed-265 kr, free Wi-Fi, Smedegade 33, tel. & fax 62 52 23 00, www.det-lille-hotel.dk, mail@det-lille -hotel.dk).

$$ Bed & Beer Guest House, while sloppily run, is good in a pinch, with seven big, modern, apartment-like rooms on the main square (Db-750 kr, breakfast-75 kr, Torvet 7, tel. 40 29 40 50, www.bedandbeer.dk).

Outside of Ærøskøbing

$$ Vindeballe Kro, about three miles from Ærøskøbing, is a traditional inn in Vindeballe at the island's central crossroads. Maria and Steen rent 10 straightforward, well-kept rooms (S-450 kr, D-650 kr, tel. 62 52 16 13, www.vindeballekro.dk, mail@vinde ballekro.dk; see page 141 for details on their restaurant).

$ Ærø Campground is set on a fine beach a few minutes' walk out of town. This three-star campground offers a lodge with a fireplace, campsites, cabins, and bike rental (camping-72 kr/ person, 4- to 6-bed cabins-125-200 kr plus per-person fee, bedding-75 kr/person, open May-Sept; facing the water, follow waterfront to the left; tel. 62 52 18 54, www.aeroecamp.dk).

Hostel: **$ Villa Blomberg**, on the edge of town, has 44 back-packer beds in simple 2- and 4-bed rooms. It's run by an organization for special-needs youth, who live nearby and help run the place as part of their job training (350 kr/person, breakfast-60 kr, sack lunch-50 kr, Internet access, shared kitchen, rental bike-55 kr/ day, Blacksmith 15, tel. 62 52 10 44, http://villablomberg.dk, info @villablomberg.dk).

Eating in Ærøskøbing

Ærøskøbing has a handful of charming and hardworking little eateries. Business is so light that chefs and owners come and go constantly, making it tough to predict the best value for the coming year. As each place has a distinct flavor, I'd spend 20 minutes enjoying the warm evening light and do a strolling survey before making your choice. While there are several simple burger-type joints, I've listed only the serious kitchens. Note that everything closes by 21:00—don't wait too late to eat (if you'll be taking the ferry that leaves Svendborg at 19:30—and arrives at Ærø at 20:45—either eat before your boat trip or call ahead to reserve a place...otherwise you're out of luck). The only places in town serving food during the winter are Addi's Brasserie, Det Lille Hotel, Hotel Ærøhus, and the Landbogården bar (see "Nightlife in Ærøskøbing," earlier).

Restaurant Mumm is where visiting yachters go for a good and classy meal. Portions are huge, and on balmy days their garden terrace out back is a hit. Call ahead to reserve (180-kr daily specials, 80-kr starters, 140-220-kr main courses, daily 16:30-21:00, closed Sun-Mon off-season, near Torvet Square, tel. 62 52 12 12, Peter Sorensen).

Café Aroma, an inexpensive Danish café that feels like a rustic old diner, has a big front porch filled with tables and good, reasonably priced entrées, sandwiches, and burgers for 60-175 kr. Ask about the daily special, which will save you money and is not listed on the confusing menu. Order at the bar (May-Aug daily 11:00-21:00, closed Sept-April, on Vestergade). They also run a high-quality, pricey fish restaurant (aptly named **Fiskerestaurant**) next door.

Ærøskøbing Røgeri serves wonderful smoked fish meals on paper plates and picnic tables. Facing the harbor, it's great for a light meal (50-75 kr for fish with potato salad and bread). Eat there or find a pleasant picnic site at the beach or at the park behind the fish house. A smoked fish dinner and a couple of cold Carlsbergs are a well-earned reward after a long bike ride (May-Sept daily 11:00-18:00, in summer until 20:00, Havnen 15, tel. 62 52 40 07).

Addi's Brasserie is a rare place that's open all year, serving fresh seafood and meat dishes. Eat in the main dining room among portraits of Danish royalty, or in the larger side room (daily lunch and dinner specials, lunch main courses-48-85 kr, dinner main courses-180 kr, daily 12:00-15:00 & 18:00-21:00, across street from Pension Vestergade, Vestergade 39, tel. 62 52 21 43).

Hotel Restaurants: Two hotels in town have dining rooms with good but expensive food; I'd eat at the restaurants I've listed above, unless they're closed. But in a pinch, try these: **Det Lille Hotel** serves meals in an inviting dining room or garden (200-kr daily specials, 70-100-kr starters, 190-240-kr main dishes, daily 12:00-21:00, dinner only off-season—but at least they're open year-round, Smedegade 33, tel. 62 52 23 00, Klaus cooks with attitude). **Hotel Ærøhus** is a last resort, serving creative but pricey French-inspired modern fare in a sprawling complex of dining rooms, big and small (115-kr starters, 225-300-kr main dishes, open daily, on Vestergade, tel. 62 52 10 03).

Grocery: Buy picnic fixings plus wine and beer at the **Spar Market** (Mon-Fri 9:00-18:00, Sat 9:00-14:00, Sun 10:00-15:00, on Torvet Square) or the bigger **Netto** supermarket (chilled beer and wine—handy for walks to the little huts on the beach at sunset,

ÆRØ

Mon-Fri 9:00-19:00, Sat 8:00-17:00, closed Sun, kitty-corner from ferry dock).

Bakery: Ærøskøbing's old-school little bakery sells homemade bread, cheese, yogurt, and tasty pastries (Tue-Fri 7:00-17:00, Sat-Sun 7:00-14:00, closed Mon, top of Vestergade).

Ice Cream: Halfway up the main drag (Vestergade), you'll smell fresh-baked waffles and see benches filled with happy ice-cream lickers. **Ærø Isen** serves good ice cream in fresh waffle cones, with whipped cream and jam topping. Their "Ærø-Isen Special" (walnut-maple syrup ice cream topped with whipped cream and maple syrup) is 9 kr more than the other flavors (daily 11:00-21:00). Be sure to check out the gallery behind the

shop to see paintings and sculptures featuring local artists.

Ærøskøbing Connections

Ærø-Svendborg Ferry

The ferry ride between **Svendborg,** with connections to Copenhagen, and **Ærøskøbing,** on the island of Ærø, is a relaxing 75-minute crossing. Just get on, and the crew will come to you for your payment. While they accept Danish credit cards, American ones don't work—so be sure to bring enough cash (184 kr round-trip per person, 406 kr round-trip per car—not including driver/passengers, you'll save a little money with round-trip tickets, you can leave the island via any of the three different Ærø ferry routes, ferry not covered by or discounted with railpass).

The ferry always has room for walk-ons, but drivers should reserve a spot in advance, especially on weekends and in summer. During these busy times, reserve as far ahead as you can—ideally at least a week in advance. Car reservations by phone or email are free and easy—simply give your name and license-plate number. If you don't know your license number (i.e., you're reserving from home and haven't yet picked up your rental car), try asking nicely if they're willing to just take your name. They may want you to call them with the number when you pick up your car, but if that's not practical, you can usually just tell the attendant your name before you drive onto the boat (office open Mon-Fri 8:00-16:00, Sat-Sun 9:00-15:30, tel. 62 52 40 00, www.aeroe-ferry.dk, info @aeroe-ferry.dk).

Ferries depart Svendborg daily at 10:15, 13:15, 16:15, 19:15, and 22:30 (plus a 7:15 departure Mon-Fri). Ferries depart Ærøskøbing daily at 8:45, 11:45, 14:45, 17:45, and 20:45 (plus a 5:45 departure Mon-Fri). Drivers with reservations just drive on (be sure to get into the *med* reservations line). If you won't use your car in Ærø, park it in Svendborg (big, safe lot two blocks in from ferry landing, or at the far end of the harbor near the Bendix fish shop). On Ærø, parking is free.

Trains Connecting with Ærø-Svendborg Ferry

The train from **Odense** dead-ends at the Svendborg harbor (2/hour Mon-Sat, 1/hour Sun, 45 minutes; don't get off at the "Svendborg Vest" station—wait until you get to the end of the line, called simply "Svendborg"). Train departures and arrivals are coordinated with the ferry schedule.

Arriving in Svendborg: The ferry leaves Svendborg about five minutes after your train arrives. If you know where you're going, it takes about that long to walk briskly from the station to the dock. Don't dawdle—the boat leaves stubbornly on time, even if the train is a minute or two late. Since trains run every half-hour during summer (except on Sundays), I recommend leaving Odense on an earlier train, so you have a little more time to absorb delays and find your way (in other words, take the train that arrives in Svendborg 35 minutes before your boat). If you're cutting it close, be ready to hop off the train and follow these directions:

To get from the Svendborg train station to the dock, turn left after exiting the train, following the sidewalk between the tracks and the station, then take a left (across the tracks) at the first street, Brogade. Head a block downhill to the harbor, make a right, and the ferry dock is ahead, across from Hotel Ærø. If you arrive early, you can head to the waiting room in the little blue building across the street from the hotel. There are several carry-out restaurants along Brogade, and a few hotels overlooking the ferry line have restaurants.

Departing from Svendborg: All Svendborg trains go to Odense (where you can connect to Copenhagen or Århus). Trains leave shortly after the ferry arrives (tight connections for hurried commuters). To reach the train from the Svendborg ferry dock, pass Hotel Ærø and continue a block along the waiting lane for the ferry, turn left and go up Brogade one block, then take a right and follow the sidewalk between the tracks and the train station. A train signed *Odense* should be waiting on the single track (departs at :20 or :50 past each hour).

ÆRØ

GREECE

The following chapter is excerpted from *Rick Steves' Greece: Athens & the Peloponnese.*

HYDRA

ΎΔΡΑ / Ύδρα

Hydra (pronounced EE-drah, not HIGH-drah)—less than a two-hour boat ride from Athens' port, Piraeus—is a glamorous getaway that combines practical convenience with idyllic Greek island ambience. After the noise of Athens, Hydra's traffic-free tranquility is a delight. Donkeys rather than cars, the shady awnings of well-worn cafés, and memorable seaside views all combine to make it clear...you've found your Greek isle.

The island's main town, also called Hydra, is one of Greece's prettiest. Its busy but quaint harbor—bobbing with rustic fishing boats and luxury yachts—is surrounded by a ring of rocky hills and blanketed with whitewashed homes. From the harbor, a fleet of zippy water taxis whisk you to isolated beaches and tavernas. Hydra is an easy blend of stray cats, hardworking donkeys, welcoming Hydriots (as locals are called), and lazy tourists on "island time."

One of the island's greatest attractions is its total absence of cars and motorbikes. Sure-footed beasts of burden—laden with everything from sandbags and bathtubs to bottled water—climb

stepped lanes. While Hydra is generally quiet, dawn teaches visitors the exact meaning of "cockcrow." The end of night is marked with much more than a distant cock-a-doodle-doo; it's a dissonant chorus of cat fights, burro honks, and what sounds like roll call at an asylum for crazed roosters. After the animal

Hydra's Hystory

While it seems tiny and low-key, overachieving Hydra holds a privileged place in Greek history. The fate of Hydriots has always been tied to the sea, which locals have harnessed to their advantage time after time.

Many Hydriot merchants became wealthy running the British blockade of French ports during the Napoleonic Wars. Hydra enjoyed its glory days in the late 18th and early 19th centuries, when the island was famous for its shipbuilders. Hydra's prosperity earned it the nickname "Little England." As rebellion swept Greece, the island flourished as a safe haven for those fleeing Ottoman oppression.

When the Greeks launched their War of Independence in 1821, Hydra emerged as a leading naval power. The harbor, with its twin forts and plenty of cannons, housed and protected the fleet of 130 ships. Hydriots of note from this period include the naval officer Andreas Miaoulis, who led the "firebrands" and their deadly "fireships," which succeeded in decimating the Ottoman navy (see page 160); and Lazaros Kountouriotis, a  wealthy shipping magnate who donated his fleet to the cause (see page 165).

Greece won its independence, but at a great cost to Hydra, which lost many of its merchant-turned-military ships to the fighting...sending the island into a deep economic funk. During those lean post-war years, Hydriots again found salvation in the sea, farming the sponges that lived below the surface (sponge-divers here pioneered the use of diving suits). Gathering sponges kick-started the local economy and kept Hydra afloat.

In 1956, Sophia Loren came here to play an Hydriot sponge-diver in the film *Boy on a Dolphin,* propelling the little island onto the international stage. And the movie's plot—in which a precious ancient sculpture is at risk of falling into the hands of a greedy art collector instead of being returned to the Greek government—still resonates with today's Greeks, who want to reclaim their heritage for the Acropolis Museum.

Thanks largely to the film, by the 1960s Hydra had become a favorite retreat for celebrities, well-heeled tourists, and artists and writers, who still draw inspiration from the idyllic surroundings. Canadian songwriter Leonard Cohen lived here for a time—and was inspired to compose his beloved song "Bird on the Wire" after observing just that here on Hydra. Today visitors only have to count the yachts to figure out that Hydra's economy is still based on the sea.

Hydra Island

SARONIC GULF

TO POROS & PIRAEUS

CAPE ZOURVA

TO ERMIONI, METOCHI & SPETSES

MANDRAKI BAY

KAMINIA

VLYCHOS

HYDRA TOWN

LIMNIONIZA

BISTI

MOLOS

NISIZA

AG. NIKOLAOS   DCH

1 MILE

1 KM

•••• HYDROFOIL/ CATAMARAN
•••• WATER TAXI
--- TRAILS
♎ BEACHES

population gets all that out of its system, the island slumbers a little longer.

Little Hydra—which has produced more than its share of military heroes, influential aristocrats, and political leaders—is packed with history. Rusted old cannons are scattered about town; black, pitted anchors decorate squares; and small museums hold engaging artifacts. But most visitors enjoy simply being on vacation here. Loiter around the harbor. Go on a photo safari for donkeys and kittens. Take a walk along the coast or up into the hills. Head for an inviting beach, near or far, to sunbathe and swim. Hang out past your bedtime in a cocktail bar. Hydra's the kind of place that makes you want to buy a bottle of ouzo and toss your itinerary into the sea.

Planning Your Time

While Hydra can be done as a long day trip from Athens, it's better to spend two nights (or more) to take full advantage of the island's many dining options, and to give yourself a whole day to relax.

To get your bearings, take my brief self-guided walk as soon as you arrive. While the walk gives you the historic context of the town, it also points out practical stops that will make your stay more efficient and enjoyable (and finishes at a wonderful little bakery). You'll still have ample time for your choice of activities—dipping into a museum that tickles your curiosity, enjoying a drink at a café, going for a hike into the hills, walking along the water to nearby villages and beaches, or catching a shuttle boat or water taxi for a spin around the island.

HYDRA

Orientation to Hydra

Remember, Hydra is the name of both the island and its main town (home to about 90 percent of the island's 3,000 residents). Hydra town climbs up the hill in every direction from the port.

Branching off from the broad café-lined walkway at the bottom of the harbor are four major streets. In order from the boat dock, these are called Tompazi, Oikonomou, Miaouli, and Lignou. Not that street names mean much in this town—locals ignore addresses, and few lanes are labeled. Though the island is small, Hydra's streets twist defiantly to and fro. If seeking a specific location, use the map in this chapter or ask a local. (Note that, like our map, most maps of Hydra show the harbor—which is actually to the north—at the bottom.) Expect to get lost in Hydra...and enjoy it when you do.

Consider venturing beyond Hydra town to settlements and beaches elsewhere on the island. The most accessible is the tiny seaside hamlet of Kaminia, which lies just over the headland west of the harbor (with a good restaurant—see "Eating in Hydra," later).

Tourist Information

Hydra has no TI. The Hydreoniki Travel Agency across from the hydrofoil/catamaran dock can help with information on transportation (tel. 22980-54007, www.hydreoniki.gr); or you can visit the Hellenic Seaways ticket office near the Alpha Bank, down the alley from the harbor by the bakery. For urgent questions, the municipal office facing the harbor between the fort and the museum is friendly (generally open Mon-Fri 9:00-14:00). Useful websites include www.hydradirect.com and www.hydra.com.gr.

Arrival on Hydra

All catamarans and hydrofoils dock in the heart of Hydra town's

harbor (along its eastern edge). All of my recommended accommodations are within a 10-minute walk (and located on the map on page 158). At the port, you can hire a donkey to carry your bags (€10-15, establish the price up front). If you ask, better hotels will often meet you at the boat and help with your bags.

HYDRA

Getting Around Hydra

As there are no cars, your options are by foot, donkey, or boat. You'll walk everywhere in town. While you can hike to neighboring beaches, it's fun to hop a **shuttle boat** (€2.50 to Vlychos with boats leaving on the half-hour, catch shuttles in front of the clock tower) or take a **water taxi** (much more expensive unless you're a small group—same rate for one person or eight). You'll see the red taxi boats stacked and waiting near the donkeys on the harborfront. Sample taxi fares: €10 to Kaminia, €14 to Mandraki Bay (there's a fare board lashed to the pole by the taxi dock, with the English translation hiding on the back side). To get back to town via water taxi, call 22980-53690.

Helpful Hints

Internet Access: Flamingo Internet Café—which has no sign and looks like a big grocery store—is 50 yards from the harbor, on Tompazi (€3/30-minute minimum, daily 12:00-23:00, right side of the street, tel. 22980-53485).

Post Office: The post office (Mon-Fri 7:30-14:00, closed Sat-Sun) faces the outdoor market (just inland from the harbor).

Bookshop: Hydra's no-name bookshop—which sells maps, books about Hydra, and a few books in English (mostly translations of Greek literature)—is just up from the harbor on the stepped lane called Lignou (Mon-Sat 10:00-13:00 & 17:00-19:00, closed Sun).

Drinking Water: While the island's name means "water" in ancient Greek, that was a long time ago. Today there's no natural water source on Hydra (other than private cisterns). Water is barged in daily. No one drinks the tap water here—cheap bottled water is sold everywhere.

Self-Guided Walk

Hydra's Harbor

Hydra clusters around its wide harbor, squeezed full of fishing boats, pleasure craft, luxury yachts, and the occasional Athens-bound hydrofoil or catamaran. Get the lay of the land with this lazy 30-minute stroll.

• *Begin at the tip of the port (to the right, as you face the sea). Climb the stairs (by the cactus) to the cannon-studded turret. From here, you have a fine...*

View of the Harbor

The harbor is the heart and soul of Hydra. Looking at the arid, barren mountains rising up along the spine of the island, it's clear that not much grows here—so the Hydriots have always turned to

HYDRA

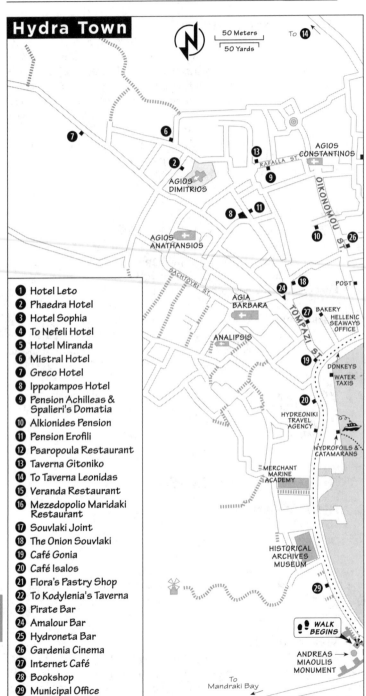

Hydra Town

50 Meters
50 Yards

To ⓮

AGIOS CONSTANTINOS

RAFALLA ST.

AGIOS DIMITRIOS

AGIOS ANATHANSIOS

OIKONOMOU ST.

BACHTOYRI ST.

AGIA BARBARA

ANALIPSIS

TOMPAZI ST.

POST

BAKERY

HELLENIC SEAWAYS OFFICE

DONKEYS

WATER TAXIS

HYDREONIKI TRAVEL AGENCY

HYDROFOILS & CATAMARANS

MERCHANT MARINE ACADEMY

HISTORICAL ARCHIVES MUSEUM

WALK BEGINS

ANDREAS MIAOULIS MONUMENT

To Mandraki Bay

❶ Hotel Leto
❷ Phaedra Hotel
❸ Hotel Sophia
❹ To Nefeli Hotel
❺ Hotel Miranda
❻ Mistral Hotel
❼ Greco Hotel
❽ Ippokampos Hotel
❾ Pension Achilleas & Spalieri's Domatia
❿ Alkionides Pension
⓫ Pension Erofili
⓬ Psaropoula Restaurant
⓭ Taverna Gitoniko
⓮ To Taverna Leonidas
⓯ Veranda Restaurant
⓰ Mezedopolio Maridaki Restaurant
⓱ Souvlaki Joint
⓲ The Onion Souvlaki
⓳ Café Gonia
⓴ Café Isalos
㉑ Flora's Pastry Shop
㉒ To Kodylenia's Taverna
㉓ Pirate Bar
㉔ Amalour Bar
㉕ Hydroneta Bar
㉖ Gardenia Cinema
㉗ Internet Café
㉘ Bookshop
㉙ Municipal Office

HYDRA

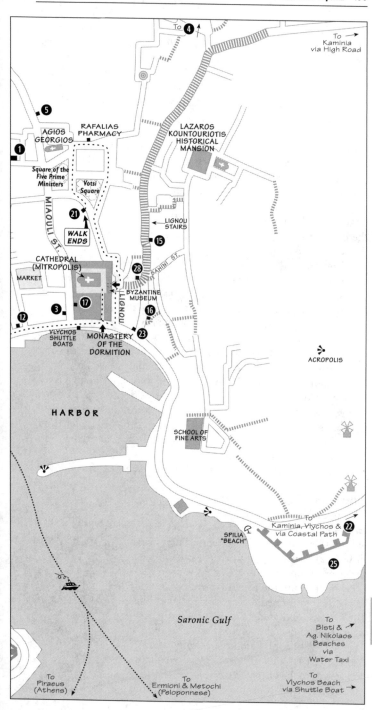

To ④

To →
Kaminia
via High Road

❺

AGIOS
GEORGIOS

RAFALIAS
PHARMACY

LAZAROS
KOUNTOURIOTIS
HISTORICAL
MANSION

❶

Square of the
Five Prime
Ministers

Votsi
Square

MIAOULI ST.

㉑

WALK
ENDS

LIGNOU
STAIRS

❶❺

CATHEDRAL
(MITROPOLIS)

SAHINI ST.

MARKET

㉘

LIGNOU

❸

❶❼

BYZANTINE
MUSEUM

❶❷

❶❻

VLYCHOS
SHUTTLE
BOATS

MONASTERY
OF THE
DORMITION

㉓

ACROPOLIS

HARBOR

SCHOOL OF
FINE ARTS

To
Kaminia, Vlychos &
via Coastal Path

㉒

SPILIA
"BEACH"

㉕

Saronic Gulf

To
Bisti &
Ag. Nikolaos
Beaches
via
Water Taxi

To
Piraeus
(Athens)

To
Ermioni & Metochi
(Peloponnese)

To
Vlychos Beach
via Shuttle Boat →

HYDRA

the sea for survival. As islanders grew wealthy from the sea trade, prominent local merchant families built the grand mansions that rise up between the modest whitewashed houses blanketing the hillsides. One of these—the Lazaros Kountouriotis Historical Mansion—is open to the public (the yellow mansion with the red roof, high on the hill across the harbor and to the left, with the small, red bell tower nearby; described later).

Another mansion, the rough stone four-story building directly across from the port (behind the imposing zigzag wall), now houses Hydra's School of Fine Arts. Artists—Greek and foreign—have long swooned over the gorgeous light that saturates Hydra's white homes, brown cliffs, and turquoise waters. The unique mix of power and art here adds to the charm of Hydra. Locals like to imagine Hydra as an ancient theater: The houses are the audience, the port is the stage, the boats are actors...and the Saronic Gulf is the scenic backdrop.

Look directly across the mouth of the harbor, to the opposite point. Along the base of the walkway, under the seafront café tables, is the town's closest "beach," called Spilia ("Cave")—a concrete pad with ladders luring swimmers into the cool blue. For a more appealing option, you can follow the paved, mostly level path around this point to the fishing hamlet of Kaminia (with a scenic seafood restaurant) and, beyond that, to Vlychos (for the best beach around). Visually trace the ridgeline above that trail, noticing the remains of two old windmills—a fixture on many Greek islands, used for grinding grain and raw materials for gunpowder. The windmills' sails are long gone, but the lower one was restored for use as a film prop (for the Sophia Loren film—see sidebar on page 154). Crowning the hill high above are the scant remains of Hydra's humble little acropolis.

• *Turn your attention to the centerpiece of this viewpoint, the...*

Andreas Miaoulis Monument

The guy at the helm is Admiral Andreas Miaoulis (1768-1835), an Hydriot sea captain who valiantly led the Greek navy in the revolution that began in 1821. This war sought to end nearly four centuries of Ottoman occupation. As war preparations ramped up, the wealthy merchant marine of Hydra transformed their vessels into warships. The Greeks innovated a clever and deadly naval warfare technique: the "fireship." (For details, see page 165.) While this kamikaze-burning strategy cost the Greeks a lot of boats, it was even more devastating to the Ottoman navy—and Miaoulis' naval victory was considered a crucial turning point in the war. For three days each June, Hydra celebrates the Miaoulia Festival, when they set fire to an old ship to commemorate the burning of the Ottoman fleet.

On the monument, the cross that hangs from the steering column represents the eventual triumph of the Christian Greeks over the Muslim Ottomans. Miaoulis' bones are actually inside the stone pedestal under the statue. The three flags above honor the EU, Greece, and Hydra.

• *Head back down the stairs and begin walking along the harborfront.*

Along the Harbor

After passing the municipal office and the port authority, you reach the stout stone mansion that houses the **Historical Archives Museum.** This small but good collection (described later, under "Sights in Hydra") does its best to get visitors excited about Hydra's history. The gap after the museum is filled with monuments honoring Hydriot heroes. The green plaque in the pillar is a gift from Argentina, to honor an Hydriot aristocrat who fought in the Argentinean war for independence. The next building is the Merchant Marine Academy, where Hydra continues to churn out sailors—many of whom often hang around out front. (During the WWII occupation of Greece, this building was used as a Nazi base.) Next, the row of covered metal benches marks the embarkation point for the hydrofoils ("Flying Dolphins") and catamarans ("Flying Cats") that connect Hydra to Athens and other Greek islands (for those of us who lack yachts of our own).

Notice the three flags—specifically the **flag of Hydra** (which you'll see all over town)—flapping in the breeze. Dating from the uprising against the Ottomans, it's loaded with symbolism: the outline of the island of Hydra topped with a cross, a flag with a warrior's helmet, and an anchor—all watched over by the protective eye of God. The inscription, Η ΤΑΝ Η ΕΠΙ ΤΑΣ, means "with it or on it," and evokes the admonition of the warlike Spartans when sending their sons into battle with their huge shields: Come back "with it," victorious and carrying your shield; or "on it," dead, with

your shield serving as a stretcher to carry your body home.

When you reach the corner of the harbor, you'll likely see **donkeys and mules** shooing flies as they wait to plod into town with visitors' luggage lashed to their backs. The donkeys are not just a touristy gimmick, but a lifestyle choice: Hydriots have decided not to allow any motorized vehicles on their island, keeping this place quiet and tranquil, and cutting down on pollution (unless you count dung). This means that, aside from a few garbage trucks, these beasts of burden are the only way to get around. It's not unusual to see one with a major appliance strapped to its back, as it gingerly navigates the steps up to the top of town. Locals dress their burros up with rugs, beads, and charms. Behind each mule-train toils a human pooper-scooper. On Hydra, a traffic jam looks like a farm show. And instead of the testosterone-fueled revving of moped engines, Hydra's soundtrack features the occasional, distant whinnying of a donkey echoing over the rooftops.

In the same corner as the donkeys is the dock for the feisty fleet of red **water taxis.** These zip constantly from here to remote points around the island.

The recommended **Café Gonia** ("Corner Café") nearby is a fun place to nurse a drink while watching the action here at the liveliest spot in town.

Hang a right and continue along the bottom of the harbor, noting the **six streets** that lead into town from here. At this corner (next to the Alpha Bank) is Tompazi, which quickly becomes a twisty warren of lanes with many hotels. Next is a tiny dead-end lane leading to a good bakery. Skinny Oikonomou Street, between the two banks, leads to shops and the open-air movie theater. A few steps farther, another narrow lane leads to the post office, public WC, and Hydra's ramshackle little outdoor market (mornings only). The next road, Miaouli, feels like Hydra's "Main Street," bustling with tavernas and a popular souvlaki joint. And the final street, Lignou, is next to the monastery at the far corner of the port. We'll venture up this lane at the end of this walk.

As you explore this harborfront area, window-shop the **cafés** and choose one to return to later. Overhead, notice the ingenious rope system the seafaring Hydriots have rigged up, so that they can quickly draw a canopy over the seating area—like unfurling the sails on a ship—in the event of rain...or, more common here, overpowering sunshine. While you sip your drink, you can watch simple fishing boats squeeze between the luxury yachts to put in and unload their catch...eyed hungrily by scrawny cats.

Shuttle boats line up in front of the clock tower. They offer cheap rides to points around the island—a service much appreciated by the owners of Hydra's many remote cafés and tavernas (but which angers the water-taxi drivers).

You'll also spot plenty of **jewelry shops** along here. Hydra is known for its jewelry. A few shops sell the handiwork of Hydriot designers and artists (such as Zoe and Elena Votsi), which you'd be hard-pressed to find anywhere but here.

• *At the end of the harbor stands a symbol of Hydra, the clock tower of the...*

Monastery of the Dormition

Hydra's ecclesiastical center is dedicated to the Dormition of the Virgin. "Dormition"—loosely translated as "falling asleep"—is a

pleasant Greek euphemism for death. While Roman Catholic views differ, Orthodox Christians believe Mary died a human death, then (like her son) was resurrected three days later, before being assumed into heaven.

Go through the archway under the tower, and you'll emerge into what was, until 1832, an active monastery. The double-decker arcade of cells circling the courtyard was once the monks' living quarters; it now houses the offices of the city government and mayor.

The monastery's church, which doubles as Hydra's *mitropolis* (cathedral), is free to enter. Stepping inside, it's clear that this was a wealthy community—compare the marble iconostasis, silver chandelier, gorgeous *Pantocrator* dome decoration, rich icons, and frescoes with the humbler decor you'll see at small-town churches elsewhere in Greece. Just inside the door (to the left), the icon of the Virgin and Child is believed to work miracles. Notice the many votive rings and necklaces draping it as a thank-you for prayers answered.

Back in the courtyard, you'll see war memorials and monuments to beloved Hydriots. The humble Byzantine Museum (up the stairs across the courtyard) displays a few rooms of glittering icons, vestments, and other ecclesiastical paraphernalia (€2, some English labels but not much information, generally Tue-Sun 10:00-14:00, closed Mon).

• *Return to the harborfront, then head inland (under the church's smaller bell tower) up Lignou Street. After a few steps, at the butcher's shop, you find a fork. The right branch climbs some steps to the upper reaches of town, including the Lazaros Kountouriotis Historical Mansion (described later), and eventually leads over the headland and down to the village of Kaminia. But let's take the left branch, to the orange-tree-filled square.*

Upper Town Squares

Tidy **Votsi Square** has a chess set, cannon, and lots of cats. Hydriots love their cats, which have a similar temperament: tender, relaxed, but secretly vigilant and fiercely independent. At the bottom of the square (on the left) is Flora's Pastry Shop, where we'll finish our stroll.

For now, keep walking about 100 feet above the square until the lane hits the old-time **Rafalias Pharmacy**. The pharmacy is an institution in town, and Vangelis Rafalias has kept it just as his grandfather did. He welcomes the browsing public, so take a look. Just inside the window (far right) is a photo of Jackie Onassis visiting Hydra. (If you like to dance, Rafalias runs tango classes each summer in the big garden behind his pharmacy.)

Facing the pharmacy, one lane leads to the right, heading uphill to the site of the original town, which was positioned inland to be safely away from marauding pirates. We'll head in the other direction, left, to the little **Square of the Five Prime Ministers.** The monument, with five medallions flanked by cannons, celebrates the five Hydriots who were chosen for Greece's highest office in the nearly two centuries since independence. It's an impressive civic contribution from a little island town, and perhaps due to Hydra's seafaring wealth and its proximity to the Greek capitals (Nafplio, then Athens). From here, narrow, stepped, cobblestone lanes invite exploration of Hydra's quiet side.

But for now, continue left and downhill, back to Votsi Square. The recommended **Flora's Pastry Shop** (daily 7:00-24:00) is at the bottom of the square, on the right. Treat yourself to a homemade ice cream or baklava. Or, for something more traditional, try the local favorite—*galaktoboureko* (gha-lahk-toh-boo-re-KOH), which is cinnamon-sprinkled egg custard baked between layers of phyllo.

Sights in Hydra

▲**Historical Archives Museum**—This fine little museum, in an old mansion right along the port, shows off a small, strangely fascinating collection of Hydra's history and has good English descriptions throughout.

Cost and Hours: €5, includes temporary art exhibit on ground floor, March-Oct daily 9:00-16:00 & 19:30-21:30, closed Nov-Feb, along the eastern side of the harbor near the hydrofoil/catamaran dock, tel. 22980-52355, www.iamy.gr.

➋ **Self-Guided Tour:** The core of the exhibit is upstairs. At the top of the stairs, look straight ahead for a tattered, yellowed **old map** by Rigas Feraios from 1797. Depicting a hypothetical and generously defined "Hellenic Republic," it claims virtually the entire Balkan Peninsula (from the Aegean to the Danube) for Greece. The map features historical and cultural tidbits of the time (such as drawings of coins from various eras), making it a treasure trove for historians. Drawn at a time when the Greeks had been oppressed by the Ottomans for centuries, the map—with 1,200 copies printed and distributed—helped to rally support for what would become a successful revolution starting in 1821.

The stairwell to the top floor is lined with portraits of "**firebrands**"—sailors (many of them Hydriots) who burned the Ottoman fleet during the war. They were considered the "body and soul" of the Greek navy in 1821. To learn more about their techniques, head behind the map and veer left into a long, narrow room; in its center, find the **model of a "fireship"** used for these attacks. These vessels were loaded with barrels of gunpowder, with large ventilation passages cut into the deck and hull. Suspended from the masts were giant, barbed, fishing-lure-like hooks. (Two actual hooks flank the model.) After ramming an enemy ship and dropping the hooks into its deck to attach the two vessels, the Greek crew would light the fuse and escape in a little dinghy... leaving their ship behind to become a giant firetrap, engulfing the Ottoman vessel in flames. Also in this room are nautical maps and models and paintings of other Hydriot vessels.

Continuing into the biggest room (immediately behind the old map), you'll see a Greek urn in the center containing the actual, embalmed **heart** of local hero Andreas Miaoulis. On the walls are portraits of V.I.H.s—very important Hydriots. Rounding out the collection is a small room of **weapons.**

Lazaros Kountouriotis Historical Mansion—Because of Hydra's merchant-marine prosperity, the town has many fine aristocratic mansions...but only this one is open to the public. Lazaros Kountouriotis (koon-doo-ree-OH-tees, 1769-1852) was a wealthy Hydriot shipping magnate who helped fund the Greek War of Independence. He donated 120 of his commercial ships to be turned into warships, representing three-quarters of the Greek navy. Today Kountouriotis is revered as a local and national hero, and his mansion offers a glimpse into the lifestyles of the 18th-century Greek rich and famous.

The main building of Kountouriotis' former estate is a fine example of aristocratic Hydriot architecture of the late 18th cen-

tury, combining elements of Northern Greek, Saronic Gulf Island, and Italian architecture. The house has barely changed since its heyday. You'll enter on the second floor, with several period-decorated rooms. These reception rooms have beautiful wood-paneled ceilings, and are furnished with all the finery of the period. Included is the statesman's favorite armchair, where you can imagine him spending many hours pondering the shape

HYDRA

of the emerging Greek nation. Then you'll head upstairs to see a collection of traditional costumes and jewelry from throughout Greece, labeled in English. The lower floor displays the art of the local Byzantinos family: father Pericles (hazy, Post-Impressionistic landscapes and portraits) and son Constantinos (dark sketches and boldly colorful modern paintings).

Cost and Hours: €4, April-Oct daily 10:00-14:00 & 18:00-21:00, closed Nov-March, on the hillside above town, signposted off the stepped Lignou Street, tel. 22980-52421.

Beaches

Although Hydra's beaches are nothing to get excited about, there's no shortage of places to swim. There's one beach in Hydra town—

the rest are reachable by foot, shuttle boat, or water taxi. Three decent beaches within a pleasant, easy walk of Hydra are Mandraki Bay, Kaminia Castello, and Vlychos. Distant beaches on the southwestern tip of the island (Bisti and Ag. Nikolaos) really get you away from it all, but are best reached by boat.

Spilia—The only spot to swim in town is Spilia ("Cave"), at the western entrance to Hydra harbor. There you'll find steps that lead down to a series of small concrete platforms with ladders into the sea—but no showers or changing rooms. (While Spilia appears to belong to the adjacent café, anyone is welcome to swim here.)

Mandraki Bay—This reasonable pebble beach is near the main coastal path to the east of Hydra (30-minute walk from the eastern end of the harbor, regular shuttle boat from Hydra). It's dominated by the Hotel Miramare, which rents windsurfing boards and other water-sports equipment, but you don't need to be a hotel guest to use the beach.

Kaminia Castello Beach—To the west of town is the delightful little harbor of Kaminia (15-minute walk). Just beyond that, you'll find a new restaurant and bar called Castello above the small Kaminia Castello Beach. While handy, the beach is bullied by the musical taste of the kids who run the bar and is often crowded with lots of families. For walking directions, see "Walks," later.

Vlychos Beach—Located past Kaminia, this is my favorite. Like a little tropical colony, 20 thatched umbrellas mark a quiet stretch of pebbly beach. You'll pay €3 for a lounge chair and €3 for an umbrella. There are showers, a café, and the Marina Taverna for a meal (daily 12:00-24:00, tel. 22980-52496). A shuttle boat zips from Hydra to Vlychos twice an hour (leaving Hydra on the

HYDRA

half-hour, until 20:00, €2.50). The 40-minute walk from Hydra to Vlychos is great (described next).

Walks

From Hydra to Kaminia and Vlychos—The walk from Hydra town to the cute cove of Kaminia and the excellent beach at Vlychos (both described earlier) is one of my favorites. While the walk leads to two beaches, it's perfectly pleasant whether or not you're taking a dip.

For the easy approach, simply follow the mostly level coastal path that runs west from Hydra town to the villages of Kaminia and Vlychos. As you curve out of Hydra, you'll pass the town's best-preserved windmill, which was reconstructed for the 1957 Sophia Loren film *Boy on a Dolphin.* Look for a plaque at the windmill honoring the film that attracted many celebrities to Hydra.

After about 15 minutes, you'll find yourself in delightful **Kaminia,** where two dozen tough little fishing boats jostle within a breakwater. With cafés, a tiny beach, and a good taverna (see page 173), this is a wonderful place to watch island life go by.

Continue through Kaminia where the donkey path climbs a cliff, passing Kaminia Castello Beach. Soon you're all alone with great sea views. Ten minutes or so later, you round a bluff, descend into a ravine, cross an Ottoman-style bridge with an evocative single-pointed arch, and drop into **Vlychos,** with its welcoming little beach.

From Vlychos, a different, high trail leads back into Hydra (30 minutes, lit at night).

The Hydra-Kaminia High Road: For an alternate route to Kaminia, find your way up Hydra's maze of stepped lanes that lace the hills just west and south of town. Here, shabby homes enjoy grand views, tethering off-duty burros seems unnecessary, and island life trudges on, oblivious to tourism. Feel your way up and over the headland, then descend into Kaminia. Along the way, look for dry, paved riverbeds, primed for the flash floods that fill village cisterns each winter. (You can also climb all the way up to the remains of Hydra's humble acropolis, topping the hill due west of the harbor.)

More Walks and Hikes—Beyond walking to a nearby beach, Hydra is popular for its network of ancient paths that link the island's outlying settlements, churches, and monasteries. Most of the paths are well maintained and clearly marked, but serious hikers should pick up a copy of Anavasi's excellent 1:25,000 map of Hydra (€5, sold locally). If you do venture into the hills, wear sturdy shoes, sunscreen, and a hat, and take your own water and picnic supplies.

HYDRA

Nightlife in Hydra

Locals, proud of the extravagant yachts that flock to the island, like to tell of movie stars who make regular visits. But the island is so quiet that, by midnight, all the high-rollers seem to be back onboard watching movies.

And yet, there are plenty of options to keep visitors busy. People enjoy watching a film at the town's outdoor cinema or nursing a drink along the harborfront—there are plenty of mellow cocktail bars proudly serving "Paradise in a Glass" for €8.

Pirate Bar is run by a hardworking family serving drinks and light bites all day long from a prime spot on the water, at the little lane just past Lignou. The son, Zeus, runs the night shift and is famous for his Lychee Martini. This is a mellow, trendy spot to be at late at night (tel. 22980-52711).

Amalour Bar, run by Alexandros and his gang of good-looking bald guys, is "the place to fall in love" (or just enjoy wonderful music and good drinks). There's no sea view here—just cool music played at the right volume inside, and tables outside tumbling down a cobbled lane. It's easy jazz until midnight, and then harder music (€6 cocktails during the 20:00-23:00 nightly "happy hour," just up Tompazi Street from the harbor, mobile 697-746-1357).

Hydroneta Bar, catering to a younger crowd with younger music, offers great sea views from under the "Sofia Loren windmill," with a bunch of romantic tables nestled within the ramparts and cannons (tel. 22980-54166). Reach it by walking along the coastline past Spilia Beach and through the Sunset Restaurant. This and the neighboring Spilia cocktail bar charge €10 for cocktails and are the most touristy of Hydra's nightlife choices.

Gardenia Cinema is part of a great Greek summer tradition: watching movies in the open air. Hydra's delightful outdoor theater is right in the center of town on Oikonomou Street; it shows movies in the original language on summer weekends (€8, May-Sept Fri-Sun at 21:00 and 23:00).

Sleeping in Hydra

Hydra has ample high-quality accommodations. Unfortunately, the prices are also high—more expensive than anywhere on the Peloponnese, and rivaling those in Athens. Prices max out in the summer (June-Sept), and I've generally listed these top rates.

Sleep Code

(€1 = about $1.40, country code: 30)
S = Single, **D** = Double/Twin, **T** = Triple, **Q** = Quad, **b** = bathroom,
s = shower only. Unless otherwise noted, breakfast is included,
credit cards are accepted, and the staff speaks English.

To help you easily sort through these listings, I've divided
the accommodations into three categories, based on the price
for a double room with bath during high season:

$$$ Higher Priced—Most rooms €110 or more.
$$ Moderately Priced—Most rooms between €65-110.
$ Lower Priced—Most rooms €65 or less.

Prices can change without notice; verify the hotel's
current rates online or by email. For other updates, see www
.ricksteves.com/update.

Outside of these times, most accommodations offer discounts (even
if not noted here)—always ask. Longer stays might also garner you
a deal. If you're stuck, the boat ticket offices on the harborfront
might be able to help you find a room. If you arrive with no reservation and sniff around, you can generally find a rough little place
with soft prices renting doubles for around €50. Some cheaper
hotels don't provide breakfast, in which case you can eat for around
€5 at various cafés around town. Communication can be challenging at a few of the cheaper places (as noted). If there's an elevator anywhere in town, I didn't see it (though no hotel has more
than three stories). Because the town has a labyrinthine street plan
and most people ignore street names, I list no addresses, so use
the map earlier in this chapter. Most accommodations in Hydra
close down for the winter (typically Nov-Feb, sometimes longer).
The lack of local spring water means that Hydra's very hard water
is shipped in from wetter islands, which can make showering or
doing laundry—and rinsing out stubborn suds—an odd frustra-
tion. When I'm here in the summer, I take several showers a day to
cool off, but I don't bother washing my hair.

Splurges with Character

$$$ Hotel Leto is the island's closest thing to a business-class
hotel, offering great service with a professional vibe, 21 elegantly
decorated rooms, and inviting public spaces (Db-€165-185, air-con,
free Wi-Fi, tel. 22980-53385, fax 22980-53806, www.letohydra.gr,
letoydra@otenet.gr, Kari).

$$$ Phaedra Hotel rents seven spacious, beautifully deco-
rated, and well-cared-for rooms. Delightfully helpful owner Hilda

HYDRA

takes pride in her hotel, and it shows (Sb-€120, standard Db-€135, superior Db with balcony-€160, apartment-€180 for four, family suites, prices soft off-season, open year-round, air-con, free Wi-Fi, tel. 22980-53330, mobile 697-221-3111, www.phaedrahotel.com, info@phaedrahotel.com).

$$$ Hotel Sophia is a plush little boutique hotel right above the harbor restaurant strip. It's been family-run since 1934; today English-speaking sisters Angela and Vasiliki are at the helm. The six thoughtfully appointed rooms are stony-chic, with heavy beams, tiny bathrooms, and good windows that manage to block out most of the noise. All the rooms have access to a little balcony, giving you a royal box seat overlooking all the harbor action (Db-€80-140 depending on the room, 10 percent discount with this book if paying cash and staying at least two nights, air-con, free Wi-Fi, tel. 22980-52313, www.hotelsophia.gr, hydra@hotelsophia.gr).

$$$ Nefeli Hotel is a place apart, providing an idyllic refuge high above the town. For the seclusion-seeking traveler, the steep 10-minute hike to get to this villa is a blessing (for €15, mule driver Giorgos can bring your bags up from the harbor on his donkey). There are nine thoughtfully appointed rooms, and the hotel's generous terraces and patios have stay-awhile lounge chairs, backgammon sets, yoga mats, and classic sunset views. With their warm expat welcome, Aussie Brett and Brit-Greek Alexandra create an ambience that forges friendships (Db-€75-130 depending on room and season, two-night minimum, air-con, free Wi-Fi, lots of helpful information, tel. 22980-53297, www.hotelnefeli.eu, info @hotelnefeli.eu).

Mid-Range Values

$$ Hotel Miranda is an early 19th-century sea captain's house with 14 rooms, a fine terrace, and classic style (Sb-€80, Db-€100, superior Db with view-€160, air-con, free Wi-Fi, tel. 22980-52230, fax 22980-53510, www.mirandahotel.gr, mirandahydra@hol.gr).

$$ Mistral Hotel is a well-run, basic place offering 17 rooms in a comfortable, modern stone building with a central lounge and breezy courtyard. It's a fine value at the very quiet, top part of town (Db-€100, big Db with view-€150, air-con, free Wi-Fi, tel. 22980-52509, www.hotelmistral.gr, info@hotelmistral.gr, Theo and Jenny).

$$ Greco Hotel, run by Maria Keramidas, rents 19 rooms set around a lovely garden where you're served a homemade breakfast. The front yard is a shady place to just relax and do nothing (Db-€75-110 depending on season and day, air-con, free Wi-Fi, tel. 22980-53200, www.grecohotel.gr, info@grecohotel.gr).

$$ Ippokampos Hotel has 16 basic rooms around a cocktail-bar courtyard (Sb-€80, Db-€80-100, prices very soft, air-con, free

Wi-Fi, bar closes at 23:00, tel. 22980-53453, fax 22980-52501, www.ippokampos.com, ippo@ippokampos.com, owner Sotiris).

$$ Pension Achilleas rents 13 small but pleasant and nicely maintained rooms in an old mansion with a relaxing courtyard terrace (Sb-€55, Db-€75, Tb-€85, prices soft off-season, cash only, air-con, tel. 22980-52050, fax 22980-53227, www.achilleas-hydra .com, kofitsas@otenet.gr, Dina speaks only a little English).

Best Cheap Beds
$ Spalieri's Domatia has three rooms in a cheery home. The units, while simple, are spacious and air-conditioned. There's a community kitchen where you enjoy a self-serve breakfast, plus a welcoming garden courtyard. Staying with the Spalieri family provides a homier experience than at most other places in town (Db-€60-70, Qb-€100, next to Pension Achilleas, tel. 22980-52894, mobile 694-414-1977, spalstef@ath.forthnet.gr, minimal English).

$ Alkionides Pension provides perhaps the best lodging value in town. It has 10 tidy rooms buried in Hydra's back lanes, around a beautiful and relaxing courtyard (Db-€60, Tb-€80, apartment-€100, breakfast-€7, air-con, free Wi-Fi, tel. & fax 22980-54055, mobile 697-741-0460, www.alkionidespension.com, info@alkionidespension.com, Kofitsas family).

$ Pension Erofili is a reliable budget standby, renting 12 basic rooms facing a skinny courtyard in the heart of town (Db-€55, Tb-€65, apartment-€90, rates soft in slow times, breakfast-€7, air-con, free Internet access and Wi-Fi, tel. & fax 22980-54049, mobile 697-768-8487, www.pensionerofili.gr, info@pensionerofili .gr, George and Irene).

Eating in Hydra

There are dozens of places to eat, offering everything from humble gyros to slick modern-Mediterranean cuisine. Harbor views come with higher prices, while places farther inland typically offer better value.

In Hydra Town
Psaropoula Restaurant fills the best spot in town, right on the harborfront, with rustic blue tables. While its interior is boring, its outside tables let you enjoy the strolling scene and almost bob with the tied-up yachts. Hydriots appreciate the classic Greek cuisine, and the prices are very fair—about what you'd pay without the prime location. Check out their big display case just inside to see what's cooking (€3-6 starters, €7-13 seafood starters, €8-12 main dishes, €15-25 seafood dishes, daily 12:00-23:00, tel. 22980-52630).

Taverna Gitoniko, better known as "Manolis and Christina" for its warm and kindly owners, is an Hydra institution. Offering wonderful hospitality, delicious food, and delightful rooftop-garden seating, this tricky-to-find taverna is worth seeking out for a memorable meal. Christina is a great cook—everything is good here. Order a selection of creative first courses (consider their delicious, smoky eggplant salad) and check their daily specials (€4-6 starters, €6-9 main dishes, seafood splurges, daily 12:00-16:00 & 18:30-24:00, closed Nov-Feb, Spilios Haramis, tel. 22980-53615).

Taverna Leonidas feels like a cross between a history museum and a friendly local home. It's been around so long it doesn't need (and doesn't have) a sign. The island's oldest taverna was the hangout for sponge-divers a century ago. Today, former New Yorkers Leonidas and Panagiota, who returned to Hydra in 1993 to take over the family business, feed guests as if they're family. Reservations are required: Call before their 10:00 shopping trip (or the day before) to order your main dish.  They prepare and cook up a great meal, including starters and dessert (sweets or fruit), for €15-17 per person (depends on the number of drinks). You'll enjoy their exuberant hospitality and traditional, rustic cooking, while appreciating the time-warp decor and rustic kitchen (daily 19:00-24:00, tel. 22980-53097). They're above town: Hike up Miaouli Street, passing Hotel Miranda, then a small church; as you curve right, watch for it on the right. Look for a lime-green door in the big white wall with a terrace, facing a staircase with blue flowerpots.

Veranda Restaurant, halfway up the steps on Sahini lane (off of Lignou), fills a terrace with fine views over the town and harbor. It's great on a summer evening; enjoy a cold drink before selecting from a menu that offers pasta served a dozen different ways and a creative assortment of salads (€8-11 seafood starters, €8-12 pastas, €10-15 traditional main dishes, €15-20 seafood dishes, better-than-average wine list, daily 18:00-24:30, upstairs with entry on Sahini, tel. 22980-52259, Andreas).

Mezedopolio Maridaki overlooks the harbor, up a set of stairs across from the Pirate Bar. A bit posh and modern, it caters more to locals than to tourists, focusing—as its name implies—on *mezedes,* or small dishes (the sardines are great). While pricey, portions are actually big, and three *mezedes* will easily and economically fill two people. Vasilias is known for his homemade *tsipouro,* the local grappa or firewater. It's worth reserving a view table (daily 11:00-24:00, tel. 22980-53046, mobile 697-741-3204).

Tavernas on Miaouli Street: Hydra's "Main Street" leading up from the port (to the left of the church bell tower) is crammed with appealing little tavernas that jostle for your attention with outdoor seating and good local food.

Souvlaki: For a quick and cheap (€2.50) meal, souvlaki is your best bet. The **hole-in-the-wall joint** on Miaouli (50 yards off the harbor, across from Hotel Sofia) serves the best in town to eat in or take away. They have a long and enticing list of variations. For a more civilized, sit-down souvlaki experience, drop by **The Onion Souvlaki,** a cute eatery filling a charming corner up Tompazi Street, next to the Amalour Bar.

Cafés on the Harbor: **Café Gonia** stakes out the best spot and serves the best Greek coffee. Nursing your drink here, you can enjoy the scene—drivers rolling their pushcarts, donkeys sneezing, taxi-boat drivers haggling, big boats coming and going—on Hydra's busiest corner. Nearby, **Café Isalos,** with a fun menu of light bites, is better for a meal (€6 sandwiches, €12 pizzas, good €3 iced coffees). In the early evening, watch for yachts trying to dock; some are driven by pros and others aren't—providing a comedic scene of naval inexperience.

Dessert: **Flora's Pastry Shop** is a hardworking little bakery cranking out the best pastries and homemade ice cream on the island. Flora has delightful tables that overlook a park on Lignou Street, just behind the monastery. She sells all the traditional local sweets, including honey treats such as baklava (two for €1). Many of her ingredients come from her farm on the nearby island of Dokos (daily 7:00-24:00).

Eating near Hydra, in Kaminia

A great way to cap your Hydra day is to follow the coastal path to the rustic and picturesque village of Kaminia, which hides behind the headland from Hydra. Kaminia's pocket-sized harbor  shelters the community's fishing boats. Here, with a glass of ouzo and some munchies, as the sun slowly sinks into the sea and boats become silhouettes, you can drink to the beauties of a Greek isle escape. Consider combining a late-afternoon stroll (along the seafront promenade) or hike (over the headland) with dinner. (For tips, see "Walks," earlier.)

Kodylenia's Taverna is perched on a bluff just over the Kaminia harbor. With my favorite irresistible dinner views on Hydra, this scenic spot lets you watch the sun dip gently into the Saronic Gulf, with Kaminia's adorable port in the foreground.

HYDRA

Owner Dimitris takes his own boat out early in the morning to buy the day's best catch directly from the fishermen. For meals, you can sit out on the shady covered side terrace above the harbor. For drinks, sit out front on the porch. Relax and take in a sea busy with water taxis, hydrofoils that connect this oasis with Athens, old freighters—like castles of rust—lumbering slowly along the horizon, and cruise ships anchored as if they haven't moved in weeks (€3-7 starters, €9-14 meat dishes—visit their display case and see what's cooking, for a seafood meal figure €15-60 per person depending on what you order, daily 11:00-24:00, closed Dec-Feb, tel. 22980-53520).

Hydra Connections

The standard way to get to Hydra is on a Hellenic Seaways high-speed hydrofoil, called a "Flying Dolphin," or the slightly larger catamaran, called a "Flying Cat." The boats leave frequently from the heart of Hydra's harbor, making it easy to connect to the mainland or other islands. While travel agencies will tell you to be at the port 30 minutes before departure, locals simply show up minutes before and walk on.

From Hydra by Hydrofoil or Catamaran to: Piraeus near Athens (9/day June-Sept, 7/day Easter-May and Oct, 4/day Nov-Easter, 1.75 hours, €25), **Ermioni** on the Peloponnese southeast of Nafplio (a.k.a. "Hermioni"; 4/day in summer, 2-3/day in winter, 20 minutes, €10), **Spetses** (6-7/day in summer, 3-4/day in winter, 30 minutes, €12), **Porto Heli** (5/day in summer, 2-3/day in winter, 45 minutes, €17), **Poros** (4-5/day year-round, 30 minutes, €14). "Summer" and "winter" seasons can vary, but summer is roughly Easter through October.

Tickets: You can buy tickets for the same price at virtually any travel agency in Greece, or at the Hellenic Seaways office in Hydra (just down an alley near the Alpha Bank; open anytime boats are running, tel. 22980-54007 or 22980-53812, www.hsw.gr). Because these boats are virtually the only game in town, it's wise to book well in advance—they can sell out during summer weekends. (It's especially important to book ahead for Sunday afternoon and evening boats to Piraeus, as they're packed with Athenians headed home after a weekend getaway.)

Book your tickets once you're comfortable locking in to a specific time or date. You can reserve a ticket on the Hellenic Seaways website and then pick it up at a travel agency, a Hellenic

Seaways ticket office, or at an automated machine at Piraeus. Or buy a ticket in person soon after you arrive in Greece. You can cancel or change your ticket (at any travel agency) up to 24 hours before departure in peak season, or three hours before departure off-season.

Possible Delays or Cancellations: Because the boats are relatively small (a Flying Dolphin holds about 150 passengers; a Flying Cat carries 200) and fast-moving, they can be affected by high winds and other inclement weather. Occasionally, departures are cancelled and they'll contact you to rebook. (For this reason, it's essential to provide a telephone number—at a minimum, your pre-boat-trip hotel—when you book.) Usually you can go later in the day, but it's possible (though rare) to get stranded overnight. Even if the sea is rocky, the ships may still run—but the ride can be very rough. If you're prone to seasickness, be prepared.

Emergency Alternative: If your boat is cancelled and you have a plane to catch in Athens, you could potentially hire a water taxi to zip you across to the mainland, and then take a taxi all the way to Athens—but this costs upwards of €200.

From Hydra to Metochi (for Drivers): The Freedom Boat connects Hydra to a parking lot immediately across the water on the Peloponnesian mainland at Metochi, about 10 miles east of Ermioni (€6.50, about 8/day in summer, 4/day in winter, 12 minutes, mobile 694-424-2141, www.hydralines.gr). If traveling with a rental car on the Peloponnese, you could park here and day-trip over, saving lots of money over the Piraeus-Hydra ferry fare.

ITALY

The following three chapters are excerpted from *Rick Steves' Italy*.

CIVITA DI BAGNOREGIO

Perched on a pinnacle in a grand canyon, the traffic-free village of Civita di Bagnoregio is Italy's ultimate hill town. In the last decade, the real Civita (chee-VEE-tah) has died—the last of its lifelong residents have moved away. But relatives and newcomers are moving in and revitalizing the village, and it remains an amazing place to visit. (It's even become popular as a backdrop for movies, soap operas, and advertising campaigns.) Civita is connected to the world and the town of Bagnoregio by a long pedestrian bridge—and a website (www.civitadibagnoregio.it, run by B&B owner Franco).

Civita's history goes back to Etruscan and ancient Roman times. In the early Middle Ages, Bagnoregio was a suburb of Civita, which had a population of about 4,000. Later, Bagnoregio surpassed Civita in size—especially following a 1695 earthquake, after which many residents fled Civita to live in Bagnoregio, fearing their houses would be shaken off the edge into the valley below. You'll notice Bagnoregio is dominated by Renaissance-style buildings while, architecturally, Civita remains stuck in the Middle Ages.

While Bagnoregio lacks the pinnacle-town romance of Civita, it's actually a healthy, vibrant community (unlike Civita, the suburb now nicknamed "the dead city"). In Bagnoregio, get a haircut, sip a coffee on the square, and walk down to the old laundry (ask, *"Dov'è la lavanderia vecchia?"*). Off-season, when Civita and Bagnoregio are deadly quiet—and cold—I'd side-trip in quickly from Orvieto rather than spend the night.

Orientation to Civita

Arrival in Bagnoregio, near Civita

If you're taking the **bus** from Orvieto, you'll get off at the bus stop in Bagnoregio. Look at the posted bus schedule and write down the return times to Orvieto, or check with the driver.

From Bagnoregio to Civita: Civita sits at the opposite end of Bagnoregio, about a mile away. From Bagnoregio, you can walk (allow around 30 minutes) or take a little **shuttle bus**—orange or white—to the base of the bridge to Civita (hourly, 10-minute ride, €1 round-trip, pay driver, first bus runs Mon-Sat at about 7:30, Sun at 8:50, last at 18:45, no buses 13:00-15:30, fewer buses June-Aug). Catch the bus at the gas station by waving your book at the driver (Bagnoregio's new mayor, a Colin Firth lookalike, is eager to welcome my readers—though the shuttle doesn't usually stop here, the mayor has instructed drivers to stop for anyone waving a copy of this book). From the base of the bridge, you have to walk the rest of the way (a 10-minute uphill hike across a pedestrian bridge). To return to Bagnoregio by bus, check the schedule posted near the bridge (at edge of parking lot, where bus let you off) before heading up to Civita, or ask at the recommended Trattoria Antico Forno.

To **walk** from the Bagnoregio bus stop to the base of Civita's bridge (at least 20 minutes, fairly level, leave heavy bags with Mauro—see "Helpful Hints," below), take the road going uphill, Via Garibaldi (overlooking the big parking lot). Once on the road, take the first right and an immediate left onto the main drag, Via Roma. Follow this straight out to the belvedere for a superb viewpoint. From the viewpoint, backtrack a few steps (staircase at end of viewpoint is a dead end) and take the stairs down to the road leading to the bridge.

A **taxi** from Orvieto to the base of the pedestrian bridge costs around €50.

Drivers coming from Orvieto or elsewhere can avoid a long walk by driving through Bagnoregio and parking under the bridge at the base of Civita (for more tips, see "Bagnoregio Connections" at the end of this chapter).

Helpful Hints

Market Day: A lively market fills the Bagnoregio bus-station parking lot each Monday.

Baggage Storage: While there's no official baggage-check service in Bagnoregio, I've arranged with Mauro Laurenti, who runs the **Bar/Enoteca/Caffè Gianfu** and **Cinema Alberto Sordi**, to let you leave your bags there (€1/bag, Fri-Wed 6:00-13:00

& 13:30-24:00, closed Thu). As you get off the bus, go back 50 yards or so in the direction that the Orvieto bus just came from, and go right around corner.

Food near Bagnoregio Bus Stop: About 100 yards from the bus stop, within a few steps of the Porta Albana (old gate to the town), you'll find both a small grocery store and a great little bakery (**L'Arte del Pane**—with fresh pizza by the slice, Via Matteotti 5, opposite the cinema).

Bus Tickets: To save money on bus fare to Orvieto, buy a ticket before boarding from the newsstand near the Bagnoregio bus stop, across from the gas station (€2 one-way or €4 round-trip; otherwise €7 one-way or €14 round-trip if purchased from driver).

Self-Guided Walk

Welcome to Civita

Civita was once connected to Bagnoregio, before the saddle between the separate towns eroded away. Photographs around town show the old donkey path, the original bridge. It was bombed in World War II and replaced in 1966 with the new footbridge that you're climbing today. The town's hearty old folks hang on to the bridge's handrail when fierce winter weather rolls through.

• *Entering the town, you'll pass through a cut in the rock and a 12th-century Romanesque...*

Arch: This was the main Etruscan road leading to the Tiber Valley and Rome. The stone passageway was cut by the Etruscans 2,500 years ago.

• *Inside the town gate, to the left, is an unmarked WC, behind the Bottega souvenir store. It faces the town's old laundry, which dates from just after World War II, when water was finally piped into the town. Until recently, this was a lively village gossip center. Nearby, inside the entry arch and on the right, are the remains of a...*

Renaissance Palace: The wooden door and windows (above the door) lead only to thin air. They were part of the facade of one of five palaces that once graced Civita. Much of the palace fell into the valley, riding a chunk of the ever-eroding rock pinnacle. Today, the door leads to a remaining section of the palace—complete with Civita's first hot tub, as it was once owned by the "Marchesa," a countess who married into Italy's biggest industrialist family. Check out the canyon viewpoint a few steps to the left of the palace. Lean over the banister and listen to the sounds of the birds and the bees. Just beyond that is the site of the long-gone home of Civita's one famous son, St. Bonaventure, known as the "second founder of the Franciscans" (look for the small plaque on the wall to your right).

• *Now wander to the main square and Civita's church.*

Piazza: Here in the town square is Wine Bar Peppone (if it's chilly, go inside for the inviting fire), two restaurants, and wild

donkey races on the first Sunday of June and the second Sunday of September. At Christmastime, a living nativity scene is enacted in this square, and if you're here at the end of July or beginning of August, you might catch a play here.

The pillars that stand like giants' bar stools are ancient Etruscan. The church with its *campanile* (bell tower) marks the spot where an Etruscan temple, and then a Roman temple, once stood.

• *Go into the church.*

Church: A cathedral until 1699, the church houses records of about 60 bishops that date back to the seventh century (church open daily 9:30-13:00 & 15:00-18:00). Inside you'll see frescoes and statues from "the school of Donatello." The central altar is built upon the relics of the Roman martyr St. Victoria, who once was the patron saint of the town. St. Marlonbrando served as a bishop here in the ninth century; an altar dedicated to him is on the right.

The fine crucifix, carved out of pear wood in the 15th century, is from the school of Donatello. It's remarkably expressive and greatly venerated by locals. Jesus' gaze is almost haunting. Some say his appearance changes based on what angle you view him from: looking alive from the front, in agony from the left, and dead from the right. Regardless, his eyes follow you from side to side. On Good Friday, this crucifix goes out and is the focus of the midnight procession.

On the left side of the nave above an altar is an intimate fresco of the Madonna of the Earthquake, given this name because—in the shake of 1695—the whitewash fell off and revealed this tender fresco of Mary and her child. (During the Baroque era, a white-and-bright interior was in vogue, and churches such as these—which were covered with precious and historic frescoes—were simply whitewashed over.) On the same wall—toward the front—find a faded portrait of Santa Apollonia, the patron saint of your teeth; notice the scary-looking pincers. Say hello to Annarita, the church attendant. Drop a coin into the offering box.

• *Just around the corner from the church, on the main street, are several...*

Eateries: At Rossana and Antonio's cool **Bruschette con Prodotti Locali,** pull up a chair and let them or their daughters, Arianna and Antonella, serve you *panini* (sandwiches), bruschetta (garlic toast with optional tomato topping), *salumi,* grilled sausages, wine, and a local cake called *ciambella.* After eating, wander down to see their cellar with its traditional winemaking gear and provisions for rolling huge kegs up the stairs. Tap on the kegs in the bottom level to see which are full (daily 11:00-17:00, in summer until 20:00, tel. 0761-793-270).

The rock below Civita is honeycombed with ancient cellars like this (for keeping wine at the same temperature all year) and cisterns (for collecting rainwater, since there was no well in town). Many date from Etruscan times.

Farther down on the left, you'll find **Antico Frantoio Bruschetteria,** a rustic, super-atmospheric place for a bite to eat. Vittoria's sons Sandro and Felice, and her grandsons Maurizio and Fabrizio, toast delicious bruschetta (roughly 10:00-20:00 in summer, off-season open weekends only 10:00-19:00, mobile 328-689-9375; Fabrizio also runs a recommended *agriturismo* outside of town). Peruse the menu, choose your topping (chopped tomato is super), and get a glass of wine for a fun, affordable snack.

While waiting for your bruschetta, take a look around to see Vittoria's mill *(mulino),* an interesting collection of old olive presses.

CIVITA

The huge **olive press** in the entry is about 1,500 years old. Until the 1960s, blindfolded donkeys trudged in the circle here, crushing olives and creating paste that filled the circular filters and was put into a second press. Notice the 2,500-year-old sarcophagus niche. The hole in the floor (with the glass top) was a garbage hole. In

ancient times, residents would toss their jewels down when under attack; excavations uncovered a windfall of treasures (if you're not eating here, a €1 donation is requested).

• *Across the street and down a tiny lane, find...*

Antica Civita: This is the closest thing the town has to a museum. The humble collection is the brainchild of Felice, Vittoria's son, who has hung old black-and-white photos, farm tools, olive presses, and local artifacts in a series of old caves. Felice wants to give visitors a feeling for life in Civita when it had its traditional economy (€1, daily 9:30-19:00, some English explanations).

• *On the left 20 yards farther down is...*

Maria's Garden (Maria's Giardino): Maria is too frail to live in Civita these days, but you may be able to peek into her garden and enjoy her view. She and her husband, Peppone (who passed away in 2009), used to carry goods on a donkey back and forth 40 times a day on the path between the old town and Bagnoregio. She's now the last native Civita resident still living. As you view the canyon in which Civita is stranded, imagine the work the two rivers did—in the same style as the Colorado River—to carve all this. Listen to the roosters and voices from distant farms.

• *At the end of town, the main drag winds downhill. On your right are small...*

Etruscan Caves: The first two caves were used as stables until a few years ago. The third cave is an unusual chapel, cut deep into the rock, with a barred door; this is the **Chapel of the Incarcerated** (Cappella del Carcere). In Etruscan times, the chapel—with a painted tile depicting the Madonna and child—may have originally been a tomb, and in medieval times, it was used as a jail. When Civita's few residents have a religious procession, they come here in honor of the Madonna of the Incarcerated.

• *After the chapel, the paving-stone path peters out into a dirt trail leading down and around to the right to an...*

Etruscan Tunnel: This tunnel dates from pre-Roman times. Tall enough for a woman with a jug on her head to pass through, it may have served as a shortcut to the river below. It was widened in the 1930s so that farmers could get between their scattered fields more easily. Think of the scared villagers who huddled here for refuge during WWII bombing raids.

• *Backtrack to return to the...*

Piazza: Evenings on Civita's town square are a bite of Italy. The same people sat on the same church steps under the same moon, night after night, year after year. I love my cool, late evenings in Civita. If you visit in the morning, have cappuccino and rolls at the small café/wine bar on the town square.

Whenever you visit, stop halfway up the donkey path and listen to the sounds of rural Italy. Reach out and touch one of the Monopoly houses. If you know how to turn the volume up on the crickets, do so.

Sleeping in Civita or Bagnoregio

In Civita and Bagnoregio, there are 15 B&B rooms up for grabs, and one newly remodeled hotel. Outside the town there are plenty of *agriturismi;* otherwise, there's always Orvieto.

In Civita

$$$ Locanda della Buona Ventura has four rooms decorated medieval-rustic-mod, filling the old mayor's house and overlooking Civita's piazza. The local-products shop just across the square functions as the reception, and has an old well down steep stairs worth checking out (Db-€100-120 depending on demand, breakfast at nearby café, mobile 347-627-5628, raffaele_rocchi@libero .it, Lara).

Sleep Code

(€1 = about $1.40, country code: 39)

S = Single, **D** = Double/Twin, **T** = Triple, **Q** = Quad, **b** = bathroom, **s** = shower only. Unless otherwise noted, credit cards are accepted and breakfast is included (but usually optional). English is generally spoken, but I've noted exceptions.

To help you sort easily through these listings, I've divided the accommodations into three categories based on the price for a double room with bath during high season:

  $$$ Higher Priced—Most rooms €100 or more.
    $$ Moderately Priced—Most rooms between €70-100.
      $ Lower Priced—Most rooms €70 or less.

Prices can change without notice; verify the hotel's current rates online or by email. For other updates, see www .ricksteves.com/update.

$ Civita B&B, run by Franco Sala (who also owns Trattoria Antico Forno), has three fine little rooms, each overlooking Civita's main square (S-€45, Sb-€50, D-€65, Db-€70, T-€90, continental breakfast, Wi-Fi, Piazza del Duomo Vecchio, tel. 076-176-0016, mobile 347-611-5426, www.civitadibagnoregio.it, fsala@pelagus.it).

In Bagnoregio

$$ Romantica Pucci B&B is a haven for city-weary travelers. Its eight spacious rooms are indeed romantic, with canopied beds and flowing veils. Both homey and elegant, it's like sleeping at Katharine Hepburn's place. Lamberto takes special care of his guests (Db-€80, air-con, free time-limited Internet access, free parking, "Pucci Speciality" €20 family-style dinner is popular with guests—non-guests are also welcome for dinner, Piazza Cavour 1, tel. 076-179-2121, www.hotelromanticapucci.it, hotelromantica pucci@libero.it). It's just above the parking lot you see when you arrive in Bagnoregio—look for a sign marking its private parking place. From the bus stop, take Via Garibaldi uphill above the parking lot, bear right at the tobacco shop onto Via Roma, then look for the hotel sign straight ahead.

$ Hotel Divino Amore has 23 bright, modern rooms, some with perfect views of a miniature Civita (Db-€70, Tb-€80, Via Fidanza 25-27, tel. & fax 076-178-0882, mobile 329-344-8950, www.hoteldivinoamore.com, info@hoteldivinoamore.com). From the bus stop, follow Via Garibaldi uphill above the parking lot, where it becomes Via Fidanza, and continue straight along for about 200 yards; #25 is on the left.

Outside of Town

$ Agriturismo Le Corone, in the valley below Civita, is an economical answer if you dream of a lazy few days relaxing among the olive trees. Flexible Fabrizio of Antico Frantoio Bruschetteria will pick you up from Bagnoregio, then drive you 10 minutes along a winding road to a simple but cozy home with a kitchen/living room, two bedrooms, and small garden. Civita is a steep- but-picturesque 45-minute uphill hike away (or persuade Fabrizio to give you a ride), and firewood is provided for romantic evenings (€35/night per person, maximum 6 people, no minimum occupancy, home-cooked pasta dinner-€10, Strade della Valle, mobile 328-689-9375, www.corone-civita.com, info@corone-civita.com).

Eating in Civita or Bagnoregio

In Civita

Osteria Al Forno di Agnese is a delightful spot where Manuela and her friends serve visitors simple yet delicious meals on a covered patio just off Civita's main square (€8 pastas, €9 *secondi*, opens daily at 12:00 for lunch and at 19:00 for dinner, sometimes closed Tue, tel. 340-1259-721).

Trattoria Antico Forno cooks up rustic dishes, homemade pasta, and salads at affordable prices. Try their homemade pasta with truffles (€7 pastas, €8 *secondi*, daily for lunch 12:30-15:30 and dinner 19:00-22:00, on main square, also rents rooms—see Civita B&B listing on previous page, tel. 076-176-0016, Franco and his assistants Gina and Nina).

In Bagnoregio

Hostaria del Ponte is *the* place for serious cooking. It offers light, creative, and traditional cuisine with a great view terrace at the parking lot at the base of the bridge to Civita. Big space heaters make it comfortable to enjoy the wonderful view as you dine from their rooftop terrace, even in spring and fall (€8 pastas, €10 *secondi*, reservations often essential, Tue-Sun 12:30-14:30 & 19:30-21:30, closed Mon; Nov-April also closed Sun eve, tel. 076-179-3565, Lorena).

Bagnoregio Connections

From Bagnoregio to Orvieto: Public buses (6/day, 1 hour, €2 one-way or €4 round-trip if purchased in advance, €7 one-way or €14 round-trip from driver) connect Bagnoregio to the rest of the world via Orvieto. Departures from Bagnoregio—daily except Sunday and some holidays—are likely to be (but confirm): 5:30, 9:55, 10:25, 13:00, 14:25, and 17:25. During the school year (roughly Sept-June), buses also run at 6:30, and 13:35. Remember to save money by buying your ticket in Bagnoregio before boarding the bus—purchase one from the newsstand near the bus stop, across from the gas station.

From Bagnoregio to Points South: Public buses run to **Viterbo,** which has a good train connection to Rome (buses go weekdays at 5:10, 7:15, 7:40, 10:00, 13:00, 13:45, 14:20, 14:50, and 18:05; less frequent Sat-Sun, 35 minutes).

Driving from Orvieto to Bagnoregio: Orvieto overlooks the autostrada (and has its own exit). The shortest way to Civita from the freeway exit is to turn left (below Orvieto) and then simply follow the signs to *Lubriano* and *Bagnoregio*.

A more winding and scenic route takes 20 minutes longer: From the freeway, pass under hill-capping Orvieto (on your right, signs to *Lago di Bolsena*, on Viale I Maggio), then take the first left (direction: Bagnoregio), winding up past great Orvieto views through Canale, and through farms and fields of giant shredded wheat to Bagnoregio.

Either way, just before Bagnoregio, follow the signs left to *Lubriano* and pull into the first little square by the church on your right for a breathtaking view of Civita. You'll find an even better view farther inside the town, from the tiny square at the next church (San Giovanni Battista). Then return to the Bagnoregio road.

Drive through the town of Bagnoregio (following yellow *Civita* signs) to the lot at the base of the steep pedestrian bridge. Park for free in spaces with no blue lines (plenty under the bridge). The €1 fee for parking in the blue-lined spaces is loosely enforced. While you're supposed to pay at the restaurant or shop opposite (same family), if no one's there, just park and don't worry. The bridge at this parking lot leads up to the traffic-free 2,500-year-old canyon-swamped pinnacle town of Civita di Bagnoregio.

LUCCA

Surrounded by well-preserved ramparts, layered with history, alternately quaint and urbane, Lucca charms its visitors. The city is a paradox. Though it hasn't been involved in a war since 1430, it is Italy's most impressive fortress city, encircled by a perfectly intact wall. Most cities tear down their wall to make way for modern traffic. But Lucca's wall effectively keeps out both traffic and, it seems, the stress of the modern world. Locals are very protective of their wall, which they enjoy like a community roof garden.

Lucca, known for being Europe's leading producer of toilet paper and Kleenex (with a monopoly on the special machinery that makes it), is nothing to sneeze at. However, the town has no single monumental sight to attract tourists—it's simply a uniquely human and undamaged, never-bombed city. Romanesque churches seem to be around every corner, as do fun-loving and shady piazzas filled with soccer-playing children.

Locals say Lucca is like a cake with a cherry filling in the middle...every slice is equally good. Despite Lucca's charm, few tourists seem to put it on their maps, and it remains a city for the Lucchesi (loo-KAY-zee).

Orientation to Lucca

Tourist Information

The main TI is just inside the Porta Santa Maria gate, on Piazza Santa Maria (daily May-Oct 9:00-20:00, Nov-April 9:00-12:30 & 15:00-18:30, pricey Internet access, WCs, no-fee room booking, Piazza Santa Maria 35, tel. 0583-919-931, www.luccatourist.it, info@luccaturismo.it).

Another TI, on Piazzale Giuseppe Verdi, offers information, a no-fee room-booking service, and baggage check (daily 9:00-18:30, futuristic WC, bike rental, 80-minute city-walk audioguide-€9, additional audioguide-€3 more; bag storage-€1.50/hour per bag, they need to photocopy your passport; tel. 0583-583-150). A third TI, just inside Porta Elisa, also has a no-fee reservations service (daily 9:00-13:30 & 14:30-18:00, WC-€0.60, baggage check, tel. 0583-495730).

Arrival in Lucca

By Train: There is no baggage check at the train station, but you may be able to leave bags at nearby Hotel Rex (see "Baggage Storage," next page). If not, you can lug them to the bag check at the TI on Piazzale Giuseppe Verdi or near Porta Elisa (TIs described above).

To reach the city center from the train station, walk toward the walls and head left, to the entry at Porta San Pietro. Taxis are sparse, but try calling 025-353 (ignore any recorded message—just wait for a live operator); a ride from the station to Piazza dell'Anfiteatro costs about €6.

By Car: The key for drivers—don't try to drive within the walls. The old town is ringed by lots (with two just inside the walls, both usually full). Parking is always free in Piazzale Don Franco, a five-minute walk north of the city walls. Otherwise, try lots just outside Porta San Donato, on Viale Europa between Porta San Pietro and Porta Sant'Anna (a.k.a. Vittorio Emanuele), or just inside Porta Santa Maria (€1/hour). Or consider parking outside the gates near the train station or on the boulevard surrounding the city (meter rates vary; also about €1/hour). Lucca's TIs have maps showing the location of free parking lots just outside the walls. Overnight parking (20:00-8:00) is free in the lots at Porta Santa Maria and on Viale Europa, and €1.50/night at Ex-Caserma Mazzini, right by Villa Guinigi, just inside Porta Elisa.

Helpful Hints

Combo-Tickets: A €6 combo-ticket includes visits to the Ilaria del Carretto tomb in San Martino Cathedral (€2), Cathedral Museum (€4), and San Giovanni Church (€2.50). A €5 combo-ticket combines the Guinigi Tower (€3.50) and the Clock Tower (€3.50). Yet another combo-ticket covers Palazzo

Mansi and Villa Guinigi for €6.50 and is valid for three days (€4 each if purchased separately).

Shops and Museums Alert: Shops close most of Sunday and Monday mornings. Many museums are closed on Monday as well.

Markets: Lucca's atmospheric markets are worth visiting. Every third weekend of the month (wherever the third Sunday falls), one of the largest **antiques markets** in Italy unfurls in the blocks between Piazza Antelminelli and Piazza San Giovanni (8:00-19:00). The last weekend of the month, local artisans sell **arts and crafts** around town, mainly near the cathedral (also 8:00-19:00). At the **general market,** held Wednesdays and Saturdays, you'll find produce and household goods (8:30-13:00, from Porta Elisa to Porta San Jacopo on Via dei Bacchettoni).

Concerts: San Giovanni Church hosts one-hour concerts featuring a pianist and singers performing highlights from home-town composer Giacomo Puccini (€17 at the door, some hotels offer tickets for the same price or cheaper, April-Oct nightly at 19:00, Nov-March check schedule and location at www.puccinielasualucca.com).

Festival: On September 13 and 14, the city celebrates Volto Santo ("Holy Face"), with a procession of the treasured local crucifix and a fair in Piazza Antelminelli.

Internet Access: You can get online (expensively) at the main **TI** (see "Tourist Information," earlier) or at **Betty Blue,** a wine bar handy to the recommended launderette (€4.50/hour, two terminals and cables to plug in your laptop, Thu-Tue 11:00-24:00, closed Wed, Via del Gonfalone 16, tel. 0583-492-166).

Baggage Storage: For train travelers, the most convenient storage spot is recommended **Hotel Rex.** However, they don't have much space, so it's best to email or call in advance (€4/bag all day, tel. 0583-955-443, info@hotelrexlucca.com). The **TIs** on Piazzale Giuseppe Verdi and near Porta Elisa are less convenient but workable options (see "Tourist Information," earlier).

Laundry: Lavanderia Self-Service Niagara is just off Piazza Santa Maria at Via Rosi 26 (€9 wash and dry, daily 7:00-23:00).

Bike Rental: A one-hour rental gives you time for two leisurely loops around the ramparts. Several places with identical prices cluster around Piazza Santa Maria (€3/hour, €12.50/day, tandem bikes available, free helmets, daily about 9:00-19:30 or sunset). Try these easygoing shops: **Antonio Poli** (Piazza Santa Maria 42, tel. 0583-493-787, enthusiastic Cristiana) and, right next to it, **Cicli Bizzarri** (Piazza Santa Maria 32,

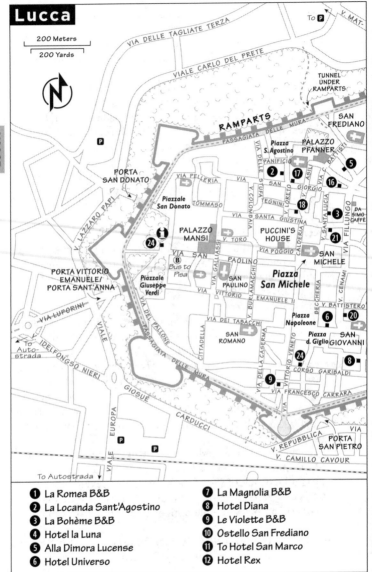

Lucca

LUCCA

200 Meters
200 Yards

1 La Romea B&B
2 La Locanda Sant'Agostino
3 La Bohème B&B
4 Hotel la Luna
5 Alla Dimora Lucense
6 Hotel Universo

7 La Magnolia B&B
8 Hotel Diana
9 Le Violette B&B
10 Ostello San Frediano
11 To Hotel San Marco
12 Hotel Rex

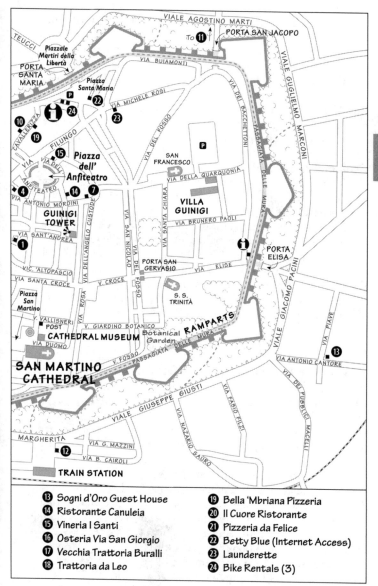

LUCCA

13 Sogni d'Oro Guest House
14 Ristorante Canuleia
15 Vineria I Santi
16 Osteria Via San Giorgio
17 Vecchia Trattoria Buralli
18 Trattoria da Leo

19 Bella 'Mbriana Pizzeria
20 Il Cuore Ristorante
21 Pizzeria da Felice
22 Betty Blue (Internet Access)
23 Launderette
24 Bike Rentals (3)

tel. 0583-496-682, Australian Dely). At the west end of town, the **TI** on Piazzale Giuseppe Verdi rents bikes. At the south end, at Porta San Pietro, you'll find **Chrono,** which rents bikes and offers guided bike tours (same rates and hours as the competition, Corso Garibaldi 93, tel. 0583-490-591, www .chronobikes.com).

Local Magazine: For insights into American and British expat life and listings of concerts, markets, festivals, and other special events, pick up a copy of *The Grapevine* (€2), available at newsstands.

Cooking Class: Gianluca invites you to the hills above Lucca to learn to make Tuscan fare. You prepare and then eat a three-course meal. Depending on how many others attend, the price ranges from €50 (a steal) to a whopping €125 per person. This is great for groups of four or more (€14 cab ride from town, 3-hour lesson plus time to dine, includes wine, reserve at least 2 days in advance, Via di San Viticchio 414, mobile 347-678-7447, www.italiancuisine.it, info@italiancuisine.it).

Local Guide: Gabriele Calabrese knows and shares his hometown well (€120/3 hours, by foot or bike, mobile 347-788-0667, www.turislucca.com, turislucca@turislucca.com).

Sights in Lucca

▲▲**Bike the Ramparts**—Lucca's most remarkable feature, its Renaissance wall, is also its most enjoyable attraction—especially when circled on a rental bike. Stretching for 2.5 miles, this is an ideal place to come for an overview of the city by foot or bike.

Lucca has had a protective wall for 2,000 years. You can read three walls into today's map: the first rectangular Roman wall, the later medieval wall (nearly the size of today's), and the 16th-century Renaissance wall that still survives.

With the advent of cannons, thin medieval walls were suddenly vulnerable. A new design—the same one that stands today—was state-of-the-art when it was built (1550-1650). Much of the old medieval wall (look for the old stones) was incorporated into the Renaissance wall (with uniform bricks). The new wall was squat: a 100-foot-wide mound of dirt faced with bricks, engineered to absorb a cannonball pummeling. The townspeople cleared a wide no-man's-land around the town, exposing any attackers from a distance. Eleven

heart-shaped bastions (now inviting picnic areas) were designed to minimize exposure to cannonballs and to maximize defense capabilities. The ramparts were armed with 130 cannons.

The town invested a third of its income for more than a century to construct the wall, and—since it kept away the Florentines and nasty Pisans—it was considered a fine investment. In fact, nobody ever bothered to try to attack the wall. Locals say that the only time it actually defended the city was during an 1812 flood of the Serchio River, when the gates were sandbagged and its ramparts kept out the high water.

Today, the ramparts seem made-to-order for a leisurely bike ride (20-minute pedal, wonderfully smooth). You can rent bikes cheaply and easily from one of several bike-rental places in town (listed earlier, under "Helpful Hints").

Piazza dell'Anfiteatro—Just off the main shopping street, the architectural ghost of a Roman amphitheater can be felt in the

delightful Piazza dell'Anfiteatro. With the fall of Rome, the theater (which seated 10,000) was gradually cannibalized for its stones and inhabited by people living in a mishmash of huts. The huts were cleared away at the end of the 19th century to better appreciate the town's illustrious past. Today, the square is a circle of touristy shops and mediocre restaurants that becomes a lively bar-and-café scene after dark. The modern street level is nine feet above the original arena floor. The only bits of surviving Roman stonework are a few arches on the northern exterior (at Via Fillungo 42 and on Via dell'Anfiteatro).

Via Fillungo—This main pedestrian drag stretches southwest from Piazza dell'Anfiteatro. *The* street to stroll, Via Fillungo takes you from the amphitheater almost all the way to the cathedral. Along the way, you'll get a taste of Lucca's rich past, including several elegant, century-old storefronts. Many of the original storefront paintings, reliefs, and mosaics survive—even if today's shopkeeper sells something entirely different.

At #97 is a classic old **jewelry store** with a rare storefront that has kept its T-shaped arrangement (when closed, you see a wooden T, and during open hours it unfolds with a fine old-time display). This design dates from a time when the merchant sold his goods in front, did his work in the back, and lived upstairs.

Di Simo Caffè, at #58, has long been the hangout of Lucca's artistic and intellectual elite. Composer and hometown boy Giacomo Puccini tapped his foot while sipping coffee here. Pop in to check out the 1880s ambience (handy €10 buffet lunch served

The History of Lucca

Lucca began as a Roman settlement. In fact, the grid layout of the streets (and the shadow of an amphitheater) survives from Roman times. Trace the rectangular Roman wall—indicated by today's streets—on the map. As in typical Roman towns, two main roads quartered the fortified town, crossing at what was the forum (main market and religious/political center)—today's Piazza San Michele.

Christianity came here early; it's said that the first bishop of Lucca was a disciple of St. Peter. While churches were built here as early as the fourth century, the majority of Lucca's elegant Romanesque churches date from about the 12th century.

Feisty Lucca, though never a real power, enjoyed a long period of independence (maintained by clever diplomacy). Aside from 30 years of being ruled from Pisa in the 14th century, Lucca was basically an independent city-state until Napoleon came to town.

In the Middle Ages, wealthy Lucca's economy was built on the silk industry, dominated by the Guinigi (gwee-NEE-gee) family. Without silk, Lucca would have been just another sleepy Italian town. In 1500, the town had 3,000 silk looms employing 25,000 workers. Banking was also big. Many pilgrims stopped here on their way to the Holy Land, deposited their money for safety...and never returned to pick it up.

In its heyday, Lucca packed 160 towers—one on nearly every corner—and 70 churches within its walls. Each tower was the home of a wealthy merchant family. Towers were many stories tall, with single rooms stacked atop each other: ground-floor shop, upstairs living room, and top-floor fire-safe kitchen, all connected by exterior wooden staircases. The rooftop was generally a vegetable garden, with trees providing shade. Later, the wealthy city folk moved into the countryside, trading away life in their city palazzos to establish farm estates complete with fancy villas. (You can visit some of these villas today—the TI has a brochure—but they're convenient only for drivers and are generally not worth the cost of admission.)

In 1799, Napoleon stormed into Italy and took a liking to Lucca. He liked it so much that he gave it to his sister as a gift. It was later passed on to Napoleon's widow, Marie Louise. With a feminine sensitivity, Marie Louise was partially responsible for turning the city's imposing (but no longer particularly useful) fortified wall into a fine city park that is much enjoyed today.

daily 12:30-14:30, café open 9:00-24:00).

A surviving five-story **tower house** is at #67. There was a time when nearly every corner sported its own tower (see the "The History of Lucca" sidebar). The stubby stones that still stick out once supported wooden staircases (there were no interior connections between floors). So many towers cast shadows over this part of town that the street just before it is called Via Buia (Dark Street). Look away from this tower and down Via San Andrea for a peek at the town's tallest tower, Guinigi, in the distance—with its characteristic oak trees sprouting from the top.

At #45 and #43, you'll see two more good examples of tower houses. Across the street, the **Clock Tower** (Torre delle Ore) has a hand-wound Swiss clock that has clanged four times an hour since 1754 (€3.50 to climb up and see the mechanism flip into action on the quarter-hour—if it's actually working, €5 combo-ticket includes Guinigi Tower, daily April-Oct 9:30-18:30, Nov-March

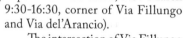

9:30-16:30, corner of Via Fillungo and Via del'Arancio).

The intersection of Via Fillungo and Via Roma/Via Santa Croce marks the center of town (where the two original Roman roads crossed). As you go right down Via Roma, you'll pass the fine Edison Bookstore on your left before reaching Piazza San Michele.

Piazza San Michele—This square has been the center of town since Roman times, when it was the forum. It's dominated by the Church of San Michele. Towering above the church's fancy Pisan Romanesque facade, the archangel Michael stands ready to flap his wings—which he was known to do on special occasions.

The square is surrounded by an architectural hodgepodge. The loggia, which dates from 1495, is the first Renaissance building in town. There's a late-19th-century interior in Buccellato Taddeucci, a 130-year old pastry shop (#34). The left section of the BNL bank (#5; in front of the church) sports an Art Nouveau facade that celebrates both Amerigo Vespucci and Cristoforo Colombo.

Perhaps you've noticed that the statues of big shots that decorate many an Italian piazza are mostly absent from Lucca's squares. That's because unlike Venice, Florence, and Milan—which were dominated by a few powerful dynasties—Lucca was traditionally run by an oligarchy of a hundred leading families, with no one central figure to commemorate in stone. But after Italian unification, when leaders were fond of saying, "We have created Italy... now we need to create Italians," stirring statues of national heroes popped up everywhere—even in Lucca. The statue on Piazza San

Michele is a two-bit local guy, dredged up centuries after his death because he favored strong central government.

Look back at the church facade, which also has an element of patriotism—designed to give roots and legitimacy to Italian statehood. Perched above many of the columns are the faces of heroes in the Italian independence and unification movement: Victor Emmanuel II (above the short red column on the right), the Count of Cavour (next to Victor, above the column with black zigzags), and Giuseppe Mazzini.

▲**San Martino Cathedral**—This cathedral, begun in the 11th century, is an entertaining mix of architectural and artistic styles. It's also home to the exquisite 15th-century tomb of Ilaria del Carretto, who married into the wealthy Guinigi family.

Cost and Hours: Cathedral-free, Ilaria tomb-€2, €6 combo-ticket includes Cathedral Museum and San Giovanni Church; Mon-Fri 9:30-17:45, Sat 9:30-18:45; Sun open sporadically between Masses: 9:30-10:45 & 12:00-17:45; Piazza San Martino.

◑ **Self-Guided Tour:** Dominating the piazza is the cathedral's elaborate Pisan Romanesque **facade,** featuring Christian teaching scenes, animals, and candy-cane-striped columns.

The central figure is St. Martin, a Roman military officer from Hungary who, by offering his cloak to a beggar, more fully understood the beauty of Christian compassion. (The impressive original, a fine example of Romanesque sculpture, hides from pollution just inside, to the right of the main entrance.) Each of the columns on the facade is unique. Notice how the facade is asymmetrical: The 11th-century bell tower was already in place when the rest of the cathedral was built, so the builders cheated on the

right side to make it fit the space. Over the right portal (as if leaning against the older tower), the architect Guideo from Como holds a document declaring that he finished the facade in 1204. On the right (at eye level on the pilaster), a labyrinth is set into the wall. The maze relates the struggle and challenge our souls face in finding salvation. (French pilgrims on their way to Rome could relate to this, as it's the same pattern they knew from the floor of the church at Chartres.) The Latin plaque just left of the main door is where moneychangers and spice traders met to seal deals (on the doorstep of the church—to underscore the reliability of their promises). Notice the date: *An Dni MCXI* (A.D. 1111).

The **interior** features Gothic arches, Renaissance paintings, and stained glass from the 19th century. On the left side of the nave, a small, elaborate, birdcage-like temple contains the wooden crucifix—beloved by locals—called Volto Santo. It's said to have been sculpted by Nicodemus in Jerusalem and set afloat in an unmanned boat that landed on the coast of Tuscany, from where wild oxen miraculously carried it to Lucca in 782. The sculpture (which is actually 12th-century Byzantine-style) has quite a jewelry collection, which you can see in the Cathedral Museum (described next).

On the right side of the nave, the sacristy houses the enchantingly beautiful **memorial tomb of Ilaria del Carretto** by Jacopo della Quercia (1407). Pick up a handy English description to the right of the door as you enter the sacristy. This young bride of silk baron Paolo Guinigi is decked out in the latest, most expensive fashions, with the requisite little dog (symbolizing her loyalty) curled up at her feet in eternal sleep. She's so realistic that the statue was nicknamed "Sleeping Beauty." Her nose is partially worn off because of a long-standing tradition of lonely young ladies rubbing it for luck in finding a boyfriend.

Cathedral Museum (Museo della Cattedrale)—This beautifully presented museum houses original paintings, sculptures, and vestments from the cathedral and other Lucca churches. The first room displays jewelry made to dress up the Volto Santo crucifix, including gigantic gilded silver shoes. Upstairs, notice the fine red brocaded silk—a reminder that this precious fabric is what brought riches and power to the city. The exhibits in this museum have very brief descriptions and are meaningful only with the slow-talking €1 audioguide—if you're not in the mood to listen, skip the place altogether.

Cost and Hours: €4, €6 combo-ticket includes Ilaria tomb and San Giovanni Church; April-Oct daily 10:00-18:00; Nov-March Mon-Fri 10:00-14:00, Sat-Sun 10:00-17:00; to the left of the cathedral as you're facing it, Piazza Antelminelli, tel. 0583-490-530, www.museocattedralelucca.it.

San Giovanni Church—This first cathedral of Lucca is interesting only for its archaeological finds. The entire floor of the 12th-century church has been excavated in recent decades, revealing layers of Roman houses, ancient hot tubs that date back to the time of Christ, early churches, and theological graffiti. Sporadic English translations help you understand what you're looking at. As you climb under the church's present-day floor and wander the lanes of Roman Lucca, remember that the entire city sits on similar ruins.

Cost and Hours: €2.50, €6 combo-ticket includes Ilaria tomb and Cathedral Museum, audioguide-€1; mid-March-Oct daily 10:00-18:00; Nov-mid-March Sat-Sun 10:00-17:00, closed Mon-Fri; see concert info on page 191; kitty-corner from cathedral at Piazza San Giovanni.

Church of San Frediano—This impressive church was built in 1112 by the pope to counter Lucca's bishop and his spiffy cathedral. Lucca was the first Mediterranean stop on the pilgrim route from northern Europe, and the pope wanted to remind pilgrims that the action, the glory, and the papacy awaited them in Rome. Therefore, he had the church made "Roman-esque." The pure marble facade frames an early Christian Roman-style mosaic of Christ with his 12 apostles. Step inside and you're struck by the sight of 40 powerful (if recycled) ancient Roman columns. The message: Lucca may be impressive, but the finale of your pilgrimage—in Rome—is worth the hike.

Inside, there's a notable piece of art in each corner: At rear left is the 12th-century baptistery, with some interesting Church propaganda showing the story of Moses (the evil Egyptians are played by Holy Roman Empire troops). At rear right is St. Zita's actual body, put there in 1278. At front left is a particularly elegant Virgin Mary, depicted at the moment she gets the news that she'll bring the Messiah into the world (carved and painted by Lucchesi artist Matteo Civitali, c. 1460). And at front right is a painting on wood of the *Assumption of the Virgin* (c. 1510), with Doubting Thomas receiving Mary's red belt as she ascends so he'll doubt no more. The pinball-machine composition serves as a virtual catalog of the fine silk material produced in Lucca—a major industry in the 16th century.

Cost and Hours: Free, Mon-Sat 8:30-12:00 & 15:00-17:30, Sun 9:00-11:30 & 15:00-17:30, Piazza San Frediano, tel. 0583-493-627.

Palazzo Mansi—Minor paintings by Tintoretto, Pontormo, Veronese, and others vie for attention, but the palace itself—a sumptuously furnished and decorated 17th-century confection—steals the show. This is your chance to appreciate the wealth of Lucca's silk merchants. Since all visitors must be accompanied by a museum employee, during high season you may have to wait a bit for your chance to enter.

Cost and Hours: €4, €6.50 combo-ticket includes Villa Guinigi, hours prone to change but generally Tue-Sat 8:30-19:30, Sun 8:30-13:30, closed Mon, no photos, request English booklet at ticket desk, Via Galli Tassi 43, tel. 0583-55-570.

Guinigi Tower (Torre Guinigi)—Many Tuscan towns have towers, but none is quite like the Guinigi family's. Up 227 steps is a small garden with fragrant trees, surrounded by fantastic views.

Cost and Hours: €3.50, €5 combo-

LUCCA

ticket includes Clock Tower, likely open daily April-Sept 9:00-19:30, Oct 10:00-18:00, Nov-March 9:30-16:30, Via Sant'Andrea 41.

Puccini's House—Opera enthusiasts (but nobody else) will want to visit the home where Giacomo Puccini (1858-1924) grew up, but—tragedy—it's been closed for several years. However, it was recently sold by Puccini's grandniece, and according to local scuttlebutt, it may reopen in 2012. The museum has the great composer's piano and a small collection of his personal belongings.

Cost and Hours: If open, likely €3, daily 10:00-18:00 though may be closed Mon, Corte San Lorenzo 9, tel. 0583-584-028.

Palazzo Pfanner—Garden enthusiasts (and anyone needing a break from churches) will enjoy this 18th-century palace built for a rich Swiss expat who came to Lucca to open a brewery. His sudsy legacy includes Baroque furniture, elaborate frescoes, a centuries-old kitchen, and a lavish garden.

Cost and Hours: Garden or residence-€4 apiece, €5.50 for both, April-Oct daily 10:00-18:00, closed Nov-March, Via degli Asili 33, tel. 0583-954-029, www.palazzopfanner.it.

Villa Guinigi—Built by Paolo Guinigi in 1418, the family villa is now a stark, abandoned-feeling museum displaying a hodgepodge of Etruscan artifacts, religious sculptures, paintings, inlaid woodwork, and ceramics. Monumental paintings by the multitalented Giorgio Vasari are the best reason to visit.

Cost and Hours: €4, €6.50 combo-ticket includes Palazzo Mansi, Tue-Sat 8:30-19:30, Sun 8:30-13:30, closed Mon, may have to wait in high season for a museum employee to accompany you, Via della Quarquonia, tel. 0583-496-033.

Sleeping in Lucca

Fancy Little Boutique B&Bs Within the Walls

$$$ La Romea B&B, in an air-conditioned, restored, 14th-century palazzo near Guinigi Tower, feels like a royal splurge. Its four posh rooms and one suite are lavishly decorated in handsome colors and surround a big, plush lounge with stately Venetian-style floors (Db-€100-135 depending on season, big suite-€160, extra bed-€20-25; 10 percent discount when you book direct, show this book, and pay cash; Wi-Fi; from the train station, take Via Fillungo, turn right on Via Sant'Andrea, then take the second right to Vicolo delle Ventaglie 2; tel. 0583-464-175, www.laromea.com, info@laromea.com, Giulio and wife Gaia).

$$$ La Locanda Sant'Agostino has three romantic, bright, and spacious rooms. The vine-draped terrace, beautiful breakfast spread, and quaint views invite you to relax (Db-€160, extra bed-€25, 5 percent discount with cash and this book, air-con, Internet access and Wi-Fi, from Via Fillungo take Via San Giorgio to

Sleep Code

(€1 = about $1.40, country code: 39)

S = Single, **D** = Double/Twin, **T** = Triple, **Q** = Quad, **b** = bathroom, **s** = shower only. Unless otherwise noted, credit cards are accepted, breakfast is included (but sometimes optional), and English is generally spoken.

To help you sort easily through these listings, I've divided the accommodations into three categories based on the price for a double room with bath during high season:

$$$ Higher Priced—Most rooms €120 or more.
  $$ Moderately Priced—Most rooms between €80-120.
    $ Lower Priced—Most rooms €80 or less.

Prices can change without notice; verify the hotel's current rates online or by email. For other updates, see www .ricksteves.com/update.

Piazza Sant'Agostino 3, best to reserve by email, tel. 0583-443-100, mobile 347-989-9069, www.locandasantagostino.it, info @locandasantagostino.it).

$$$ La Bohème B&B has a cozy yet elegant ambience, offering six large, charming, chandeliered rooms, each painted with a different rich color scheme (Db-€120, less off-season, 10 percent discount with this book if you pay cash and book direct, air-con, free Wi-Fi, Via del Moro 2, tel. & fax 0583-462-404, www .boheme.it, info@boheme.it, Sara).

Sleeping More Forgettably Within the Walls

$$ Hotel la Luna, run by the Barbieri family, has 29 rooms in a great location, right in the heart of the city. Updated rooms are split between two adjacent buildings just off of the main shopping street. The annex may have an elevator, but I prefer the rooms in the main building, which are larger and classier (Sb-€83, Db-€113, suite-€175, these prices for Rick Steves readers who book direct, air-con, pay Internet access, parking-€15/day, Via Fillungo at Corte Compagni 12, tel. 0583-493-634, fax 0583-490-021, www .hotellaluna.com, info@hotellaluna.com, Sara).

$$ Alla Dimora Lucense's seven newer rooms are bright, modern, clean, and peaceful, with all the comforts. Enjoy their relaxing, sunny interior courtyard (Db-€115, suite for 2-4 people-€150-200; 10 percent discount if you pay cash, book direct, and show this book; optional breakfast-€5, air-con, Wi-Fi, half a block from Via Fillungo at Via Fontana 17, tel. 0583-495-722, fax 0583-441-210, www.dimoralucense.it, info@dimoralucense.it).

$$ Hotel Universo, renting 56 rooms right on Piazza Napoleone and facing the theater and Palazzo Ducale, is a 19th-century town fixture. While it clearly was once elegant, now it's old and tired, with a big Old World lounge and soft prices ("comfort" Db-€100, "superior" Db with updated bath-€130, Wi-Fi, Piazza del Giglio 1, tel. 0583-493-678, www.universolucca.com, info@universolucca.com).

$$ La Magnolia B&B offers five basic rooms and one apartment with an intimate atmosphere and relaxing garden. It's buried in a ramshackle old palace in a central location (Sb-€65, Db-€85, Qb-€90, includes breakfast at nearby bar, 5 percent discount with this book if you pay cash and book direct, a block behind amphitheater at Via Mordini 63, tel. 0583-467-111, www.lamagnolia .com, info@lamagnolia.com, Andrea and Laura).

$ Hotel Diana is a dreary little family-run hotel, with nine rooms in the main building and another six slightly nicer, soundproofed, and air-conditioned rooms in the annex just around the corner (D-€50, Db-€65, annex Db-€85, south of the cathedral at Via del Molinetto 11, tel. 0583-492-202, fax 0583-467-795, www .albergodiana.com, info@albergodiana.com).

$ At Le Violette B&B, friendly Anna (who's still learning English; her granddaughter Sara speaks English) will settle you into one of her six homey rooms near the train station inside Porta San Pietro (D-€60, Db-€75, extra bed-€15, Wi-Fi, communal kitchen, €5 to use washer and dryer, Via della Polveriera 6, tel. 0583-493-594, mobile 349-823-4645, fax 0583-429-305, www .leviolette.it, leviolette@virgilio.it).

$ Ostello San Frediano, in a central, sprawling ex-convent with a peaceful garden, is a cut above the average hostel, though it's still filled mainly with a young crowd. Its 29 rooms are bright and modern, and some have fun lofts (€20 beds in 6- to 8-person dorms, 140 beds, Db-€60, Tb-€78, Qb-€100, includes sheets, €3 extra/night for non-members, cash only, breakfast extra, no curfew, lockers, Internet access, cheap restaurant, free parking, Via della Cavallerizza 12, tel. 0583-469-957, fax 0583-461-007, www .ostellolucca.it, info@ostellolucca.it).

Outside the Walls

$$$ Hotel San Marco, a seven-minute walk outside the Porta Santa Maria, is a postmodern place decorated à la Stanley Kubrick. Its 42 recently remodeled rooms are sleek, with all the comforts (Sb-€87, Db-€126, extra bed-€10, includes nice breakfast spread, air-con, Wi-Fi, elevator, pool, bikes-€5/half-day, free parking, taxi from station-€6, Via San Marco 368, tel. 0583-495-010, fax 0583-490-513, www.hotelsanmarcolucca.com, info@hotelsan marcolucca.com).

$$ Hotel Rex rents 25 rooms in a practical modern building on the train station square. While in the modern world, you're just 200 yards away from the old town and get more space for a better price (Db-€80-100, 10 percent discount with this book if you pay cash and book direct, air-con, Wi-Fi, free bike rental, a few steps from the train station at Piazza Ricasoli 19, tel. 0583-955-443, www.hotelrexlucca.com, info@hotelrexlucca.com).

$ Sogni d'Oro Guest House ("Sleep like Gold"), run by Davide, is a handy budget option for drivers, with five basic rooms and a cheery communal kitchen (grocery store next door). It's a 10-minute walk from the train station and a five-minute walk from the city walls (D-€50, Db-€65, Q-€70, 10 percent discount with cash; free ride to and from station with advance notice—then call when your train arrives in Lucca; from the station, head straight out to Viale Regina Margherita and turn right, follow the main boulevard as it turns into Viale Giuseppe Giusti, at the curve turn right onto Via Antonio Cantore to #169; tel. 0583-467-768, mobile 329-582-5062, fax 0583-957-612, www.bbsognidoro.com, info@bbsognidoro.com).

Eating in Lucca

Ristorante Canuleia makes everything fresh in their small kitchen. While the portions aren't huge, the food is tasty. You can eat in their dressy little dining room or outside on the garden courtyard (€10 pastas, €17 *secondi*, Mon-Sat 12:30-14:00 & 19:30-21:30, closed Sun, Via Canuleia 14, tel. 0583-467-470, reserve for dinner).

Vineria I Santi is pricey but good if you appreciate quality food and fine wine, and just want to lie back and be pampered. Leonardo serves food with a sexy jazz ambience that would work well in a bordello. Relax in the peaceful indoors among wine bottles, or on a quiet square outside (€11 pastas, €18 *secondi*, Thu-Tue 12:30-14:30 & 19:30-22:00, closed Wed, Via dell'Anfiteatro 29, tel. 0583-496-124).

Osteria Via San Giorgio, owned by Daniela and her brother Piero, is a cheery family eatery that satisfies both fish-lovers and meat-lovers. Sample the splittable *antipasto fantasia*—five small courses such as *ceviche* (seafood salad), scallops au gratin, squid sautéed with potatoes, or whatever else was caught that day in Viareggio; they also offer a meatier version. Dinner-size salads are bright and fresh, pasta is homemade, and Daniela's desserts tempt (daily 12:00-16:00 & 19:00-23:00, Via San Giorgio 26, tel. 0583-953-233).

Vecchia Trattoria Buralli, on quiet Piazza Sant'Agostino, is a good bet for traditional cooking and juicy steaks, with fine

Specialties in Lucca

Lucca has some tasty specialties worth seeking out. *Ceci* (CHEH-chee), also called *cecina* (cheh-CHEE-nah), makes an ideal cheap snack any time of day. This garbanzo-bean crepe is sold in pizza shops and is best accompanied by a nip of red wine.

Farro, a grain (spelt) dating back to ancient Roman cuisine, shows up in restaurants in soups or as a creamy rice-like dish *(risotto di farro)*.

Tordelli, the Lucchesi version of *tortelli,* is homemade ravioli. It's traditionally stuffed with meat and served with more meat sauce, but chefs creatively pair cheeses and vegetables, too.

Meat, not fish, is the star at most restaurants, especially steak, which is listed on menus as *filetto di manzo* (filet), *tagliata di manzo* (thin slices of grilled tenderloin), or the king of steaks, *bistecca alla fiorentina.* Order *al sangue* (rare), *medio* (medium rare), *cotto* (medium), or *ben cotto* (well). Anything more than *al sangue* is considered a travesty for steak connoisseurs.

Note that steaks (as well as fish) are often sold by weight, noted on menus as *s.q.* (according to quantity ordered) or *l'etto* (cost per 100 grams—250 grams is about an 8-ounce steak).

For something sweet, bakeries sell *buccellato,* bread dotted with raisins, lightly flavored with anise, and often shaped like a wreath. It's only sold in large sizes, but luckily it stays good for a few days (and it also pairs well with *vin santo*—fortified Tuscan dessert wine). An old proverb says, "Coming to Lucca without eating the *buccellato* is like not having come at all." *Buon appetito!*

indoor and piazza seating (€7 pastas, €10 *secondi,* €12-30 fixed-price meals, Thu-Tue 12:00-14:45 & 19:00-22:30, closed Wed, Piazza Sant'Agostino 10, tel. 0583-950-611).

Trattoria da Leo, a brother of Vecchia Trattoria Buralli, packs in chatty locals for typical, cheap home-cooking in a hash-slingin' Mel's-diner atmosphere. This place is a high-energy winner...you know it's going to be good as soon as you step in. Arrive early or reserve in advance (€6 pastas, €10 *secondi,* Mon-Sat 12:00-14:30 & 19:30-22:30, sometimes open Sun, cash only, leave Piazza San Salvatore on Via Asili and take the first left to Via Tegrimi 1, tel. 0583-492-236).

Bella 'Mbriana Pizzeria focuses on doing one thing very well: turning out piping-hot, wood-fired pizzas to happy locals in a welcoming wood-paneled dining room. Order and pay at the counter, take a number, and they'll call you when your pizza's ready.

Consider take-out to munch on the nearby walls. Prices range from €5 for your basic *Napolitano* to €8 for their specialty, with buffalo mozzarella and other gourmet ingredients (Wed-Mon 12:30-14:30 & 18:30-23:00, closed Tue, to the right as you face the Church of San Frediano, Via della Cavallerizza 29, tel. 0583-495-565).

Il Cuore Enogastronomia includes a delicatessen and restaurant. For a fancy picnic, drop in the deli for ready-to-eat lasagna, saucy meatballs, grilled and roasted vegetables, vegetable soufflés, Tuscan bean soup, fruit salads, and more, sold by weight and dished up in disposable trays to go. Ask them to heat your order *(riscaldare)*, then picnic on nearby Piazza Napoleone. For curious traveling foodies on a budget who want to eat right there, they can assemble a €10 "degustation plate"—just point to what you want from among the array of tasty treats under the glass (Tue-Sun 9:30-19:30, closed Mon, Via del Battistero 2, tel. 0583-493-196, Marianna and Cristina).

Il Cuore Ristorante, located across the way, is a trendy find for wine-tasting or a meal on a piazza. Try the €8 *aperitivo* (available 18:00-20:00), which includes a glass of wine and a plate of cheese, *salumi*, and snacks, or feast on fresh pastas and other high-quality dishes from their lunch and dinner menus (Wed-Sun 12:00-22:00 with limited menu 15:00-19:30, Tue 12:00-15:00, closed Mon, Via del Battistero, tel. 0583-493-196).

Pizzeria da Felice is a little mom-and-pop hole-in-the-wall serving *cecina* (chickpea crepes) and slices of freshly baked pizza to throngs of snackers. Grab a *cecina* and a short glass of wine for €2.50 (Mon-Sat 10:00-20:30, closed Sun and 3 weeks in Aug, Via Buia 12, tel. 0583-494-986).

Lucca Connections

From Lucca by Train to: Florence (2/hour, 1.5 hours), **Pisa** (roughly 1-2/hour Mon-Sat, 30 minutes, bus is better), **Milan** (2/hour except Sun, 4-5 hours, transfer in Florence), **Rome** (1/hour except Sun, 3-4 hours, change in Florence).

From Lucca by Bus to Pisa: Direct buses from Lucca's Piazzale Giuseppe Verdi drop you right at the Leaning Tower, making Pisa an easy day trip (hourly, 30 minutes, €3.50). Even with a car, I'd opt for this much faster and cheaper option.

VOLTERRA

Encircled by impressive walls and topped with a grand fortress, Volterra sits high above the rich farmland surrounding it. More than 2,000 years ago, Volterra was one of the most important Etruscan cities, a city much larger than the one we see today. Greek-trained Etruscan artists worked here, leaving a significant stash of art, particularly funerary urns. Eventually Volterra was absorbed into the Roman Empire, and for centuries it was an independent city-state. Volterra fought bitterly against the Florentines, but like many Tuscan towns, it lost in the end and was given a fortress atop the city to "protect" its citizens.

Unlike other famous towns in Tuscany, Volterra feels not cutesy or touristy...but real, vibrant, and almost oblivious to the allure of the tourist dollar. A refreshing break from its more commercial neighbors, it's my favorite small town in Tuscany.

Orientation to Volterra

Compact and walkable, the city stretches out from the pleasant Piazza dei Priori to the old city gates.

Tourist Information

The helpful TI is on the main square, at Piazza dei Priori 19 (daily 10:00-13:00 & 14:00-18:00, tel. 0588-87257, www.volterratur.it). The TI's excellent €5 audioguide narrates 20 stops (2-for-1 discount on audioguides with this book).

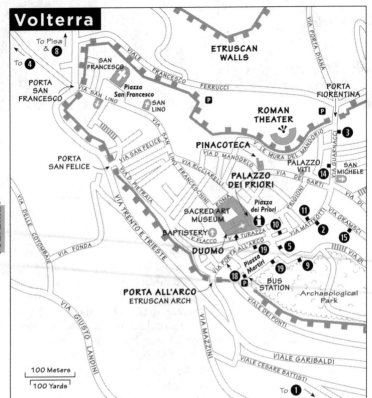

Arrival in Volterra

By Public Transport: Buses stop at Piazza Martiri della Libertà in the town center. Train travelers can reach the town with a short bus ride (see "Volterra Connections," at the end of this chapter.)

By Car: Drivers will find the town ringed with easy numbered parking lots (#3 and #5 are free; #3 is most likely to have a place, but comes with a steeper hike into town). The most central lots are the pay lots at Porta Fiorentina and underground at Piazza Martiri della Libertà (€1.50/hour, €11/24 hours).

Helpful Hints

Market Day: The market is on Saturday morning near the Roman Theater (8:00-13:00, in Piazza dei Priori in winter).

Festivals: Volterra's Medieval Festival takes place the third and fourth Sundays of August. Fall is a popular time for food festivals—check with the TI for dates and events planned.

Internet Access: Web & Wine has a few terminals, fine wine by the glass, and organic food (€3/hour, no minimum, summer

- ❶ To Park Hotel Le Fonti
- ❷ Albergo Etruria
- ❸ Hotel La Locanda
- ❹ To Albergo Villa Nencini
- ❺ Albergo Nazionale
- ❻ Seminario Vescovile Sant'Andrea
- ❼ To Volterra Youth Hostel & Trattoria da Bado
- ❽ To Podere Marcampo
- ❾ Ristorante Enoteca del Duca
- ❿ Trattoria Don Beta
- ⓫ La Vecchia Lira
- ⓬ Ristorante il Sacco Fiorentino
- ⓭ La Vena di Vino Wine Bar
- ⓮ Ombra della Sera & Pizzeria Tavernetta
- ⓯ Despar Market
- ⓰ Alab'Arte Alabaster Showroom
- ⓱ Alab'Arte Alabaster Workshop
- ⓲ "Artisan Lane"
- ⓳ Internet Cafés (2)

VOLTERRA

daily 9:30-1:00 in the morning, off-season closed Thu, Via Porta all'Arco 11-15, tel. 0588-81531, www.webandwine.com, Lallo speaks English). **Enjoy Café Internet Point** has a couple of terminals in their basement (€3/hour, daily 6:30-1:00 in the morning, Piazza dei Martiri 3, tel. 0588-80530).

Local Guide: American **Annie Adair** is an excellent city guide. She and her husband Francesco, a sommelier, organize private food and wine tours and even Tuscan weddings for Americans (€50/hour, minimum 2 hours, tel. 0588-87774, mobile 347-143-5004, www.tuscantour.com, info@tuscantour.com).

Sights in Volterra

▲▲**Guided Volterra Walk**—Annie Adair and her colleagues offer a great one-hour, English-only introductory walking tour of Volterra for €10. The walk touches on Volterra's Etruscan, Roman, and medieval history, as well as the contemporary cultural scene (April-July and Sept-Oct daily, rain or shine, at 18:00; meet in front of alabaster shop on Piazza Martiri della Libertà, no need to reserve—just show up, they need a minimum of 3 people—or €30—to make the tour go, www.volterrawalkingtour.com or www .tuscantour.com, info@volterrawalkingtour.com). There's no better way to spend €10 and one hour in this city.

▲▲**Self-Guided Historic Town Walk**—You can easily lace the town's top sights and my descriptions together to make your own handy little town walk. Here's the spine of the walk (all described in this order below): Start with the Etruscan Arch, browse up what I call "Artisan Lane," follow my tour of Via Matteotti, side-trip to the main square and Duomo, detour (if you like) to the Pinacoteca and Roman Theater, head over to the Etruscan Museum and Alabaster Workshop, and finish with a drink under all the bras with Bruno and Lucio at La Vena di Vino. The town's other sights are easily grafted onto this route.

▲**"Porta all'Arco" Etruscan Arch**—Volterra's most famous sight is its Etruscan arch, built of massive, volcanic tuff stones in the fourth century B.C. Volterra's
original wall was four miles around—twice the size of the wall that encircles it today. With 25,000 people, Volterra was a key Etruscan trade center—one of 12 leading towns that made up the Etruscan *Dodecapolis* (a league of Etruscan cities). The three seriously eroded heads, dating from

the first century B.C., show what happens when you leave something outside for 2,000 years. The newer stones are part of the 13th-century city wall, which incorporated parts of the much older Etruscan wall.

A plaque just outside remembers June 30, 1944. That night, Nazi forces were planning to blow up the arch to slow the Allied advance. To save their treasured landmark, Volterrans ripped up the stones that pave Via Porta all'Arco and plugged the gate, managing to convince the Nazi commander that there was no need to blow up the arch. Today, all the stones are back in their places, and like silent heroes, they welcome you through the oldest standing Etruscan gate into Volterra. Locals claim this as the only surviving round arch of the Etruscan age and believe this is where Romans got the idea for using a keystone in their arches.

"Artisan Lane"—Via Porta all'Arco (which leads to and from the Etruscan arch) is lined with interesting shops featuring the work of artisans and producers. Because of its alabaster heritage, Volterra attracted artisans and artists, who brought with them a rich variety of crafts (shops generally open Mon-Sat 10:00-13:00

Vampire Volterra

Sitting on its stony main square at midnight, watching bats dart about as if they own the place, I realized there really is something supernatural about Volterra. The cliffs of Volterra inspired Dante's "cliffs of hell." In the winter, the town's vibrancy is smothered under a deadening cloak of clouds. The name Volterra means "land that floats"—referring to the clouds that often seem to cut it off from the rest of the world below.

The people of Volterra live in a cloud of mystery, too. Their favorite cookie, crunchy with almonds, is called Ossi di Morta ("bones of the dead"). The town's first disco was named Catacombs. And in the 1970s, when Volterra was the set of a wildly popular TV horror series called *Ritratto di Donna Velata (Portrait of a Veiled Woman)*, all of Italy tuned in to Volterra every week for a good scare.

In recent years, the town has attracted international attention for its connection to the bestselling *Twilight* series of vampire romance novels and movies. Part of the second movie, *New Moon* (2009), is set in Volterra. Even though most of it was actually filmed in Montepulciano, the TI plays a video clip of *New Moon* continuously and is proud of Volterra's Hollywood connection.

As a result, the town is seeing lots of "Twihards," who come not for the Etruscan Museum, but to run across the sun-drenched square at noon and retrace the footsteps of Edward and Bella down dark alleyways. The enthusiasm may be past its peak, but the tourism board clings to the vampire vibe—it's in their blood.

& 16:00-19:00, closed Sun; the TI produces a free booklet called *Handicraft in Volterra*).

From the Etruscan Arch, browse your way up the hill, checking out these shops and items (listed from bottom to top): La Mia Fattoria, a co-op of producers of cheese, salami, and olive oil, letting you buy direct at farm prices (#52); alabaster shops (#57, #50, and #45); book bindery and papery (#26); jewelry (#25); etchings and silk screening (#23); leather (#16); Web & Wine (Internet access; #11-15); and bronze work (#6).

▲**Via Matteotti**—The town's main drag, named after the popular Socialist leader killed by the Fascists in 1924, provides a good cultural scavenger hunt. The street starts 30 yards from Palazzo dei Priori (City Hall and cathedral, described later).

At #1 is a typical Italian bank security door. (Step in and say, "Beam me up, Scotty.") Look up and all around. Find the medieval griffin torch holder—symbol of Volterra—and imagine it holding a lit torch. The pharmacy sports the symbol of its medieval guild.

As you head down Via Matteotti, notice how the doors show centuries of refitting work.

At #2, look up and imagine heavy beams cantilevered out, supporting extra wooden rooms and balconies crowding out over the street. Throughout Tuscany, today's stark and stony old building fronts once supported a tangle of wooden extensions. Doors that once led to these extra rooms are now partially bricked up to make windows. Contemplate urban density in the 14th century, before the plague thinned out the population. Be careful: There's a wild boar (a local delicacy) at #10.

At #12, notice the line of doorbells: This typical palace, once the home of a single rich family, is now occupied by many middle-class families. After the social revolution in the 18th century and the rise of the middle class, former palaces were condominiumized. Even so, like in *Dr. Zhivago,* the original family still lives here. Apartment #1 is the home of Count Guidi.

At #16, pop in to an alabaster showroom. Alabaster, mined nearby, has long been a big industry here. Volterra alabaster—softer and more porous than marble—was sliced thin to serve as windows for Italy's medieval churches.

At #19, the recommended La Vecchia Lira is a lively cafeteria. The Bar L'Incontro across the street is a favorite for homemade gelato and pastries.

Across the way, up Vicolo delle Prigioni, is a fun bakery *(panificio).* They're happy to sell small quantities if you want to try the local *cantuccini* (almond biscotti) or munch a cannoli.

At #51, a bit of Etruscan wall is artfully used to display more alabaster art. And #56A is the alabaster art gallery of Paolo Sabatini.

Locals gather early each evening at Osteria dei Poeti (at #57) for the best cocktails in town—served with free munchies. The cinema is across the street. Movies in Italy are rarely in *versione originale*; Italians are used to getting their movies dubbed into Italian.

At #66, another Tuscan tower marks the end of the street. This noble house has a ground floor with no interior access to the safe upper floors. Rope ladders were used to get upstairs. The tiny door was wide enough to let in your skinny friends...but definitely not anyone wearing armor and carrying big weapons.

Across the street stands the ancient Church of St. Michael. After long years of barbarian chaos, the Lombards moved in from the north and asserted law and order in places like Volterra. That generally included building a Christian church on the old Roman forum to symbolically claim and tame the center of town. The church standing here today is Romanesque, dating from the 12th century. Find the crude little guys under its eaves—they've been making faces at the passing crowds for 800 years.

Palazzo dei Priori—Volterra's City Hall (c. 1209) claims to be the oldest of any Tuscan city-state. It clearly inspired the more famous Palazzo Vecchio in Florence. Town halls like this were emblematic of an era when city-states were powerful. They were architectural exclamation points declaring that, around here, no pope or emperor called the shots. Towns such as Volterra were truly city-states—proudly independent and relatively democratic. They had their own armies, taxes, and even weights and measures. Notice the horizontal "cane" cut into the City Hall wall. For a thousand years, this square hosted a market, and the "cane" was the local yardstick. When not in use for meetings or weddings, the city council chambers—lavishly painted and lit with fun dragon lamps, as they have been for centuries of town meetings—are open to visitors.

Cost and Hours: €1.50, April-Oct daily 10:30-17:30, Nov-March Sat-Sun only 10:00-17:00.

Duomo—A common arrangement in the Middle Ages was for the church to face the baptistery (you couldn't enter the church until you were baptized)...and for the hospital to face the cemetery. All of these overlooked the same square. That's how it is in Pisa, and that's how it is here. This 12th-century church is not as elaborate as its cousin in Pisa, but the simple facade and central nave, flanked by monolithic stone columns, are beautiful examples of the Pisan Romanesque style.

Cost and Hours: Free, daily 8:00-12:30 & 15:00-17:00.

Touring the Church: The chapel to the left of the entry has painted terra-cotta statue groups. The interior was decorated mostly in the late 16th century, during Florentine rule under the Medici family. You'll see a lot of the Medici coat of arms (with the six pills, representing the family's first trade—as doctors, or *medici*). The 12th-century marble pulpit is beautifully carved. All of the apostles are together except Judas, who's under the table with the evil dragon (his name is the only one not carved onto the relief).

Just before the pulpit (in the Rosary Chapel, on the left), check out the *Annunciation* by Fra Bartolomeo (who was a student of Fra Angelico and painted this in 1497). Bartolomeo delicately gives worshippers a way to see Mary "conceived by the Holy Spirit." Note the vibrant colors, exaggerated perspective, and Mary's *contrapposto* pose—all attributes of the Renaissance.

To the right of the main altar is a dreamy painted-and-gilded-wood *Deposition* (Jesus being taken down from the cross), restored to its original form. Painted in 1228, a generation before Giotto, it shows emotion and motion way ahead of its time.

The glowing windows in the transept and behind the altar

are sheets of alabaster. These, along with the recorded Gregorian chants, add to the church's wonderful ambience.

Sacred Art Museum—This humble four-room museum collects sacred art from deconsecrated churches and small, unguarded churches from nearby villages.

Cost and Hours: €10 combo-ticket includes Etruscan Museum and Pinacoteca, daily 9:00-13:00 & 15:00-18:00, morning only in winter, well-explained in English, next to the Duomo at Via Roma 1, tel. 0588-86290.

Pinacoteca—This museum fills a 14th-century palace with fine paintings that feel more Florentine than Sienese—a reminder of whose domain this town was in. Its highlights are Luca Signorelli's beautifully lit *Annunciation,* an example of classic High Renaissance (from the town cathedral), and (to the right) *Deposition from the Cross,* the groundbreaking Mannerist work by Rosso Fiorentino (note the elongated bodies and harsh emotional lighting and colors). Notice also Ghirlandaio's *Christ in Glory.* The two devout-looking kneeling women are actually pagan, pre-Christian Etruscan demigoddesses, Attinea and Greciniana, but the church identified them as obscure saints to make the painting acceptable.

Cost and Hours: €6, €10 combo-ticket includes Etruscan and Sacred Art museums, daily 9:30-19:00, Nov-mid-March until 13:45, Via dei Sarti 1, tel. 0588-87580.

Palazzo Viti—Go behind the rustic, heavy, stone walls of the city and see how the nobility lived (in this case, rich from 19th-century alabaster wealth). One of the finest private residential buildings in Italy, with 12 rooms open to the public, Palazzo Viti feels remarkably lived in because it is. You'll also find Senora Viti herself selling admission tickets. It's no wonder this time warp is so popular with Italian movie directors. Remember, you're helping keep a noble family in leotards.

Cost and Hours: €5 includes a glass of wine, samples of cheese, and olive oil; pick up the loaner English description, April-Oct daily 10:00-13:00 & 14:30-18:30, closed Nov-March, Via dei Sarti 41, tel. 0588-84047, www.palazzoviti.it.

Roman Theater—Built in about 10 B.C., this well-preserved theater is considered to have some of the best acoustics of its kind. Because of the fine aerial view you get from the city wall promenade, you may find it unnecessary to pay admission to enter. Belly up to the 13th-century wall and look down. The wall that you're standing on divided the theater from the town center...so, naturally, the theater became the town dump. Over time, the theater was forgotten—covered in the garbage of Volterra. Luckily, it was rediscovered in the 1950s.

The stage wall was standard Roman design—with three levels

from which actors would appear: one for mortals, one for heroes, and the top one for gods. Parts of two levels still stand. Gods leaped out onto the third level for the last time in the fourth century A.D., when the town decided to abandon the theater and to use its stones to build fancy baths instead. You can see the remains of the baths behind the theater, including the round sauna with brick supports to raise the heated floor.

From the vantage point on the city wall promenade, you can trace Volterra's vast Etruscan wall. Find the church in the distance, on the left, and notice the stones just below. They are from the Etruscan wall that followed the ridge into the valley and defined Volterra five centuries before Christ.

Cost and Hours: €3.50, but you can view the theater free from Via Lungo le Mure, April-Oct daily 10:30-17:30, Nov-March Sat-Sun only 10:00-16:00.

▲▲Etruscan Museum (Museo Etrusco Guarnacci)—Filled top to bottom with rare Etruscan artifacts, this museum—even with few English explanations and its dusty, almost neglectful, old-school style—makes it easy to appreciate how advanced this pre-Roman culture was.

Cost and Hours: €8, €10 combo-ticket includes—like it or not—the Pinacoteca and Sacred Art Museum; daily April-Oct 9:00-19:00, Nov-March 9:00-13:45; ask at the ticket window for mildly interesting English pamphlet, €3 audioguide fleshes out your visit well, Via Don Minzoni 15, tel. 0588-86347, www .comune.volterra.pi.it/english.

Touring the Museum: The collection starts with pre-Etruscan Villanovian artifacts (c. 1500 B.C.), but its highlight is a seemingly endless collection of Etruscan funerary urns (designed to contain the ashes of cremated loved ones).

Each urn is tenderly carved with a unique scene, offering a peek into the still-mysterious Etruscan society. While contempo-

raries of the Greeks, the Etruscans were more libertine. Their religion was less demanding, and their women were a respected part of both the social and public spheres. Women and men alike are depicted lounging on Etruscan urns. While they seem to be just hanging out, the lounging dead were actually offering the gods a banquet—in order to gain their favor in the transition to the next life. The outcome of the banquet had eternal consequences.

On urns dating from the seventh to the first century B.C., the dearly departed are often depicted holding scrolls, blank wax

Under the Etruscan Sun

Around 550 B.C.—just before the Golden Age of Greece—the Etruscan people of central Italy had their own Golden Age. Though their origins are mysterious, their mix of Greek-style art with Roman-style customs helped lay a civilized foundation for the rise of the Roman empire. As you travel through Italy—particularly in Tuscany (from "Etruscan"), Umbria, and North Latium—you'll find traces of the long-lost Etruscans.

The Etruscans first appeared in the ninth century B.C., when a number of cities sprouted up in sparsely populated Tuscany and Umbria. Possibly immigrants from Turkey, but more likely local farmers who moved to the city, they became traders and craftsmen, and welcomed new ideas from Greece.

More technologically advanced than their neighbors, the Etruscans mined metal, exporting it around the Mediterranean, both as crude ingots and as some of the finest-crafted jewelry in the known world. They drained and irrigated large tracts of land, creating the fertile farmland of central Italy's breadbasket. With their disciplined army, warships, merchant vessels, and (from the Greek perspective) pirate galleys, they ruled central Italy and the major ports along the Tyrrhenian Sea. For nearly two centuries (c. 700-500 B.C.), much of Italy lived a Golden Age of peace and prosperity under the Etruscan sun.

Judging from the frescoes and many luxury items that have survived, the Etruscans enjoyed the good life: They look healthy, vibrant, and well-dressed (including the slaves), as they play flutes, dance with birds, or play party games. Etruscan artists celebrated individual people, showing their wrinkles, crooked noses, silly smiles, and funny haircuts.

Thousands of surviving ceramic plates and cups attest to the importance of food. Men and women ate together, propped on their elbows on dining couches, surrounded by colorful decor. The banqueters were entertained with music and dancing, and served by elegant and well-treated slaves.

Scholars today have deciphered the Etruscans' Greek-style alphabet and some individual words, but they have yet to crack the code. Much of what we know of the Etruscans comes from their tombs. The tomb was a home in the hereafter, complete with all of the deceased's belongings. The sarcophagus might have a statue on the lid of the deceased at a banquet—lying across a dining couch, spooning with his wife, smiles on their faces, living the good life for all eternity.

Seven decades of wars with the Greeks (545-474 B.C.) disrupted the trade routes and drained the Etruscan League, just as a new Mediterranean power was emerging: Rome. In 509 B.C., the Romans overthrew their Etruscan king, and Rome expanded, capturing Etruscan cities one by one (the last in 264 B.C.). Etruscan resisters were killed, the survivors intermarried with Romans, and their kids grew up speaking Latin. By Julius Caesar's time, the only remnants of Etruscan culture were its priests, who became

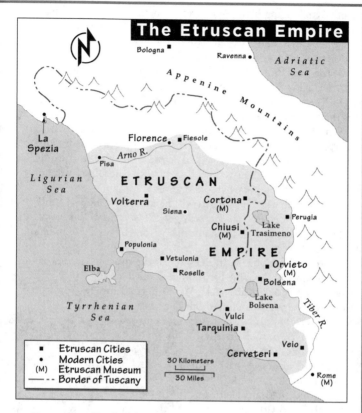

The Etruscan Empire

Rome's professional soothsayers. Interestingly, the Etruscan prophets had foreseen their own demise, having predicted that Etruscan civilization would last 10 centuries.

But Etruscan culture lived on in Roman religion (pantheon of gods, household gods, and divination rituals), art (realism), lifestyle (the banquet), and in a taste for Greek styles—the mix that became our "Western civilization."

Etruscan Sights in Italy

Here are some of the more important and more accessible Etruscan sights:

Rome: Traces of original Etruscan engineering projects (e.g., Circus Maximus), Vatican Museum artifacts, and Villa Giulia Museum, with the famous "husband and wife sarcophagus."

Orvieto: Archaeological Museum (coins, dinnerware, and a sarcophagus), necropolis, and underground tunnels and caves.

Volterra: Etruscan gate (Porta dell'Arco, from fourth century B.C.) and Etruscan Museum (funerary urns).

Chiusi: Museum, tombs, and tunnels.

Cortona: Museum and dome-shaped tombs.

tablets (symbolizing blank new lives in the next world), and libation cups—offering wine to the gods. Realistic scenes show the fabled horseback-and-carriage ride to the underworld, where the dead are greeted by Caron, with his hammer and pointy ears. While the finer urns are carved of alabaster, most are made of volcanic tuff. Most lids are mismatched—casualties of reckless 18th- and 19th-century archaeology. Look at the faces, and imagine the lives they lived and the loved ones they left behind.

On the top floor is a re-created grave site, with several urns and artifacts that would have been buried with the deceased. Some of these were funeral dowry (called *corredo*) that the dead would pack along. You'll see artifacts such as mirrors, coins, hardware for vases, votive statues, pots, pans, and jewelry.

Fans of Alberto Giacometti will be amazed at how the tall, skinny figure called *The Shadow of Night (L'Ombra della Sera)* looks just like the modern Swiss sculptor's work—but is 2,500 years older.

Nearby: After your visit, duck across the street to the alabaster showroom and the wine bar (both described next).

▲**Alabaster Workshop**—Alab'Arte offers a fun peek into the art of alabaster. Their showroom is across from the Etruscan Museum. A block downhill, in front of Porta Marcoli, is their powdery workshop, where you can watch Roberto Chiti and Giorgio Finazzo at work. They are delighted to share their art with visitors. Lighting shows off the translucent quality of the stone and the expertise of these

artists. For more artisans in action, visit "Artisan Lane," described earlier, or ask the TI for their list of the town's many workshops open to the public.

Cost and Hours: Free, showroom—daily 10:30-13:00 & 15:30-19:00, Via Don Minzoni 18; workshop—March-Oct Mon-Sat 9:30-13:00 & 15:00-19:00, closed Sun, usually closed Nov-Feb—call ahead, Via Orti Sant'Agostino 28; tel. 0588-87968, www.alabarte.com.

▲**La Vena di Vino (Wine-Tasting with Bruno and Lucio)**—La Vena di Vino, also just across from the Etruscan Museum, is a fun *enoteca* where two guys have devoted themselves to the wonders of wine and share it with a fun-loving passion. Each day Bruno and Lucio open six or eight bottles, serve your choice by the glass, pair it with characteristic munchies, and offer fine music (guitars available for patrons) and an unusual decor (the place is strewn with bras). Hang out here with the local characters. This is your chance to try the Super Tuscan wine—a creative mix of international grapes grown in Tuscany. According to Bruno, "While the Brunello (€7/glass) is just right for wild boar, the Super Tuscan (€6) is just right for meditation." Food is served all day, including some hot dishes or a plate of meats and cheeses. Although Volterra is famously quiet late at night, this place is full of action. There's a vintage dentist chair attached to the karaoke machine downstairs.

Cost and Hours: Pay per glass, open Wed-Mon 11:30-1:00 in the morning, closed Tue, 3- and 5-glass wine tastings, shipping options available, Via Don Minzoni 30, tel. 0588-81491, www.lavenadivino.com.

Medici Fortress and Archaeological Park—The Parco Archeologico marks what was the acropolis of Volterra from 1500 B.C. until A.D. 1472, when Florence conquered the pesky city and burned its political and historic center, turning it into a grassy commons and building the adjacent Medici Fortezza. The old fortress—a symbol of Florentine dominance—now keeps people in rather than out. It's a maximum-security prison housing only about 60 special prisoners. (When you're driving from San Gimignano to Volterra, you pass another big, modern prison—almost surreal in the midst of all the Tuscan wonder.) Authorities prefer to keep organized crime figures locked up far away from their family ties in Sicily. To the right of the meadows and playground is an archaeological dig, which costs €3 to enter, but can be viewed through a fence for free.

Cost and Hours: Park—free to enter, closes at 20:00 in summer, 17:00 in winter.

Sleeping in Volterra

$$$ Park Hotel Le Fonti, a 10-minute walk downhill from Porta all'Arco, is a spacious, imposing building with 67 rooms, many with views. While overpriced at peak times, the hotel can be a good value if you manage to snag a deal. In addition to the swimming pool, guests can use a small spa with sauna, hot tub, and an intriguing "emotional shower" (Db-€89-165 but prices vary wildly depending on season, elevator, on-site restaurant, wine bar, free parking, Via di Fontecorrenti 5, tel. 0588-85219, fax 0588-92728, www.parkhotellefonti.com, info@parkhotellefonti.com).

$$$ Hotel La Locanda is well-located and rents 18 decent rooms (Db-€93-125, air-con, Wi-Fi, Via Guarnacci 24/28, tel.

VOLTERRA

Sleep Code

(€1 = about $1.40, country code: 39)
S = Single, **D** = Double/Twin, **T** = Triple, **Q** = Quad, **b** = bathroom, **s** = shower only. Unless otherwise noted, credit cards are accepted and breakfast is included (but usually optional). English is generally spoken, but I've noted exceptions.

To help you sort easily through these listings, I've divided the accommodations into three categories based on the price for a double room with bath during high season:

$$$ Higher Priced—Most rooms €100 or more.
 $$ Moderately Priced—Most rooms between €70-100.
  $ Lower Priced—Most rooms €70 or less.

Prices can change without notice; verify the hotel's current rates online or by email. For other updates, see www.ricksteves.com/update.

0588-81547, www.hotel-lalocanda.com, staff@hotel-lalocanda.com, Jenny, Stefania, and Irina).

$$ Albergo Etruria, on Volterra's main drag, rents 21 fresh, modern, and spacious rooms within an ancient stone structure. They have a welcoming TV lounge and a peaceful garden out back (Sb-€75, Db-€95, Tb-€115, 10 percent discount with cash and this book when you book direct, fans, Wi-Fi, Via Matteotti 32, tel. 0588-87377, fax 0588-92784, www.albergoetruria.it, info@albergoetruria.it, Lisa and Giuseppina are fine hosts).

$$ Albergo Villa Nencini, just outside of town, is big, modern, and professional, with 36 fine rooms. A few rooms have terraces and many have views. Guests also enjoy the large pool and free parking (Sb-€67, Db-€88, Tb-€115, 10 percent discount with cash and this book, Borgo Santo Stefano 55, a 15-minute uphill walk to main square, tel. 0588-86386, fax 0588-80601, www.villanencini.it, info@villanencini.it, Nencini family).

$$ Albergo Nazionale, with 38 big rooms, is simple, a little musty, short on smiles, popular with school groups, and steps from the bus stop (Sb-€60-70, Db-€80-90, Tb-€105, 10 percent discount with cash and this book if you book direct, reception closes at midnight, Via dei Marchesi 11, tel. 0588-86284, fax 0588-84097, www.hotelnazionale-volterra.it, info@hotelnazionale-volterra.it).

$ Seminario Vescovile Sant'Andrea has been training priests for more than 500 years. Today, the remaining eight priests still train students, but when classes are over, their 16 rooms—separated by vast and holy halls in an echoing old mansion—are rented very cheaply. Look for the 15th-century Ascension ceramic by Andrea della Robbia, tucked away in a corner upstairs (S-€17, Sb-€22, D-€30, Db-€38, T-€44, Tb-€56, breakfast-€3, elevator, closes at 24:00, groups welcome, free parking, easy 7-minute walk from Etruscan Museum, Viale Vittorio Veneto 2, tel. 0588-86028, semvescovile@diocesivolterra.it; Alberto, Angela, and Sergio).

$ Volterra Youth Hostel fills a wing of the restored Convent of San Girolamo with 85 beds. It's spacious and has lots of services, but it's a 15-minute hike out of town, in a boring area, and no cheaper than the more memorable seminary option closer to town (bed in 6-bed dorm-€17, Db-€60, breakfast-€3, lockers, tel. 0588-86613, www.ostellovolterra.it, info@ostellovolterra.it).

Near Volterra

$$ Podere Marcampo is a newer *agriturismo* about four miles outside Volterra on the road to Pisa. Run by Genuino (owner of the recommended Ristorante Enoteca del Duca) and his wife, this peaceful spot has three well-appointed rooms and three apartments, plus a swimming pool with panoramic views. Genuino produces his award-winning Merlot on site and offers €15 wine-tastings with cheese and homemade salami. Cooking classes are also available (Db-€94, apartment-€125-160, includes breakfast, air-con, Wi-Fi, free parking, tel. 0588-85393, mobile 348-514-9782, www.agriturismo-marcampo.com, info@agriturismo-marcampo.com).

Eating in Volterra

Menus feature a Volterran take on regional dishes. *Zuppa alla Volterrana* is a fresh vegetable-and-bread soup, similar to *ribollita* (except that it isn't made from leftovers). *Torta di ceci*, also known as *cecina*, is a savory-pancake-like dish made with garbanzo beans. Those with more adventurous palates dive into *trippa* (tripe; comes in a bowl like stew), the traditional breakfast of the alabaster carvers.

Ristorante Enoteca del Duca, with a locally respected chef named Genuino, serves well-presented and creative Tuscan cuisine. You can dine under a medieval arch with walls lined with wine bottles, in a stark dining room (with an Etruscan statuette at each table), or on a nice little patio out back. It's a good place for truffles, and has a fine wine list (which includes Genuino's own merlot) and friendly staff. The spacious seating, dressy clientele, and calm atmosphere make this a good choice for a romantic meal (€42 food-sampler fixed-price meal, €10 pastas, €17 *secondi*, Wed-Mon 12:30-15:00 & 19:30-22:00, closed Tue, near City Hall at Via di Castello 2, tel. 0588-81510).

Trattoria da Bado, a 10-minute hike out of town, is every local's favorite for its *tipica cucina Volterrana*. Giacomo and family offer a rustic atmosphere and serve food with no pretense—"the way you wish your mamma cooked" (meals from 12:30 and 19:30, closed Wed, Borgo San Lazzero 9, tel. 0588-86477, reserve before you go as it's often full).

Don Beta is a family-run trattoria on the main drag, popular with travelers for its stylish home cooking. Mirko supervises the lively young team as they whisk out steaming plates of seafood pasta and homemade desserts (€7 pastas, €15 *secondi*, daily 12:00-14:30 & 18:45-22:00, reservations smart, Via Matteotti 39, tel. 0588-86730; Paolo, Azzura, and Mamica).

La Vecchia Lira, bright and cheery, is a classy self-serve eatery that's a hit with locals as a quick and cheap lunch spot by day, and a fancier restaurant at night (Fri-Wed 12:00-14:30 & 19:00-22:30, closed Thu, Via Matteotti 19, tel. 0588-86180, Lamberto and Massimo).

Ristorante il Sacco Fiorentino is a local favorite for traditional cuisine and seasonal seafood specials (€8 pastas, €15 *secondi*, Thu-Tue 12:00-15:00 & 19:00-22:00, closed Wed, Piazza XX Settembre 18, tel. 0588-88537).

La Vena di Vino is an *enoteca* serving up simple and traditional dishes and the best of Tuscan wine in a fun atmosphere (closed Tue, Via Don Minzoni 30, tel. 0588-81491). For more details, read the description on page 218.

Pizzerias: Ombra della Sera dishes out what local kids consider the best pizza in town. At €6 a pop, their pizzas make for a cheap date (Tue-Sun 12:00-15:00 & 19:00-22:00, closed Mon, Via Guarnacci 16, tel. 0588-85274). **Pizzeria Tavernetta**, next door, is more romantic, with delightful indoor and on-the-street seating. Its upstairs has a romantically frescoed dining room. Marco, who looks like Billy Joel, serves €7 pizzas (closed Wed, Via Guarnacci 14, tel. 0588-87630).

Picnic: You can assemble a picnic at the few *alimentari* around town (try Despar Market at Via Gramsci 12, Thu-Tue 7:30-13:00 & 17:00-20:00, Wed only 7:30-13:00) and eat in the breezy Archaeological Park.

Volterra Connections

The nearest train station is in **Saline di Volterra,** a 15-minute bus ride away (7/day, 4/day Sun). In Volterra, buses come and go from Piazza Martiri della Libertà (buy tickets at any tobacco shop).

From Volterra by Bus to: **Florence** (4/day, 1/day Sun, 2 hours, change in Colle Val d'Elsa), **Siena** (4/day, none on Sun, 2 hours, change in Colle Val d'Elsa), **San Gimignano** (4/day, 1/day Sun, 2 hours, change in Colle Val d'Elsa), **Pisa** (9/day, 2 hours, change in Pontedera). For Siena, Florence, and San Gimignano, C.P.T. bus tickets get you only as far as Colle Val d'Elsa (4/day, 50 minutes, €2.75); you must then buy another ticket (from another bus company) at the newsstand near the bus stop.

MOROCCO

The following chapter is excerpted from *Rick Steves' Spain.*

TANGIER

Tanja

Go to Africa. As you step off the boat, you realize that the crossing (less than an hour) has taken you further culturally than did the trip from the US to Spain. Morocco needs no museums; its sights are living in the streets. For decades its once-grand coastal city of Tangier deserved its reputation as the "Tijuana of Africa." But that has changed. The current king is enthusiastic about Tangier, and there's a fresh can-do spirit in the air. The town is as Moroccan as ever...yet more enjoyable and less stressful.

Morocco in a Day?

Though Morocco certainly deserves more than a day, many visitors touring Spain see it in a quick side-trip. And, though such a short sprint through Tangier is only a tease, it's far more interesting than another day in Spain. A day in Tangier gives you a good introduction to Morocco, a legitimate taste of North Africa, and a nonthreatening slice of Islam. All you need is a passport (no visa or shots required) and €67 for the round-trip ferry crossing. Your big decisions: where to sail from; whether to go on your own or buy a ferry/guided tour day-trip package; and whether to make it a day trip or spend the night. Of these, the biggest decision is:

With a Tour or On My Own?: Because the ferry company expects you to do a lot of shopping (providing them with kickbacks), it's actually a bit cheaper to join a one-day tour than to buy a round-trip ferry ticket. The question is: Do you want the safety and comfort of having Morocco handed to you on a user-friendly platter; or do you want the independence to see what you want to see, with a more authentic experience, fewer cultural clichés, and less forced shopping? There are pros and cons to each approach, depending on your travel style. My preferred approach is sort of a hybrid: Go to Morocco "on your own," but arrange in advance to meet up with a local guide to ease your culture shock and accompany you to your choice of sights (I've listed several guides on page 238, or you can book a tour with the ferry company and pay for the "VIP" option). While this costs a bit more than joining a package tour, ultimately the cost difference (roughly €10-20 more per person) is pretty negligible, considering the dramatically increased cultural intimacy. Doing it entirely on your own (no guide at all) can be a great adventure, but potentially more stressful.

Time Difference: Morocco is on Greenwich Mean Time (like Great Britain)—that means one hour behind Spain. It typically observes Daylight Saving Time, but "springs forward" and "falls back" at different times than Europe. In general, Moroccans change their clocks in early April (a week after Spain), then again just before Ramadan (in 2011, that date was July 31—nearly three months before Spain). Therefore, during the summer months, Morocco is either one hour (if they've changed) or two hours (if they haven't changed, or have already changed back) behind Spain. In general, ferry and other schedules use the local time (if your boat leaves Tangier "at 17:00," that means 5:00 p.m. Moroccan time—not Spanish time)...be sure to change your watch when you get off the boat.

Terminology: Note that the Spanish refer to Morocco as "Marruecos" (mar-WAY-kohs) and Tangier as "Tánger" (TAHN-*h*air, with a guttural *h*).

Going on Your Own, by Ferry from Tarifa

While the trip to Tangier can be made from various ports, only the ferry from Tarifa, Spain takes you to Tangier's city-center port, called the Tangier Medina Port (Spaniards call it the *Puerto Viejo*, "Old Port"). Boats from Algeciras or Gibraltar dock instead at the Tangier MED Port (Spaniards call it the *Puerto Nuevo*, "New Port"), about 25 miles east of the city center. (Note: Confusingly, because the city-center port is being remodeled, some Moroccans call it the "new port"—exactly the opposite of the Spaniards.) Tangier's city-center port has been closed to cargo shipping, and is in the midst of a massive renovation and beautification project, which will extend the pier to accommodate large cruise ships and create a marina for yachts. Most sources indicate that ferries from Tarifa will continue to use the city-center port, though it's possible (temporarily—due to construction at the port) that Tarifa ships could be sent to the MED port. I'll describe the trip assuming you're sailing from Tarifa to Tangier's city-center Medina Port— the most logical route for the typical traveler.

Ferry Crossing: Two different companies make essentially

the same 35-minute crossing from Tarifa to Tangier, on alternating hours: **FRS** (tel. 956-684-847, www.frs.es) and **Comarit** (tel. 956-657-462, www.comarit.es). Prices are about the same with either company (€37 one-way, €67 round-trip). Between them, boats leave Tarifa at the top of every hour from about 8:00 to 22:00—so go with the boat that best suits your schedule. For the return trip from Tangier to Tarifa, boats run from about 7:00 to 21:00.

Tickets are very easy to get: You can buy one at the port, through your hotel in Tarifa, from a local travel agency, or at FRS's ticket office in Tarifa. You can almost always just buy a ticket and walk on, though in the busiest summer months (July-Aug), the popular 9:00 departure could be booked up with tours. Boats are most crowded in July (when Moroccans in Spain go home for Ramadan) and in August (when the Costa del Sol groups come en masse). A few crossings a year are canceled because of storms or wind, mostly in winter.

Procedure: The ferry from Tarifa is a fast Nordic hydrofoil that theoretically takes 35 minutes to cross. It often leaves late.

You'll go through Spanish customs at the port and Moroccan customs on the ferry. Whether taking a tour or traveling on your own, you *must* get a stamp (available on board) from the Moroccan immigration officer. After you leave Spain, find the customs desk on the boat, line up, and get your passport and entry paper stamped. If you're coming back the same day and know your return time, the immigration official may also give you an exit stamp (for your return from Morocco), which  prevents delays at the port at departure time. The ferry is equipped with WCs, a shop, and a snack bar. Tarifa's modern little terminal has a cafeteria and WCs.

Hiring a Guide: Even if you're visiting Morocco independently, I recommend hiring a local guide to show you around Tangier (for a list of recommended guides, see "Guides," on page 238).

Tangier MED Port: Ferries from Algeciras and Gibraltar (and, potentially but unlikely, ferries from Tarifa) arrive at the Tangier MED Port, 25 miles from downtown. While this wastes time (it's about an hour each way from the boat to downtown Tangier), the connection is simple: A free shuttle bus picks up passengers at the Tangier MED Port terminal and brings them right to the entrance of the Tangier Medina Port, in the city center. Remember that if you're coming from Tarifa, your ship will most likely dock at the Tangier Medina Port (covered under "Arrival in Tangier—By Ferry," page 235).

Returning to Tarifa: It's smart to return to the port about 20 minutes before your ferry departs. If you didn't get your passport's exit stamp on the way over, you must wait in line to get it stamped at the Tangier ferry terminal before you board the boat.

Taking a Tour

Taking a tour is easier but less rewarding than doing it on your own or with a private guide. A typical day-trip tour includes a round-trip crossing and a guide who meets your big group at a prearranged point in Tangier, then hustles you through the hustlers and onto your tour bus. Several guides await the arrival of each ferry in Tangier and assemble their groups. (Tourists wear stickers identifying which tour they're with.) All offer essentially the same five-hour Tangier experience: a city bus tour, a drive

through the ritzy palace neighborhood, a walk through the Medina (old town), and an overly thorough look at a sales-starved carpet shop (where prices include a 20 percent commission for your guide and tour company; some carpet shops are actually owned by the ferry companies). Longer tours may include a trip to the desolate Atlantic Coast for some rugged African scenery, and the famous ride-a-camel stop (five-minute camel ride for a couple of euros). Any tour wraps up with lunch in a palatial Moroccan setting with live music (and non-Moroccan belly dancing), topped off by a final walk back to your boat through a gauntlet of desperate merchants.

Sound cheesy? It is. But no amount of packaging can gloss over this exotic and different culture. This kind of cultural voyeurism is almost embarrassing, but it's nonstop action.

The day trip is so tightly organized that tourists have hardly any time alone in Tangier. For many people, that's just fine. But frankly, seeing a line of day-trippers clutching their bags nervously like paranoid kangaroos reminded me of a self-imposed hostage crisis. It was pathetic.

You rarely need to book a tour more than a day in advance, even during peak season. Tours generally cost about €60 (less than a round-trip ferry ticket alone—they make their money off commissions if you shop, and get a group rate on the ferry tickets). Prices are roughly the same no matter where you buy. While some agencies run their own tours, others simply sell tickets on excursions operated by the two big ferry companies, FRS and Comarit. If you're choosing between these two companies, the more-established FRS has a better reputation for tours than the cheaper, newer Comarit. But ultimately, it's the luck of the draw as to which guide you're assigned. Don't worry about which tour company you select. (They're all equally bad.)

Tours leave Tarifa on a variable schedule: For example, one tour may depart at 9:00 and return at 15:00, the next could run 11:00-19:00 (offering a longer experience), and the next 13:00-19:00. If you're an independent type on a one-day tour, you could stay with your group until you return to the ferry dock, and then just slip back into town on your own, thinking, "Freedom!" You're welcome to use your return ferry ticket on any later boat run by the same company (FRS or Comarit; each has departures every two hours).

You can pay extra for various add-ons. For an extra €15 per person beyond the cost of a standard tour, they will arrange a **"VIP tour"** for up to four people—you'll get a private guide and vehicle, plus lunch. This is actually quite economical, especially if you're traveling as a foursome and would prefer a more personalized experience.

If you want a longer visit, it's cheap to book a package through the ferry company that includes staying in a Tangier hotel for one night (only €30-35 more than the regular tour, €10 extra in peak season, includes guiding and 2 lunches and 1 dinner). If you stay overnight, the first day is the same as the one-day tour, but rather than catching the boat that afternoon, you take the same boat—on your own—24 hours later. There's also a two-day option that includes no guiding or meals (€25-30 more than regular tour, €12 extra in peak season).

Booking a Tour: If you're taking one of these tours, you may as well book direct with the **ferry company** (see contact information earlier, under "Ferry Crossing," or visit their offices at the port in Tarifa), or through your **hotel** (you'll pay the same, but the hotel gets a commission; if you know you want to visit Morocco with a tour, ask your hotel to book it when you reserve). There's not much reason to book with a **travel agency,** but offices all over southern Spain and in Tarifa sell ferry tickets and seats on tours. In Tarifa, Luís and Antonio at Baelo Tour offer my readers a 10 percent discount (daily in summer 7:40-21:00, across from TI at Avenida de la Constitución 5, tel. 956-681-242); other Tarifa-based agencies are Tarifa Travel and Travelsur (both on Avenida de Andalucía, above the old-town walls).

Tangier

Artists, writers, and musicians have always loved Tangier. Delacroix and Matisse were drawn by its evocative light. The Beat generation, led by William S. Burroughs and Jack Kerouac, sought the city's multicultural, otherworldly feel. Paul Bowles found his sheltering sky here. From the 1920s through the 1950s, Tangier was an "international city," too strategic to give to any one nation, and jointly governed by as many as nine different powers, including France, Spain, Britain, Italy, Belgium, the Netherlands...and Morocco. The city was a tax-free zone (since there was no single authority to collect taxes), which created a booming free-for-all atmosphere, attracting playboy millionaires, bon vivants, globetrotting scoundrels, con artists, and expat romantics. Tangier enjoyed a cosmopolitan golden age that, in many ways, shaped the city visitors see today.

Tangier is always defying expectations. Ruled by Spain in the 19th century and France in the 20th, it's a rare place where signs are in three languages...and English doesn't make the cut. In this Muslim city, you'll find a synagogue, Catholic and Anglican churches, and the town's largest mosque in close proximity.

Because of its "international zone" status, Morocco's previous king effectively disowned the city, denying it national funds for improvements. Over time, neglected Tangier became the armpit of Morocco. But when the new king—Mohammed VI—was crowned in 1999, the first city he visited was Tangier. His vision is to restore Tangier to its former glory. Prodding his countrymen with the slogan "Morocco is moving," he's nudging the country into the future.

Thanks to King Mohammed VI, Tangier (with a population of 700,000 and growing quickly) is experiencing a rebirth. While the city has a long way to go, restorations are taking place on a grand scale: The beach has been painstakingly cleaned, pedestrian promenades are popping up, and gardens bloom with lush new greenery. A brand-new futuristic soccer stadium opened in 2011, and the city-center port is being converted into a huge, slick leisure-craft complex that will handle cruise megaships, yachts, and ferries from Tarifa.

I'm uplifted by the new Tangier—it's affluent and modern without having abandoned its roots and embraced Western values. Many visitors are impressed by the warmth of the Moroccan people. Notice how they touch their right hand to their heart after shaking hands or saying, "thank you"—a kind gesture meant to emphasize sincerity. (In Islam, the right hand is holy, while the left hand is evil. Moroccans who eat with their hands—as many civilized people do in this part of the world—always eat with their right hand; the left hand is for washing.)

A visit to Morocco—so close to Europe, yet embracing the Arabic language and script and Muslim faith—lets a Westerner marinated in anti-Muslim propaganda see what Islam aspires to be and can be...and realize it is not a threat.

Planning Your Time

If you're not on a package tour, pre-arrange for a guide to meet you at the ferry dock (see "Guides," later), hire a guide upon arrival, or head on your own to the big square called the Grand Socco to get oriented (you can walk or catch a Petit Taxi from the port to the Grand Socco). Get your bearings with my Grand Socco spin-tour, then delve into the old town (the lower Medina, with the Petit Socco, market, and American Legation Museum; and the upper Medina's Kasbah, with its museum and residential lanes). With more time, take a taxi to sightsee along the beach and then along Avenue Mohammed VI, through the urban new town, and back to the port. You'll rarely see other tourists outside the tour-group circuit.

After Dark: Nighttime is great in Tangier. If you're spending the night, don't relax in a fancy hotel restaurant. Get out and about in the old town after dark. It's an entirely different experience and a highlight of any visit. (But remember, this isn't night-owl Spain—things die down by around 22:00.)

Orientation to Tangier

Like almost every city in Morocco, Tangier is split in two: old and new. From the ferry dock you'll see the old town (Medina)—

encircled by its medieval wall— on your right, behind Hotel Continental. The old town has the markets, the Kasbah (with its palace and the mosque of the Kasbah—marked by the higher of the two minarets you see), cheap hotels, characteristic guest houses, homes both decrepit and recently renovated, and 2,000 wannabe guides. The twisty, hilly streets of the old town are caged within a wall accessible by keyhole gates. The larger minaret (on the left) belongs to the modern Mohammed

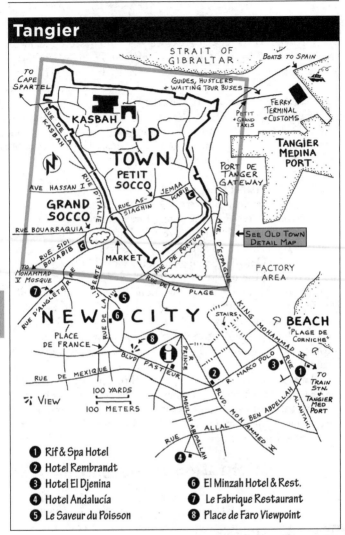

Tangier

- ❶ Rif & Spa Hotel
- ❷ Hotel Rembrandt
- ❸ Hotel El Djenina
- ❹ Hotel Andalucía
- ❺ Le Saveur du Poisson
- ❻ El Minzah Hotel & Rest.
- ❼ Le Fabrique Restaurant
- ❽ Place de Faro Viewpoint

V mosque—the biggest one in town.

The new town, with the TI and modern international-style hotels, sprawls past the industrial port zone to your left. The big square, Grand Socco, is the hinge between the old and new parts of town.

Note that while tourists (and this guidebook) refer to the twisty old town as "the Medina," locals consider both the old and new parts of the city center to be medinas.

Tangier is the fifth-largest city in Morocco, and many visitors assume they'll get lost here. While the city could use more street signs, it's laid out simply—although once you enter the mazelike Medina, all bets are off. Nothing listed under "Sights in Tangier" is more than a 20-minute walk from the port. Petit Taxis (described later, under "Getting Around Tangier") are a remarkably cheap godsend for the hot and tired tourist. Use them liberally.

Because so many different colonial powers have had a finger in this city, it goes by many names: In English, it's Tangier (or Tangiers); in French, Tanger (tahn-zhay); in Arabic, it's Tanja (TAHN-zhah); in Spanish, Tánger (TAHN-hair, with a guttural *h*); and so on. Unless you speak Arabic, French is the handiest second language, followed by Spanish and (finally) English.

Tourist Information

The TI, about a 15-minute gradual uphill walk from the Grand Socco, is not particularly helpful (English is in short supply, but a little French goes a long way). But at least you can pick up a free town brochure—in French only—with a town map (Mon-Fri 8:30-16:30, closed Sat-Sun, in new town at Boulevard Pasteur 29, tel. 0539-94-80-50). There's also a TI desk at the Tangier MED Port, and there may be one at the city-center Tangier Medina Port in the future.

The urban area around the Tangier TI has a few interesting features. The yellow building across the small street from the TI (toward the Grand Socco) is a synagogue. A block farther is the beautiful Place de Faro terrace, with its cannons and views back to Spain. (Nicknamed "Terrace of the Lazy Ones," this momentum-killing spot is usually lined with men relaxing and enjoying the views.) Beyond that, Rue de la Liberté leads directly into the Grand Socco square, the hub of old Tangier.

Arrival in Tangier
By Ferry

If you're taking a tour, just follow the leader. If you're on your own, you'll want to head for the Grand Socco to get oriented. You can

either take a taxi (cheap) or walk (about 10 gently uphill minutes through the colorful but confusing lanes of the Medina). Note that the entire port area is slated for an extensive reconstruction in the coming years, so you may find some changes from the way things are described here.

A small blue **Petit Taxi** is your easiest way to get from the port into town (described later, under "Getting Around Tangier"); unfortunately, prices are not regulated from the port. An honest cabbie will charge you 10 dh (about $1.25) for a ride from the ferry into town; less scrupulous drivers will try to charge closer to 100 dh. Set your price before hopping in.

To **walk** into town, head out through the port entrance checkpoint (by the mosque) and bear left at the stubby wall, passing the big bus parking lot and the white Hotel Continental on your right-hand side. After a few minutes, at the end of the bus lot, look for a mosque's white minaret with green tile high on the hill, and head toward it by going up the street just beyond the long, high white wall (behind the buses). Go through the yellow gateway (Bab Dar Dbagh) marked *1921* and *1339*. Bear right/uphill at the T-intersection, then turn left/uphill on Rue de la Marine. You'll pass a school on the right, then the mosque with the green minaret on your left. Continue straight up to the café-lined Petit Socco square, then continue to the top of the street and turn left before the white gate to enter the Grand Socco. Leave mental breadcrumbs as you walk, so you can find your way back to your boat.

By Plane

The Tangier Airport (Aeroport Ibn Battouta) is very new-feeling, slick, and well-organized, with ATMs, cafés, and other amenities. Iberia, Royal Air Maroc, easyJet, and Ryanair fly from here to Madrid (easyJet also has a route to Paris). Jet4you, another low-cost airline, is based in Casablanca, but offers flights from Tangier to Barcelona and Brussels (www.jet4you.com). To get into downtown Tangier, taxis should run you about 150 dh and take 30-45 minutes.

Getting Around Tangier

There are two types of taxis: Avoid the big, beige Mercedes "Grand Taxis," which are the most aggressive and don't use their meters (they're designed for longer trips outside of the city center, but have been known to take tourists for a ride in town...in more ways than one). Look instead for Petit Taxis—blue with a yellow stripe (they fit up to three people). These generally use their meters, are very cheap, and only circulate within the city. However, at the port, Petit Taxis are allowed to charge whatever you'll pay without using the meter, so it's essential to agree on a price up front (see "Arrival in Tangier," earlier).

Be aware that Tangier taxis "double up"—if you're headed somewhere, the driver may pick up someone else who's going in the same direction. However, in this case you don't get to split the fare—each of you pays full price (even though sometimes the other passenger's route takes you a bit out of your way).

Women in Morocco

Most visitors to Tangier expect to see the women completely covered head-to-toe by their kaftans. In fact, only about one-

quarter of Moroccan women still adhere strictly to this religious code. Some just cover their head (allowing their face to be seen), while others eliminate the head scarf altogether. Some women wear only Western-style clothing. This change in dress visibly reflects deeper, more fundamental shifts in Moroccan attitudes about women's rights.

Morocco happens to be one of the most progressive Muslim countries around. As in any border country, contact with other cultures fosters the growth of new ideas. Bombarded with Spanish television and visitors like you, change is inevitable. Another proponent of change is King Mohammed VI, who was only 35 years old when he rose to the throne in 1999. For the first time in the country's history, the king personally selected a female adviser to demonstrate his commitment to change. The king also married a commoner for...get this...*love*. And even more shocking, she's seen in public. (It's a first—locals don't even know what King Mohammed VI's mother looks like, as she is never in the public view.)

Recent times have brought even more sweeping transformations to Moroccan society. In order to raise literacy levels and understanding between the sexes, schools are now co-ed—something taken for granted in the West for decades. In 2004, the Mudawana, or judiciary family code, was shockingly overhauled. The legal age for women to marry is now 18 (just like men) instead of 15. Other changes make it more difficult to have a second wife. Verbal divorce and abandonment are no longer legal—disgruntled husbands must now take their complaints to court before divorce is granted. And for the first time, women can divorce their husbands. If children are involved, whoever takes care of the kids gets the house. Of course, not everyone has been happy with the changes, and Islamic fundamentalists were blamed for a series of bombings in Casablanca in 2003. But the reforms became law, and Morocco became a trendsetter for women's equality in the Islamic world.

Helpful Hints

Money: While most businesses happily take euros or dollars, it's classier to use the local currency—and you'll save money. If you're on a tour, they'll rip you off anyway, so just stick with euros. If you're on your own, it's fun to get a pocket full of dirhams.

A few ATMs are around the Grand Socco (look for one just to the left of the archway entrance into the Medina); more are opposite the TI along Boulevard Pasteur. ATMs work as you expect them to. Exchange desks are quick, easy, and fair. (Just understand the buy-and-sell rates—there should be no other fee. If you change €50 into dirhams and immediately change the dirhams back, you should have about €45.) Look for the official *Bureaux de Change* offices, where you'll get better rates than at the banks. There are some on Rue Pasteur, and a handful between the Grand and Petit Soccos. The official change offices all offer the same rates, so there's no need to shop around.

Convert your dirhams back to euros before catching the ferry—it's cheap and easy to do here (change desks at the port keep long hours), but very difficult once you're back in Spain.

Navigation: Tangier's maps and street signs are frustrating. I ask in French for the landmark: *Où est...?* ("Where is...?," pronounced oo ay, as in *"oo ay Medina?"* or *"oo ay Kasbah?"*). It can be fun to meet people this way. However, most people who offer to help you (especially those who approach you) are angling for a tip—young and old, locals see dollar signs when a traveler approaches. To avoid getting unwanted company, ask for directions only from people who can't leave what they're doing (such as the only clerk in a shop) or from women who aren't near men. There are fewer hustlers in the new (but less interesting) part of town. Be aware that most people don't know the names of the smaller streets (which don't usually have signs), and tend to navigate by landmarks. In case you get the wrong directions, ask three times and go with the consensus. If there's no consensus, it's time to hop into a Petit Taxi.

Mosques: Tangier's mosques (and virtually all of Morocco's) are closed to non-Muslim visitors.

Guides

If you're on your own, you'll be to street guides what a horse's tail is to flies...all day long. Seriously—it can be exhausting to constantly deflect come-ons from anyone who sees you open a guidebook. In order to have your own translator, and a shield from less scrupulous touts who hit up tourists constantly throughout the old town, I recommend hiring a guide. Stress your interest in the people and culture rather than shopping. Guides, hoping to get a huge commission from your purchases, can cleverly turn your Tangier day into the Moroccan equivalent of  the Shopping Channel. Truth be told, some of these guides would work for free, considering all the money they make on commissions when you buy stuff.

I've worked with a variety of guides who speak great English, are easy to get along with, will meet you at the ferry dock, and charge fixed rates. They've promised me they won't make you do any more shopping than you want to—so be very clear about your interests. If one of these guides is busy (or takes a long time responding to your email), try the others. Any of these guides will make your Tangier experience more enjoyable for a negligible cost. They can also book your ferry tickets for the same cost as booking direct: They'll give you a reference number to give at the ticket office in Tarifa, then you'll pay them for the tickets when you meet in Tangier. While each has their own specific itineraries, the two basic options are more or less the same: a half-day walking tour around the Medina and Kasbah (generally 3-5 hours); or a full-day "grand tour" that includes the walk around town as well as a mini-bus ride to outlying viewpoints—the Caves of Hercules and Cape Spartel (7-8 hours, generally also includes lunch at your expense in a restaurant the guide suggests). Prices are fairly standard from guide to guide. If you're very pleased with your guide, he'll appreciate a tip.

Aziz Begdouri, who enjoys teaching about Moroccan society and culture, has been a big help to me with my guidebook-writing and TV production in Tangier (half-day walking tour-€15/person, groups limited to 4-5 people; 8-hour grand tour-€35/person; mobile 06-6163-9332, from Spain dial 00-212-6-6163-9332, aziz tour@hotmail.com).

Ahmed Taoumi, who has been guiding for more than 30 years, is a great teacher—almost professorial—but also a good storyteller and fun to be around. He takes pride in tailoring his tours to his customers' interest (half-day walking tour-€18/person, full-day grand tour with minibus-€35/person, also offers mini-bus side-trips to nearby destinations and discounted ferry tickets, mobile 06-6166-5429, from Spain dial 00-212-6-6166-5429, www .visitangier.com, taoumitour@hotmail.com,).

If Aziz Begdouri and Ahmed are both busy, consider one of

TANGIER

the following youthful go-getters who are a bit lighter on information, but enjoyable to spend time with and dedicated to making visitors comfortable: **Aziz Benami** (half-day walking tour-€15/person; all-day minibus and walking tour-€79/person, price includes ferry tickets from Spain; mobile 06-6126-3335, from Spain dial 00-212-6-6126-3335, www.tangierprivateguide.com, info@tangierprivateguide.com) and **Abdellatif ("Latif") Chebaa** (half-day walking tour-€15/person, grand tour-€35/person, mobile 06-6107-2014, from Spain dial 00-212-6-6107-2014, visittangier @gmail.com).

Other Options: If you don't want to plan too far ahead, and any guide will do, you can book a **"VIP" tour** through the ferry companies in Tarifa for approximately the same prices listed above (for details, see page 231). I've also had good luck with the **private guides who meet the boat.** If you're a decent judge of character, try interviewing guides when you get off the ferry to find one you click with, then negotiate a good price. These hardworking, English-speaking, and licensed guides offer their services for the day for €15.

Sights in Tangier

▲▲The Grand Socco

This big, bustling square is a transportation hub, market, popular meeting point, and the fulcrum between the new town and the

old town (Medina). Five years ago, it was a pedestrian nightmare and a perpetual traffic jam. But now, like much of Tangier, it's on the rise. Many of the sights mentioned in this spin-tour are described in more detail later in this chapter.

◐ **Self-Guided Spin Tour:** The Grand Socco is a good place to get oriented to the heart of Tangier. Stand on the square between the fountain and the mosque (the long building with arches and the tall tower). We'll do a slow clockwise spin.

Start by facing the **mosque**— newly remodeled with a long arcade of keyhole arches, and with a colorfully tiled minaret. Morocco is a decidedly Muslim nation, though its take on Islam is progressive, likely owing to the

Tangier's Old Town

NOTE: TANGIER'S OLD TOWN (MEDINA) IS A MAZE OF TINY STREETS. ONLY MAJOR STREETS ARE SHOWN.

TO CAPE SPARTEL

KASBAH GATE

PLACE DU TABOR

STRAIT OF GIBRALTAR

100 YARDS

100 METERS

TOWN WALLS

R. RIAD

SULTAN

Museum

KASBAH

PLACE DE LA KASBAH

TO PORT

VIEW

R. JEN. CAPTAN RAISSOULI

DAR EL BAROUD

BAB EL-MARSA (GATE)

GERMAN GRAVES

OLD

R. ALMANZOR

TORRES

ALMOHADES

COMM.

JEMAA EL-KEBIR

Mosque

MENDOUBIA GARDENS

Gate

RUE D'ITALIE

RUE AS-SIAGHIN

PETIT SOCCO

MOKHTAR AHARDAN

TOWN

R. BOUARRAQUIA

SIDI BOUABIB

Mosque

GRAND SOCCO

TOUAHINE

PORT DE TANGER GATEWAY

D'ANGLETERRE

RUE DE LA PLAGE

RUE DE PORTUGAL

DCH

R. DE LA LIBERTE

JEWISH CEMETERY

TO BEACH PROMENADE & TANGIER MED PORT

NEW TOWN

TANGIER

❶ Dar Chams Tanja
❷ La Maison Blanche
❸ La Tangerina
❹ Dar Nour
❺ Dar Sultan
❻ Hotel Continental
❼ Maison Communitaire des Femmes (Café)
❽ Le Salon Bleu Restaurant
❾ Le Nabab Restaurant
❿ Hamadi Restaurant
⓫ Marhaba Palace Restaurant
⓬ Mamounia Palace Rest.
⓭ Tangier American Legation Mus.
⓮ Cinema Rif
⓯ Anglican Church
⓰ Market
⓱ Bureau de Change

country's crossroads history. For example, women are relatively free to dress as they like. Five times a day, you'll hear the call to prayer echo across the rooftops of Tangier, from minarets like this one. Unlike many Muslim countries, Morocco doesn't allow non-Muslims to enter its mosques (with the exception of its biggest and most famous one, in Casablanca). This custom may have originated decades ago, when occupying French foreign legion troops spent the night in a mosque, entertaining themselves with wine and women. Following this embarrassing desecration, it was the French government—not the Moroccans—who instituted the ban that persists today.

Locals say that in this very cosmopolitan city, anytime you see a mosque, you'll find a church nearby. Sure enough, peeking up behind the mosque, you can barely make out the white, crenellated top of the **Anglican Church**'s tower (or at least the English flag above it—a red cross on a white field). A fascinating architectural hybrid of Muslim and Christian architecture, this house of worship is well worth a visit.

Also behind the mosque, you can see parts of a sprawling **market.** (This features mostly modern goods; the far more colorful produce, meat, and fish market is across the square.) Those market stalls used to fill the square you're standing in; traditionally the Grand Socco was Tangier's hub for visiting merchants. The gates of town would be locked each evening, and vendors who did not arrive in time spent the night in this area. (Nearby were many caravanserai, old-fashioned inns.) But a few years ago, this square was dramatically renovated by the visionary king, Mohammed VI, and given a new name: "April 9th Square," commemorating the date in 1947 when an earlier king, Mohammed V, appealed to his French overlords to grant his country its independence. (France eventually complied, peacefully, in 1956.) In just the last few years, Mohammed VI tamed the traffic, added the fountain you're standing next to (there was never a fountain here before), and turned this into a delightfully people-friendly space.

Spin a few more degrees to the right, where you'll see the crenellated gateway marked *Tribunal de Commerce*—the entrance to the **Mendoubia Garden,** a pleasant park with a gigantic tree and a quirky history that reflects the epic story of Tangier (particularly from the 1920s to the 1950s, when multiple foreign powers shared control of this city). At the top of the garden gateway, notice the Moroccan flag: a green five-pointed star on a red field. The five points of the star represent the five pillars of Islam; green is the color of peace; and red represents the struggles of hard-fought Moroccan history.

Spinning farther right, you'll see the **keyhole arch** marking the entrance to the Medina. (If you need cash, notice the exchange booths and ATM just to the left of this gateway.) To reach the heart of the Medina—the Petit Socco (the café-lined little brother of the square you're on now)—go through this arch and take the first right.

In front of the arch, you'll likely see **day laborers** looking for work. Each one stands next to a symbol of the kind of work he specializes in: a bucket of paintbrushes for a painter, a coil of wiring for an electrician, and a loop of hose for a plumber.

Speaking of people looking for work, how many locals have offered to show you around ("Hey! What you looking for? I help you!") since you've been standing here, holding this guidebook? Get used to it. While irritating, it's understandable. To these very poor people, you're impossibly rich—your pocket change is at least a good day's wage. If someone pesters you, you can simply ignore them, or say *"Lah shokran"* (No, thank you). But be warned: The moment you engage them, you've just prolonged the sales pitch.

Back to our spin-tour: To the right of the main arch, and just before the row of green rooftops, is the low-profile entrance to the **market** *(souk).* A barrage on all the senses, this is a fascinating place to explore. The row of green rooftops leads toward Rue de la Plage, with more market action.

Continue spinning another quarter-turn to the tall, white building at the top of the square labeled **Cinema Rif.** This historic movie house still plays films (in Arabic and French). The street to the left of the cinema takes you to Rue de la Liberté, which eventually leads through the modern town to the TI (about a 15-minute walk). Just to the right of the cinema, notice the yellow terrace, which offers the best view over the Grand Socco (just go up the staircase). It's also part of a café, where you can order a Moroccan tea (green tea, fresh mint, and lots of sugar), enjoy the view over the square, and plot your next move.

Near the Grand Socco

These sights are near the Grand Socco, but still outside the Medina (old town).

▲**Anglican Church**—St. Andrew's Anglican Church, tucked behind a showpiece mosque, embodies Tangier's mingling of Muslim and Christian tradition. The land on which the church sits was a gift from the sultan to the British community in 1881, during

Queen Victoria's era. Shortly thereafter, this church was built. Although fully Christian, the church is designed in the style of a Muslim mosque. The Lord's Prayer rings the arch in Arabic, as verses of the Quran would in a mosque. Knock on the door—Ali or his son Yassin will greet you and give you a "thank you very much" tour (a tip of about 20 dh is appreciated; daily 9:00-18:00 except closed during Sunday services). The garden surrounding the church is a tranquil, parklike cemetery.

Mendoubia Garden—This pleasant park, through the castle-like archway off of the Grand Socco, is a favorite place for locals to hang out, but also has a surprising history.

Walk through the gateway to see the trunk of a gigantic banyan tree, which, according to local legend, dates from the 12th century. Notice how the extra supportive roots have grown from the branches down to the ground. The large building to the left—today the business courthouse *(Tribunal de Commerce)*—was built to house the representative of the Moroccan king, back in the early 20th century when Tangier was ruled as a protectorate of various European powers and needed an ambassador of sorts to keep an eye out for Moroccan interests. The smaller house on the right (behind the giant tree) is currently the marriage courthouse (used exclusively for getting married or divorced), but it was once the headquarters of the German delegation in Tangier. France originally kept Germany out of the protectorate arrangement by giving them the Congo. But in 1941, when Germany was on the rise in Europe and allied with Spain's Franco, it joined the mix of ruling powers in Tangier. Although Germans were only here for a short time (until mid-1942), they had a small cemetery in what's now the big park in front of you. If you go up the stairs and around the blocky Arabic monument, at the bases of the trees beyond it you'll find headstones of German graves...an odd footnote in the very complex history of this intriguing city.

The Medina (Old Town)

Tangier's Medina is its convoluted old town—a twisty mess of narrow stepped lanes, dead-end alleys, and lots of local life spilling out into the streets. It's divided roughly into two parts: the lower

Medina, with the Petit Socco, market, American Legation, and bustling street life; and, at the top, the more tranquil Kasbah.

The Lower Medina and Petit Socco

A maze of winding lanes and tiny alleys weave through the old-town market area.

Petit Socco—This little square, also called Souk Dahel ("Inner Market"), is the center of the lower Medina. Lined with tea shops and cafés, it has a romantic quality that has long made it a people magnet. In the 1920s, it was the meeting point for Tangier's wealthy and influential elite; by the 1950s and '60s, it drew Jack Kerouac and his counterculture buddies. Nursing a coffee or a mint tea here, it's easy to pretend you're a Beat Generation rebel, dropping out from Western society and delving deeply into an exotic, faraway culture. More recently, filmmakers have been drawn here. Scenes from both *The Bourne Ultimatum* and *Inception* were filmed on the streets between the Grand and Petit Soccos.

The Petit Socco is ideal for some casual people-watching over a drink. You can go to one of the more traditional cafés, but Café Central—with the modern awning—is the most accessible, and therefore the most commercialized and touristy (7-12-dh coffee drinks, 20-45-dh meals, daily 6:00-24:00).

▲▲Market (Souk)—The Medina's market, just off the Grand Socco, is a highlight. Wander past piles of fruit, veggies, and olives, countless varieties of bread, and fresh goat cheese wrapped in palm leaves. Phew! You'll find everything but pork.

Entering the market through the door from the Grand Socco, turn right to find butchers, a cornucopia of produce (almost all of it from Morocco), more butchers, piles of olives, and yet more butchers. The chickens are plucked and hung to show they have been killed according to Islamic guidelines (Halal): Animals are slaughtered with a sharp knife in the name of Allah, head to Mecca, and drained of their blood. The far aisle (parallel and to the left of where you're walking) has more innards and is a little harder to stomach.

You'll see women vendors wearing straw hats decorated with ribbons, and often also striped skirts, scattered around the market; these are Berbers from the nearby Rif mountains. (Before taking photos of these women, or any people you see here, it's polite to ask permission.)

TANGIER

Eventually you'll emerge into the large white market of fish-sellers; with the day's catch from both the Mediterranean and the Atlantic, this is like a textbook of marine life. The door at the far end of the fish market pops you out on the Rue Salah El-dine Al Ayoubi; a right turn takes you back to the Grand Socco, but a left turn leads to the (figurative and literal) low end of the market—a world of very rustic market stalls under a corrugated plastic roof. While just a block from the main market, this is a world apart, and not to everyone's taste. Here you'll find cheap produce, junk shops, electronics (such as recordable CDs and old remote controls), old ladies sorting bundles of herbs from crinkled plastic bags, and far less sanitary-looking butchers than the ones inside the main market hall (if that's possible). Peer down the alley filled with a twitching poultry market, which encourages vegetarianism.

The upper part of the market (toward the Medina and Petit Socco) has a few food stands, but more non-perishable items, such as clothing, cleaning supplies, toiletries, and prepared foods. Scattered around this part of the market are spice and herb stalls (usually marked *hérboriste*), offering a fragrant antidote to the meat stalls. In addition to cooking spices, these sell homegrown Berber cures for ailments. Pots hold a dark-green gelatinous goo—a kind of natural soap.

If you're looking for souvenirs, you won't have to find them... they'll find you, in the form of aggressive salesmen who approach you on the street and push their conga drums, T-shirts, and other trinkets in your face. Most of the market itself is more focused on locals, but the Medina streets just above the market are loaded with souvenir shops. Aside from the predictable trinkets, the big-ticket items here are tilework (such as vases) and carpets. You'll notice many shops have tiles and other, smaller souvenirs on the ground floor, and carpet salesrooms upstairs.

▲▲▲Exploring the Medina

—Appealing as the market is, one of the most evocative Tangier experiences is to simply lose yourself in the lanes of the Medina. A first-time visitor cannot stay oriented—so don't even try. I just wander, knowing that uphill will eventually get me to the Kasbah and downhill will eventually lead me to the port. Expect to get a little lost...going around in circles is part of the fun. Pop in to see artisans working in their shops: mosaic tile-makers, thread spinners, tailors. While shops are on the ground

Bargaining Basics

No matter what kind of merchandise you buy in Tangier, the shopping is...Moroccan. Bargain hard! The first price you're offered is simply a starting point, and it's expected that you'll try to talk the price way down. Bargaining can become an enjoyable game if you follow a few basic rules:

Determine what the item is worth to you. Before you even ask a price, decide what the item's value is to you. Consider the hassles involved in packing it or shipping it home.

Determine the merchant's lowest price. Many merchants will settle for a nickel profit rather than lose the sale entirely. Work the cost down to rock bottom, and when it seems to have fallen to a record low, walk away. That last price the seller hollers out as you turn the corner is often the best price you'll get. If the price is right, go back and buy.

Look indifferent. As soon as the merchant perceives the "I gotta have that!" in you, you'll never get the best price.

Employ a third person. Use your friend who is worried about the ever-dwindling budget or who doesn't like the price or who is bored and wants to return to the hotel. This trick can work to bring the price down faster.

Show the merchant your money. Physically hold out your money and offer him "all you have" to pay for whatever you are bickering over. He'll be tempted to just grab your money and say, "Oh, OK."

If the price is too much, leave. Never worry about having taken too much of the merchant's time. They are experts at making the tourist feel guilty for not buying. It's all part of the game.

level, the family usually lives upstairs.

Many people can't afford private ovens, phones, or running water, so there are economical communal options: phone desks (called *teleboutiques*), baths, and bakeries. If you smell the aroma of baking bread, look for a hole-in-the-wall bakery, where locals drop off their ready-to-cook dough (as well as meat, fish, or nuts to roast). You'll also stumble upon

communal taps, with water provided by the government, where people come to wash. Cubby-hole rooms are filled with kids playing video games on old TVs—they can't afford their own at home, so they come here instead.

Go on a photo safari for ornate "keyhole" doors, many of which lead to neighborhood mosques. Green doors are the color of Islam and symbolize peace. The ring-shaped door knockers double as a place to hitch a donkey.

As you explore, notice that some parts of the Medina seem starkly different, with fancy wrought-iron balconies. This is the approximately 20 percent of the town that was built and controlled by Spaniards and Portuguese living here (with the rest being Arabic and Berber). The two populations were separated by a wall, the remains of which you can still trace running through the Medina. It may seem at first glance that these European zones are fancier and "nicer" compared to the poorer-seeming Arabic/Berber zones. But the Arabs and Berbers take more care with the inside of their homes—if you went behind these humble walls, you'd be surprised how pleasant the interiors are. While European cultures externalize resources, Arab and Berber cultures internalize them.

Tangier American Legation Museum—Located at the bottom end of the Medina (just above the port), this unexpected museum is worth a visit. Morocco was one of the first countries to recognize the newly formed United States as an independent country (in 1777). The original building, given to the United States by the sultan of Morocco, became the fledgling government's first foreign acquisition.

This was the US embassy (or consulate) in Morocco from 1821 to 1961, and it's still American property—our only National Historic Landmark overseas. Today this nonprofit museum and research center, housed in a 19th-century mansion, is a strangely peaceful oasis within Tangier's intense old town. It offers a warm welcome and lots of interesting artifacts—all well-described in English in an evocative building. The ground floor is filled with an art gallery. In the stairwell, you'll see photos of kings with presidents, and a letter with the news of Lincoln's assassination. Upstairs are more paintings, as well as model soldiers playing out two battle scenes from Moroccan history. These belonged to American industrialist Malcolm Forbes, who had a home in Tangier (his son donated these dioramas to the museum). Rounding out the upper floor are more paintings, and evocative old maps of Tangier and Morocco. A visit here is a fun reminder of how long the US and Morocco have had good relations.

Cost and Hours: Free entry but donations appreciated, Mon-Thu 10:00-13:00 & 15:00-17:00, Fri 10:00-12:00 & 15:00-17:00, during Ramadan holiday 10:00-15:00, closed Sat-Sun, ring bell, Rue d'Amérique 8, tel. 0539-935-317, www.legation.org.

• *When you've soaked in enough old-town atmosphere, make your way to the Kasbah (see map, page 241). Within the Medina, head uphill, or exit the Medina gate and go right on Rue de la Kasbah, which follows the old wall uphill to Bab Kasbah (a.k.a. Porte de la Kasbah), a gateway into the Kasbah.*

Kasbah

Loosely translated as "fortress," a *kasbah* is an enclosed, protected residential area near a castle that you'll find in hundreds of Moroccan towns. Originally this was a place where a king or other leader could protect his tribe. Tangier's Kasbah comprises the upper quarter of the old town. A residential area with twisty lanes and some nice guest houses, this area is a bit more sedate and less claustrophobic than parts of the Medina near the market below.

▲**Kasbah Museum**—On Place de la Kasbah, you'll find the Dar el-Makhzen, a former sultan's palace that now houses a history

museum with a few historical artifacts. While there's not a word of English, some of the exhibits are still easy to appreciate, and the building itself is beautiful. Most of the exhibits surround the central, open-air courtyard; rooms proceed roughly chronologically as you move counter-clockwise, from early hunters and farmers to prehistoric civilizations, Roman times, the region's conversion to Islam, and the influence of European powers. The two-story space at the far end of the courtyard focuses on a second-century mosaic floor depicting the journey of Venus. The big 12th-century wall-size map (in Arabic) shows the Moorish view of the world: with Africa on top (Spain is at the far right). Nearby is an explanation of terra-cotta production (a local industry), and upstairs is an exhibit on funerary rituals. Near the entrance, look for signs to *jardin* and climb the stairs to reach a chirpy (if slightly overgrown) garden courtyard. While the building features some striking tilework, you just can't shake the feeling that the best Moorish sights are back in Spain.

Cost and Hours: 10 dh, Wed-Mon 9:00-16:00, closed for prayer Fri 12:30-14:30, closed all day Tue, tel. 0539-932-097.

Place de la Kasbah—Because the Kasbah Museum (while modest) is the city's main museum, the square in front of the palace

attracts more than its share of tourists. That means it's also a vivid gauntlet of amusements waiting to ambush parading tour groups: snake charmers, squawky dance troupes, and colorful water vendors. These colorful Kodak-moment hustlers make their living off the many tour groups passing by daily. (As you're cajoled, remember that the daily minimum wage here for men as skilled as these beggars is $10. That's what the gardeners you'll pass in your walk earn each day. In other words, a €1 tip is an hour's wage for these people.) If you draft behind a tour group, you won't be the focus of the hustlers. But if you take a photo, you must pay.

Before descending out of the Kasbah, don't miss the ocean viewpoint—as you stand in the square and face the palace, look to the right to find the hole carved through the thick city wall (Bab Dhar, "Sea Gate"). This leads out to a large natural terrace with fine views over the port, the Mediterranean, and Spain.

The lower gate of the Kasbah (as you stand in Place de la Kasbah facing the palace, it's on your left) leads to a charming little alcove, between the gates, where you can see a particularly fine tile fountain: The top part is carved cedarwood, below that is carved plaster, and the bottom half is hand-laid tiles. In this area, poke down the tiny lane to

the left of the little shop—you'll find that it leads to a surprisingly large courtyard ringed by fine homes.

Matisse Route—The artist Matisse, who traveled to Tangier in 1912, was inspired by his wanderings through this area, picking up themes that show up in much of his art. The diamond-shaped stones embedded in the street (you'll see them on the narrow lane leading up along the left side of the palace) mark a "Matisse Route" through the Kasbah, from the lower gate to the upper;

those familiar with his works will recognize several scenes along this stretch.

Tangier Beach
(Plage de Corniche, a.k.a. Playa)

Lined with lots of fishy eateries and entertaining nightclubs, this fine, wide, white-sand crescent beach stretches eastward from

the port. The locals call it by the Spanish word *playa*. It's packed with locals doing what people around the world do at the beach—with a few variations. Traditionally clad moms let their kids run wild. Along with lazy camels, you'll see people—young and old—covered in hot sand to combat rheumatism. Early, late,

and off-season, the beach becomes a popular venue for soccer teams. The palm-lined pedestrian street along the waterfront was renamed for King Mohammed VI, in appreciation for recent restorations. While the beach is cleaner than it once was, it still has more than its share of litter—great for a stroll, but maybe not for sunbathing or swimming. If you have a beach break in mind, do it on Spain's Costa del Sol.

Just past the beach on the port side (between here and the Medina) is a zone of nondescript factories. Here local women sew clothing for big, mostly European companies that pay about $8 a day. Each morning and evening rush hour, the street is filled with these women commuters...on foot.

Nightlife in Tangier

Most important: Be out in the **Medina** around 21:00. In the cool of the evening, the atmospheric squares and lanes become even more evocative. Then at about 22:00 things get dark, lonely, and foreboding.

El Minzah Hotel hosts **traditional music** most nights for those having dinner there (see "Eating in Tangier," later; 85 Rue de la Liberté, tel. 0539-935-885).

The **Rif Cinema,** the landmark theater at the top of the Grand Socco, shows movies in French—which the younger generation must learn—and Arabic. The cinema is worth popping into, if only to see the Art Deco interior. As movies cost only 20 dh, consider dropping by to see a bit of whatever's on...in Arabic (closed Mon, tel. 0539-934-683).

Sleeping in Tangier

I've recommended two vastly different types of accommodations in Tangier: cozy Moroccan-style (but mostly French-run) guest houses in the maze of lanes of the Kasbah neighborhood, at the top of the Medina (old town); and big, modern international-style hotels in the urban-feeling new town, a 10-to-20-minute walk from the central sights.

If you want to call Tangier from Europe, dial 00 (Europe's international access code), 212 (Morocco's country code), then the local number (dropping the initial zero). June through mid-September is high season, when rooms may be a bit more expensive and reservations are wise. Most hotels charge an extra tax of 15-25 dh per person per night (typically not included in the prices I've listed here).

Moroccan-Style Guest Houses in the Kasbah

In Arabic, *dar* means "guest house." You'll find these in the Medina, or atmospheric old quarter. While the lower part of the Medina is dominated by market stalls and tourist traps, and can feel a bit seedy after dark, the upper part (called the Kasbah, for the castle that dominates this area) is more tranquil and feels very residential. All of these are buried in a labyrinth of lanes that can be very difficult to navigate; the map on page 241 gives you a vague sense of where to go, but it's essential to ask for very clear directions when you reserve. If you're hiring a guide in Tangier, ask them to help you find your *dar*. (If you're on your own, you can try asking directions when you arrive—but many local residents

TANGIER

Sleep Code

(8 dh = about $1, country code: 212, area code: 539)
S = Single, **D** = Double/Twin, **T** = Triple, **Q** = Quad, **b** = bathroom, **s** = shower only. Unless otherwise noted, credit cards are accepted, English is spoken, and breakfast is included.

To help you easily sort through these listings, I've divided the accommodations into three categories, based on the price for a double room with bath during high season:

$$$ Higher Priced—Most rooms 1,000 dh or more.
$$ Moderately Priced—Most rooms between 500-1,000 dh.
$ Lower Priced—Most rooms 500 dh or less.

Prices can change without notice; verify the hotel's current rates online or by email. For other updates, see www.ricksteves.com/update.

take that as an invitation to tag along and hound you for tips.) All of these are in traditional old houses, with rooms surrounding a courtyard atrium, and all have rooftop terraces where you can relax and enjoy sweeping views over Tangier. There are rarely stand-alone showers; instead, in Moroccan style, you'll find a handheld shower in a corner of the bathroom.

$$$ Dar Chams Tanja, just below the Kasbah gate, has seven elegant, new-feeling rooms with all the comforts surrounding a clean-white inner courtyard with lots of keyhole windows. While pricey, it's impeccably decorated, calm, and stylish (five big Db-1,580 dh, two small Db-1,240 dh, sometimes discounts in slow times—check website, air-con, free Wi-Fi, hammam—Turkish-style bath, massage service, Rue Jnan Kabtan 2, tel. 0539-332-323, www.darchamstanja.com, darchamstanja@gmail.com).

$$$ La Maison Blanche ("The White House"), run by tour guide Aziz Begdouri, has nine rooms in a traditional Moroccan house with modern amenities in the Kasbah (Sb-1,000 dh, Db-1,100 dh, all with bathtubs, air-con, free Wi-Fi, just inside the upper gate of the Kasbah at Rue Ahmed Ben Ajiba 2, tel. 0539-373-545, www.lamaisonblanchetanger.com, info@lamaison blanchetanger.com).

$$ La Tangerina, run by Jürgen (who's German) and his Moroccan wife Farida, has 10 comfortable rooms that look down into a shared atrium. At the top is a gorgeous rooftop seaview balcony (Db-600-935 dh in April and June-mid-Sept, otherwise Db-500-770; suite-1,520-1,650 dh in April and June-mid-Sept, otherwise 1,100-1,320 dh; prices depend on size and include tax, cash only, free Wi-Fi, wood-fired hammam, Riad Sultan 19, tel. 0539-947-731, www.lantangerina.com, info@latangerina.com).

$$ Dar Nour, run with funky French style by Philippe, Jean-Olivier, and Catherine, has an "Escher-esque" floor plan that sprawls through five interconnected houses (it's "labyrinthine like the Medina," says Philippe). The 10 homey rooms feel very tradi-tional, with lots of books and lounging areas spread throughout (Db-735 dh, junior suite Db-970 dh, suite Db-1,330 dh, cash only, free Wi-Fi in lobby, Rue Gourna 20, mobile 06-6211-2724, www .darnour.com, contactdarnour@yahoo.fr).

$$ Dar Sultan rents six romantically decorated rooms on a pleasant street in the heart of the Kasbah (Db-990 dh, larger Db-1,210 dh, Db with terrace-1,320 dh, free Wi-Fi in lobby and cable Internet in rooms, Rue Touila 49, tel. 0539-336-061, www .darsultan.com, dar-sultan@menara.ma).

Modern Hotels in the Modern City

These hotels are centrally located, near the TI, and within walking distance of the Grand Socco, Medina, and market. The first two are three-star hotels and take credit cards; the others are cash-only.

$$$ Rif & Spa Hotel, recently restored to its 1970s glamour, is a worthy splurge. Offering 127 plush, modern rooms, sprawling public spaces, a garden, a pool, and grand views, it feels like an oversized boutique hotel. The great Arabic lounge—named for Winston Churchill—with a harbor view compels you to relax (Sb-1,200 dh, Db-1,400 dh, 200-dh more July-Aug, 200-dh extra for sea view, see website for specials, breakfast-100 dh, air-con, elevator, free Wi-Fi in lobby, 3 restaurants, spa and sauna, Avenue Mohammed VI 152, tel. 0539-349-300, fax 0539-944-569, www.hotelsatlas.com, riftanger@menara.ma).

$$ Hotel Rembrandt feels just like the 1940s, with a restaurant, a bar, and a swimming pool surrounded by a great grassy garden. Its 70 rooms are outdated and simple, but clean and comfortable, and some come with views (Sb-450-550 dh, Db-600-710 dh, higher prices are for June-Aug, sea view-100 dh extra, includes tax, breakfast often included, otherwise-80 dh, air-con, elevator, free Wi-Fi, a 5-minute walk above the beach in a busy urban zone at Boulevard Mohammed VI 1, tel. 0539-937-870, fax 0539-930-443, www.hotel-rembrandt.com, hotelrembrandt@menara.ma).

$$ Hotel Continental—actually in the Medina (at the bottom of the old town, facing the port)—is the Humphrey Bogart option, a grand old place sprawling along the old town. It has lavish, atmospheric, and recently renovated public spaces, a chandeliered breakfast room, and 70 spacious bedrooms with rough hardwood floors and new bathrooms. Jimmy, who's always around and runs the shop adjacent to the lobby, says he offers everything but Viagra. When I said, "I'm from Seattle," he said, "206." Test him—he knows your area code (Sb-495 dh, Db-635 dh, about 100 dh more July-Sept, includes tax and breakfast, free Wi-Fi, Dar Baroud 36, tel. 0539-931-024, fax 0539-931-143, hcontinental@iam.net.ma). This hotel's terrace aches with nostalgia. Back during the city's glory days, a ferry connected Tangier and New York. American novelists would sit out on the terrace of Hotel Continental, never quite sure when their friends' boat would arrive from across the sea...

$ Hotel El Djenina is a local-style business-class hotel—extremely plain, reliable, safe, and well-located. Its 40 rooms are a block off the harbor, midway between the port and the TI. Request a room on the back side to escape the street noise (Sb-319-357 dh, Db-382-463 dh, higher prices are for mid-May-Sept, cash only, no breakfast, no air-con, elevator, free Wi-Fi, tel. 0539-942-244, fax 0539-942-246, Rue al-Antaki 8, eldjenina@menara.ma).

$ Hotel Residencia Andalucía is solid, clean, and minimal. It's buried in a totally non-touristy area in the new town, about a 20-minute walk from the Grand Socco. It has 19 rooms, a small reception, and a peaceful lobby (Sb-200-230 dh, Db-230-260 dh, higher prices are for mid-June-mid-Sept, cash only, Rue Omar Ben Abdelaziz 14, tel. 0539-941-334, Azdeen speaks a little English). Don't confuse it with the similarly named but very exclusive Hotel Andalucía Golf across town.

Eating in Tangier

Moroccan food is a joy to sample. First priority is a glass of the refreshing "Moroccan tea"—green tea that's boiled and steeped once, then combined with fresh mint leaves to boil and steep some more, before being loaded up with sugar. Tourist-oriented restaurants have a predictable menu. For starters, you'll find Moroccan vegetable soup *(harira)* or Moroccan salad (a combination of fresh and stewed vegetables). Main dishes include couscous (usually with chicken, potatoes, carrots, and other vegetables and spices); *tagine* (stewed meat served in a fancy dish with a cone-shaped top); and *briouates* (small savory pies). Everything comes with Morocco's distinctive round, flat bread. For dessert, it's pastries—typically, almond cookies.

I've mostly listed places in or near the Medina. (If you'd prefer the local equivalent of a yacht-club restaurant, survey the places along the beach.) Moroccan waiters expect about a 10 percent tip.

Le Saveur du Poisson is an excellent bet for the more adventurous, featuring one room cluttered with paintings adjoining a busy kitchen. There are no choices here. Just sit down and let owner Muhammad or his son, Hassan, take care of the rest. You get a rough hand-carved spoon and fork. Surrounded by lots of locals and unforgettable food, you'll be treated to a multicourse menu. Savor the delicious fish dishes—Tangier is one of the few spots in Morocco where seafood is a major part of the diet. The fruit punch—a mix of seasonal fruits brewed overnight in a vat—simmers in the back room. Ask for an explanation, or even a look. The desserts are full of nuts and honey. The big sink in the room is for locals who prefer to eat with their fingers (150-dh fixed-price meal, Sat-Thu 13:00-17:00 & 20:00-23:00, closed Fri and during Ramadan; walk down Rue de la Liberté roughly a block toward the Grand Socco from El Minzah Hotel, look for the stairs leading down to the market stalls and go down until you see fish on the grill; Escalier Waller 2, tel. 0539-336-326).

Maison Communitaire des Femmes, a community center for women, hides an inexpensive, hearty lunch spot that's open to everyone. A tasty three-course lunch is only 60 dh. Profits support the work of the center (Mon-Sat 12:00-16:00, last order at 15:30, also open 8:00-11:00 & 15:30-18:00 for cakes and tea, closed Sun, pleasant terrace out back, near slipper market just outside Grand

Socco, Place du 9 Avril).

El Minzah Hotel offers a fancier yet still authentic experience. The atmosphere is classy but low-stress. It's where unadventurous tourists and local elites dine. Dress up and choose between two dining zones: The white-tablecloth continental (French) dining area, called El Erz, is stuffy (80-150-dh starters, 120-240-dh main dishes); while in the Moroccan lounge, El Korsan, you'll be serenaded by live traditional music (music nightly 20:00-23:30, belly-dance show at 20:30 and 22:30, no extra charge for music; 70-120-dh starters, 170-260-dh main dishes). There's also a cozy wine bar here—a rarity in a Muslim country (50-120-dh starters, 120-190-dh main dishes, decorated with photos of visiting celebrities). At lunch, light meals and salads are served poolside (all dining areas open daily 13:00-16:00 & 20:00-22:30, Rue de la Liberté 85, tel. 0539-935-885, www.elminzah.com).

Le Salon Bleu has decent Moroccan food and some of the most spectacular seating in town: perched on a whitewashed terrace overlooking the square in front of the Kasbah Museum, with 360-degree views over the rooftops. Hike up the very tight spiral staircase to the top level, with the best views and lounge-a-while sofa seating. French-run (by the owners of Dar Nour guest house), it offers a simple menu of Moroccan fare—the 80-dh appetizer plate is a good sampler for lunch or to share for an afternoon snack. While there is some indoor seating, I'd skip this place if the weather's not ideal for lingering on the terrace (30-40-dh starters, 80-120-dh main dishes, Place de la Kasbah, mobile 06-5432-7618). You'll see it from the square in front of the Kasbah; to reach it, go through the gate to the left (as you face it), then look right for the stairs up.

Le Fabrique has nothing to do with old Morocco. But if you want a break from couscous and keyhole arches, this industrial-mod brasserie with concrete floors and exposed brick has a menu of purely French classics—a good reminder that in the 20th century, Tangier was nearly as much a French city as a Moroccan one (70-140-dh starters, 130-230-dh main dishes, Tue-Sat 12:00-14:30 & 20:00-23:00, closed Sun-Mon, Rue d'Angleterre 7, tel. 0539-374-057). It's a steep 10-minute walk up from the Grand Socco: Head up Rue d'Angleterre (left of Cinema Rif) and hike up the hill until the road levels out—it's on your left.

Le Nabab is geared for tourists, but offers more style and less crass commercialism than the tourist traps listed below. Squirreled away in a mostly residential neighborhood just below the lower Kasbah gate (near the top of the Medina), it has a menu of predictable Moroccan favorites in a sleek concrete-and-white-tablecloths dining room with a few echoes of traditional Moroccan decor (170-dh three-course meal is a good deal to sample several items,

40-55-dh starters, 100-150-dh main dishes, Mon-Sat 12:00-15:30 & 19:30-23:30, closed Sun; below the lower Kasbah gate—bear left down the stairs, then right, and look for signs; Rue Al Kadiria 4, mobile 06-6144-2220).

Tourist Traps

Tangier seems to specialize in very touristy Moroccan restaurants that are designed to feed and entertain dozens or even hundreds of tour-group members with overpriced and predictable menus of Moroccan classics, and often live music and belly-dancing. The only locals you'll see here are the waiters. For day-trippers who just want a safe, comfortable break in the heart of town, these restaurants' predictability and Moroccan clichés are just perfect. For other travelers, these places are tour-group hell and make you thankful to be free. Each local guide has their own favorite, but these are the best-known.

Hamadi is as luxurious a restaurant as a tourist can find in Morocco, with good food at reasonable prices (25-40-dh starters, 60-80-dh main dishes, long hours daily, Rue Kasbah 2, tel. 0539-934-514).

Marhaba Palace has the most impressive interior, with huge keyhole arches ringing a grand upstairs hall slathered in colorful tilework. It also has the highest prices—hardly a good value. It's near the upper gate to the Kasbah, so it's convenient for a meal just before heading downhill through town to the Medina and market (170-240-dh fixed-price meals, daily 10:00-23:00, Rue Kasbah, tel. 0539-937-927).

Mamounia Palace, considered by most the bottom of the barrel, is right on the Petit Socco and more in the middle of the action. At least it has a Hollywood connection: The Moroccan tea-house scenes from the movie *Inception* were filmed on its upstairs balcony. A meal here will cost you about 100 dh for four courses (no à la carte, daily 11:00-22:00, tel. 0539-935-099).

Tangier Connections

In Tangier, all train traffic comes and goes from the suburban Gare Tanger Ville train station, one mile from the city center and a short Petit Taxi ride away (10-20 dh). If you're traveling inland, check the information booth at the entrance of the train station for schedules (www.oncf.ma).

From Tangier by Train to: Rabat (5/day, 5 hours), **Casablanca** (station also called **Casa Voyageurs,** 6/day, 5 hours; a new train line will cut the trip to about 2 hours by 2014), **Marrakech** (4/day, 12 hours), **Fès** (4/day, 4.5 hours).

From Tangier by Bus to: Ceuta and **Tétouan** (hourly, 1 hour).

From Fès to: Casablanca (9/day, 4.5 hours), **Marrakech** (7/day, 7 hours), **Rabat** (9/day, 4 hours), **Meknès** (10/day, 45 minutes), **Tangier** (5/day, 5.5 hours).

From Rabat to: Casablanca (2/hour, 45 minutes), **Fès** (9/day, 3.5 hours), **Tétouan** (2 buses/day, 4.5 hours, 3 trains/day, 6 hours).

From Casablanca to: Marrakech (9/day, 3.5 hours).

From Marrakech to: Meknès (7/day, 7 hours), **Ouarzazate** (4/day, 4 hours).

By Plane: Flights within Morocco are convenient and reasonable (about $180 one-way from Tangier to Casablanca).

SLOVENIA

THE JULIAN ALPS

Vršič Pass • Soča River Valley • Bovec • Kobarid

The countryside around Lake Bled is plenty spectacular. But to crescendo your Slovenian mountain experience, head for the hills. The northwestern corner of Slovenia —within yodeling distance of Austria and Italy—is crowned by the Julian Alps (named for Julius Caesar). Here, mountain culture has a Slavic flavor.

The Slovenian mountainsides are laced with hiking paths, blanketed in a deep forest, and speckled with ski resorts and vacation chalets. Beyond every ridge is a peaceful alpine village nestled around a quaint Baroque steeple. And in the center of it all is Mount Triglav—ol' "Three Heads"—Slovenia's symbol and tallest mountain.

The single best day in the Julian Alps is spent driving up and over the 50 hairpin turns of the breathtaking Vršič Pass (vur-SHEECH, open May-Oct) and back down via the Soča (SOH-chah) River Valley, lined with offbeat nooks and Hemingway-haunted crannies. As you curl on twisty roads between the cut-glass peaks, you'll enjoy stunning high-mountain scenery, whitewater rivers with superb fishing, rustic rest stops, thought-provoking World War I sights, and charming hamlets.

A pair of Soča Valley towns holds watch over the region. Bovec is all about good times (it's the whitewater adventure-sports hub), while Kobarid attends to more serious matters (WWI history). Though neither is a destination in itself, both Bovec and Kobarid are pleasant, functional, and convenient home bases for exploring this gloriously beautiful region.

Getting Around the Julian Alps

The Julian Alps are best by **car.** Even if you're doing the rest of your trip by train, consider renting a car here for maximum mountain day-trip flexibility. I've included a self-guided driving tour incorporating the best of the Julian Alps (Vršič Pass and Soča Valley).

It's difficult to do the Vršič Pass and Soča Valley without your own wheels. Hiring a **local guide** with a car can be a great value, making your time not only fun, but also informative. Cheaper but less personal, you could join a day-trip **excursion** from Bled. (You can hire Bled-based guides Tina Hiti and Sašo Golub to take you over the pass—€150 roundtrip from Bled; www.pg-slovenia.com.) A public **bus** follows more or less this same route, leaving Ljubljana each morning at 6:30, arriving in Bovec at 10:45 (daily July-Aug, Sat-Sun only Sept-June, none Oct-May). Or stay closer to Bled, and get a taste of the Julian Alps by taking advantage of easy and frequent bus connections to more convenient day-trip destinations (Radovljica, the Vintgar Gorge, and Lake Bohinj).

Julian Alps Self-Guided Driving Tour

This all-day, self-guided driving tour, rated ▲▲▲, takes you over the highest mountain pass in Slovenia, with stunning scenery and a few quirky sights along the way. From waterfalls to hiking trails, World War I history to queasy suspension bridges, this trip has it all.

Orientation to the Julian Alps

Most of the Julian Alps are encompassed by the Triglav National Park (Triglavski Narodni Park). This drive is divided into two parts: the Vršič Pass and the Soča River Valley. While not for stick-shift novices, all but the most timid drivers will agree the scenery is worth the many hairpin turns. Frequent pull-outs offer plenty of opportunity to relax, stretch your legs, and enjoy the vistas.

Planning Your Time: This drive can be done in a day, but consider spending the night along the way for a

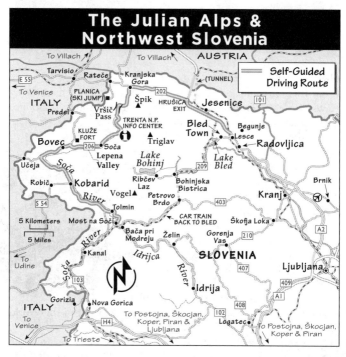

The Julian Alps &
Northwest Slovenia

more leisurely pace. You can start and end in Bled or Ljubljana. For efficient sightseeing, I prefer to begin in Bled (after appreciating the mountains from afar for a day or two) and end in the capital.

Length of This Tour: These rough estimates do not include stops: Bled to the top of Vršič Pass—1 hour; Vršič Pass to Trenta (start of Soča Valley)—30 minutes; Trenta to Bovec—30 minutes; Bovec to Kobarid—30 minutes; Kobarid to Ljubljana or Bled—2 hours (remember, it's an hour between Ljubljana and Bled). In other words, if you started and ended in Bled and drove the entire route without stopping, you'd make it home in less than five hours...but you'd miss so much. It takes at least a full day to really do the region justice.

Tourist Information: The best sources of information are the Bled TI (www.bled.si), the Triglav National Park Information Centers in Trenta (page 267) and Bled (www.trip.si), and the TIs in Bovec and Kobarid (both listed in this chapter).

Maps: Pick up a good map before you begin (available at local TIs, travel agencies, and gas stations). The all-Slovenia *Autokarta Slovenija* or the TI's *Next Exit: Goldenhorn Route* map both include all the essential roads, but several more detailed options are also available. The 1:50,000 Kod & Kam *Posoče* map covers the entire

THE JULIAN ALPS

Vršič Pass and Soča Valley (but doesn't include the parts of the drive near Bled and Ljubljana).

OK...let's ride.

Part 1: Vršič Pass

From Bled or Ljubljana, take the A-2 expressway north, enjoying views of Mount Triglav on the left as you drive. About 10 minutes past Bled, you'll approach the industrial city of **Jesenice**, whose iron- and steelworks— once called the "Detroit of Yugoslavia"— filled this valley with multicolored smoke until most of them closed in the 1980s. The city plans to convert these old factories into a sort of theme park.

Just after the giant smokestack with the billboards, the little gaggle of colorful houses on the right (just next to the free-way) is **Kurja Vas** ("Chicken Village"). This unassuming place is locally famous for pro-ducing hockey players: 18 of the 20 play-ers on the 1971 Yugoslav hockey team—which went to the World Championships—were from this tiny hamlet.

As you zip past Jesenice, keep your eye out for the exit marked *Jesenice-zahod, Trbiž/Tarvisio, Kr. Gora,* and *Hrušica* (it's after the gas station, just before the tunnel to Austria). When you exit, turn left toward *Trbiž/Tarvisio* and *Kranjska Gora* (yellow sign).

Just after the exit, the big, blue building surrounded by tall lights was the former border station (the overpass you'll go under leads into Austria). Locals have fond memories of visiting Austria during the Yugoslav days, when they smuggled home forbidden Western goods. Some items were simply not available back home (VCRs, Coca-Cola, designer clothes); other goods were simply better over there (chocolate, coffee, dishwasher soap).

Slovenes brag that their country—"with 56 percent of the land covered in forest"—is Europe's second-greenest. As you drive toward Kranjska Gora, take in all this greenery...and the char-acteristic Slovenian hayracks (recognized as part of the national heritage and now preserved). The Vrata Valley (on the left) is a popular starting point for climbing Mount Triglav. Paralleling the road on the left is a rails-to-trails bike path that loops from here through Italy and Austria, allowing bikers to connect three countries in one day. On the right, watch for the statue of Jakob Aljaž, who actually bought Triglav, back when such a thing was possible (he's pointing at his purchase). Ten minutes later, in Gozd Martuljek, you'll cross a bridge and enjoy a great head-on view of Špik Mountain.

Entering Kranjska Gora (once Yugoslavia's leading winter resort and still popular with Croatian skiers), you'll see a turnoff to the left marked for *Bovec* and *Vršič*. This leads up to the pass, but winter sports fanatics may first want to take a 15-minute detour to see the biggest ski jump in the world, a few miles ahead (stay straight through Kranjska Gora, then turn left at signs for **Planica,** the last stop before the Italian border). Every year, tens of thousands of sports fans flock here to watch the ski-flying world championships. This is where a local boy was the first human to fly more than 100 meters (328 feet) on skis. Today's competitors routinely set new world records (currently 784 feet—that's 17 seconds in the air). From the ski jump, you're a few minutes' walk from Italy or Austria. This region—spanning three nations—lobbied unsuccessfully under the name Senza Confini (Italian for "without borders") to host the 2006 Winter Olympics. This philosophy is in tune with the European Union's vision for a Europe of regions, rather than nations.

Back in Kranjska Gora, follow the signs for *Vršič*. Before long, you'll officially enter **Triglav National Park** and come to the first of this road's 50 hairpin turns (24 up, then 26 down)—each one numbered and labeled with the altitude in meters. Notice that they're cobbled to provide better traction. If the drive seems daunting, remember that 50-seat tour buses routinely conquer this pass... if they can do it, so can you. (Better yet, imagine the bicyclists who routinely pedal to the top. The best can do it in less than 30 minutes—faster than driving.)

After switchback #8, with the cute waterfall, park your car on the right and hike up the stairs on the left to the little **Russian chapel.** This road was built during World War I by at least 10,000 Russian POWs of the Austro-Hungarian Empire to supply the front lines of the Soča Front. The POWs lived and worked in terrible conditions, and several hundred died of illness and exposure. On March 8, 1916, an avalanche thundered down the mountains, killing hundreds more workers. This chapel was built where the final

casualty was found. Take a minute to pay your respects to the men who built the road you're enjoying today. Because it's a Russian Orthodox chapel, notice that the crosses topping the steeples have three crossbars.

Back on the road, after #17, look as high as you can on the cliff face to see sunlight poking through a **"window"** in the rock. This

Mount Triglav

Mount Triglav ("Three Heads") stands watch over the Julian Alps and all of Slovenia. Slovenes say that its three peaks are the guardians of the water, air, and earth. This mountain defines Slovenes, even adorning the nation's flag: Look for the national seal, with three peaks. The two squiggly lines under it represent the Adriatic. Or take a look at one of Slovenia's €0.50 coins.

From the town of Bled, you'll see Triglav peeking up over the ridge on a clear day. (You'll get an even better view from nearby Lake Bohinj.)

It's said that you're not a true Slovene until you've climbed Triglav. One native took these words very seriously and climbed the mountain 853 times...in one year. Climbing to the summit—at 9,396 feet—is an attainable goal for any hiker in decent shape. If you're here for a while and want to become an honorary Slovene, befriend a local and ask if he or she will take you to the top.

If mountain climbing isn't your style, relax at an outdoor café with a piece of cream cake and a view of Triglav. It won't make you a Slovene...but it's close enough on a quick visit.

THE JULIAN ALPS

natural formation, a popular destination for intrepid hikers, is big enough for the Statue of Liberty to crawl through.

After #22, at the pullout for Erjavčeva Koča restaurant, you may see tour-bus groups making a fuss about the mountain vista. They're looking for a ghostly face in the cliff wall, supposedly belonging to the mythical figure **Ajda.** This village girl was cursed by the townspeople after correctly predicting the death of the Zlatorog (Golden Horn), a magical, beloved, chamois-like animal. Her tiny image (with a Picasso nose) is just above the tree line, a little to the right—try to get someone to point her out to you (you

can see her best if you stand at the signpost near the road).

After #24, you reach the **summit** (5,285 feet). Consider getting out of the car to enjoy the views (in peak season, you'll pay an attendant to park here). Hike up to the hut for a snack or drink on the grand view terrace. On the right, a long gravel chute gives hikers a thrilling glissade down. (From the pullout just beyond #26, it's easy to view hikers "skiing" down.)

As you begin the descent, keep an eye out for old WWI debris. A lonely guard tunnel stands after #28, followed by a tunnel marked *1916* (on the left) that was part of the road's original path. Then you'll see abandoned checkpoints from when this was the border between Italy and the Austro-Hungarian Empire. At #48 is a statue of **Julius Kugy,** an Italian botanist who wrote books about alpine flora.

At #49, the road to the right (marked *Izvir Soče*) leads to the **source of the Soča River.** If you feel like stretching your legs after all that shifting, drive about five minutes down this road to a restaurant parking lot. From here, you can take a challenging 20-minute uphill hike to the Soča source. This is also the starting point for a new, well-explained Soča Trail (Soška Pot) that leads all the way to the town of Bovec, mostly following the road we're driving on today. With plenty of time and a hankering to hike rather than drive, consider taking this trail (about 12 miles one-way).

Nearing the end of the switchbacks, follow signs for *Bovec*. Crossing the Soča River, you begin the second half of this trip.

Part 2: Soča River Valley

During World War I, the terrain between here and the Adriatic made up the Soča (Isonzo) Front. As you follow the Soča River south, down what's nicknamed the "Valley of the Cemeteries," the scenic mountainsides around you tell the tale of this terrible warfare. Imagine a young Ernest Hemingway driving his ambulance through these same hills (see sidebar next page).

But it's not all so gloomy. There are plenty of other diversions—interesting villages and churches, waterfalls and suspension bridges, and lots more. Perhaps most impressive is the remarkable clarity and milky-blue color of the Soča itself, which Slovenes proudly call their "emerald river."

After switchback #49, you'll cross a bridge, then pass a church and a botanical garden of alpine plants (Alpinum Juliana). Across the street (on the right) is the parking lot for the Mlinarica Gorge. While the gorge is interesting, the bridge leading to it was damaged in a severe storm and hasn't yet been rebuilt—so it's best left to hardy hikers.

The last Vršič switchback (#50) sends you into the village of **Trenta.** As you get to the cluster of buildings in Trenta's "downtown," look on the left for the **Triglav National Park Information Center,** which also serves as a regional TI (daily May-Oct 10:00-18:00, Dec-April 10:00-14:00, closed Nov, tel. 05/388-9330,

THE JULIAN ALPS

Hemingway in the Julian Alps

It was against the scenic backdrop of the Slovenian Alps that a young man from Oak Park, Illinois, first came to Europe—the continent with which he would forever be identified. After graduating high school in 1917 and working briefly as a newspaper reporter, young Ernest Hemingway wanted to join the war effort in Europe. Bad vision kept him out of the army, but he craved combat experience—so he joined the Red Cross Ambulance Corps instead.

After a short detour through Paris, Hemingway was sent to the Italian Front. On his first day, he was given the job of retrieving human remains—gruesomely disfigured body parts—after the explosion of a munitions factory. Later he came to the Lower Piave Valley, not far from the Soča Front. In July 1918, his ambulance was hit by a mortar shell. Despite his injuries, he saved an Italian soldier who was also wounded. According to legend, he packed his own wound with cigarette butts to stop the flow of blood.

Sent to Milan to recuperate, Hemingway fell in love with a nurse, but she later left him for an Italian military officer. A decade later, Hemingway wrote about Kobarid (using its Italian name, Caporetto), the war, and his case of youthful heartbreak in the novel *A Farewell to Arms*.

www.tnp.si). The humble €4 museum here provides a look (with English explanations) at the park's flora, fauna, traditional culture, and mountaineering history. A poetic 15-minute slide show explains the wonders and fragility of the park (included in museum entry, ask for English version as you enter).

After Trenta, you'll pass through a tunnel; then, on the left, look for a classic **suspension bridge.** Pull over to walk out for a bounce, enjoying the river's crystal-clear water and the spectacular mountain panorama.

About five miles beyond Trenta, in the town of Soča, is the **Church of St. Joseph** (with red onion dome, hiding behind the big tree on the right). The church was damaged in the earthquakes of 1998 and 2004, so the interior is likely covered with scaffolding. But if it's not covered, you'll see some fascinating art. During World War II, an artist hiding out in the mountains filled this church with patriotic symbolism. The interior is bathed in Yugoslav red, white, and blue—a brave statement made when such nationalistic sentiments were dangerous. On the ceiling is St. Michael (clad in Yugoslav colors) with Yugoslavia's three WWII enemies at his feet: the eagle (Germany), the wolf (Italy), and the serpent (Japan). The tops of the walls along the nave are lined with saints, but these are Slavic, not Catholic. Finally, look carefully at the Stations of the Cross and find the faces of hated Yugoslav enemies:

Hitler (fourth from altar on left) and Mussolini (first from altar on right). Behind the church, the stylized cross on the hill marks a World War I **cemetery**—the final resting place of some 600 Austro-Hungarian soldiers who were killed in action.

For another good example of how the Soča River cuts like God's band saw into the land, stop about two minutes past the church at the small gravel lot (on the left) marked *Velika Korita Soče* ("Grand Canyon of Soča"). Venture out onto the suspension bridge over the gorge...and bounce if you dare. Just beyond this bridge is the turnoff (on the left) to the Lepena Valley, home of the recommended Pristava Lepena pension—and their Lipizzaner horses (described later, under "Sleeping in Bovec").

Roughly five miles after the town of Soča, you exit the National Park, pass a WWI graveyard (on the left), and come to a fork in the road. The main route leads to the left, through Bovec.

But first, take a two-mile detour to the right (marked *Trbiž/Tarvisio* and *Predel/Kluže*), where the WWI **Kluže Fort** keeps a close watch over the narrowest part of a valley leading to Italy (€3; July-Aug daily 9:00-20:00; June and Sept

Sun-Fri 9:00-17:00, Sat 9:00-18:00; May and Oct Sat-Sun 10:00-18:00, closed Mon-Fri; closed Nov-April). In the 15th century, the Italians had a fort here to defend against the Ottomans. Half a millennium later, during World War I, it was used by Austrians to keep Italians out of their territory. Notice the ladder rungs fixed to the cliff face across the road from the fort—allowing soldiers to quickly get up to the mountaintop.

Back on the main road, continue to **Bovec**. This town, which saw some of the most vicious fighting of the Soča Front, was hit hard by earthquakes in 1994 and 1998 (and another tremor in 2004). Today, it's been rebuilt and remains the adventure-sports capital of the Soča River Valley—also known as the "Adrenaline

Valley," famous for its whitewater activities. (Since the water comes from high-mountain runoff, the temperature of the Soča never goes above 68 degrees Fahrenheit.) For a good lunch stop in Bovec, take the turnoff as you first reach the town, and you'll pass a pair of inviting restaurant terraces on the right (Martinov Hram, then Letni Vrt; for details, see "Eating in Bovec," later). But if you're not eating or spending the night in Bovec, you could skip the town (continue along the main road to bypass the town center).

Heading south along the river—with water somehow both perfectly clear and spectacularly turquoise—watch for happy kayakers. When you pass the intersection at Žaga, you're just four miles from Italy. Along the way, you'll also pass a pair of waterfalls: the well-known Boka ("Slovenia's second-longest waterfall," on the right just before Žaga) and the hidden gem Veliki Kozjak (unmarked, on the left just before Kobarid). For either, you'll have to park your car and hike uphill to see the falls.

Signs lead to the town of **Kobarid,** home to a sleepy main square and some fascinating WWI sights. Even if you don't think you're interested in the Soča Front, consider dropping in the Kobarid Museum. Driving up to the Italian mausoleum hovering over the town is a must. (These sights are described later, under "Sights in Kobarid.")

Leaving Kobarid, continue south along the Soča to **Tolmin.** Before you reach Tolmin, decide on your route back to civilization...

Finishing the Drive

To Ljubljana: From Tolmin, you have two possible driving routes to the capital. Either option brings you back to the A-1 expressway south of Ljubljana, and will get you to the city in about two hours (though the second route has fewer miles).

The option you'll encounter first (turnoff to the right before Tolmin) is the smoother, longer route southwest to **Nova Gorica.** This fairly dull city is divided in half by the Italian border (the Italian side is called "Gorizia"). Because Italians aren't allowed to gamble in their home towns, Nova Gorica is packed with casinos catering to Italian gamblers. In fact, it's home to Europe's biggest casino. Rocks spell out the name "TITO" on a hillside above town—a strange relic of an earlier age. From Nova Gorica, you can hop on the H-4 expressway, which links easily to the main A-1 expressway. Also notice that the road from Nova Gorica to Ljubljana takes you through the heart of the Karst region—if you have time and daylight to spare, you could tour a cave, castle, or Lipizzaner stud farm on your way back up to Ljubljana.

I prefer the more rural second option: Continue through

Tolmin, then head southeast through the hills back toward Ljubljana. Along the way, you could stop for a bite and some sightseeing at the town of **Idrija** (EE-dree-yah), known to all Slovenes for three things: its tourable mercury mine, fine delicate lace, and tasty *žlikrofi* (like ravioli). Back at the expressway (at Logatec), head north to Ljubljana or on to Bled.

To Bled: The fastest option is to load your car onto a **"Car Train"** (Autovlak) that cuts directly through the mountains. The train departs at 18:30 from Most na Soči (just south of Tolmin, along the Idrija route described above) and arrives at Bohinjska Bistrica, near Lake Bohinj, at 19:14 (€12 for the car; confirm schedule at the Bled TI before making the trip). From Bohinjska Bistrica, it's just a half-hour drive back to Bled. No reservations are necessary, but arrive at the train station about 30 minutes before the scheduled departure to allow time to load the car.

To **drive** all the way back, the fastest route (about 2 hours) is partially on a twisty, rough, very poor-quality road (go through Tolmin, turn off at Bača pri Modreju to Podbrdo, then from Petrovo Brdo take a very curvy road through the mountains into Bohinjska Bistrica and on to Bled). For timid drivers, it's more sane and not too much longer to start out on the Idrija route toward Ljubljana (described above), but turn off in Želin (before Idrija) toward Skofja Loka and Kranj, then on to Bled. Or take one of the two routes described above for Ljubljana, then continue on the expressway past Ljubljana and back up to Bled (allow 3 hours).

Bovec

The biggest town in the area, Bovec (BOH-vets) has a happening main square and all the tourist amenities. It's best known as a hub for whitewater adventure sports. While not exactly quaint, Bovec is charming enough to qualify as a good lunch stop or overnight home base. If nothing else, it's a nice jolt of civilization wedged between the alpine cliffs.

Orientation to Bovec

(area code: 05)
Tourist Information
The helpful TI on the main square offers fliers on mountain biking and water sports (flexible hours, generally June-Sept daily 8:30-20:30, shorter hours off-season, Trg Golobarskih Žrtev 8, tel. 05/389-6444, www.bovec.si).

Arrival in Bovec

The main road skirts Bovec, but you can turn off (watch for signs on the right) to take the road that goes through the heart of town, then rejoins the main road farther along. As you approach the city center, you can't miss the main square, Trg Golobarskih Žrtev, with the TI and a pair of good restaurants (described later, under "Eating in Bovec").

Sleeping in Bovec

$$$ Dobra Vila is a gorgeous hotel with classy traditional-meets-contemporary decor that feels out of place in little, remote Bovec. Not that I'm complaining. Its 12 rooms are swanky, and the public spaces (including a sitting room/library, breakfast room/restaurant, wine cellar, winter garden porch, and terrace with cozy mountain-view chairs) are welcoming. As it's under new management, some details might change (high season: Db-€127-134, Db with balcony-€137-172; low season: Db-€112-119, Db with balcony-€122-157; Sb-€20 less than Db rate, price depends on size of room, 10 percent extra for 1-night stays, includes breakfast and dinner, fun old-fashioned elevator, on the left just as you enter town on the main road from the Vršič Pass at Mala Vas 112, tel. 05/389-6400, fax 05/389-6404, www.dobra-vila-bovec.com, welcome@dobra-vila-bovec.com).

$$ Martinov Hram has 11 nondescript modern rooms over a popular restaurant a few steps from Bovec's main square. While

Sleep Code

(€1 = about $1.40, country code: 386, area code: 05)
S = Single, **D** = Double/Twin, **T** = Triple, **Q** = Quad, **b** = bathroom. Unless otherwise noted, breakfast is included and credit cards are accepted. Everyone speaks English and all of these accommodations include breakfast. These prices don't include the €1.01 tourist tax per person, per night.

To help you sort easily through these listings, I've divided the accommodations into three categories based on the price for a double room with bath during high season:

  $$$ Higher Priced—Most rooms €100 or more.
    $$ Moderately Priced—Most rooms between €50-100.
      $ Lower Priced—Most rooms €50 or less.

Prices can change without notice; verify the hotel's current rates online or by email. For other updates, see www.ricksteves.com/update.

the rooms are an afterthought to the busy restaurant (reception at the bar), they're comfortable (very flexible rates, in peak season figure Sb-€40, Db-€70, a few euros less off-season, no extra charge for 1-night stays, Trg Golobarskih Žrtev 27, tel. 05/388-6214, sara .berginc@volja.net).

Near Bovec

$$$ Pristava Lepena is a relaxing oasis hiding out in the Lepena Valley just north of Bovec. Well-run by Milan and Silvia Dolenc, this place is its own little village: a series of rustic-looking cabins, a restaurant, and a sauna/outdoor swimming pool. Hiding behind the humble split-wood shingle exteriors is surprising comfort: 13 cozy apartments (with wood-burning stoves, TV, telephone, and all the amenities) that make you feel like relaxing. This place whispers "second honeymoon" (July-Aug: Db-€138; May-June and Sept: Db-€122; early Oct and late April: Db-€106; closed in winter, multi-night stays preferred, 1-night stays may be possible for 20 percent extra, dinner-€19, lunch and dinner-€31, nonrefundable 30 percent advance payment when you reserve; just before Bovec, turn left off the main road toward Lepena, and follow the white horses to Lepena 2; tel. 05/388-9900, fax 05/388-9901, www .pristava-lepena.com, pristava.lepena@siol.net). The Dolences also have three Welsh ponies and four purebred Lipizzaner horses (two mares, two geldings) that guests can ride (in riding ring-€16/hour, on trail-€20/hour, riding lesson-€24; non-guests may be able to ride for a few euros more—call ahead and ask).

$ Tourist Farm Pri Plajerju, on a picturesque plateau at the edge of Trenta (the first town at the bottom of the Vršič Pass road), is your budget option. Run by the Pretner family, this organic farm raises sheep and goats, and rents four apartments and one room in three buildings separate from the main house. While not quite as tidy as other tourist farms I recommend, it's the best one I found in the Soča Valley (July-Aug: Db-€38-50; Sept-June: Db-€34-45; price depends on size of room or apartment, breakfast-€6, dinner-€10, watch for signs to the left after passing through the village of Trenta, Trenta 16a, tel. & fax 05/388-9209, www.eko-plajer .com, info@eko-plajer.com).

Eating in Bovec

Martinov Hram, run by the Berginc family, has an inviting outdoor terrace under a grape trellis. Inside, the nicely traditional decor goes well with Slovenian specialties focused on sheep (good homemade bread, €6-9 pastas, €9-15 main courses, closed Mon, on the main road through Bovec, just before the main square on the right at Trg Golobarskih Žrtev 27, tel. 05/388-6214).

Letni Vrt Pizzeria, dominating the main square, is the busiest place in town—with pizzas, pastas, salads, and more (closed Sun, Trg Golobarskih Žrtev 12, tel. 05/388-6335).

Kobarid

Kobarid (KOH-bah-reed) feels older, and therefore a bit more appealing, than its big brother Bovec. This humble settlement was

immortalized by a literary giant, Ernest Hemingway, who drove an ambulance in these mountains during World War I. He described Kobarid as "a little white town with a campanile in a valley. It was a clean little town and there was a fine fountain in the square." Sounds about right. Even though Kobarid loves to tout its Hemingway connection, historians believe that Papa did not actually visit Kobarid until he came back after the war to research his book.

Aside from its brush with literary greatness, Kobarid is known as a hub of Soča Front information (with an excellent WWI museum, a hilltop Italian mausoleum, and walks that connect the nearby sights). You won't find the fountain Hemingway wrote about—it's since been covered up by houses (though the town government hopes to excavate it as a tourist attraction). You will find a modern statue of Simon Gregorčič (overlooking the main intersection), the beloved Slovenian priest-slash-poet who came from and wrote about the Soča Valley.

Orientation to Kobarid

(area code: 05)
The main road cuts right through the heart of little Kobarid, bisecting its main square (Trg Svobode). The Kobarid Museum is along this road, on the left before the square. To reach the museum from the main square, simply walk five minutes back toward Bovec.

Tourist Information
The TI has good information on the area and Internet access (daily July-Sept 9:00-19:00, Oct-April 10:00-13:00 & 14:00-15:00, May-June 9:00-13:00 & 14:00-18:00, tel. 05/380-0490, on the main square at Trg Svobode 16, www.lto-sotocje.si and www.kobarid.si).

THE JULIAN ALPS

Sights in Kobarid

▲▲▲**Kobarid Museum (Kobariški Muzej)**—This modest but world-class museum, offering a haunting look at the tragedy of the Soča Front, was voted Europe's best museum in 1993. The tasteful exhibits, with fine English descriptions and a pacifist tone, take an even-handed approach to the fighting—without getting hung up on identifying the "good guys" and the "bad guys." The museum's focus is not on the guns and heroes, but on the big picture of the front and on the stories of the common people who fought and died here.

Cost and Hours: €4, good €8 *Soča Front* book; April-Sept Mon-Fri 9:00-18:00, Sat-Sun 9:00-19:00; Oct-March Mon-Fri 10:00-17:00, Sat-Sun 9:00-18:00; Gregorčičeva 10, tel. 05/389-0000, www.kobariski-muzej.si.

◒ Self-Guided Tour: The entry is lined with hastily made cement and barbed-wire gravestones, flags representing all the nationalities involved in the fighting, and pictures of soldiers and nurses from diverse backgrounds who were brought together here (for example, the men wearing fezzes were from Bosnia-Herzegovina, annexed by the Austro-Hungarian Empire shortly before the war).

Buy your ticket and ask to watch the English version of the 19-minute film on the history of the Soča Front (informative but dry, plays on top floor).

The first floor up is divided into several rooms. The White Room, filled with rusty crampons, wire-cutters, pickaxes, and shovels, explains wintertime conditions at the front. What looks like a bear trap was actually used to trap enemy soldiers. The Room of the Rear shows the day-to-day activities away from the front line, from supplying troops to more mundane activities (milking cows, washing clothes, getting a shave, playing with a dog). The Black Room is the museum's most somber, commemorating the more than one million casualties of the Soča Front. These heartbreaking exhibits honor the common people whose bodies fertilized the battlefields of Europe. Horrific images of war injuries are juxtaposed with a display of medals earned by soldiers such as these—prompting the question, was it worth it? The little altar was purchased by schoolchildren, who sent it to the front to offer the troops some solace.

Through the door marked *Room of the Krn Range* (also on the

The Soča (Isonzo) Front

The valley in Slovenia's northwest corner—called Soča in Slovene and Isonzo in Italian—saw some of World War I's fiercest fighting. While the Western Front gets more press, this eastern border between the Central Powers and the Allies was just as significant. In a series of 12 battles involving 22 different nationalities along a 60-mile-long front, 300,000 soldiers died, 700,000 were wounded, and 100,000 were declared MIA. In addition, tens of thousands of civilians died. A young Ernest Hemingway, who drove an ambulance for the Italian army in nearby fighting, would later write the novel *A Farewell to Arms* about the battles here (see "Hemingway in the Julian Alps" sidebar on page 268).

On April 26, 1915, Italy joined the Allies. A month later, it declared war on the Austro-Hungarian Empire (which included Slovenia). Italy unexpectedly invaded the Soča Valley, quickly taking the tiny town of Kobarid, which it planned to use as a home base for attacks deeper into Austro-Hungarian territory. For the next 29 months, Italy launched 10 more offensives against the Austro-Hungarian army on the mountain-tops. All of these Italian offensives were unsuccessful, even though the Italians outnumbered their oppo-

nents three to one. This was unimaginably difficult warfare—Italy had to attack uphill, waging war high in the mountains, in the harshest of conditions. Trenches were carved into rock instead of mud, and many unprepared conscripts—brought here from faraway lands and unaccustomed to the harsh winter conditions atop the Alps—froze to death. During one winter alone, some 60,000 soldiers were killed by avalanches.

Visitors take a look at this tight valley, hemmed in by seemingly impassible mountains, and wonder: Why would people fight so fiercely over such an inhospitable terrain? At the time, Slovenia was the natural route from Italy to the Austro-Hungarian capital at Vienna. The Italians believed that if they could hold this

first floor up), find your way to the Kobarid Rooms, which trace the history of this region from antiquity to today. High on the wall, look for the timelines explaining the area's turbulent history. The one in the second room shows wave after wave of invaders (including Ottomans, Habsburgs, and Napoleon). In the next room, above a display case with military uniforms, another timeline shows the many flags that flew over Kobarid's main square in the 20th century.

On the top floor, across from the room where the film plays

valley and push over the mountains, Vienna—and victory—would be theirs. Once committed, they couldn't turn back, and the war devolved into one of exhaustion—who would fall first?

In the fall of 1917, Austro-Hungarian Emperor Karl appealed to his ally Germany, and the Germans agreed to assemble an army for a new attack to retake Kobarid and the Soča Valley. In an incredible logistical puzzle, they spent just six weeks building and supplying this new army by transporting troops and equipment high across the mountaintops under cover of darkness...over the heads of their oblivious Italian foes dozing in the valley.

On October 24, Austria-Hungary and Germany launched a downhill attack of 600,000 soldiers into the town of Kobarid. This crucial 12th battle of the Soča Front, better known as the Battle of Kobarid, was the turning point—and saw the introduction of battlefield innovations that are commonplace in the military today. German field commanders were empowered to act independently on the battlefield, reacting immediately to developments rather than waiting for approval. Also, for the first time ever, the Austrian-German army used elements of a new surprise-attack technique called *Blitzkrieg*. (One German officer, Erwin Rommel, made great strides in the fighting here, and later climbed the ranks to become famous as Hitler's "Desert Fox" in North Africa.)

The attack caught the Italian forces off-guard, quickly breaking through three lines of defense. Within three days, the Italians were forced to retreat. (Because the Italian military worked from the top down, the soldiers were sitting ducks once they were cut off from their commanders.) The Austrians called their victory the "Miracle at Kobarid." But Italy felt differently. The Italians see the battle of Caporetto (the Italian name for Kobarid) as their Alamo. To this day, when an Italian finds himself in a mess, he says, "At least it's not a *Caporetto*."

A year later, Italy came back—this time with the aid of British, French, and US forces—and easily retook this area. On November 4, 1918, Austria-Hungary conceded defeat. After more than a million casualties, the fighting at Soča was finally over.

(described above), you'll see a giant model of the surrounding mountains, painstakingly tracing the successful Austrian-German *Blitzkrieg* attack during the Battle of Kobarid.

▲▲**Italian Mausoleum (Kostnica)**—The 55 miles between here and the Adriatic are dotted with more than 75 cemeteries, reminders of the countless casualties of the Soča Front. One of the most dramatic is this mausoleum, overlooking Kobarid. The access road, across Kobarid's main square from the side of the church, is marked by stone gate towers (with the word *Kostnica*—one tower is topped with a cross and the other with a star for the Italian army).

Take the road up Gradič Hill—passing Stations of the Cross—to the mausoleum. Built in 1938 (when this was still part of Italy) around the existing Church of St. Anthony, this octagonal pyramid holds the remains of 7,014 Italian soldiers. The stark, cold, Neoclassical architecture is pure Mussolini. Names are listed alphabetically, along with mass graves for more than 1,700 unknown soldiers *(militi ignoti)*.

Walk behind the church and enjoy the **view.** Find the WWI battlements high on the mountain's rock face (with your back to church, they're at 10 o'clock). Incredibly, the fighting was done on these treacherous ridges; civilians in the valleys only heard the distant battles. Looking up and down the valley, notice the "signal churches" evenly spaced on hilltops, each barely within view of the next—an ancient method for spreading messages or warnings across long distances quickly.

If the **church** is open, go inside and look above the door to see a brave soldier standing over the body of a fallen comrade and fending off enemies with nothing but rocks.

When Mussolini came to dedicate the mausoleum, local revolutionaries plotted an assassination attempt that couldn't fail. A young man planned to suicide-bomb Mussolini as he came back into town from this hilltop. But as Mussolini's car drove past, the would-be assassin looked at his fellow townspeople around him, realized the innocent blood he would also spill, and had a last-minute change of heart. Mussolini's trip was uneventful, and fascism continued to thrive in Italy.

World War I Walks—At the Kobarid Museum (and local TIs), you can pick up a free brochure outlining the **"Kobarid Historical Walk"** tracing WWI sites in town and the surrounding countryside (3 miles, mostly uphill, allow 3-5 hours; or you can just do a shorter stretch along the river, 1-2 hours). A newer **"Walk of Peace"** links several WWI sights all along the Soča Valley (details and map at TI). History buffs can also call ahead to arrange a private guide (€15/hour, tel. 05/389-0000).

Sleeping in Kobarid

(€1 = about $1.40, country code: 386, area code: 05)
My first listing is right on the main square. The other two hide on side streets about a block off the main road through town, between the museum and the main square (about a 3-minute walk

to either).

$$$ Hotel Hvala is the only real hotel in town. Run by the Hvala family, its 31 contemporary rooms are comfortable, and the location can't be beat. The mural on the wall in the elevator shaft tells the story of the Soča Valley as you go up toward the top floor (mid-July-Aug: Sb-€76, Db-€112; April-mid-July and Sept-mid-Nov: Sb-€72, Db-€104; cheaper off-season; pricier superior Db with air-con and sleek new decor-€160-200, hotel closed Feb and most of Nov, elevator, Trg Svobode 1, tel. 05/389-9300, fax 05/388-5322, www.hotelhvala.si, topli.val@siol.net).

$ Picerija Fedrig is a pizzeria that rents five simple but fine rooms upstairs (Db-€40, less for more than 1 night, 10 percent more in Aug, between the main square and the Kobarid Museum at Volaričeva 11, tel. 05/389-0115, jernej.grahli@volja.net).

$ Apartma-Ra has four rooms and three apartments in a cozy, family-friendly house (D-€30, Db-€40-50, apartment-€80-110, cash only, also runs a rafting company, Gregorčičeva 6C, mobile 041-641-899, apartma-ra@siol.net).

Eating in Kobarid

Topli Val ("Heat Wave"), Hotel Hvala's restaurant, is pricey but good, with a menu that emphasizes fish (€9-15 pastas, €10-30 main courses, lengthy list of Slovenian wines, daily 12:00-15:00 & 18:00-23:00, Trg Svobode 1, tel. 05/389-9300).

Kotlar Restaurant, across the square from Hotel Hvala, is similarly priced and well-regarded (Thu-Mon 12:00-23:00, closed Tue-Wed, Trg Svobode 11, tel. 05/389-1110). Kotlar also rents rooms if you're in a pinch.

Picerija Fedrig (also listed under "Sleeping in Kobarid," earlier) serves up good €5-7 pizzas (Tue-Sun 12:00-22:00, closed Mon, Volaričeva 11, tel. 05/389-0115).

SPAIN

The following chapter
is excerpted from
Rick Steves' Spain.

SAN SEBASTIÁN/DONOSTIA

Shimmering above the breathtaking Concha Bay, elegant and prosperous San Sebastián (Donostia in Euskara) has a favored location with golden beaches, capped by twin peaks at either end, and with a cute little island in the center. A delightful beachfront promenade runs the length of the bay, with an intriguing Old Town at one end and a smart shopping district in the center. It has 183,000 residents and almost that many tourists in high season (July-Sept). With a romantic setting, a soaring statue of Christ gazing over the city, and a late-night lively Old Town, San Sebastián has a mini-Rio de Janeiro aura. Though the actual "sightseeing" isn't much, the scenic city itself provides a pleasant introduction to Spain's Basque Country. And as a culinary capital of Spain, it dishes up some of the top tapas anywhere.

In 1845 Queen Isabel II's doctor recommended she treat her skin problems by bathing here in the sea. (For modesty's sake, she would go inside a giant cabana that could be wheeled into the surf—allowing her to swim far from prying eyes, never having to set foot on the beach.) Her visit mobilized Spain's aristocracy, and soon the city was on the map as a seaside resort. By the turn of the 20th century, San Sebastián was the toast of the belle époque, and a leading resort for Europe's beautiful people. Before World War I, Queen María Cristina summered here and held court in her Miramar Palace overlooking the crescent beach (the turreted, red-brick building partway around the bay). Hotels, casinos, and theaters flourished. Even Franco enjoyed 35 summers in a place he was sure to call San Sebastián, not Donostia.

Planning Your Time

San Sebastián's sights can be exhausted in a few hours, but it's a great place to be on vacation for a full, lazy day (or longer). Stroll the two-mile-long promenade and scout the place you'll grab to work on a tan. The promenade leads to a funicular that lifts you to the Monte Igueldo viewpoint. After exploring the Old Town and port, walk up to the hill of Monte Urgull. If you have more time, enjoy the delightful aquarium. Art-lovers can venture to the Museum of San Telmo, the largest of its kind on Basque culture. A key ingredient of any visit to San Sebastián is enjoying tapas in the Old Town bars.

Orientation to San Sebastián

The San Sebastián that we're interested in surrounds Concha Bay (Bahía de la Concha). It can be divided into three areas: Playa de la Concha (best beaches), the shop-ping district (called Centro), and the skinny streets of the grid-planned Old Town (called Parte Vieja, to the north of the shopping district). Centro, just east of Playa de la Concha, has beautiful turn-of-the-20th-century architecture, but no real sights. A busy drag called Alameda del Boulevard (or just "Boulevard") stands where the city wall once ran, and separates the Centro from the Old Town.

It's all bookended by mini-mountains: Monte Urgull to the north and east, and Monte Igueldo to the south and west. The river (Río Urumea) divides central San Sebastián from the district called Gros, which—contrary to its name—is actually quite nice, with a lively night scene and surfing beach.

Tourist Information

San Sebastián's TI, conveniently located right on the Boulevard, has information on city and regional sights, bike rentals (see "Helpful Hints," later), and bus and train schedules. Pick up the free map and the *Donostia/San Sebastián Holiday Guide* booklet, which has English descriptions of the three walking tours—the Old Town/Monte Urgull walk is best (July-Sept daily 9:00-20:00; Oct-June Mon-Thu 9:00-13:30 & 15:30-19:00, Fri-Sat 10:00-19:00, Sun 10:00-14:00; Boulevard 8, tel. 943-481-166, www.sansebastianturismo.com).

Arrival in San Sebastián

By Train: The town has two train stations (neither has luggage storage, but you can leave bags at Zarranet Internet café downtown—see "Helpful Hints," later).

If you're coming on a regional Topo train from Hendaye/Hendaia on the French border, get off at the **EuskoTren Station** (end of the line, called Amara). It's a level 15-minute walk to the center: Exit the station and walk across the long plaza, then veer right and walk eight blocks down Calle Easo (toward the statue of Christ hovering on the hill) to the beach. The Old Town will be ahead on your right, with Playa de la Concha to your left. To speed things up, catch bus #21, #26, or #28 along Calle Easo and take it to the Boulevard stop, near the TI at the bottom of the Old Town.

If you're arriving by train from elsewhere in Spain (or from France after transferring in Irún), you'll get off at the main **RENFE Station.** It's just across the river from the Centro shopping district. There are no convenient buses from the station—to get to the Old Town and most recommended hotels, catch a taxi (stand out front, €6 to downtown). Or just walk—cross the fancy dragon-decorated María Cristina Bridge, turn right onto the busy avenue called Paseo de los Fueros, and follow the Urumea River until the last bridge.

By Bus: A few buses—such as those from Hondarribia and the airport—can let you off at pretty Plaza de Gipuzkoa (first stop after crossing the river, in Centro shopping area, one block from the Boulevard, TI, and Old Town). But most buses—including those from Bilbao—take you instead to San Sebastián's makeshift "bus station" (dubbed Amara) at a big roundabout called Plaza Pío XII. It's basically a parking lot with a few bus shelters and a TI kiosk (open July-Aug only). At the end of the lot nearest the big roundabout, you'll see directional signs pointing you toward the town center (about a 30-minute walk). To save time and energy, catch local bus #21, #26, or #28 from the bus stop at the start of Avenida de Sancho el Sabio and get off at the Boulevard stop, near the TI at the start of the Old Town.

By Plane: San Sebastián Airport is beautifully situated along the harbor in the nearby town of Hondarribia, 12 miles east of the city (just across the bay from France). An easy bus (#E21) connects the airport to San Sebastián's Plaza de Gipuzkoa, just a block south of the Boulevard and TI (€2; about hourly Mon-Sat 6:30-21:15, Sun 10:00-20:00; 35 minutes, timetable at TI). A taxi into town costs about €30. For flight information, call 943-668-500 (airport info: www.aena.es).

If you arrive at **Bilbao Airport,** go out front and take the Pesa bus directly to San Sebastián (€15.40, pay driver, runs hourly, 1 hour, drops off at Plaza Pío XII, www.pesa.net).

By Car: Take the Amara freeway exit, follow *centro ciudad* signs into the city center, and park in a pay lot (many are well-signed). If you're picking up or returning a rental car, you'll find **Europcar** at the RENFE train station (tel. 943-322-304). Less centrally located are **Hertz** (Centro Comercial Garbera, Travesía de Garbera 1, bus #16 connects with downtown, tel. 943-392-223) and **Avis** (a taxi ride away at Hotel Barceló Costa Vasca, Pío Baroja 15, tel. 943-461-556).

Helpful Hints

Internet Access: A half-dozen Internet cafés are well-advertised throughout the Old Town, most offering fast access for about €2/hour; try **Zarranet** (Mon-Sat 10:00-22:00, Sun 16:00-22:00, closed for lunch in winter, Calle San Lorenzo 6, tel. 943-433-381, helpful Juan). These days, government-subsidized Wi-Fi access is available just about everywhere (including at most hotels).

Bookstore: Elkar, an advocate of Basque culture and literature, has two branches on the same street in the Old Town. Both have a collection of Basque literature, and one has a wide selection of guidebooks, maps, and books in English (Mon-Sat 10:00-14:00 & 16:00-20:00, Sun 11:00-14:00 & 16:30-20:30, Calle Fermín Calbetón 30, tel. 943-420-080).

Baggage Storage: There's no baggage storage at the train or bus stations. **Zarranet** Internet café, listed above, has space for about 80 bags (first-come, first-served; €0.50/hour, overnight-€5, 24 hours-€10).

Laundry: Wash & Dry is in the Gros neighborhood, across the river (self-service daily 8:00-22:00, drop-off service Mon-Fri 9:30-13:00 & 16:00-20:00, Iparragirre 6, tel. 943-293-150).

Bike Rental: The city has some great bike lanes and is a good place to enjoy on two wheels. Like many cities in Europe, San Sebastián has an automated bike-sharing program. Purchase a dBizi Card from the **TI** and use it to unlock your bike—there are nine stands spread around the city. Bikes must be returned to any stand within four hours, but you can pick up another one after 30 minutes (€8/day, €15/3 days, €20 cash-only deposit, return dBizi Card to TI during office hours to retrieve deposit; rental office hours Mon-Sat 10:00-13:00 & 15:30-18:00, Sun 10:30-13:00, longer in summer; TI at Boulevard 8; tel. 943-481-166).

For longer-term bike rentals, try **Bici Rent Donosti** (also rents scooters in summer, Avenida de Zurriola 22, 3 blocks across river from TI, mobile 639-016-013) or **Bicicletas Alai** (behind Amara bus station, Mon-Sat 11:00-13:00 & 17:00-

20:00, Sun by appointment only, Avenida de Madrid 24, tel. 943-470-001).

Marijuana: While Spain is famously liberal about marijuana laws, the Basque Country is even more so. Walking around San Sebastián, you'll see "grow shops" sporting the famous green leaf (shopkeepers are helpful if you have questions). The sale of marijuana is still illegal, but the consumption of marijuana is decriminalized and people are allowed to grow enough for their personal use at home. With the town's mesmerizing aquarium and delightfully lit bars filled with enticing munchies, it just makes sense here.

Getting Around San Sebastián

By Bus: Along the Boulevard at the bottom edge of the Old Town, you'll find a line of public buses ready to take you anywhere in town; give any driver your destination, and he'll tell you the number of the bus to catch (€1.40, pay driver).

Some handy bus routes: #21, #26, and #28 connect the Amara bus and EuskoTren stations to the TI (get off at the Boulevard stop); #16 begins at the Boulevard/TI stop, goes along Playa de la Concha and through residential areas, and eventually arrives at the base of the Monte Igueldo funicular. The TI has a bus-route map (or see www.ctss.es).

By Taxi: Taxis start at €6, which covers most rides in the center. You can't hail a taxi on the street—you must call one (tel. 943-404-040 or 943-464-646) or find a taxi stand (most convenient along the Boulevard).

By Metro: A new Metro system is currently under construction in San Sebastián—it will connect the main areas of the city and eventually extend to the airport.

Tours in San Sebastián

Walking Tours—The TI runs English-language walking tours. Options include Essential San Sebastián (€10, 1.5 hours), Flavors of San Sebastián (€18, 2 hours, includes three *pintxos* and three drinks), and San Sebastián—A Film City (€16, 2 hours, includes one *pintxo* and one drink). Schedules vary—ask at the TI or call 943-217-717 for info and reservations.

Local Guides—Itsaso Petrikorena is good (mobile 647-973-231, betitsaso@yahoo.es). **Gabriella Ranelli,** an American who's lived in San Sebastián for 20 years, specializes in culinary tours. She can take you on a sightseeing spin around the Old Town, along with a walk through the market and best *pintxo* bars (€160/half-day, €210/day, more for driving into the countryside, mobile 609-467-381, www.tenedortours.com, info@tenedortours.com). Gabriella

San Sebastián

☐ = See Old Town Detail Map

P Parking

↙ View

300 YARDS
300 METERS

CASTILLO DE

SANTA CLARA ISLAND

AQUARIUM

MONTE IGUELDO

FUNICULAR

CON B

PLAYA DE ONDARRETA

BEAC

SWIM

AV. SATRUSTEGUI

PASEO

DCH

❶ Hotel Arrizul & Pensión Kursaal
❷ Hotel Arrizul Gros & Launderette
❸ Hotel Niza
❹ Pensión Bellas Artes
❺ Miramar Palace
❻ La Perla Spa & Café de la Concha

also organizes cooking classes—where you shop at the market, then join a local chef to cook up some tasty *pintxos* of your own (€120/person for a small group)—as well as wine-tastings (€50-130/person).

Gastronomic Tours—**Ramón Barea,** who owns the San Sebastián Gastronomic Club, offers travelers the opportunity to enter one of San Sebastián's exclusive "private eating clubs" (described on page 290) and even participate in preparing a gourmet dinner. Prices start around €80 per person, including ingredients but excluding wine. Ramón also can organize *pintxo* tours (mobile 650-862-202, www.bidainet.com, ramonbarea@bidainet.com).

Tours on Wheels—Two tour options on wheels (following a similar route around the bay) are available, but most travelers won't find them necessary in this walkable city: the **"txu-txu"** tourist train (€4.50, daily 11:00-14:00 & 15:00-19:00, until 21:00 in sum-

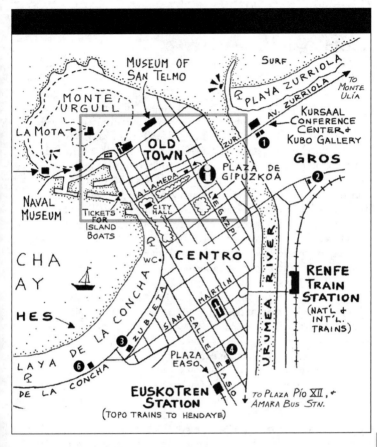

mer, 40-minute round-trip, tel. 943-422-973) and the **Donosti Tours** hop-on, hop-off bus tour along the bay and around the city (€12, full loop takes about one hour, ticket good for 24 hours, leaves from Victoria Eugenia theater on the Boulevard, tel. 696-429-847, www.busturistikoa.com, Raquel).

Basque Excursions—Based in San Sebastián, **Agustin Ciriza** leads minibus tours for up to eight people through the Spanish and French Basque Country, with destinations including Hondarribia, Biarritz, the Biscay Coast, Bayonne, and Pamplona (even during the running of the bulls). He also offers guided kayaking expeditions, pilgrimages, mountain treks, surf lessons, surfing trips, wine tours to the Rioja region, and wine tastings, food tours, and cooking classes in town. Prices start at €65 per person for a half-day excursion (minimum two people, mobile 686-117-395, www.gorilla-trip.com, agus@gorilla-trip.com).

Sights in San Sebastián

▲▲Old Town (Parte Vieja)

Huddled in the shadow of its once-protective Monte Urgull, the Old Town is where San Sebastián was born about 1,000 years ago. Because the town burned down in 1813 (as Spain, Portugal, and England fought the French to get Napoleon's brother off the Spanish throne), the architecture you see is generally Neoclassical and uniform. Still, the grid plan of streets hides heavy Baroque and Gothic churches, surprise plazas, and fun little shops, including venerable pastry stores, rugged produce markets, Basque-independence souvenir shops, and seafood-to-go delis. The highlight of the Old Town is its array of incredibly lively tapas bars—though here these snacks are called *pintxos* (PEEN-chohs; see "Eating in San Sebastián," later). To see the fishing industry in action, wander out to the port (described later).

Although the struggle for Basque independence is currently in a relatively calm stage, with most people opposing violent ETA tactics, there are still underlying tensions between Spain and the Basque people. In the middle of the Old Town, **Calle Juan de Bilbao** is the political-action street. Here you'll find people more sympathetic to the struggle (whereas for others, it's a street to avoid). Speaking Basque is encouraged.

Flagpoles mark **"private eating clubs"** throughout the Old Town (otherwise unmarked). Basque society is matrilineal and very female-oriented. A husband brings home his paycheck and hands it directly to his wife, who controls the house's purse strings (and everything else). Basque men felt they needed a place where they could congregate and play "king of the castle," so they formed these clubs where members could reserve a table and cook for their friends. The clubs used to be exclusively male; women are now allowed as invited guests...but never in the kitchen, which remains the men's domain.

▲Plaza de la Constitución

—The Old Town's main square is where bullfights used to be held. Notice the seat numbering on the balconies: Even if you owned an apartment here, the city retained rights to the balconies, which it could sell as box seats. (Residents could peek over the paying customers' shoulders.) Above the clock, notice the seal of San Sebastián: A merchant ship with sails billowing in the wind.

The city was granted trading rights by the crown—a reminder of the Basque Country's importance in Spanish seafaring. Inviting café tables spill into the square from all corners.

Museum of San Telmo—After several years of renovation, this museum reopened in 2011 and is now the largest museum of Basque culture in the country. The permanent collection has 19th- and 20th-century paintings by Basque artists that offer an interesting peek into the spirit, faces, and natural beauty of this fiercely independent region (other featured artists include El Greco and Rubens). Rooms are arranged around the peaceful cloister of a former Dominican monastery. The modern addition holds artifacts spanning the history of this region, dating back to ancient Roman times.

Cost and Hours: €5, free on Tue, open Tue-Sun 10:00-20:00, closed Mon, Plaza Zuloaga 1, tel. 943-481-580, www.santelmo museoa.com.

▲**Bretxa Public Market (Mercado de la Bretxa)**—Wandering through the public market is a fun way to get in touch with San Sebastián and Basque culture. Although the big, white market building facing the Boulevard has been converted into a modern shopping mall, the farmers produce market thrives here (lined up along the left side of the building), as well as the fish and meat market (behind it and underground).

Hours: Mon-Fri 8:00-14:00 & 17:00-20:00, Sat 8:00-14:00, closed Sun, Plaza de Sarriegi.

Visiting the Market: To get to the fish and meat market, walk past the produce vendors (look under the eaves of the modern building to see what the farmers are selling), and find a big glass cube in the square, where an escalator will take you down into the market.

At the bottom of the escalator, notice the **fish stall** on the left (marked *J. Ma. Mujika*). In the case you'll see different cuts of *bacalao* (cod). Entire books have been written about the importance of cod to the evolution of seafaring in Europe. The fish could be preserved in salt to feed sailors on ever-longer trips into the North Atlantic, allowing them to venture beyond the continental shelf (into deeper waters where they couldn't catch fresh fish). Cod was also popular among Catholic landlubbers on Fridays. Today cod remains a Basque staple. People still buy the salted version, which must be soaked for 48 hours (and the water changed three times) to become edible. If you're in a rush, you can buy de-salted cod...but at a cost in flavor. Stroll behind this stall to explore the fresh fish market—often with the catch of the day set up in cute little scenes. There's a free **WC** in the market—just ask *"¿Dónde está el servico, por favor?"*

When you're done exploring, take the escalator up and cross the busy street to the **Aitor Lasa** cheese shop (Mon-Fri 8:30-14:00 & 17:15-20:00, Sat 8:30-14:30, closed Sun, Aldamar 12, tel.

SAN SEBASTIÁN

943-430-354). Pass the fragrant piles of mushrooms at the entrance and head back to the display case, showing off the Basque specialty of *idiazábal*—raw sheep's milk cheese. Notice the wide variety, which depends on the specific region it came from, whether it's smoked or cured, and for how long it's been cured *(curación)*. If you're planning a picnic, this is a very local (and expensive) ingredient. To try the cheese that won first prize a few years back in the Ordizia International Cheese Competition, ask for *"El queso con el premio de Ordizia, por favor."* The owners are evangelical about the magic of combining the local cheese with walnuts and *casero* (homemade) apple jam.

The Port

At the west end of the Old Town, protected by Monte Urgull, is the port. Take the passage through the wall at the appropriately named Calle Puerto, and jog right along the level, portside promenade, Paseo del Muelle. You'll pass fishing boats unloading the catch of the day (with hungry locals looking on), salty sailors' pubs, and fishermen mending nets. Also along this strip are the skip-

pable Naval Museum and the entertaining aquarium. Trails to the top of Monte Urgull are just above this scene, near Santa María Church (or climb the stairs next to the aquarium).

Cruises—Small boats cruise from the Old Town's port to the island in the bay (Isla Santa Clara), where you can hike the trails and have lunch at the lone café, or pack a picnic before setting sail (€3.80 round-trip, small ferry departs June-Sept only, on the hour 10:00-20:00). The *City of San Sebastián* catamaran gives 30-minute tours of the bay for €8.

Naval Museum (Museo Naval)—This museum's two floors of exhibits describe the seafaring city's history, revealing the intimate link between the Basque culture and the sea.

   Cost and Hours: €1.20, free on Thu, borrow English description at entry, Tue-Sat 10:00-13:30 & 16:00-19:30, Sun 11:00-14:00, closed Mon, Paseo del Muelle 24, tel. 943-430-051.

▲▲**Aquarium**—San Sebastián's aquarium is surprisingly good. Exhibits are thoughtfully described in English and include a history of the sea, a collection of naval vessels, and models showing various drift-netting techniques. You'll see a petting tank filled with nervous fish; a huge whale skeleton; a trippy, illuminated, slowly tumbling tank of jellyfish; and a mesmerizing 45-foot-long tunnel that lets you look up into a wet world of floppy rays, menacing sharks, and local fish. The local section ends with a tank of shark fetuses safely incubating away from hungry predators. Local kids see the tropical wing and holler, "Nemo!"

Cost and Hours: €12, €6 for kids under 13; July-Aug daily 10:00-21:00; Sept-June Mon-Fri 10:00-19:00, Sat-Sun 10:00-20:00; last entry one hour before closing, at the end of Paseo del Muelle, tel. 943-440-099, www.aquariumss.com.

▲**Monte Urgull**—The once-mighty castle (Castillo de la Mota) atop the hill deterred most attackers, allowing the city to prosper in

the Middle Ages. The free museum within the castle, featuring San Sebastián history, is mildly interesting. The best views from the hill are not from the statue of Christ, but from the ramparts on the left side (as you face the hill), just above the port's aquarium. **Café El Polvorín,** nestled in the park, is a free-spirited place with salads, sandwiches, and good sangria.

A walkway allows you to stroll the mountain's entire perimeter near sea level. This route is continuous from Hotel Parma to the aquarium, and offers an enjoyable after-dinner wander. You can also walk a bit higher up over the port (along the white railing)—called the *paseo de las curas,* or "priest's path," where the clergy could stroll unburdened by the rabble in the streets below. These paths are technically open only from sunrise to sunset (daily May-Sept 8:00-21:00, Oct-April 8:00-19:00), but you can often access them later.

The Beach and Beyond

▲▲**La Concha Beach and Promenade**—The shell-shaped Playa de la Concha, the pride of San Sebastián, has one of Europe's

loveliest stretches of sand. Lined with a two-mile-long promenade, it allows even backpackers to feel aristocratic. Although it's pretty empty off-season, sunbathers pack its shores in summer. But year-round it's surprisingly devoid of eateries and money-grubbing businesses.

There are free showers, and *cabinas* provide lockers, showers, and shade for a fee. For a century the lovingly painted wrought-iron balustrade that stretches the length of the promenade has been a symbol of the city; it shows up on everything from jewelry to headboards. It's shaded by tamarisk trees, with branches carefully pruned into knotty bulbs each winter that burst into leafy shade-giving canopies in the summer—another symbol of the city. **Café de la Concha** serves reasonably priced mediocre food, and you can't beat the location of its terrace overlooking the beach (€14 weekday lunch special, tel. 943-473-600).

The Miramar palace and park, which divides the crescent beach in the middle, was where Queen María Cristina held court when she summered here. Her royal changing rooms are used today as inviting cafés, restaurants, and a fancy spa. You can walk in the park, although the palace, used as a music school, is closed to the public.

La Perla Spa—The spa overlooking the beach attracts a less royal crowd today and appeals mostly to visitors interested in sampling "the curative properties of the sea." You can enjoy its Talasso Fitness Circuit, featuring a hydrotherapy pool, a relaxation pool, a panoramic Jacuzzi, cold-water pools, a seawater steam sauna, a dry sauna, and a relaxation area.

Cost and Hours: €25 for 2-hour fitness circuit, €32 for 3-hour circuit, daily 8:00-22:00, €3 caps and €1 rental towels, bring a swimsuit or buy one for €33, on the beach at the center of the crescent, Paseo de la Concha, tel. 943-458-856, www.la-perla.net.

Monte Igueldo—For commanding city views (if you ignore the tacky amusements on top), ride the funicular up Monte Igueldo, a mirror image of Monte Urgull. The views over San Sebastián, along the coast, and into the distant green mountains are sensational day or night. The entrance to the funicular is on the road behind the tennis club on the far western end of Playa de Ondarreta, which extends from Playa de la Concha to the west.

Cost and Hours: Funicular—€2.70 round-trip; July-mid-Sept daily 10:00-22:00; April-June and mid-Sept-Oct daily 11:00-20:00; Nov-March Mon-Tue and Thu-Fri 11:00-18:00, Sat-Sun 11:00-20:00, closed Wed). If you drive to the top, you'll pay €1.90 to enter. The #16 bus takes you from the Old Town to the base of the funicular in about 10 minutes.

In Gros

Gros and Zurriola Beach—The district of Gros, just east across the river from the Old Town, offers a distinct Californian vibe. Literally a dump a few years ago, today it has a surfing scene on Zurriola Beach (popular with students and German tourists) and a futuristic conference center (described next). Long-term plans call for a new promenade that will arc over the water and under Monte Ulía.

▲Kursaal Conference Center and Kubo Gallery—These two Lego-like boxes (just east and across the river from the Old Town, in Gros) mark the spot of what was once a grand casino, torn down by Franco to discourage gambling. Many locals wanted to rebuild it as it once was, in a similar style to the turn-of-the-20th-century buildings in the Centro, but, in an effort to keep up with the postmodern trends in Bilbao, city leaders opted instead for Rafael Moneo's striking contemporary design. The complex is supposed to resemble the angular rocks that make up the town's breakwater. The Kursaal houses a theater, conference facilities, some gift shops and travel agencies, a restaurant, and the Kubo Gallery. The gallery offers temporary exhibits by international artists and promotes contemporary Basque artists. Each exhibit is complemented by a 10-minute video that plays continuously in the gallery theater.

Cost and Hours: Free, daily 11:30-13:30 & 17:00-21:00.

Chillida-Leku Museum—Unfortunately, this fine museum showcasing the abstract sculptures of Eduardo Chillida has closed due to financial troubles, and it is uncertain when it will reopen. Check at the TI, call 943-336-006, or visit www.museochillidaleku.com.

Sleeping in San Sebastián

Rates in San Sebastián fluctuate with the season. When you see a range of prices in these listings, the top end is for summer (roughly July-Sept), and the low end is for the shoulder season (May-June and Oct); outside of these times, you'll pay even less. Since breakfast is often not included, I've recommended some good options elsewhere in town (see "Eating in San Sebastián," later).

Sleep Code

(€1 = about $1.40, country code: 34)

S = Single, **D** = Double/Twin, **T** = Triple, **Q** = Quad, **b** = bathroom, **s** = shower only. Unless otherwise noted, credit cards are accepted and English is spoken, but breakfast is generally not included. The word *ostatua* (which you'll see throughout the Basque Country) means "pension."

To help you sort easily through these listings, I've divided the accommodations into three categories based on the price for a double room with bath in high season:

  $$$ Higher Priced—Most rooms €90 or more.
  $$ Moderately Priced—Most rooms €60-90.
  $ Lower Priced—Most rooms €60 or less.

Prices can change without notice; verify the hotel's current rates online or by email. For other updates, see www.ricksteves.com/update.

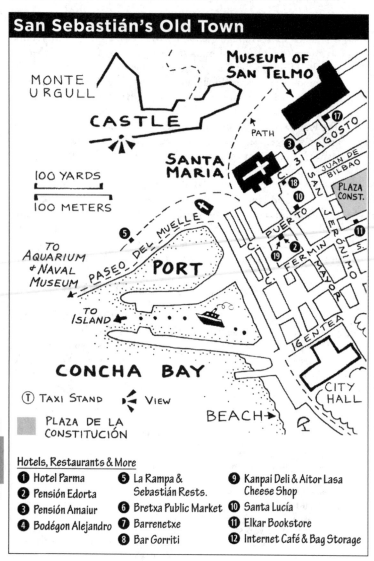

San Sebastián's Old Town

MONTE URGULL

CASTLE

MUSEUM OF SAN TELMO

PATH

SANTA MARIA

100 YARDS

100 METERS

PASEO DEL MUELLE

TO AQUARIUM & NAVAL MUSEUM

PORT

TO ISLAND

CONCHA BAY

(T) TAXI STAND   VIEW

PLAZA DE LA CONSTITUCIÓN

BEACH

CITY HALL

AGOSTO

JUAN DE BILBAO

PLAZA CONST.

C. 31

C. SAN

PUERTO

C. FERMIN

SAN JERÓNIMO

MAYOR

IGENTEA

Hotels, Restaurants & More

❶ Hotel Parma
❷ Pensión Edorta
❸ Pensión Amaiur
❹ Bodégon Alejandro
❺ La Rampa & Sebastián Rests.
❻ Bretxa Public Market
❼ Barrenetxe
❽ Bar Gorriti
❾ Kanpai Deli & Aitor Lasa Cheese Shop
❿ Santa Lucía
⓫ Elkar Bookstore
⓬ Internet Café & Bag Storage

SAN SEBASTIÁN

In or near the Old Town

$$$ Hotel Parma is a business-class place with 27 fine rooms and family-run attention to detail and service. It stands stately on the edge of the Old Town, away from the bar-scene noise, and over-looks the river and a surfing beach (Sb-€70-99, windowless interior Db-€103-151, view Db-€124-165, breakfast-€10, air-con, modern lounge, free Wi-Fi, Paseo de Salamanca 10, tel. 943-428-893, fax 943-424-082, www.hotelparma.com, hotelparma@hotelparma

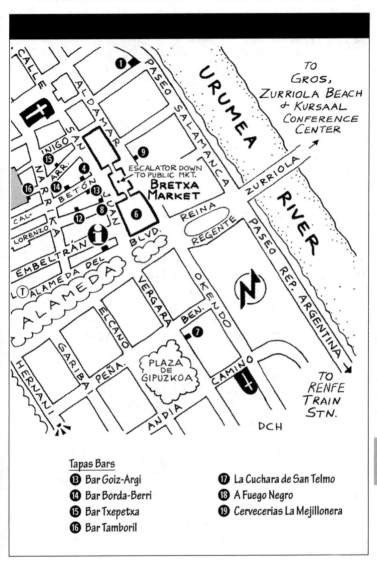

Tapas Bars
- ⑬ Bar Goiz-Argi
- ⑭ Bar Borda-Berri
- ⑮ Bar Txepetxa
- ⑯ Bar Tamboril

- ⑰ La Cuchara de San Telmo
- ⑱ A Fuego Negro
- ⑲ Cervecerias La Mejillonera

.com; Iñaki, Pino, Maria Eugenia, and Ana).

$$ Pensión Edorta ("Edward"), deep in the Old Town, elegantly mixes wood, brick, and color into nine modern, stylish rooms (D-€40-70, Db-€60-90, extra bed-€20-25, elevator, Calle Puerto 15, tel. 943-423-773, fax 943-433-570, www.pensionedorta .com, info@pensionedorta.com, Javier).

$ Pensión Amaiur is a flowery place with long, narrow halls and great-value rooms within the Old Town. Kind Virginia gives the justifiably popular *pensión* a homey warmth. Her 13 color-ful, cozy rooms share seven bathrooms (S-€34-42, quiet interior D-€44-50, exterior D-€54-60, T-€69-75, family room €84-90, kitchen facilities, pay Internet access, free Wi-Fi, next to Santa María Church at Calle 31 de Agosto 44, tel. 943-429-654, www .pensionamaiur.com, amaiur@telefonica.net).

Across the River, in Gros

The pleasant Gros district—San Sebastián's "uptown"—is marked by the super-modern, blocky Kursaal conference center. The nearby Zurriola Beach is popular with surfers. These hotels are less than a five-minute walk from the Old Town. For locations, see the map on page 288.

$$$ Hotel Arrizul is bright and fresh, with mod and mini-malist decor in each of its 12 rooms (Sb-€62-105, Db-€90-142, Db suite-€110-178, Qb-€140-225, breakfast-€7, air-con, elevator, free Wi-Fi, parking-€15, Peña y Goñi 1, tel. 943-322-804, fax 943-326-701, www.arrizul.com, info@arrizulhotel.com). Their sister hotel, **Hotel Arrizul Gros,** is about five blocks away and has 17 rooms with similar decor (slightly lower rates, includes small breakfast) plus seven apartments (apartments: €145-189/2 people, €185-229/4 people, €215-249/6 people, Iparraguirre 3, same contact info as main Hotel Arrizul).

$$ Pensión Kursaal has 19 basic but colorful and modern rooms in the original building, with white and beige decor (Db-€50-83, family room, elevator, pay Internet access, free Wi-Fi, park-ing-€12, Peña y Goñi 2, tel. 943-292-666, fax 943-297-536, www .pensionesconencanto.com, kursaal@pensionesconencanto.com).

On the Beach

$$$ Hotel Niza, set in the middle of Playa de la Concha, is often booked well in advance. Half of its 40 rooms (some with balconies) overlook the bay. From its chandeliered and plush lounge, a clas-sic elevator takes you to its comfortable pastel rooms with wed-ding-cake molding (tiny interior Sb-€58-64, Db-€128-152, view rooms cost the same—requests with reservation considered...but no promises, extra bed-€22, only streetside rooms have air-con, fans on request, great buffet breakfast-€11, free Internet access and Wi-Fi, parking-€15/day—must reserve in advance, Zubieta 56, see map on page 288 for location, tel. 943-426-663, fax 943-441-251, www.hotelniza.com, niza@hotelniza.com). The breakfast room has a sea view and doubles as a bar with light snacks throughout the day (Bar Biarritz, daily 7:30-24:00).

Between the Beach and EuskoTren Station

$$$ Pensión Bellas Artes, while farther from the Old Town than my other listings, is worth the 15-minute walk. Lively Leire, who lived in New York and runs her *pensión* with pride, rents 10 small, well-appointed, tidy rooms with thoughtful extra touches like fresh flowers in each room and a free loaner laptop. Leire loves to give her guests sightseeing and dining tips. She can also tell you about apartment rentals in the area (Sb-€69-89, Db-€89-109, extra bed-€20, elevator, free Internet access and Wi-Fi, near EuskoTren Station at Urbieta 64, tel. 943-474-905, fax 943-463-111, www .pension-bellasartes.com, info@pension-bellasartes.com). For the location, see the map on page 288.

Eating in San Sebastián

Basque food is regarded as some of the best in Spain, and San Sebastián is the culinary capital of the Basque Country. What the city lacks in museums and sights, it more than makes up for in food. San Sebastián is proud of its many Michelin-rated fine-dining establishments, but they require a big commitment of time and money. Most casual visitors will prefer to hop from pub to pub through the Old Town, following the crowds between Basque-font signs. I've listed a couple of solid traditional restaurants, but for the best value and memories, I'd order top-end dishes with top-end wine in top-end bars.

Pintxo Bar-Hopping

San Sebastián's Old Town provides the ideal backdrop for tapas-hopping; just wander the streets and sidle up to the bar in the

liveliest spot. Calle Fermín Calbetón has the best concentration of bars; the streets San Jerónimo and 31 de Agosto are also good. I've listed these top-notch places in order as you progress deeper into the Old Town. Note that there are plenty of other options along the way. Before you begin, study the sidebar on the next page.

Bar Goiz-Argi ("Morning Light"), every local's top recommendation, serves its tiny dishes with pride and attitude. Advertising *pintxos calientes,* they cook each treat for you, allowing you a montage of petite gourmet snacks. Try their *tartaleta de txangurro* (spider-crab spread on bread) or their signature shrimp

Do the Txikiteo Tango—
Tapas Cheat Sheet

Txikiteo (chih-kee-TAY-oh) is the Basque word for hopping from bar to bar, enjoying small sandwiches and tiny snacks (*pintxos,*

PEEN-chohs) and glasses of wine. Local competition drives small bars to lay out the most appealing array of *pintxos.* The selection is amazing, but the key to eating well here is going for the *pintxos calientes*—the hot tapas advertised on blackboards and cooked to order. Tapas are best, freshest, and accompanied by the most vibrant crowd from 12:00 to 14:00 and from 20:00 to 22:30. Watch what's being served—the locals know each bar's specialty. No matter how much you like a place, just order one dish; you want to be mobile.

Later in the evening, bars get more crowded and challenging for tourists. To get service amid the din, speak loudly and direct (little sweet voices get ignored), with no extra words. Expect to share everything. Double-dipping is encouraged. It's rude to put a dirty napkin on the table; it belongs on the floor.

If you can't get the bartender's attention to serve you a particular *pintxo,* don't be shy—just grab it and a napkin, and munch away. You pay when you leave; just keep a mental note of the tapas you've eaten. There's a code of honor. Everyone is part of the extended Basque family.

If you want a meal instead of *pintxos,* some bars—even ones that look only like bars from the street—have attached dining rooms, usually in the back.

Pintxos

antxoas	anchovies (not the cured, heavily salted kind you always hated)
bocadillos	baguette sandwiches
bacalao	cod (served lots of ways)
txampis (chahm-pees)	mushrooms
gambas	shrimp
patatas bravas	crisp potato cubes served with a spicy sauce
tortilla	big, round omelet pie served by the slice (many varieties)

txangurro (chang-GOO-roh)	spider crab, a delicacy, often mixed with onions, tomatoes, and wine, served hot or made into a spread to put on bread

Descriptions

brocheta	anything on a stick
calientes	served hot and cooked to order (listed on chalkboard, not already on the bar)
cazuelas	hot meal-size servings (like raciones in Spanish)

Drinks

caña (KAHN-yah)	draft beer
mosto	non-alcoholic grape juice that comes in red or white (for when you've had enough beer and wine)
Rioja	a better wine
sidra	a dry cider that's a bit more alcoholic than beer
sin (seen)	non-alcoholic beer (literally means "without")
tinto	red house wine
txakoli (chah-koh-lee)	fresh white wine, poured from high to "break against the glass" and aerate it to add sparkle. Good with seafood, and therefore fits the local cuisine well.
un crianza	a glass of nicely aged wine. It's smart to ask for this instead of "un tinto" to get better quality for nearly the same price.
vaso de agua	glass of tap water (they'll ask you "bottled?"—embotellada—and you say no)
zurito (thoo-ree-toh)	small beer

Paying the Bill

Zenbat da?	"How much?"
Me cobras?	"What's the damage?" (a fun way to say "The bill, please")

SAN SEBASTIÁN

kebab. A good selection of open wine bottles are clearly priced and displayed on the shelf (great prices, no chairs, congregate at bar, Mon lunch only, closed Tue, Calle Fermín Calbetón 4, tel. 943-425-204).

Bar Borda-Berri (loosely, "Mountain Hut"), a couple of doors down, features a more low-key ambience and top-quality €3 *pintxos*. There are only a few items at the bar; check out the chalkboard menu for today's options, order, and they'll cook it fresh. The specialty here is melt-in-your-mouth beef cheeks *(carrillera de tenera)* in a red-wine sauce, risotto with wild mushrooms, and foie gras (grilled goose liver) with apple jelly, which is even better paired with a glass of their best red wine (closed Mon, Calle Fermín Calbetón 12, tel. 943-425-638).

Bar Txepetxa is *the* place for anchovies. A plastic circle displaying a variety of *antxoas* tapas makes choosing your anchovy treat easy. These fish are fresh—not cured and salted like those most Americans hate (€2.20/*pintxo*, Tue lunch only, closed Sun-Mon, Calle Pescaderia 5, tel. 943-422-227).

Bar Tamboril is a traditional place right on the main square favored for its seafood, mushrooms *(txampis tamboril)*, and anchovy tempura along with its good prices. Their list of hot *pintxos* (grab the little English menu on the bar) makes you want to break the one-tapa-per-stop rule (Calle Pescaderia 2, tel. 943-423-507).

La Cuchara de San Telmo, with cooks taught by a big-name Basque chef, Alex Mondiel, is a cramped place that devotes as much space to its thriving kitchen as its bar. It has nothing precooked and set on the bar—order your mini-gourmet plates with a spirit of adventure from the constantly changing blackboard. Their foie gras with apple jelly is rightfully famous (€3 *pintxos,* closed Mon, tucked away on a lonely alley called Santa Corda behind Museum of San Telmo at 31 de Agosto #28, tel. 943-435-446).

A Fuego Negro is cool and upscale compared with the others, with a hip, slicker vibe and a blackboard menu of *pintxos* and drinks (there's an English translation sheet). They have a knack for mixing gourmet pretentiousness with whimsy here: Try their *txangurro* (crab), *aguacate* (avocado), and *regaliz* (licorice ice cream) trio for a unique taste-bud experience (€3.60). Enjoy their serious and extensive wine selection (closed Mon, 31 de Agosto #31, tel. 650-135-373). An inviting little section in the back makes this a sit-down dining opportunity.

Cervecerias La Mejillonera is famous among students for its big cheap beers, *patatas bravas,* and mussels ("*tigres*" is the spicy favorite). A long, skinny stainless-steel bar and lots of photos make ordering easy—this is the only place in town where you pay when served (Puerto 15, tel. 943-428-465).

Restaurants

Bodégon Alejandro is a good spot for modern Basque cuisine in a dark and traditional setting (three-course fixed-price lunch-€15, Tue-Sun 13:00-15:30 & 20:00-22:30 except closed Sun night, closed Mon, in Old Town on Calle Fermín Calbetón 4, tel. 943-427-158).

Seafood Along the Port: For seafood with a salty sailor's view, check out the half-dozen hardworking, local-feeling restaurants that line the harbor on the way to the aquarium. **La Rampa** is an upscale eatery, specializing in crab *(txangurro)* and lobster dishes and seafood *parillada* (€30-50 for dinner, closed Tue-Wed, Paseo Muelle/Kaiko Pasealekua 26-27, tel. 943-421-652). Also along here, locals like **Sebastián** (more traditional, closed Tue).

Picnics and Takeout

A picnic on the beach or atop Monte Urgull is a tempting option. You can assemble a bang-up spread at the **Bretxa Public Market** at Plaza de Sarriegi (described earlier).

Upscale **Barrenetxe** has an amazing array of breads, prepared foods, and some of the best desserts in town. In business since 1699, their somewhat formal service is justified (daily 8:00-20:00, Plaza de Gipuzkoa 9, tel. 943-424-482).

Kanpai, a high-quality deli serving Basque and international cuisine, is run by David and his mother. Step up to the display case and get something "to go" for an easy and tasty picnic (daily 10:00-15:00 & 17:00-20:30, shorter hours off-season, Calle Aldamar 12, tel. 943-423-884).

Breakfast

If your hotel doesn't provide breakfast—or even if it does—consider one of these places. The first is a traditional stand-up bar; the second is a greasy spoon.

Bar Gorriti, delightfully local, is packed with market workers and shoppers starting their day. You'll stand at the bar and choose a hot-off-the-grill *francesca jamon* omelet (fluffy mini-omelet sandwich topped with a slice of ham) and other goodies (€2 each). This and a good cup of coffee makes for a very Basque breakfast (daily, breakfast served 7:00-10:00, facing the side of the big white market building at San Juan 3, tel. 943-428-353). By the time you get there for breakfast, many market workers will be taking their mid-morning break.

Santa Lucía, a 1950s-style diner, is ideal for a cheap Old Town breakfast or *churros* break (*churros* are like deep-fried doughnut sticks that can be dipped in pudding-like hot chocolate). Photos of two dozen different breakfasts decorate the walls, and plates of fresh *churros* keep patrons happy. Grease is liberally applied to the grill...from a squeeze bottle (daily 8:30-21:30, Calle Puerto 6, tel. 943-425-019).

San Sebastián Connections

By Train

San Sebastián has two train stations: RENFE and EuskoTren (described under "Arrival in San Sebastián" on page 285). The station you use depends on your destination.

RENFE Station: This station handles long-distance destinations within Spain (most of which require reservations). Connections include **Irún** (9/day, 25 minutes), **Hendaye**, France (6/day, 30 minutes), **Madrid** (2/day, 5-6 hours), **Burgos** (6/day, 3 hours), **León** (1/day, 5 hours), **Pamplona** (2/day, 2 hours), **Salamanca** (2/day, 6 hours), **Vitoria** (8/day, 1.75 hours), **Barcelona** (2/day, 5.5 hours), and **Santiago de Compostela** (1/day direct, 11 hours, final destination A Coruña).

EuskoTren Station: If you're going into France, take the regional Topo train (which leaves from the EuskoTren Station) over the French border into **Hendaye** (2/hour, 35 minutes, departs EuskoTren Station at :15 and :45 after the hour 6:15-21:45). From Hendaye connect to France's SNCF network (www.sncf.com), where connections include **Paris** (4/day direct, 5.5-6 hours, or 8.5-hour night train, reservations required). Unfortunately, San Sebastián's EuskoTren Station doesn't have information on Paris-bound trains from Hendaye. Don't buy the Spanish ticket too far in advance—EuskoTren tickets to Hendaye must be used within two hours of purchase (or else they expire).

Also leaving from San Sebastián's EuskoTren Station are slow regional trains to destinations in Spain's Basque region, including **Bilbao** (hourly, 2.5 hours—the bus is faster, €8.50 round-trip ticket saves €1.50; EuskoTren info: toll tel. 902-543-210, www.euskotren.es). Although the train ride from San Sebastián to Bilbao takes twice as long as the bus, it passes through more interesting countryside. The Basque Country shows off its trademark green and gray: lush green vegetation and gray clouds. It's an odd mix of heavy industrial factories, small homegrown veggie gardens, streams, and every kind of livestock you can imagine.

By Bus

San Sebastián's "bus station," called **Amara** for the neighborhood, is a congregation of bus parking spots next to the big Hotel Amara Plaza, at the roundabout called Plaza Pío XII (on the river, four blocks south of EuskoTren Station). Some schedules are posted at various stops, but confirm departure times. You must buy your tickets in advance at the bus companies, with offices on either side of the block north of the station area (toward downtown, along Avenida de Sancho el Sabio and Paseo de Vízcaya). Bus tickets are not available from the driver. The Pesa office, which serves St. Jean-de-Luz and Bilbao, is located at Avenida de Sancho el Sabio 33 (toll tel. 902-101-210, www.pesa.net). The Alsa office—which serves Madrid, Burgos, and León—is just beyond Pesa at Sancho el Sabio 31 (toll tel. 902-422-242, www.alsa.es). The Roncalesa office is in the same office as Alsa (tel. 943-461-064, www.condasa.com). The Vibasa office—which serves Burgos, Pamplona, and Barcelona—is on the other side of the block, at Calle Vizcaya 15 (closed 13:30-15:00, toll tel. 902-101-363, www.vibasa.es).

From San Sebastián, buses go to **Bilbao** (get ticket from Pesa office, 2/hour, hourly on weekends, 6:30-22:00, 1.25 hours, €10, departs from Amara; morning buses fill with tourists, commuters, and students, so consider buying your ticket the day before; once in Bilbao, buses leave you at Termibús stop with easy tram connections to the Guggenheim modern-art museum); **Bilbao Airport** (a Pesa bus goes directly to the airport from San Sebastián's Plaza Pío XII, hourly, 1.25 hours, €15.40), **Pamplona** (Roncalesa office, 8/day, 1 hour, €7), **León** (Alsa office, 1/day, 6 hours, €30), **Madrid** (Alsa office, 8/day, 6 hours direct, otherwise 7 hours, €30-42), **Burgos** (Alsa or Vibasa office, 6/day, 3 hours, €16), and **Barcelona** (Vibasa office, 2/day and 1 at night, 7 hours, €30).

To visit **Hondarribia,** you can catch buses #E21 or #E23 much closer to the center at Plaza de Gipuzkoa (1 block south of TI; about 3/hour, 35 minutes, #E21 goes to airport en route to Hondarribia, €2).

Buses to French Basque Country: A bus goes from San Sebastián's Amara bus station to **St. Jean-de-Luz** (Mon-Sat only, 2/day at 9:00 and 14:30, none on Sun, 1 hour, return trips at 12:45 and 19:15, get ticket from Pesa office, only 1/week off-season, €4.50), then continues directly to **Biarritz** (1.25 hours from San Sebastián, €6.60) and **Bayonne** (1.5 hours from San Sebastián, €7.75).

APPENDIX

Tourist Information

Most European countries have a national tourist office (TI) in the US. They can be a wealth of information, with maps, information on festivals and holidays, details on public transportation, and more. Many TI websites allow you to download free brochures.

Austria: US tel. 212/944-6880, www.austria.info

Bosnia & Herzegovina: US tel. 036/580-275, www.bhtourism.ba

Croatia: US tel. 800-829-4416, http://us.croatia.hr

Czech Republic: US tel. 212/288-0830, www.usa.czechtourism.com

Denmark: US tel. 212/885-9700, www.goscandinavia.com

Greece: US tel. 212/421-5777, www.visitgreece.gr

Italy: US tel. 212/245-5618, www.italiantourism.com

Morocco: From the US, dial 011-212-537-674-013; www.visitmorocco.com

Slovenia: US tel. 011-386-1-589-8550, www.slovenia.info

Spain: US tel. 212/265-8822, www.spain.info

European Calling Chart

Just smile and dial, using this key:
AC = Area Code, LN = Local Number.

European Country	Calling long distance within...	Calling from the US or Canada to...	Calling from a European country to...
Austria	AC + LN	011 + 43 + AC (without the initial zero) + LN	00 + 43 + AC (without the initial zero) + LN
Belgium	LN	011 + 32 + LN (without initial zero)	00 + 32 + LN (without initial zero)
Bosnia-Herzegovina	AC + LN	011 + 387 + AC (without initial zero) + LN	00 + 387 + AC (without initial zero) + LN
Britain	AC + LN	011 + 44 + AC (without initial zero) + LN	00 + 44 + AC (without initial zero) + LN
Croatia	AC + LN	011 + 385 + AC (without initial zero) + LN	00 + 385 + AC (without initial zero) + LN
Czech Republic	LN	011 + 420 + LN	00 + 420 + LN
Denmark	LN	011 + 45 + LN	00 + 45 + LN
Estonia	LN	011 + 372 + LN	00 + 372 + LN
Finland	AC + LN	011 + 358 + AC (without initial zero) + LN	999 (or other 900 number) + 358 + AC (without initial zero) + LN
France	LN	011 + 33 + LN (without initial zero)	00 + 33 + LN (without initial zero)
Germany	AC + LN	011 + 49 + AC (without initial zero) + LN	00 + 49 + AC (without initial zero) + LN
Gibraltar	LN	011 + 350 + LN	00 + 350 + LN
Greece	LN	011 + 30 + LN	00 + 30 + LN
Hungary	06 + AC + LN	011 + 36 + AC + LN	00 + 36 + AC + LN
Ireland	AC + LN	011 + 353 + AC (without initial zero) + LN	00 + 353 + AC (without initial zero) + LN

APPENDIX

European Country	Calling long distance within ...	Calling from the US or Canada to ...	Calling from a European country to ...
Italy	LN	011 + 39 + LN	00 + 39 + LN
Montenegro	AC + LN	011 + 382 + AC (without initial zero) + LN	00 + 382 + AC (without initial zero) + LN
Morocco	LN	011 + 212 + LN (without initial zero)	00 + 212 + LN (without initial zero)
Netherlands	AC + LN	011 + 31 + AC (without initial zero) + LN	00 + 31 + AC (without initial zero) + LN
Norway	LN	011 + 47 + LN	00 + 47 + LN
Poland	LN	011 + 48 + LN (without initial zero)	00 + 48 + LN (without initial zero)
Portugal	LN	011 + 351 + LN	00 + 351 + LN
Slovakia	AC + LN	011 + 421 + AC (without initial zero) + LN	00 + 421 + AC (without initial zero) + LN
Slovenia	AC + LN	011 + 386 + AC (without initial zero) + LN	00 + 386 + AC (without initial zero) + LN
Spain	LN	011 + 34 + LN	00 + 34 + LN
Sweden	AC + LN	011 + 46 + AC (without initial zero) + LN	00 + 46 + AC (without initial zero) + LN
Switzerland	LN	011 + 41 + LN (without initial zero)	00 + 41 + LN (without initial zero)
Turkey	AC (if there's no initial zero, add one) + LN	011 + 90 + AC (without initial zero) + LN	00 + 90 + AC (without initial zero) + LN

- The instructions above apply whether you're calling a land line or mobile phone.
- The international access codes (the first numbers you dial when making an international call) are 011 if you're calling from the US or Canada, or 00 if you're calling from virtually anywhere in Europe (except Finland, where it's 999 or another 900 number, depending on the phone service you're using).
- To call the US or Canada from Europe, dial 00, then 1 (the country code for the US and Canada), then the area code and number. In short, 00 + 1 + AC + LN = Hi, Mom!

Begin Your Trip at www.ricksteves.com

At ricksteves.com, you'll discover a wealth of free information on European destinations, including fresh monthly news and helpful tips from thousands of fellow travelers. You'll find my latest guidebook updates (www.ricksteves.com/update), a monthly travel e-newsletter (easy and free to sign up), my personal travel blog, and my free Rick Steves Audio Europe smartphone app (if you don't have a smartphone, you can access the same content via podcasts). You can even follow me on Facebook and Twitter.

Our **online Travel Store** offers travel bags and accessories specially designed by Rick Steves to help you travel smarter and lighter. These include my popular carry-on bags (roll-aboard and backpack versions), money belts, totes, toiletries kits, adapters, other accessories, and a wide selection of guidebooks, planning maps, and DVDs.

Choosing the right **railpass** for your trip—amidst hundreds of options—can drive you nutty. We'll help you choose the best pass for your needs and ship it to you for free, plus give you a bunch of free extras.

Rick Steves' Europe Through the Back Door travel company offers **tours** with more than three dozen itineraries and 450 departures reaching the best destinations in this book... and beyond. We offer a 14-day Ireland tour, as well as multiple tours in nearby England, Wales, and Scotland. You'll enjoy great guides, a fun bunch of travel partners (with small groups of generally around 24-28 travelers), and plenty of room to spread out in a big, comfy bus. You'll find European adventures to fit every vacation length. For all the details, and to get our Tour Catalog and a free Rick Steves Tour Experience DVD (filmed on location during an actual tour), visit www.ricksteves.com or call the Tour Department at 425/608-4217.

APPENDIX

INDEX

A

Accommodations: *See* Sleeping

Ærø: 129–149; biking, 137–142; map, 138; transportation, 129–130, 148–149

Ærø Brewery: 142

Ærø Museum: 136

Ærøskøbing: 130–149; eating, 146–148; helpful hints, 131–132; map, 133; nightlife, 143–144; planning tips, 131; sights/ activities, 132–137; sleeping, 144–146; tourist information, 131; transportation, 148–149; walking tour, 132–136

Ærø-Svendborg Ferry: 148–149

Ajda: 266

Alabaster Workshop (Volterra): 218

Ali Baba (Mostar): 50–51

Altaussee: 21

American Legation Museum (Tangier): 248–249

Andreas Miaoulis Monument (Hydra): 160–161

Aquariums: Rovinj, 89; San Sebastián, 292–293

Austria: 9–30; tourist information, 307. *See also* Hallstatt

B

Bagnoregio: *See* Civita di Bagnoregio

Balbi Arch (Rovinj): 84

Balota Beach (Rovinj): 89

Barber's Bridge (Český Krumlov): 113

Baroque Theater (Český Krumlov): 115–116

Bars: *See* Nightlife

Batana boats, in Rovinj: 87–88, 91

Beaches: Ærø, 142, 143–144; Hallstatt, 11; Hydra, 166–167; Rovinj, 89; San Sebastián, 284, 293–294; Tangier, 251

Bear Pits (Český Krumlov): 113

Beneš, Edvard: 110–111

Biking (bike rentals): Ærø, 132, 137–142; Český Krumlov, 107; Hallstatt, 22; Lucca, 191, 194–195; Rovinj, 89–90; San Sebastián, 286–287

Bilbao Airport: 285–286

Bileća: 59

Bilećko Lake: 58–59

Bišćevića Kuća (Mostar): 48

Bišćević Turkish House (Mostar): 48

Blagaj: 57

Bled: 271

Boat travel: Ærø, 148–149; Český Krumlov, 118–119; Hallstatt, 11, 18, 24; Hydra, 156, 157, 162, 174–175; Plitvice Lakes, 67; Rovinj, 79, 84, 88, 91. *See also* Ferries

Bone Chapel (Hallstatt): 17–18

Borgnaes (Ærø): 139

Bosnia-Herzegovina: 33–59; tourist information, 307. *See also* Mostar

Bottle Peter Museum (Ærøskøbing): 136–137

Bovec: 269–270, 271–274; eating, 273–274; sleeping, 272–273; tourist information, 271; transportation, 272

Braće Fejića (Mostar): 47–50

Bregninge (Ærø): 140

Bregninge Church (Ærø): 139–140

Bretxa Public Market (San Sebastián): 291–292

Bulevar (Mostar): 38–39

C

Calle Juan de Bilbao (San Sebastián): 290

Canoeing, in Český Krumlov: 118–119

Celebration of the Rose (Český Krumlov): 106–107

Český Krumlov: 103–125; eating,

Rick's free app and podcasts

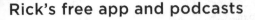

The FREE Rick Steves Audio Europe™ app for iPhone, iPad, iPod Touch and Android gives you self-guided audio tours of Europe's top museums, sights and historic walks—plus hundreds of tracks filled with cultural insights and sightseeing tips from Rick's radio interviews—all organized into geographic-specific playlists.

Let Rick Steves Audio Europe™ amplify your guidebook. This free app includes self-guided audio tours for all the most important museums and historical walks in London, Paris, Rome, Venice, Florence, Athens, and more.

With Rick whispering in your ear, Europe gets even better.

Thanks Facebook fans for submitting photos while on location! From top: John Kuijper in Florence, Brenda Mamer with her mother in Rome, and Alyssa Passey with her friend in Paris.

Find out more at ricksteves.com

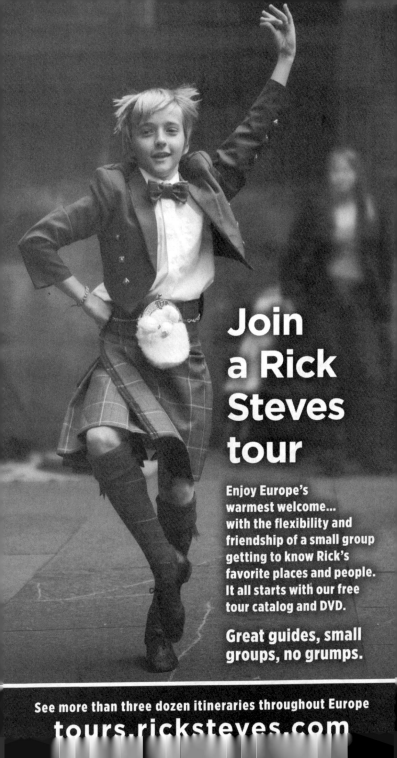

Join a Rick Steves tour

Enjoy Europe's warmest welcome... with the flexibility and friendship of a small group getting to know Rick's favorite places and people. It all starts with our free tour catalog and DVD.

Great guides, small groups, no grumps.

Free information and great gear to

▸ Plan Your Trip

Browse thousands of articles and a wealth of money-saving tips for planning your dream trip. You'll find up-to-date information on Europe's best destinations, packing smart, getting around, finding rooms, staying healthy, avoiding scams and more.

▸ Eurail Passes

Find out, step-by-step, if a railpass makes sense for your trip—and how to avoid buying more than you need. Get free shipping on online orders

▸ Graffiti Wall & Travelers Helpline

Learn, ask, share—our online community of savvy travelers is a great resource for first-time travelers to Europe, as well as seasoned pros.

Rick Steves' Europe Through the Back Door, Inc.

turn your travel dreams into affordable reality

▶ Free Audio Tours & Travel Newsletter

Get your nose out of this guide book and focus on what you'll be seeing with Rick's free audio tours of the greatest sights in Paris, London, Rome, Florence, Venice, and Athens.

Subscribe to our free Travel News e-newsletter, and get monthly articles from Rick on what's happening in Europe.

▶ Great Gear from Rick's Travel Store

Pack light and right—on a budget—with Rick's custom-designed carry-on bags, roll-aboards, day packs, travel accessories, guidebooks, journals, maps and DVDs of his TV shows.

130 Fourth Avenue North, PO Box 2009 • Edmonds, WA 98020 USA
Phone: (425) 771-8303 • Fax: (425) 771-0833 • www.ricksteves.com

Rick Steves

www.ricksteves.com

Rick Steves guidebooks are published by Avalon Travel,
a member of the Perseus Books Group.

NOW AVAILABLE:
eBOOKS, APPS & BLU-RAY

eBOOKS

Most guides are available as eBooks from Amazon, Barnes & Noble, Borders, Apple, and Sony. Free apps for eBook reading are available in the Apple App Store and Android Market, and eBook readers such as Kindle, Nook, and Kobo all have free apps that work on smartphones.

RICK STEVES' EUROPE DVDs

10 New Shows 2011–2012
Austria & the Alps
Eastern Europe
England & Wales
European Christmas
European Travel Skills & Specials
France
Germany, BeNeLux & More
Greece & Turkey
Iran
Ireland & Scotland
Italy's Cities
Italy's Countryside
Scandinavia
Spain
Travel Extras

BLU-RAY

Celtic Charms
Eastern Europe Favorites
European Christmas
Italy Through the Back Door
Mediterranean Mosaic
Surprising Cities of Europe

PHRASE BOOKS & DICTIONARIES

French
French, Italian & German
German
Italian
Portuguese
Spanish

JOURNALS

Rick Steves' Pocket Travel Journal
Rick Steves' Travel Journal

APPS

Select Rick Steves guides are available as apps in the Apple App Store.

PLANNING MAPS

Britain, Ireland & London
Europe
France & Paris
Germany, Austria & Switzerland
Ireland
Italy
Spain & Portugal

Rick Steves books and DVDs are available at bookstores and through online booksellers.

Credits

Researchers

Amanda Buttinger

Amanda moved to Madrid in 1998, thinking she'd be there a year. Since then she's found many reasons to stay, from learning more Spanish to guiding and travel writing to the best of all—sunny city walks with her dog and her boys.

Helen Inman

After graduating with a law degree, Helen left England for the Mediterranean, finding sunshine, vibrant energy, and Latin culture and languages. Currently working as a guide for Rick Steves tours and as a guidebook researcher, she enjoyed five years in bella Roma before moving to Spain, where she thrives on a diet of dancing, laughter, cava, and seafood.

Karin Kibby

Having lived in Italy for more than 10 years, Karin guides Rick Steves tours, researches guidebooks, and helps private travelers get in touch with the real Tuscany. When she's not working, you'll find her with her husband skiing in the Alps, exploring Italian islands by boat, and hanging out with friends and family in Tuscany.

Ian Watson

Ian has worked with Rick's guidebooks since 1993, after starting out with Let's Go and Frommer's guides. Originally from upstate New York, Ian speaks several European languages, including German, and makes his home in Reykjavík, Iceland.

Contributors and Co-Authors

Cameron Hewitt

Cameron Hewitt grew up listing to the Polish nursery rhymes of his grandfather, Jan Paweł Dąbrowski. Today, Cameron researches and writes guidebooks for Rick Steves. When he's not on the road, Cameron lives in Seattle with his wife Shawna.

Gene Openshaw

Gene is the co-author of 10 Rick Steves books. For this book, he wrote material on Europe's art, history, and contemporary culture. When not traveling, Gene enjoys composing music, recovering from his 1973 trip to Europe with Rick, and living everyday life with his daughter.

Honza Vihan

Honza grew up roaming the Czech countryside in search of the Wild West. Once the borders opened, he set off for South Dakota. His journey took him to China, Honduras, India, and Iran, where he contributed to several travel guides. Honza lives in Prague with his family, teaches Chinese, and leads Rick Steves' tours through Eastern Europe.

Chapter Images

The following list identifies the chapter-opening images and credits their photographers.

Introduction: Hydra Harbor	Rick Steves
Austria: Hallstatt	Rick Steves
Hallstatt & the Salzkammergut: Town View	Gretchen Strauch
Bosnia-Herzegovina: Mostar	Cameron Hewitt
Mostar: Old Bridge	Cameron Hewitt
Croatia: Plitvice Waterfall	Cameron Hewitt
Plitvice Lakes National Park: Boardwalk	Rick Steves
Rovinj: Old Town	Cameron Hewitt
Czech Republic: Český Krumlov at Night	Cameron Hewitt
Český Krumlov: Český Krumlov	Rick Steves
Denmark: Ærøskøbing Guide	Dominic Bonuccelli
Ærø: Aero Bungalows	Dominic Bonuccelli
Greece: Hydra	Cameron Hewitt
Hydra: Hydra Harbor	Rick Steves
Italy: Civita di Bagnoregio	Dominic Bonuccelli
Civita di Bagnoregio: Civita	Rick Steves
Lucca: Back Street	Cameron Hewitt
Volterra: Street Scene	Rick Steves
Morocco: Grand Socco, Tangier	Dominic Bonuccelli
Tangier: Market Vendor	Rick Steves
Slovenia: Julian Alps	Cameron Hewitt
Julian Alps: Mountain Hut	Cameron Hewitt
Spain: San Sebastián	Cameron Hewitt
San Sebastián: San Sebastián	Cameron Hewitt

Rick Steves' Guidebook Series

City, Regional, and Country Guides

Rick Steves' Amsterdam, Bruges & Brussels
Rick Steves' Best of Europe
Rick Steves' Budapest
Rick Steves' Croatia & Slovenia
Rick Steves' Eastern Europe
Rick Steves' England
Rick Steves' Florence & Tuscany
Rick Steves' France
Rick Steves' Germany
Rick Steves' Great Britain
Rick Steves' Greece: Athens & the Peloponnese
Rick Steves' Ireland
Rick Steves' Istanbul
Rick Steves' Italy
Rick Steves' London
Rick Steves' Paris
Rick Steves' Portugal
Rick Steves' Prague & the Czech Republic
Rick Steves' Provence & the French Riviera
Rick Steves' Rome
Rick Steves' Scandinavia
Rick Steves' Spain
Rick Steves' Switzerland
Rick Steves' Venice
Rick Steves' Vienna, Salzburg & Tirol

Snapshot Guides

Excerpted from country guidebooks, the Snapshots Guides cover many of my favorite destinations, such as *Rick Steves' Snapshot Barcelona, Rick Steves' Snapshot Scotland,* and *Rick Steves' Snapshot Hill Towns of Central Italy.*

Pocket Guides

My new Pocket Guides are condensed, colorful guides to Europe's top cities, including Paris, London, Rome, and more. These combine the top self-guided walks and tours from my city guides with vibrant full-color photos, and are sized to slip easily into your pocket.

Rick Steves' Phrase Books

French
French/Italian/German
German
Italian
Portuguese
Spanish

More Books

Rick Steves' Europe 101: History and Art for the Traveler
Rick Steves' Europe Through the Back Door
Rick Steves' European Christmas
Rick Steves' Mediterranean Cruise Ports
Rick Steves' Postcards from Europe
Rick Steves' Travel as a Political Act